Books should be returned on or before the
last date stamped below.

27 FEB 1996

10 APR 1996

- 4 JUN 1996

11 JUL 1996

20 NOV 1997

The Castles of Scotland

By the same author

Maurice Lindsay

The Castles of Scotland

Constable · London

First published in Great Britain 1986
by Constable and Company Limited
10 Orange Street London WC2H 7EG
Copyright © 1986 by Maurice Lindsay
Set in Monophoto Garamond 11pt. by
Servis Filmsetting Ltd Manchester
Printed in Great Britain by
BAS Printers Ltd Over Wallop

British Library CIP data
Lindsay, Maurice
The castles of Scotland
1.   Castles – Scotland
I.   Title
941.1   DA875

ISBN 0 09 464600 7

To Jack, for the fun of the early years
of The Scottish Civic Trust

Contents

Illustrations

Acknowledgements

The standard work on Scottish castles is *The Castellated and Domestic Architecture of Scotland* by David MacGibbon and Thomas Ross, a magisterial achievement which appeared in five large well-illustrated volumes published in Edinburgh between 1887 and 1892. No one could thereafter attempt to deal with the subject without acknowledging a debt to these two busy Edinburgh architects, whose story has been told for the first time by David Walker in 'The Architecture of MacGibbon and Ross: The Background to the Books', an essay in the splendid *festschrift* presented to Stewart Cruden, *Studies in Scottish Antiquity* (1984). Apart from his long and distinguished years as Scotland's Principal Inspector of Historic Buildings and Ancient Monuments, Cruden's many publications included his fascinating and scholarly study *The Scottish Castle* (1960, revised 1981). Between 1962 and 1970, Nigel Tranter produced his five-volume survey of Scottish Castles, *The Fortified House in Scotland*, with helpful historical notes, but perhaps the unique usefulness of which is the series of drawings of each made by him especially for these volumes. He thus provides an interesting visual comparison stressing the gains and losses in this aspect of our heritage over nearly a century. The tower house, or castle, is without doubt Scotland's one unique contribution to European architecture, and Mr Tranter's books did much to widen popular interest in this aspect of Scotland's heritage.

Other authorative studies essential to the subject include the *Proceedings of the Society of Antiquaries*, in particular the articles by Douglas Simpson, John Dunbar and Harry Gordon Slade; W. Mackay Mackenzie's *The Medieval Castle In Scotland* (1927); W. Douglas Simpson's studies on many individual castles as well as *The Ancient Stones of Scotland* (2nd edition 1968) and, of course, the Royal Commission on the Ancient and Historical Monuments of Scotland's series of inventories (by no means yet complete) and the Ancient Monuments individual guides to the buildings in State care. Valuable, too, is Oliver Hill's *Scottish Castles of the 16th and 17th Centuries* (1953) and *The Painted Ceilings of Scotland* by M.R. Apted (1966).

As a member for the best part of a decade of the Historic Buildings Council for Scotland, I have had the benefit in the course of duty of reading merit reports on many of the castles which that body has assisted with essential repair grants and, happily, in some cases, the wherewithal to bring about more or less complete restoration. My colleague on that body, Marc Ellington, himself the restorer of Towie Barclay, read my typescript and made several most useful observations. I have also had the benefit of the comments of Dr Richard Fawcett and his staff of the Ancient Monuments, on the castles now in State care.

Above all, however, I cannot too warmly thank David Walker, the present Principal Inspector of the Historic Buildings Council for Scotland, whose encyclopaedic knowledge has so generously been put at my disposal. He read my typescript and made invaluable comments. But for him, above all, this book would have been much less informative than I hope it is.

In spite of the help of these authorities, both dead and living, needless to say any errors or shortcomings are entirely my own.

I must also warmly thank my daughter, Mrs Kirsteen Stokes, who, in the midst of a busy family life, and while also acting as the Managing Editor of *The Scottish Review*, typed both the first draft of this book and the final version.

The photographs are acknowledged separately, but I must record a special word of thanks to Mrs Geraldine Simpson of Muchalls Castle, who most kindly drew my attention to her large collection of photographs of castles taken by herself, and made these available to me.

Finally, I would like to thank Benjamin Glazebrook, the Chairman and Managing Director of Constable Publishers, for his courtesy and patience in waiting for the delivery of my text, delayed for over a year because of my unexpected involvement with various conservation interests, in particular, my becoming Honorary Secretary-General of *Europa Nostra*.

Introduction

Man is a fighting animal. As his technical knowledge has advanced, his methods of defending himself have adapted accordingly. Consequently, there is no such thing as *the* Scottish castle; rather a series of castles of different kinds designed to meet dangers ranging from the relatively straightforward assaults with fire and sword of whoever were the enemies of the broch people to the primitive firearms in general use when Scotland's King James VI succeeded Elizabeth of England on the London throne. The Union of the Crowns then brought about a sort of peace between the two countries which made future practical defensive evolutions of style in Scottish castle-building unnecessary.

Castles did, of course, get built for a further three centuries, at first aping the defensive needs of former times. Some built by the Victorians and Edwardians used sixteenth- and seventeenth-century motifs as a style applied to modern plans with modern techniques, at their best openly enjoying their allusions to the past. Latterly, a few, like Formakin and Broughton Place, were simply 'pretend' castles; grand houses usurping a designation to which their purely domestic role did not really entitle them.

The castles dealt with in this book were intended to repel attackers, and all of them were erected before 1707. The Union of Parliaments of Scotland and England appeared to ensure – at least from England's point of view – that the Scots could offer no further trouble. The Jacobite risings of 1715 and 1745 were neither static enough, nor, indeed, of long enough duration, to affect the long process of stylistic change as the Scottish castle underwent a gradual transformation over two centuries to the opulent servant-laden turreted Edwardian country house; the last flourish of a scale of private building for a society whose *ancien régime* was finally blown to bits on the battlefields of the 1914–18 war.

Strictly speaking, then, the earliest Scottish castles to survive are the brochs, those round hollow towers built of dry stone masonry and externally rather like miniature twentieth-century industrial cooling towers. Their thick walls contained mural galleries surmounted by a fighting platform on the wall head, and encircling a courtyard which, in all probability, was roofed over with timber. Nobody can be absolutely certain who the broch people were, though it is generally assumed that they must have been Picts. Nor do we know why they built these impressive defensive structures, apparently siting them in clusters. Brochs have survived in the greatest number in two areas; in the Northern Isles and the neighbouring mainland former counties of Caithness and Sutherland; and in the Hebrides and along the adjoining coast of the old counties of Ross-shire and Inverness-shire. Brochs have also been discovered, however, in what were once Angus, Perthshire, Stirlingshire, Selkirkshire, Berwickshire and even in Galloway, though those in the extreme south may simply have been outposts for a defensive civilisation that had a northern centre.

W. Douglas Simpson[1] suggests that there were perhaps in all about five hundred brochs in Scotland at the height of the broch period, the first and second centuries AD. He also notes that all of those whose stones survive stood on good farmland. The mystery of why they were built remains.

It seems likely that brochs were in some way connected with the Roman occupation of Western Europe, which, of course, included Britain. One theory is that from about the time of the Roman conquest of Gaul during the first century BC, slave-catchers, 'whether Roman or middle-men, such as the Belgae of southern Britain amongst whose remains slave chains have been found',[2] ranged far and wide in search of a supply of slaves, but met with resistance in the far north of the country. One possible explanation for the main concentration of brochs in the northern and more isolated regions of Scotland could thus be the fact that the Roman sphere of influence never effectively extended north of Inverness in the east, beyond the western seaboard, or into Galloway in the south-west.

Many investigators, struck by the remarkable similarity of constructional methods employed by the broch builders, have wondered if broch design was the work of a single master-mind. Defensive architecture down the ages, however, has tended to evolve in recognisably derivative patterns in response to whatever happened to be the latest and most dangerous military threat. What proved effective in one location was simply copied in another, where similar dangers had to be countered.

The majority of surviving brochs bear evidence of adaptation for later activities, mostly agricultural. Many have been extensively if not completely destroyed. The sites of a few have been excavated

---

[1] *The Ancient Stones of Scotland* (2nd ed., 1968)
[2] Stewart Cruden: *The Scottish Castle* (3rd ed., 1981)

scientifically, notably those at Mid Hoy and Gurness in Orkney, Skitten in Caithness, and Torwoodlee in Selkirkshire. Fascinating as is the broch culture, the scale of this guide does not permit more than the mention here of two examples, Mousa in Shetland and Dun Carloway in Lewis, both relatively complete and, particularly the latter, accessible.

Also apparently occupied over a long period were the small stone-walled forts known as 'duns', found in the Hebrides. Sometimes it has been claimed that they were related to the brochs, but whether they represent the original form of what later developed into the more sophisticated structure or exemplify the broch tradition in decline must remain a matter of conjecture.

In the twelfth century, the early Canmore kings were responsible for the transformation of Scotland into a feudal kingdom organised along Anglo-Norman lines. A large number of structures of a new type, known as motte-and-bailey castles, was put up by the Norman settlers and soon imitated by Celtic chiefs in other parts of Scotland, notably Aberdeenshire. The Norman name for the new defensive device came from the earthen mound on which the castle itself was erected (the derivative word *moat* representing the defensive ditch surrounding it, from which the earth was dug out). On the top of the motte or mound was a timber tower surrounded by an inner palisade and a fosse or wet ditch. The bailey consisted of a larger but lower enclosure, also surrounded by an inner palisade and fosse, in which were located the domestic buildings, including the solar or lord's private apartment, and shelter for his dependants in time of danger. They, too, were surrounded by an inner palisade. The bailey and the motte were linked by a timber bridge spanning the fosse. The whole thing was further surrounded by an outer palisade of timber, and yet another fosse.

We have quite a clear idea of what motte-and-bailey castles looked like, because several are illustrated in the Bayeux Tapestry. Needless to say none of the actual structures has come down to us, although many of the earthen tumuli thrown up to carry them are still to be found, especially in the Border river valleys. The mound known as the Motte of Urr, in the Dumfries and Galloway Region, has, indeed, been excavated.

The sites of a few of the larger motte-and-bailey castles carry later structures; notably Huntly, in Grampian Region, and Castle Duffus and Castle Urquhart, in Highland Region. At Duffus, where the outer fosse appears to have encompassed about eight

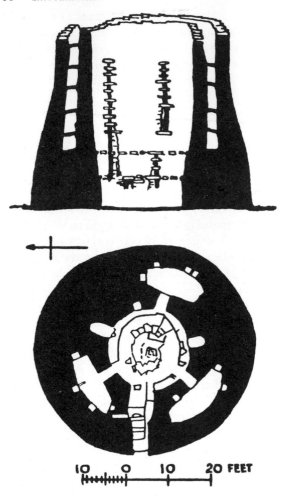

10   0   10   20 FEET

Broch of Mousa, Shetland: A cross-section of the circular interior.

acres in all, the original wooden castle on the mound was replaced by a stone building, perhaps about the year 1300; at about the same time a stone wall was thrown around the bailey. The weight of the stone castle on a mound originally built to support a wooden one eventually proved too great. The stone tower split in two and part of the original wall collapsed. It held up long enough, however, to

Broch of Mousa, Shetland, the most complete broch to come down to us.

Motte-and-Bailey Castle: an imaginary reconstruction of one of these early wooden castles.

provide shelter for David I, who visited it in 1151 when engaged in founding Kinloss Abbey.

The rebuilding at Duffus provides a link with the next stage of Anglo-Norman development in Scotland; the thirteenth-century stone castle of enceinte, or enclosure behind a high embattled curtain wall. There were, of course, stone castles of an intermediary sort put up during the twelfth century in those parts of Scotland where the Norse Jarls held sway. Kolbein Hruga, colloquialised to Cubbie's Roo, on the Orkney island of Wyre, is a miniature keep about twenty feet square skilfully constructed of local flagstone. When it was built – c.1145, according to the *Orkneyenga Saga* – it probably had two or three storeys topped with a saddle-backed roof, and would be entered by means of a ladder leading to the first floor. It was surrounded by a circular rampart and fosse.

Castle Sween, on the shores of Loch Sween, is perhaps of an even earlier date. It has a sea-gate as well as its mainland entrance through a round arched door in one of its mid-wall buttresses. It appears to have been floored and roofed, and therefore a keep of Norse type similar to Cubbie's Roo. In the fifteenth century, a large square tower with pointed openings was added to the north-east corner of Castle Sween. In the sixteenth century, a round tower was tacked on to the north-west corner.

Rothesay Castle, on the island of Bute, is another transitional building. It is basically a twelfth-century circular keep erected on a flat motte. To this, four round towers were added outside the wall in the thirteenth century. A forework was provided to defend the entrance. About 1500, a much larger forework was added, which encompassed royal apartments and a great hall. At the time of this addition the walls were raised and a small postern was added. The put-log holes for the boarding, or external over-laying gallery – which would be removed when not needed for defensive purposes but covered with wet hides when in use – are still to be seen. The bailey contained not only the usual domestic buildings but also a chapel. The end result was thus a castle of enceinte, though its circular pattern has remained unique in Scotland.

Many of the earliest castles of enceinte were originally devised simply as curtain walls to protect a range of buildings. To these walls towers were later added so that covering fire-power for archers and crossbowmen could be provided. One such example is the thirteenth-century Comyn Castle of Balvenie, in Grampian Region; quadrangular, and surrounded by a huge wall of rubble and a ditch cut out of rock. The use of dressed ashlar for curtain walls was, of course, much more common. Much of the Balvenie that we see today, however, dates from the fifteenth and sixteenth centuries.

A splendidly preserved castle of this kind is Loch Doune, in Dumfries and Galloway Region, dismantled from its original island site to make way for a hydro-electric development and reconstructed in its present position during the 1930s. It has a plain entrance through an archway, a portcullis, drawbars for the defence of the door, and walls with battar, or thickening spread, round the base to afford additional protection.

Related in purpose to Castle Sween, already mentioned, is an interesting group of thirteenth-century curtain-walled castles scattered along the west coast and throughout the Western Isles. All stand on rocky sites by the sea, their purpose being the defence of the surrounding area against the Norsemen who came to Scotland.

Castle Tioram stands fast on a tidal island in Loch Moidart, its roughly pentagonal shape governed by the contour of the rock which carries it. It has rounded curtain-wall corners and an easily defended narrow entrance in the north wall. This leads into the courtyard, where there is a keep of later date. An outside stair against the inner wall leads to the battlement walk.

Mingarry, on the cliff where Loch Sunart meets the Sound of Mull, is of a similar type. Kisimull Castle, on the island of Barra, has a square keep set into the curtain wall. The seat of the Macneils of Barra, it has been restored in post-World-War-II years.

Dunstaffanage, on the Firth of Lorne, near Oban, has a quadrangular enceinte with round towers set into the angles, such as are to be found at Rothesay. Though thirteenth-century in origin, it now has sixteenth- and eighteenth-century additions. One of its original towers takes the form of a keep, and it has been suggested that this represents a transitional stage towards the 'concentric castle' of Edward I,[1] which represented the highest development of fortification in the days before the introduction of gunpowder. Inverlochy, in Highland Region, once another Comyn stronghold, is a quadrangular structure with four round towers at the angles, one of which was the keep, or donjon, from which in emergencies the defenders were supposed in the last resort to make a concerted stand. The surrounding moat was filled by the River Lochy, control of the inflow being provided by a water-gate.

The principle of retreat to the donjon was fundamentally somewhat defeatist. The Edwardian castles of North Wales, like their Scottish near-counterparts, therefore thrust the defence forward to a massive gate-house, supported by parapeted curtain-walls punctuated at regular intervals by projecting towers capable of providing an extensive field of covering fire. This improved system was probably copied from Byzantine castles, the efficacy of whose defensive arrangements would have been painfully noted by the Crusaders.

Broadly speaking, the medieval castle had two functions. In times of peace it was the centre of local administration. In times of war it had to defend both its lord and his dependants. As methods of warfare changed, so did architectural needs. Until about the time of Edward I, castles had to be able to repel sudden onslaught with the use of ladders, and – if the invaders were successful in scaling them – the hand-to-hand fighting which ensued.

In Edward I's time, when an assault was to be made upon a sufficiently important target, great wooden towers protected by wet hides would be moved on wooden rollers up against the curtain walls. They could then be used not only to rain arrows and crossbow fire upon the defendants within, but also to lob missiles

[1] T.W. West, *A History of Architecture in Scotland* 1967

Bothwell Castle: an imaginary reconstruction, published by
MacGibbon and Ross in 1887.

from catapults. While all this was going on wooden tunnels,
similarly protected, would be pushed against the base of the wall to
enable sappers to attempt to burrow an entrance from beneath.

It now seems to be generally accepted that Edward I did not
himself order the building of any of the Scottish castles that
featured prominently in the Wars of Independence. An English-
trained master mason, John Kilburne, had a hand in the reconstruction of Bothwell, in Strathclyde Region, between 1331–7. It still
retains the concept of the keep, since as well as its curtain-walls with
round and square towers, and a gate house (later demolished), it
also possessed a massive cylindrical donjon, probably the second
largest in Britain, exceeded in dimension only by that at Conisborough, in Yorkshire. Scottish lairds who found themselves
having to recapture their own castles after having lost them to the
English frequently dismantled their defences; a process called
'slighting'. Half the donjon of Bothwell was thrown down into the

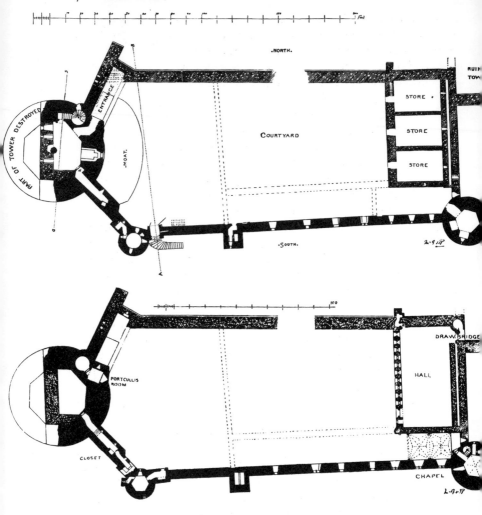

Bothwell Castle: plans of the ground floor and the first floor.

Clyde by its owner, Sir Andrew de Moray, in 1337 during just such a 'slighting'. When the donjon was eventually replaced, a straight wall was substituted for the previous circular one. Even so, the tower still rises to a height of ninety feet. A moat separates the keep from the bailey, within which a hall and a chapel were added in the fourteenth century by its Douglas owners. Machicolations were added in the fifteenth century.

Kildrummy, in Grampian Region, built to a pentagonal plan, resembles Bothwell in several respects. It, too, has the largest of its four towers as the donjon, situated to the rear of the enceinte. The hall and chapel are in one of the smaller angle towers. The magnificent gate-house is of a kind associated with Edward I's master mason, James of St George. It boasts two large jutting drum towers, suggesting an offensive rather than a purely defensive posture. One of the towers probably enabled the laird to sleep safely at night. The term 'keep-gate-house' has been applied to dual-purpose structures of this kind. Although some fifteenth- and sixteenth-century work was carried out at Kildrummy, this castle probably retains more of its thirteenth-century original design than any other similar Scottish secular building.

Caerlaverock, in Dumfries and Galloway Region, was built to a mid-thirteenth-century triangular plan, still clearly distinguishable in spite of many later additions. It has two round towers at the rear angles of its high wall, and a magnificent twin-tower keep-gate-house enclosing a rib-vaulted hall. The machicolated wall-heads, as at Bothwell, are fifteenth-century additions.

On the other side of Scotland, at Dirleton, in Lothian Region, on a rocky outcrop which dictated the original plan, stands another castle of enceinte from the high period of its kind. Captured by the English in 1298, it was duly retaken by the Scots and 'slighted'. The original castle formed a group of three towers ranged round a small courtyard. The bailey, indeed, is so small that it is little more than an adjunct to the towers. Again, the keep-gate-house thrusts forward aggressively, providing not only the main element in the defensive arrangements, but also two polygonal vaulted halls, one above the other. Later work at Dirleton included a fifteenth-century hall over the cellarage, and a Renaissance house.

Mention should perhaps be made at this point of a type of architecture which, though it found great favour in England, failed to become popular in the Scotland of the early Middle Ages. This was the fortified manor house. Surviving Scottish examples are few, but include Morton Castle, in Dumfries and Galloway Region, an unvaulted hall house with a defended gate-house, and Rait Castle in Grampian Region, built by two brothers, Sir Gervais and Sir Andrew Rait, both strong supporters of Edward I in an area of Scotland vigorously opposed to his rule. Rait has a long rectangular hall built upon vaulted cellarage and a round tower containing the Lord's private rooms. In its older parts, Hailes Castle, Lothian

Region, owned by a Northumbrian family, the Gourlays, has architectural features copied from their English seat, Aydon Castle, on Tyneside.

These are exceptions. For some reason the fashion simply never caught on. The concept of the fortified manor house was virtually abandoned once the Scots passion for building vertically, dating from the broch days, found new expression over many centuries in the fortified tower house.

There were, however, some further developments of earlier castle patterns before the tower house entered upon its long period of supremacy. While the War of Independence in Scotland was raging, siege and destruction rather than building were the order of the day. About this time the feudal law whereby men had to make themselves available for specified periods in support of their lord's military needs gave place to the establishment of paid mercenaries, or liverymen, who could be hired for as long as they might be required. Because these liverymen had to be paid, they could insist on reasonable standards of accommodation, which was generally provided within the lord's castle. The need to meet these changing circumstances led to the construction of a number of major buildings sometimes known as 'livery and maintenance castles'.

Tantallon, built by the Douglas family (who provided the most serious of all the baronial threats to the Crown), stands gripping a dramatic rocky outcrop on the Lothian's coast. Two previous castles may have occupied the same near-impregnable site in turn; but the existing ruin, that of one of the most impressive castles of enceinte ever built in Scotland, was a new building in 1374. The fifty-feet-high curtain wall, later strengthened against firearms, straddles the headland. The mid tower acted as the gate-house and once contained five storeys, providing accommodation for the lord as well as both a laich (lower) hall and a long hall above it. As the vaulted entrance-way passed through the tower, it was protected by a portcullis and no fewer than three pairs of swinging gates. The lord thus had full command of his own defences. A secondary hall for housing his mercenaries was situated within the curtain-wall.

Clearly, the protective use of cliffs, plunging down to the sea, dictated Tantallon's uncharacteristic shape. Much more usual is Doune, in Central Region, almost quadrangular in layout. It is an impressive and singularly well-preserved example of a kind sometimes described in Europe as the castle of 'bastard feudalism'; the term applied to castles constructed according to the old pattern when the social order which dictated its characteristics had begun to decline. Doune was built for the Regent Albany during the minority and enforced English captivity of the poet-king James I. Its forceful keep-gate-house provided not only accommodation for the lord, but also separate quarters for his servants. Its frontal mass faces the only possible angle of attack, while at the rear there is simply a curtain wall against which the minor domestic buildings were erected. Gone is the principle of the donjon and separate gate-house. The curtain walls rise to forty feet, just above the height against which at that time it was possible effectively to place scaling ladders. The undulating nature of the surrounding ground ensured that a wooden assault tower could not possibly be wheeled near the curtain walls.

Two other medieval castles should perhaps be mentioned in this introductory survey. On the remote Hebridean island of Coll, Breachacha Castle survives to remind us that a sufficiently determined and influential man could always import craftsmen from the mainland to meet his desire to have a castle of his own in the latest fashion. In this once remote island there is thus a fortress with a central donjon, inner curtain, flanking tower linked to a hall, outer curtain and surrounding palisade; in fact, a mainland medieval castle in miniature.

Individual in a different sense is Ravenscraig, Fife Region, now overlooked by blocks of Kirkcaldy flats. Begun by James II in 1460, it was left half-completed on the death of his widow, Mary of Guelders, for whom it was intended as a dower-house. The Scots first had firearms used against them by Edward III in 1327. Scots kings thereafter naturally paid great attention both to the development of firearms for offence, and to defensive measures against their application. Ravenscraig was the first castle in Britain to be constructed to resist attack by artillery, anticipating even Henry VIII's English coastal forts by some eighty years.

Ravenscraig somewhat resembles Tantallon in plan. The lord's apartments were presumably located in one of its two massive round towers, the garrison quarters in the other. The frontal range has a passage entrance and vaulted basement. It also has inverted keyhole-shaped gun posts, topped by an open gun platform with breastworks and wide-mouthed embrasures. Mary of Guelders was a Burgundian princess, and it is known that Burgundian technicians and craftsmen were employed in Scotland after her marriage to James II.

After the decline of baronial power about the middle of the fourteenth century, the form of major building which surpassed all others was the tower house. It could be argued that from the early brochs to the 'lands' of the seventeenth and eighteenth centuries – through, indeed, to the tenements of the nineteenth century and the high-rise flats of the twentieth – the Scots have always preferred to build upwards rather than horizontally, in the English fashion; the early reflection, perhaps, of an insecurity that over centuries has become an inbred national characteristic. The purpose of the tower house, which remained in fashion for almost three hundred years, was to provide both a home and a place of defence in the one building. It offered the triple advantages of economy and of gratifying both private dignity and local pride.

The earliest tower houses were either square or rectangular, their unornamented thick ashlar walls rising to a crenellated parapet, often with unroofed turrets or rounds set at the summit angles. Usually there was a low stone-vaulted basement, suitably ventilated, above which was a higher vault divided in two by a timber floor resting on stone corbels. The Great Hall would be situated on this first floor with the solar, or lord's private apartment, above it.

The house would be entered by wooden stairs leading directly to the first, sometimes even to the second floor. A spiral or turnpike internal stair often twisted round a newel up one corner of the thick walls, frequently switching direction from one side of the wall to the other halfway up as an additional defensive device.

Unlike the Norman keep to be found in England, the Scottish tower house had no forebuilding, outer wall or pilaster buttresses. Now and then a barmkin, or courtyard, would be thrown round the tower house, such as was also constructed round many a Norman keep. More usually, however, the Scots resorted to ramparts or ditches as their form of outer defence.

The island castle of Loch Leven, near Kinross, is a good early example of a tower house with angle turrets and a curtain wall. More characteristic, though only islanded at high tide by the River Dee, is Threave, in Dumfries and Galloway Region, a Douglas stronghold built at about the same time as the family was constructing their great castle of Tantallon, on the other side of the country, in the older style.

Threave has five stories. It was entered from the upper floor of a curtain wall linked to the second floor of the tower by a wooden bridge. This formidable structure seems once to have had permanent timber boarding over the wall-top.

Drum, in Grampian Region, and Crichton, in Lothian Region, are other early examples. Hallforest, in Grampian, illustrates the attempts of late-fourteenth century owners to expand their accommodation by adding a wing, thus making the structure L-shaped. The adoption of this plan eventually led to the construction of the entrance door in the internal angle, thus affording protection from two sides.

Craigmillar, now engulfed by the environs of Edinburgh, is basically an L-shaped tower house with many later additions, including a fifteenth-century curtain wall with angle towers. Castle Campbell, sightlessly staring down on the prosperous little town of Dollar from the Ochil Hills, possesses a similar late addition.

Hermitage, in the Border Region, was formed out of an English-style manor house with tower blocks flanking an open court. Around 1400, projecting square towers were added to each of the corners, creating an appearance of aggressive strength which still impresses us today.

There are similarities between Hermitage and Borthwick, Lothian Region, built about 1430, and happily still intact and occupied. Borthwick has two wings, or jambs, projecting from the same wall. Other roughly similar structures of the period include the now almost totally collapsed Elphinstone, in Lothian Region. Except for Comlongon, in Dumfries and Galloway Region, among Scottish castles it was never to be surpassed either in scale of construction or strength.

From about 1480 until the Reformation – a period of eighty or so years – the impetus to build tower houses slackened. This can reasonably be attributed to the disaster of Flodden in 1513, when virtually an entire generation of the nation's leaders was wiped out along with their king, James IV.

A few notable tower houses went up during these years; notably Craig Castle, Delgaty, Towie Barclay and Balbegno, all employing rib vaulting.

Legislation of 1535 had stipulated that every landed man dwelling 'in the inland or upon the borders' having land valued at £100 must build 'a sufficient Barmekin' of stone and lime on his land to ensure their defence, with 'a tour in the samen for himsel', if he thought that expedient. Smaller landowners were similarly enjoined to build peel-towers of sufficient strength to defend their property. All this was to be done within two years, but until the troublous religious questions of the day which resulted in the eruption of the Reformation were settled, violent public controversy made more urgent demands than private defence.

The most characteristic addition to Scotland's secular architectural heritage in the years leading up to the Reformation was the adornment of the 'palatial' royal castles; Stirling, Holyroodhouse, Falkland and Linlithgow. Falkland was a tower house at the end of the fourteenth century, though already one with additional facilities added. The major period of its reconstruction, from 1537 to 1542, transformed it from the 'old ludging' known to James II into the French style Renaissance building which has come down to us today, effulgently decorated with effigies carved by Peter Flemisman in 1538-9. It bears witness to its somewhat hybrid character, for as Stewart Cruden has so aptly observed,[1] the south range is really a 'Renaissance screen which hangs in front of an unaffected Gothic range a corridor's breadth behind'. Linlithgow Palace underwent an equally dramatic transformation during the reign of James V, who was born in it. He was responsible for the fine fountain in the centre of the quadrangle, the detached gateway to the south which then led into an enclose court, and the alterations to the south and west elevations. James VI had further alterations made to the west side, as well as rebuilding the north side between 1617 and 1628, the master mason being William Wallace, who was also responsible for Heriot's Hospital in Edinburgh. James IV and James V commissioned much of the fine Renaissance work in Stirling Castle, notably in Parliament Hall, completed *c.*1505. It is a large medieval hall of traditional plan, flanked by two impressive mullioned bay windows crossed by transomes, or stone bars, and rising to the full height of the building. Buttresses and little effigies in framed niches emphasise the older Gothic influence, but that of the Renaissance is to be seen in the intersecting tracery of the bay windows. The hall forms the east side of a quadrangle. The north side is the Chapel Royal, built in 1594, replacing an earlier chapel. It has a painted frieze and a classical doorway flanked by Roman Doric columns. On the south side is The Royal Palace, begun by Andrew Aytoun for James IV in 1496 and completed in 1540 during James V's reign, which exemplifies further the working in of Renaissance detail to a structure essentially Gothic in conception. Sculptured Renaissance

[1] *op. cit.*

statues stand on baluster wall-shafts. Drawing upon classical subject-matter, they display a vigorous Renaissance exuberance almost Baroque in its energy. A lion supporting a crown surmounts the crow-stepped gabled and battlemented parapet. The parapet, which projects over the main face of the wall, is supported by a cornice decorated with puffy-faced *putti* inspired by French or Italian patterns. Indeed, they may even have been carved by the same probably foreign hand as that which fashioned the famous 'Stirling Roundels', the fifty-six oak panels once set inside the flat ceiling of the king's chamber. They were removed when the building was in later use as a barracks after one had fallen, fatally injuring a soldier. Happily, they will be replaced (in some cases in replica) as part of the late-twentieth-century restoration.

Edinburgh Castle also had its palatial quarter added about this time. In spite of being a self-contained centre of administration equipped with a treasure house, a mint, and an arsenal and its associated workshops, Edinburgh, however, was not much favoured as a royal residence by the Stuart kings. Indeed, it was the Earl of Arran who was responsible for a good deal of expenditure on what were no doubt much-needed improvements in its residential quarters during his years as Regent for the young Mary, Queen of Scots, inserting or modernising the glazing, which did not come into general use in Scottish castles until the early fifteenth century.

There was also the early work at Holyroodhouse. James V had Sir James Hamilton of Finnart design the south-western corner of the Palace, an edifice altered in the capping of the towers, and internally, by Sir William Bruce's work for Charles II, though it still contains the rooms associated with Rizzio's murder.

While post-Reformation tower houses in no way attempted to reflect the external splendour of the great Elizabethan country houses of England, they did, however, aim at providing greater spaciousness and improved amenities for their owners than could be accommodated in the older towers. Today, most of the tower houses that have come down to us have either been altered internally, in greater or lesser degree, to take account of nineteenth- and twentieth-century living standards, or are sad shells; ruins often still reflecting the architectural features and qualities which once distinguished their exteriors, particularly in the upper works, but stripped of the accoutrements of daily living which must have lent them at least a certain colourful graciousness and made them pleasingly habitable homes by the standards of their times.

Quite why the Scots maintained their medieval fondness for building vertically in the teeth of changing fashion is hard to explain. Perhaps the relatively few people required to defend a tower as compared to the Elizabethan house, with its larger plan and mullioned windows, offers one explanation; shortage of land within the walled towns, of course, and perhaps the high cost of timber everywhere, as well as the difficulty of obtaining long lengths of it, another. Yet when money and the advance of taste did allow the Scots to fulfil the family demand for extra accommodation, they achieved it either by building to a still greater height, as at Amisfield (1600), in Dumfries and Galloway Region, where the inventiveness of the crowded upper works still manages to create a remarkable sense of balance; or, more frequently, simply by linking towers together in one form or another.

A tower was certainly regarded as a symbol of authority, as we know from Lyndsay of Pitscottie's reference to James V founding 'ane fair palice in the abbey of Halirudhous and ane greit towre to himself to rest into quhene he pleissit to come to the toun'; a 'towre' which, significantly, contained the king's private suite.

Originally, the tower house had been a relatively classless structure, size and strength alone indicating differences of wealth or social position. With new wealth available in Protestant Scotland – wealth which, in Catholic times, had been spent on votive masses, in founding chapels or cathedrals, or on monastic churches – to say nothing of the redistribution of the old Church's plundered riches, there was every encouragement for a resumption of secular building. Thus between 1570, when the upheaval that preluded and accompanied the establishment of the Reformation had more or less subsided, and the outbreak of the Covenanting troubles in 1637, the list of newly erected tower houses is a long one. It includes such distinguished examples as Claypotts (1569–88), with its use of corbelling to provide square-roomed structures like cottages on top of round towers, defensive measures being confined to the ground floor; Balbegno (1569); Tolquhon (1584–9), where the defensive arrangements were little more than wide-mouthed gun ports covering the curtain walls; and Fyvie (c.1600), its great showy front linking two towers with an immense imposing gate-house in the middle. There was also McLellan's castle in Kirkcudbright (1582), Elcho (1580) and Noltland a few years later, amongst many others.

Most tower houses had one room per floor and were usually without corridors. Where there were adjacent rooms, one was entered through the other. The L-plan castles, built before as well as after the Reformation, allowed for better domestic planning, as well as better defence, one part being able to protect the other along the adjoining faces. In the case of the Z-plan castle,[1] 'the whole of the four walls of the main building were covered and defended from slotholes in the two diagonally opposite towers'. Tiny Terpersie, in Grampian Region (1561), is one of the first Z-plan castles, though Beldorney (*c*.1545) is an earlier example. Claypotts (1569–88), much more ambitious, is another. The earliest of all, however, was probably Strathbogie, in Grampian Region, put up about 1552 after the Earl of Moray had destroyed its predecessor. Drochil, in the Border Region, a Z-plan castle built for the Regent Morton, has a central corridor on each of its floors, virtually a unique feature at the time of its building and anticipating later domestic planning.

Defensive arrangements were increasingly taken less and less account of, the early possibilities of ordinance weapons, with their low trajectories, not always being fully appreciated. By 1630, a lawsuit decision over a disputed building ruled that the subject in question 'was not a Tower or Fortalice . . .' having 'neither Fosse nor Barmekin wall about it, nor Battling, but was only an ordinary house'.[2] By 1677, the Earl of Strathmore, who owned Huntly and Glamis, could confidently declare that towers were 'truly out of fashion, as feuds are . . . the country being generally more civilised than it was of ancient times'.[3]

European influences are increasingly reflected in many of the later tower houses; that of France in the case of Huntly, with its oriel windows and richly ornamented corbelling, probably inspired by a similar feature at Blois; in the symmetrically balanced sixteenth-century section of Thirlstane, which has no counterpart in Scotland; Fyvie's extended frontage, part of a quadrangle formed around an earlier castle of enceinte but never completed, though reflected in a somewhat similar way by Sir William Bruce's

---

[1] MacGibbon and Ross, *The Castellated and Domestic Architecture of Scotland*
[2] *Duries Decisions*, quoted by W.M. Mackenzie in *The Medieval Castle in Scotland* (1921)
[3] Cruden: *op. cit.*

remodelling of Holyroodhouse for Charles II in 1671;[1] the influence of Italy in the Italianate formidable-looking diamond-patterned courtyard façade of the Earl of Bothwell's Crichton (1580–90); and that of Germany in the additions made to Edzell Castle in Tayside Region by Sir Patrick Lindsay, Lord Edzell, where the decorations on the wall of his pleasance openly acknowledge their inspiration to a pupil of Dürer.

The pepper-pot turrets, really roofed-in angle rounds, so long to be perpetuated in Scottish architecture, though also popular in France, do, however, seem to be a native feature, a development, perhaps, of the rounded angles to be found at Drum.

Apart from the untypical Elizabethan-like extravaganza which is the Earl's Palace of Kirkwall, Orkney, erected by the despotic Earl Patrick Stewart about 1600 but never actually finished, because his crimes caught up with him, the finest group of later tower house castles is that found in Grampian Region, comprising Fyvie, Midmar, Castle Fraser, Craigievar and Crathes, all but Midmar (still owned privately) now in the safe keeping of the National Trust for Scotland.

The stylistic hands that wrought their distinctions have left behind some identifying clues. The sophisticated stairway at Crichton and some of the detail in the castles of the north-east were clearly the work of a few hands and inventive minds. We know of 'ane gentilman, Andrew Crawfurd, sumtym servand and maister of vark to the Earl of Orkney', whose broken tombstone in the old churchyard at Tingwall, near Scalloway, records that he died on '1 Mai 160–'. In the churchyard at Midmar (formerly called Balogy) another tombstone states, 'Heir lyis Georg Bel mason Deceisit in Balogy Ano 1575', while on the front of Castle Fraser a tablet commemorates 'I. Bell 1617', a member of the same family. A relative, David Bell, was employed at Pitfichie in 1617. Another family who worked as designing masons in Scotland were the Leipers, the initials of Thomas Leiper surviving on a skew-putt at Tolquhon. Although Sir William Bruce is thought by some to have had a hand in Drumlanrig because of similarities in the crowned

---

[1] David Walker has commented that although James V's tower at Holyrood was not duplicated before Bruce's day, the main front was otherwise symmetrical (as a drawing of 1650 by F. de Witt in MacGibbon and Ross's *The Castellated and Domestic Architecture of Scotland* shows). Mr Walker adds that unfinished Barnes, Birsay and the old palace at Scone were all to have been symmetrically planned courtyard houses on the English model, as would Fyvie had it been completed.

centre-piece, arched loggias and huge square piers in the courtyards of the Dumfriesshire castle to his work at Holyroodhouse, the only known name connected with Drumlanrig is that of William Lukup, commemorated on the tombstone of one of his children in the nearby churchyard of Durisdeer. Crathes, an L-shaped house, seems to have been begun in 1553 and finished in 1596. It has sometimes been criticised for presenting a 'lumpish elevation', created by the large stair tower which links the two wings. But of course neither it nor Craigievar stood alone, as we now see them, both (like Castle Menzies, in Tayside) having once extensive walled outworks. Nevertheless, imaginative use of bold cable-moulding, the confidence of the corbelling and the sculptural inventiveness, dating from the late sixteenth and early seventeenth centuries, distinguish each of the group. Craigievar, completed in 1626 and happily little altered, is generally regarded as the finest of all the late tower houses and, indeed, as a piece of architecture by European standards outstanding, internally and externally. By the time it was first lived in, defensive arrangements had entirely ceased to be a serious consideration, as indeed they had also in the hall houses of England built during the same period.

Other methods of increasing accommodation while still retaining the tower tradition included U-shaped structures – virtually two Ls laid tail to tail – and, more spectacular, the quadrangular structure. One of the earliest of the quadrangular castles was the Earl's Palace on the Orkney island of Birsay, now badly ruined and neglected. Apparently Earl Robert, father of the despotic Earl Patrick, never got round to building a fourth corner tower. The three towers that did go up contained gun-ports which, in such a place and in turbulent times, were clearly not intended merely for decoration. John Seton's Barnes Castle (*c.*1599), in Lothian Region, now similarly neglected, also had enfilading gun positions built into its not dissimilar four towers.

Three later quadrangular buildings of undeniable distinction which clearly still acknowledge the influence of the tower house are Holyroodhouse (1671–9), George Heriot's Hospital (completed 1650, and now a school) and, more ornate but not dissimilar, Drumlanrig (1679–89), in Dumfries and Galloway Region. The Drumlanrig towers have small overhanging corner roundels, and on three elevations there is that elaborate cable moulding pattern which became fashionable in the sixteenth century. In overall design and in confident Baroque swagger, however, Drumlanrig resembles to some degree the English country seat of the period, and anticipates the castellated country houses that were to replace castle homes in Scotland during the eighteenth and nineteenth centuries.

Not that peace and industrial opulence were to end the romantic hankering of wealthy Scots for the old tower house with its defensive features. During the nineteenth century, re-created castles boasting towers and turrets, corbelling roundels and machicolations, often bearing no real relationship to any through-conceived design, proliferated throughout Scotland, particularly in the Highlands. The direct inspiration for much of this exercise of fantasy was probably the four-volumed study *Baronial and Ecclesiastical Antiquities of Scotland* by Robert William Billings, who was first invited to Scotland in 1845 by the architect William Burn. The final part of Billings's survey appeared in 1852. Many of these elaborate and extensive castellated Victorian and Edwardian structures, depending on large staffs of servants to run them, have succumbed to neglect or suffered demolition as a result of changed economic circumstances. A few, the more fortunate though not necessarily always the best, have been turned into institutions or hotels.

Many of the finest of the Victorian castles not only adapted and reinterpreted the external features of the past, but also developed the processional features which make such an impression in Baroque castles; for example, the grand *piano nobile* stair at Drumlanrig, reached only after crossing the courtyard through an open screen of arches, and the internal sequence of dining room, drawing room, bedchamber and closet. But after about 1700, the great houses were homes, not fortalices. Such troubles as their owners sometimes brought down upon their heads were the result of political intrigue or unyielding religious conviction, and rarely involved the defence of their property against military siege. These country-house castles therefore lie outside the scope of this book, although the best of them have become as irreplaceable as our dwindling stock of real castles, and as vital a part of our heritage, constantly in need of care and vigilant defence. Such famous castles as Culzean and Inveraray, which are notably 'country house' castles not built for defence, are excluded.

In the individual entries which deal with the more important castles, the arrangement is alphabetical. An Appendix, however, groups the castles alphabetically by Region. A large number of castles so radically altered as to be unrecognisable have been excluded, as have shapeless heaps of stone.   Inevitably, opinions will differ along the borderlines of categorisation, but a line has to be drawn somewhere if a guide intended for pleasurable practical use is not to swell to unmanageable and uneconomic proportions.

Abbot Hunter's Tower

This rectangular fifteenth-century tower stands in a Mauchline garden, part of an abbatial residence related to a Cistercian grange, in lands granted to Melrose Abbey in the twelfth century. Ranges abutted into the walls suggest that a quadrangular plan for the grange buildings was anticipated. What survives is dated by the arms of Abbot Hunter (*c.*1444–71), on a boss in the vaulting of the first-floor Hall.

As it now stands, the red rubble tower rises to four storeys with a crow-step gabled garret storey formerly contained within the modern crenellated parapet. It was replaced in the nineteenth century but has again been removed. At the north gable, overlooking the stream, is an unusual double garderobe chute. The basement contains two poorly-lit vaults. The tower's entrance is at ground level to the south, and there is a turnpike stair rising to the left of it. The fine Hall on the first floor is, very unusually, rib-vaulted in two bays and has a window with stone seats. A seventeenth-century house, much Georgianised, adjoins the tower against the west wall.

In 1521, Hew Campbell of Loudon was appointed Bailie of Barony by arrangement with the Abbot, and in 1606 gained the temporal lordship, when he turned it into a fortified house. The tower was once occupied by Gavin Hamilton, Burns's friend, as a tenant of Lord Loudon.

Badly modernised at a later date, by 1974 it was in poor condition, though attempts are being made to find a new use for it.

Aberdour Castle

Aberdour Castle, by the village of the same name, lies along a ridge of ground above the Dour burn a few yards before it falls into the Firth of Forth. The castle once consisted of three sections, two of which have been ruinous since the late eighteenth century and freely used as quarries for other buildings. The oldest section was a massive keep on the north-west corner, standing on the highest ground. Unfortunately, it collapsed in 1844, the fall destroying most of the internal arrangements. The first addition was probably the work of the Regent Morton, possibly unfinished at his death in 1581. The second addition, little later in date, further increased the

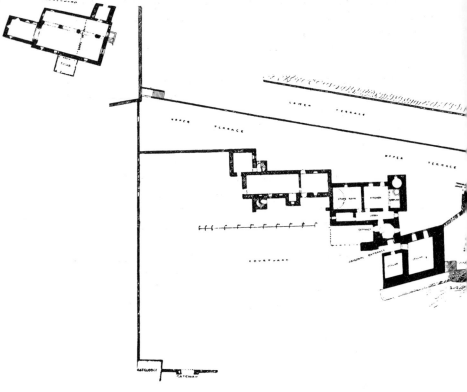

Aberdour Castle: a plan showing the extent of the ground floor.

domestic amenities. These buildings are also ruinous. It has been claimed that, though incorporated in the ancient keep, in concept they showed a freedom from the traditional restraints of keep or courtyard in achieving expanded, well-lit accommodation. The ruins of a chapel, on the south side of the garden, are still extant. Part of the walls of the chapel date from the Norman period, when Aberdour belonged to the Priory of St Colme's Inch.

All that survives intact today is the extreme eastern range of this once vast and splendid castle, a part of which consists of an oblong main block with two small projections to the north, and a square wing to the south, dating probably from the early seventeenth century. There is a low square tower in the re-entrant angle now containing the entrance and the stairway, but which may once have been a larger flanking tower forming part of the courtyard.

The basement has two unvaulted rooms. The upper floor has a long gallery which communicated on the west side with a sixteenth-century section of the castle. Its eastern window, generous for the period, has a pediment above its pilasters with the initials of William, seventh Earl of Morton, who died in 1648. His initials and those of his wife also adorn a sundial on the corner of the south wing. A seventeenth-century Renaissance gateway guarded by gunloops protects the entrance to the castle. The Ancient Monuments have carried out an ambitious restoration of the terraced garden.

James Douglas of Dalkeith became Lord Aberdour and Earl of Morton in 1458, but after three generations an heiress took the property by marriage to Sir George Douglas of Pittendreich, who, through his wife, rather strangely, became fourth Earl of Morton, Chancellor of Scotland, Regent, one of the murderers of Darnley and a notable cashier-in on the spoils of the Reformation.

The last inhabitant of the castle, Robert Watson of Muirhouse, died in it in 1791. Thereafter, it was neglected, plundered, 'used as cow-byres and piggeries' in MacGibbon and Ross's day, and only rescued when it was taken into care as an Ancient Monument.

Abergeldie Castle

Abergeldie Castle stands six miles west of Ballater, on the banks of the Dee. A small oblong tower probably dating from the late sixteenth century, it has similarities to Balfluig. Abergeldie has a turret at its north-east angle, and a semi-circular stair tower at the south-west corner corbelled square at eaves level to provide a watch-room. This now has a balustraded flat roof from which an ogee-capped belfry rises, replacing a Georgian railed parapet and iron cupola. There is a mid-Georgian dormer window, emerging out of the eaves nearby, and a tower clock, *c*.1840, by James Henderson. A large plain mid-Georgian mansion, mildly baronialised by Henderson, formerly adjoined to the west.

The castle is three storeys and an attic in height, with a vaulted basement. The Hall, is on the first floor and is vaulted. The interior is in an excellent and original state, restored to a high standard by a descendant of the builder, John Gordon of Abergeldie.

Abergeldie has been a Gordon stronghold since Sir Alexander Gordon of Midmar, second son of the first Earl of Huntly, acquired the lands. James, his grandson, was killed at the Battle of Pinkie. A Gordon laird lost all seven sons, killed by the Forbes while digging peat. A grandson in due course exacted revenge. Alexander Gordon of Abergeldie fought against the Covenanters, when the castle had a near escape from destruction.

The Birks of Abergeldie were 'transferred' poetically to Aberfeldy in a famous song by Burns, Dorothy Wordsworth correctly observing that Aberfeldy possessed no Birks!

Abergeldie Castle, though remaining in Gordon ownership, was long leased as a royal home. Prince Albert had the lease for forty years from 1848. The then Duchess of Kent used it as a summer home from 1850 to 1861. Following the death of the Prince Imperial, the Empress Eugénie stayed there in 1879. Thereafter, it was the Scottish home of the future Edward VII and Queen Alexandra when Prince and Princess of Wales. After a period of disuse, the lease was broken, and the castle returned to John Gordon, who demolished the Georgian mansion and restored the tower house.

Aberuchill Castle

On the slopes of the Glenartney hills two miles south-west of Comrie, Aberuchill Castle is a seventeenth-century L-plan structure with angle turrets and a circular stair tower in the re-entrant angle. At roof level, where the main gable and the wing join, there are unusual twin gables each flanked by an angle turret.

The castle is three storeys high with an attic. The walls are harled and whitewashed. A pediment from an original dormer carries the date 1607, though the present dormers are Victorian, as is the porch built out to the south. The re-entrant angle on the other side has been filled in with mid-Victorian additions by John Bryce. The original arrangement of cellarage, first floor Hall and bedrooms above was altered to suit Georgian requirements when a pleasant two-storey-and-attic Georgian wing with pepperpots and raking crenellations was added c.1805.

Comrie was MacGregor country, but the lands of Aberuchill were taken by the Campbells in 1596, and Colin, second son of Campbell of Lawers, was given Crown leave to build this castle. In Rob Roy's day the laird of Aberuchill, Lord Aberuchill, though Lord Justice Clerk, still thought it prudent to pay the outlaw 'mail',

Aboyne Castle: freed from massive Victorian additions, as remodelled by Ian Begg.

or protection money, to ensure that his cattle would not be stolen. After 1715, Lord Aberuchill's Hanoverian son, Sir James Campbell, discontinued the practice. Rob Roy himself arrived while Sir James was giving a dinner party, forcing the host to leave his guests and pay the traditional 'premium'.

Aboyne Castle

Aboyne Castle, once a mighty stronghold, stands one mile north of Aboyne village. It is a tall, compact building the oldest known part of which was rebuilt in 1671 by Charles Gordon, first Earl of Aboyne (the hero of the ballad 'Lord Aboyne', though his wife was Lady Elizabeth Lyon, and not 'Peggy Irvine' as the balladier suggests). This is the north-west section of what was the full nineteenth-century structure and contains the initials of husband and wife, the religious monogram IHS and the date. It has a five-storey circular stair tower corbelled out to a square top and with a crow-stepped pitched roof. The north tower is square, similarly roofed but with small ogee-capped towers, and open outlook turrets on the north corners. There is an open timber bartisan walk on the west face at third-floor level.

The property was much altered and added to. An east wing was constructed in 1801. In 1869, the range containing the domestic buildings was pulled down, and a new block with crow-stepped gables put up. Much of the structure, eventually in high Baronial style, was subsequently allowed to become ruinous, but restored ancillary buildings were long the home of the owner, the Marquess of Huntly, 'Cock o' the North', whose ancestors got the lands in the early fifteenth century from the Knights Templar. George, fifth Earl of Aboyne, succeeded the last Duke of Gordon as clan chief and ninth Marquis of Huntly in 1836. Aboyne fell to the Covenanters and was occupied by Argyll and his troops in 1640. The building has been much reduced in size and reconstructed in our own day by the architect Ian Begg. It is lived in by the present Earl and Countess of Aboyne. Thus the family seat, long ruinous and even for a time sold to other hands, has now been restored in seventeenth-century Scottish castellated style.

Achanachie Castle

Five miles north-west of Huntly, Achanachie began as a late-sixteenth-century tall tower which was probably reduced in height when a two-storey eastern extension at right angles – an extension a little later on still further extended – was added in the seventeenth century. The tower now has three storeys. A large circular stair-tower occupies the angle between the tower and its extension, and this has arrow-slit windows at three levels and, under the eaves, a series of shot-holes. The massive chimney stack on the east front has had the fireplace it once served built over, but it remains a commanding feature. Over the doorway by the chimney stack is a panel with the inscription FROM OUR ENEMIES DEFENDE US O CHRIST and the date 1594.

The basement of the tower is vaulted, with bosses carrying the Gordon, Fraser and Campbell arms. There is a steep turnpike stair leading to the very small vaulted first floor Hall. The rest of the castle, which is lived in and part of a farm, has been modernised.

Achanachie was the home of the eldest son of the Gordons of

Avochie – now a shattered ruin, a few miles to the east – and was eventually passed to the second son of the fourth laird, with whose descendants it has remained.

Ackergill Castle

Ackergill Tower, as it is usually known, overlooks the sea from the rocky Caithness cliffs three miles or so north of Wick and just over a mile west of Girnigoe Castle, whose Sinclair owners coveted it, and who had to be restrained by law from actually seizing it. Ackergill would probably once have been surrounded by a ditch or moat, no traces of which remain.

Built in the late fifteenth or early sixteenth century, it is a massive square five-storey tower erected for the Keiths of Inverugie. Oliphants had it for a time, but it later passed to the Dunbars of Hempriggs, who still own it.

The main entrance is by a round-headed door with cable moulding in the north-west elevation. This leads to the vaulted ground floor, and a straight Bryce baronial main stair to the first-floor Hall, replacing the original mural stair. The vaulted sixteenth-century Hall rose through two storeys, but was transformed by Bryce into an oak-panelled Baronial dining-hall. The upper floors are reached by turnpike stairs in the north-east and south-east corners, and from a service stair beyond the tower to the north. The third and fourth floors each have two rooms with garderobes, now simply mural chambers, and have eighteenth-century Gothic windows on the flanking elevations to the towers.

The two-storey addition to the south houses a library, two drawing-rooms and offices. It has been said, with some justification, that 'the importance of the sixteenth-century tower has been enhanced rather than overpowered' by Bryce's work. There were eighteenth-century window enlargements, as a William Daniell etching of 1821 shows, but as already indicated, the main alterations were carried out by David Bryce in 1851 for Sir George Dunbar. These included the battlemented turret, parapets, a new cap-house and other details, as well as additions built to the south and east of the tower.

Affleck Castle

Affleck, or Auchenleck Castle, stands on high ground a mile west of the parish church of Monikie. A tall oblong tower of five storeys, sixty feet high, its walls of coursed rubble are thick enough to accommodate several mural rooms. It is a splendid example of a free-standing fifteenth-century tower in a good state of preservation, though it has been unoccupied since 1760, when it was superseded by a new mansion.

Internally, it has several interesting features. The basement, a few steps down from the entrance, is sub divided. The first-floor Hall has a vaulted ceiling, supporting the with-drawing room above. The Hall has a tiny staircase of eleven steps in the east wall leading to an entresol bedroom almost seven feet square, above the principal staircase. From this room, a spy-hole looks into the Hall below. As the entrance turnpike leads only to this floor and anyone wishing to come higher would have to cross the Hall, no one could have reached the ascending turnpike stair in the opposite corner without being observed.

One step up from the second-floor withdrawing room, which has a fine shafted fireplace, window seats and wall closets, there is a beautiful circular vaulted little chapel or oratory, complete with holy-water stoup, piscina, aumry and decorative stone candle holders. Evidently, it was once closed off with an iron railing. Above, there is a bedroom on each floor.

Externally, there is a projection by the door to house the stairs with a square caphouse at the top. Uniquely, there is also a second square caphouse over the south-west angle. Open rounds are placed at all the other angles. Over the arched doorway there is a device for dropping missiles or liquid on unwelcome guests, with a similar device on the west front. The parapet appears to have been restored at some stage.

The Auchenlecks of that Ilk, hereditary armour-bearers to the Earls of Crawford, were already on their lands during the reign of James I. Affleck came early in the eighteenth century to a family of Reids, one of whom was a Jacobite and 'out' in the Forty-Five.

Aiket Castle

Aiket, which stands above the Water of Glazert, two miles south-west of Dunlop, is a late-fifteenth-century tower bonded quite clearly at its western end to a late-sixteenth-century addition. In the eighteenth century the tower, once four storeys in height, was reduced, probably to make the building more fashionable and to prevent rain penetration. The castle was lived in until twenty-five years ago when it was burned down. It was restored in 1979 by Robert and Katrina Clow to its pre-eighteenth-century form.

The land was owned by Alexander Cunninghame, who married the daughter of the first Earl of Cassillis about 1479.

The fifth of the line was involved in the murder of Hugh, Earl of Eglinton, in 1586, and was himself shot dead near his own house of Aiket soon afterwards by the murdered man's kinsmen. The line ended with the ninth laird, James, who played a leading part in the ill-fated Darien Scheme and strenuously opposed the Union of 1707. Thereafter the tower was owned by one of the branches of the Dunlops of Dunlop, until let as a farm labourers' dwelling, when it went on fire, twice in one day.

Airdrie House

Three miles west of Crail stands Airdrie House. According to a nineteenth-century writer it was a 'mansion embosomed in wood' crowning 'a swelling ground ... and includes an ancient tower which commands a magnificent view from Edinburgh to the ocean and from St Abb's Head to the Bell Rock lighthouse'.

It is an oblong main block with the windows later enlarged and with a square wing rising a storey higher than the rest – a very odd T-shaped structure, perhaps dating from the sixteenth century. The corbelled turret in the re-entrant angle carries a stair rising above roof level to provide a square parapeted look-out platform with dummy open roundels. In David II's time, Airdrie belonged to the Dundemons of that Ilk. The estate then came to the Lumsdaines. The initials M.C.L.O.A. – apparently for Magister C. Lumsdaine of Airdrie – and the date 1588 are to be found on a lintel and panel-space respectively. The house was later owned by Prestons, Anstruthers and Erskines, Earls of Kellie, the Earl dying in it in 1830.

Airlie Castle

Once-great Airlie Castle, the 'Bonnie Hoose o' Airlie', stands in a strong position on the banks of the Isla, where it is joined by the Melgam Water.

What survives is a large and massive section of the east wall of enceinte and part of the northern tower, both from the original fifteenth-century fortalice. The gate-house was altered in the late sixteenth century. Behind this once well-defended front is the simple late Georgian residence of the Earls of Airlie, restored and reoccupied by the Dowager Countess.

James I gave Sir Walter Ogilvy of Lintrathan (a descendant of the first Thane of Angus) a licence in 1432 to build his 'tower of Eroly'. In 1458 his son, Sir John, had a grant of the castle and barony. It must have been an imposing structure, for the gate-house has a strongly guarded arched gateway fitted for a portcullis, and a second inner iron grille door. Above the entrance arch is a flue for pouring down boiling liquid. There was also a corbel-supported timber gallery on the inner side of the tower, a caphouse with a flat parapet and a walkway along the curtain-wall. Yet in 1640, when the Covenanting Earl of Argyll attacked it with four thousand Covenanters, he took it (admittedly while the Earl of Airlie was absent, his son, Lord Ogilvy, fled as the enemy approached). Argyll demolished much of the castle, helping, it is said, in the work of destruction with his own vengeful hands.

Airth Castle

The earliest section of Airth Castle is a squat square tower built some time after 1488 when one 'Robert Brus of Erht' was given by James IV official payment of one hundred pounds 'to the byggin (building) of his place that was byrnt (burnt).' This portion is now known as Wallace's Tower, though it must have been a previous castle which Wallace sacked when a hundred Englishmen held his uncle, the priest of Dunipace, in it. The tower has a basement, two main floors and an attic within a crenellated parapet. The crow-stepped gabled roof was probably put on when the castle was extended to the east early in the sixteenth century, and again by Sir Alexander Bruce in 1581, who added a wing to the north. It appears that this was then balanced by a wing at the west end of the main block (but by 1762, according to a plan for a road, this wing had already been demolished and the castle had assumed an L-shape) and the wing of 1581 over the doorway of which is the date and the motto LAT THAIM SAY. David Hamilton concealed the inward façade to the castle in 1807, by a triangular addition of ingenious plan with a Tudorish castellated frontage, at the same time enlarging the windows and greatly altering the interior.

The property came to Sir Robert Bruce of Clackmannan early in the fifteenth century through his marriage to Agnes, the Airth heiress who probably built the tower burnt by James III in 1488 just before the Battle of Sauchieburn – the tower for which subsequent reimbursement was made by James IV. Sir Robert's grandson, who no doubt built 'Wallace's Tower', married the daughter of the Earl of Linlithgow in 1547. Through the marriage of a Bruce heiress the castle went to the Elphinstones and Dundases. James Graham, Judge Advocate of Scotland, bought it in 1717, and his family retained it until comparatively recent times.

The garden retains two sundials, one dated 1690, put up by the Elphinstones.

Aldie Castle

Aldie Castle, situated in hilly country two miles or so south of Crook of Devon and five miles south-west of Kinross, dates from four periods in the sixteenth and seventeenth centuries. Originally, Aldie was a freestanding ashlar rectangular tower of three storeys and an attic. It has conically roofed angle towers with windows and gun-loops at three corners, and a small watch-room at the stair-head in the south-west angle. The original doorway stood at the bottom of the stair-tower. A large chimney stack rises above the north front alongside which is a small dormer window.

There is a vaulted basement. The Hall is on the first floor. There is one room in each of the upper floors.

The first extension was a two storey structure to the south-west, no doubt intended to provide a kitchen, which was in the vaulted basement. Later, a three-storey unvaulted range was added parallel to the main tower. The final addition linked this wing to the main tower. There is a string-course over the entrance, situated in this final addition, and an heraldic panel with the arms of Mercer of Aldie.

Before its restoration in the 1950s by the architect Ian Lindsay for Hope Dickson, who had spent most of his life in the Orient, Aldie, though not wholly ruinous, was in danger of becoming so, having been unoccupied for the best part of a century. Known locally as the 'House of Aldie', it had belonged to the Perth family of Mercer, who were supposed to have acquired it as part of the dowry of Alidia of Tullibardine in the mid-fourteenth century. It passed in a similar manner to the family of the Lords Nairne, and later still by marriage to the Anglo-Irish Landsdownes, who took the name Mercer-Nairne.

Allardyce Castle

Two miles west of Inverbervie, in a valley of the Bervie Water, Allardyce Castle is a late-sixteenth-century mansion, later a farmhouse. Both arms of its L-plan were extended a century or so after the original structure was built. It was much altered in the following century, but is remarkable for the use of label mouldings in the corbelling, a device much favoured in the north east, and here probably unique in the intricacy of its application to support the stair turret in the re-entrant angle.

The main block rises to three storeys and an attic. The castle once formed two sides of a courtyard, the remainder being enclosed by a barmkin. Access to the courtyard was through a still-surviving pend in the main block.

A few years ago the castle suffered severe fire damage, but has now been successfully restored, and is the home of an architect.

The ancestors of Allardyce of that Ilk, variously spelt, had their land from Robert the Bruce. An heiress carried them by marriage to the Barclays at the turn of the eighteenth century. The last of the Allardyces of Allardyce was Captain Barclay-Allardyce, a famous walker, who died in 1854.

Alloa Tower

Alloa Tower, in the grounds of Alloa House, on the edge of the town of Alloa, is supposed to date back to 1223. The present building appears, however, to be no older than the beginning of the fifteenth century.

The building is a simple rectangle, but big and lofty, with four storeys and a garret inside a parapet which rises flush with the walling rather than resting in the more usual manner on corbelling. Each corner has an open round with shot-holes, and there is a fifth round over the door for added protection. The walling is eleven feet thick, making the task of throwing out symmetrically planned additional windows in the seventeenth century no light undertaking. The end windows in each row, however, are dummies.

There is a turnpike stair in the thickness of the south-west angle, topped by a conical roofed cap-house. At one end of the broad parapet walk there is a garderobe for the guard.

Internally, the tower was substantially altered around 1700 by the architect-engineer Earl of Mar, 'Bobbing John' of 1715 fame. His may be the simple but impressive semi-domed stair to first-floor level. Above this, all the interior work has gone. The roof is ancient and of impressive construction.

The entrance on the north front has a Renaissance doorway. The ground floor is vaulted. The first floor once carried the Hall, which has lateral passages in the thickness of its walls, one of which connects with the turnpike stair.

The tower was given to Sir Robert Erskine, Great Chamberlain of Scotland, by David II in 1360, and has remained with his descendants, the Earls of Mar, ever since. Later additions to it were completely destroyed in the great fire of 28 August 1800, when one of the casualties was a portrait of Mary, Queen of Scots, who, like James IV and Prince Henry after her, knew Alloa well in childhood.

Amisfield Tower

Amisfield, which stands five miles north of Dumfries, is one of the most attractive of all the Border towers, and an outstanding example of the crowning of upper works upon a simple square without any loss of balance or style. It was completed in 1600 and it is thought to have been constructed by the same builder who put up nearby Elshieshields.

The tower is square, its walls rising four storeys to the eaves, above which there is both an attic and a garret storey within the steeply pitched roof. There is a circular stair-tower projecting from the south-east angle at first-floor level. Two storeys higher it is

Amisfield Tower: a sophisticated balance of intricacy and symmetry.

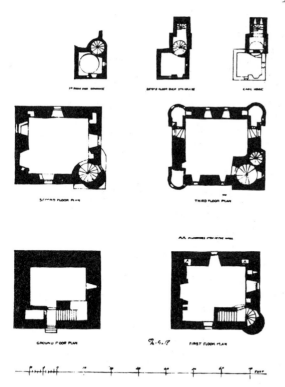

Amisfield Castle: the floor plans of a tower house extended upwards.

corbelled out to become square. It then rises a further two storeys, and is roofed and gabled on a level with the main roof. Above it, on the main east gable, is a gabled watch tower. The remaining three corners of the tower have conically capped angle turrets of two storeys. At the level of the eaves above the ground-level door there is a machicolated projection for the dropping of objects or substances on unwelcome guests.

Stewart Cruden's[1] reaction to the external exuberance of Amisfield cannot be bettered 'All manner of new combinations of forms are exploited although none of the components are new. This is not just a matter of applied ornament, but also of volumes, their size and shape, and an arbitrary disposition regardless of floor levels ... Projecting parts, round and rectangular, of different sizes

[1] *op. cit.*

and lengths hang as much as they rise. They seem to be draped above the upper part of the square tower, descending with different lengths down the corners ... one is filled with wonder that so much could have been erected upon so small a plan without looking cheap and overdressed, which it does not, for the scale is faultless.' The ornamental finishings combine Gothic survival with Renaissance features.

The basement is vaulted, its only illumination three gun-loops. Because of the inward projection of the stair, the first-floor room is L-shaped, having three windows and its own garderobe. The turnpike stair leads to the second floor, which has windows in each wall, two with stone seats, a fine fireplace and garderobes at both ends of the south wall, and would seem to have surviving traces of tempera plaster-painting in the Hall. The third floor has two bedrooms with fireplaces, and the squared turret contains another room. Access to the lower storeys of the turrets is from the third floor, access to the upper storeys through the attic. The lower storeys of the turrets house garderobes, and have windows and shot-holes. Otherwise, the only defensive measures are small gun-loops in the basement and a single machicolation at the sill of the dormer window above the door.

The tower was built by the Anglo-Norman family of Charteris, which now holds the Wemyss title. A second-floor window gives the date of completion along with the initials I.C. and A.M., representing Sir John Charteris and his wife Anne Maxwell, a daughter of Lord Herries, as well as the arms of Charteris and Maxwell of Herries. The Charteris family had the lands from the late thirteenth century. One of them was Chancellor to Alexander II, another – Deputy Warden of the West Marches to James V – found himself punished by his monarch for wronging a widow.

There is a nineteenth-century mansion adjacent to the old tower which is, however, kept in good repair.

Ardblair Castle

Ardblair Castle, a mile west of Blairgowrie, is one of the few castles to retain its courtyard entire, and gives a much more complete picture of seventeenth-century living than most, even although it has been a good deal altered. The oldest part is an L-plan tower house in the north-west angle rising to three storeys and an attic, though now with a simplified roof-line. Later buildings complete the courtyard on all but the north side, where it is enclosed by a wall with a central arched gateway. According to the date on the handsome pediment above, this gateway was built in 1668. The tower house has its wing attached to the main block by the middle of the gable, thus producing two re-entrant angles. Use is made of the additional wall space so provided for the siting of an extra gun-loop. The stair tower, resting on corbels at first-floor level and conically capped, rises in the outer re-entrant.

The entrance to the house is in the inner re-entrant angle, and has an ornate but uninscribed panel space above it. The vaulted basement in the main block probably housed the original kitchen, having a wide fireplace underneath a massive chimney-stack that forms a feature of the south side of the main building.

The wing carries a wide staircase to the former first-floor Hall, now the panelled eighteenth-century dining-room. The turret stair gives access to the higher floor.

David II granted the estates, then amounting to a fifth of the entire parish of Blairgowrie, to Thomas Blair in 1399. Blair was a scion of a troublesome family one of whom, Patrick, was beheaded in 1554 for his part in the murder of George Drummond of Ledcrieff. The castle passed by marriage in 1792 to the Oliphants of Gask, who still own it. When Gask itself was sold just after the turn of the twentieth century, many of the family's Jacobite relics were brought to Ardblair. Lady Nairne – the author of 'Caller Herrin', 'The Auld Hoose' and 'Will Ye No Come Back Again' and the most popular song-writer after Burns – was a sister of the lady who became mistress of Ardblair, and was consequently a frequent visitor. Their father had been an aide-de-camp to Prince Charles Edward Stuart.

Ardchonell

An Argyll fortress, on a small island in Loch Awe a few hundred yards from the shore, near Port Sherrach, Ardchonell was a rudimentary stronghold, perhaps of the thirteenth century, consisting of two courts, the southern, the castle proper, about sixty-three feet square within the walls with buildings on the south and east sides. Its south, west and north walls are of great thickness. On the north is an outer court with out-buildings about fifty-five feet long, with a landing-place and a smaller postern approached by steps. Within the inner court it had an open staircase to the battlements. The main building lies along the south side of the inner court. The Hall on the first floor apparently had a private apartment leading off it, and there was also on the first floor another small room in the angle tower. Towards the end of the fifteenth century it became a prison for the infant heir to the Lordship of the Isles, Donald Dubh. He escaped when a young man, raised an army, invaded Badenoch, was captured, and thereafter spent forty years in Edinburgh Castle. He escaped again in 1545 and became Lord of the Isles, but was almost at once involved in the troubles preceding the Reformation and fled to Ireland, where he died.

Arnage Castle

An attractive Z-plan castle, built about 1650 about four miles north of Ellon, Arnage was much added to and altered in mid-Victorian times by the Aberdeen architect James Matthews; notably by the enlargement of its first-floor windows. In its original state it was the work of the local master mason, Thomas Leiper. It has three storeys, with an extra storey in the stair wing. The original entrance has been built up. There is a vaulted basement – its original stair from wine cellar to Hall now gone – a Hall on the first floor and the usual bedroom accommodation above. All that survives of a courtyard is an original well.

Above first-floor level two turnpike stairs in conically roofed turrets in the re-entrant angles give access to the upper floors. These are unusual in that they appear only as minimal splays until they break through the roofline. Another small turret provides access to the garret.

Arnage came by marriage to the Cheyne family in the latter part of the fourteenth century. The last of the line sold their lands in 1643 to John Sibbald, but Arnage was bought in 1702 by Baillie John Ross, later Provost of Aberdeen, in which city his town house has been restored. Arnage remained with his family – the Leith Rosses as a result of his grand-daughter's marriage – until recent times.

Ascog House

Ascog House, flatted and in the grounds of a later mansion two miles from Rothesay, began as an L-shaped fortalice probably in the early sixteenth century, though it has been much altered, alterations being recorded on a dormer as early as 1687. The original door, now blocked up, was in the re-entrant angle of the stair-tower. A watch-room, corbelled out at eaves level, has a projection for dropping missiles on unwanted guests. The modern entrance is in the re-entrant angle of the south extension.

A Stewart family were the first owners, and retained the castle until the middle of the eighteenth century, after which it seems to have been in the hands of distant descendants for some further decades before coming into the possession of the Marquess of Bute.

Ashintully Castle

Ashintully Castle stands two miles north of Kirkmichael, and is an L-shaped tower house dating from the late sixteenth century to a wing of which a large extension was added in the late seventeenth century. The whole was radically regularised and rebuilt in late Georgian times. The western jamb, which resembles a keep, has four storeys and a garret, but with altered upper works. A simple open parapet, restored in 1831, guards the south-facing doorway in the re-entrant angle. This carries the initials of the builder, Andro Spalding, the date 1583, and the hope that THE LORD DEFEND THIS HOUS. Wide splayed gun-loops at basement and second-floor levels were inserted to assist the Almighty towards that end.

The interior has been largely Georgianised and a rib-ceilinged long gallery was added to the rear in 1831 to provide better circulation. In the original part, a straight stair rises to the first-floor Hall, and a turnpike stair in the opposite wall leads up to the bedroom floors.

In 1587, a gang of local lairds besieged Ashintully and maltreated the unfortunate Andro, taking him prisoner. The Earl of Atholl had to stand caution – an early form of bail – to James VI for the behaviour of his Stewart kinsmen. Since the culprits failed to appear for their trial, they were put to the horn – declared outlaws – and the Earl lost his one hundred Scots merks.

Andro's son, David, was summoned four times for supporting

the Ruthvens after the Gowrie Conspiracy of 1600, and once again in 1618 for appropriating timber from woods belonging to the Earl of Mar.

Auchans Castle

Auchans Castle, one mile west of Dundonald, is now a sad ruin. It was built in 1644, probably incorporating an earlier structure, and may originally have been intended to be of the Z-plan variety. As it finished up, it was a long east–west main block of three storeys and an attic, and with a wing to the north-west in L-plan arrangement, a storey lower. A tall stair tower of square construction rises in the re-entrant angle, a Renaissance entrance at its foot. A wide stair rose to the third floor, after which access was by turnpike stair. A circular stair-tower also rises right up the east front of the north wing, with a square corbelled-out watch-room at its head. Apart from the vaulted kitchens, the floors have fallen in and the whole structure is much collapsed. Restoration of this superb house would now be a formidable undertaking.

The previous Auchans was a Wallace stronghold until the property was purchased by the builder of the present house, Sir William Cochrane of Coldoun. Sir William, a royalist, suffered severely during the Civil War, though he was rewarded afterwards with the earldom of Dundonald for his services to the king's cause. Later, Auchans came into the possession of the Earls of Eglinton. As a dower house it was the home of the widow of the ninth Earl, formerly the beautiful Susanna Kennedy of Culzean, his third wife. She remained a staunch Jacobite until her death in 1780 at the age of ninety-one. The poet Allan Ramsay dedicated to her his pastoral opera *The Gentle Shepherd*, the original manuscript of which she presented to James Boswell when he and Dr Johnson arrived at Auchans during their Scottish tour. According to Boswell 'her figure was majestick, her manners high-bred, her reading extreme and her conversation elegant'. Discovering that she had been married the year before Johnson was born, she declared that he might have been her son, so 'adopted' him. On parting she embraced him with the words: 'My dear son, farewell!', which greatly pleased the sixty-four-year-old Dr Johnson. She was, however, eccentric in other ways, training rats to come from behind the panelling of the dining-room to eat up any unfinished scraps from her meals, and disciplining them with a wand which she kept by her.

The 'Auld House o' Auchans' ended its days divided into workers' flats, fell into disrepair and was allowed to become ruinous. The estate, the ruin and the neighbouring later mansion, was recently reacquired by the Earl of Dundonald.

Auchenbowie House

Auchenbowie House, just under two miles south-west of Bannock-burn, incorporates older structures, but is now a handsome example of an L-plan building of *c.*1666 with a semi-hexagonal and conically capped stair tower in the re-entrant angle rising to the full height of three storeys and an attic. It was enlarged to the south-west in 1768 when the interior was largely refitted with interior work of some quality. All its defensive features have disappeared, and it is now harled and washed in yellow.

Robert Bruce, Provost of Stirling in 1555, bought the lands of Auchenbowie from the Cunninghams of Polmaize, and built the oldest surviving part of the house. It was probably added to at the end of the seventeenth century by Captain William Bruce, a hot-tempered man who killed a relative, Charles Elphinstone of Airth Castle, in a duel. In 1708 the Bruce heiress married Major-General Monro, with whose descendants the property remains.

Auchness Castle

Auchness Castle stands near the coast a mile south of the village of Ardwell. A late-sixteenth-century tower house, it was McDouall property. It is a large three-storey structure with a garret within the steeply pitched crow-step gabled roof. Now a farmhouse, its windows have been enlarged and dummy angle-turrets added to its corners.

Auchterhouse

Midway between Dundee and Newtyle stands early-sixteenth-century Auchterhouse, much remodelled in the seventeenth century and subsequently simplified externally in late Georgian times. It does, however, retain an entrance hall and a drawing-room *en suite* with superb Jacobean plaster ceilings with pendants, the finest and best-preserved plasterwork display in Scotland, and a sixteenth-century fireplace. Probably built for the Earls of Buchan, the seventh Earl being responsible for the plasterwork, it passed by succession to James, Earl of Moray, then, in 1648 to Patrick, Earl of Panmure, before coming to the Earl of Airlie. It is now an hotel.

Balbegno Castle

Balbegno is a large and unusually fine L-shaped tower house of 1569 half a mile south-west of Fettercairn, attached to a small, neat later-eighteenth-century mansion, now a farmhouse, which replaced what must once have been extensive outbuildings. The castle has an intact roof, but is unoccupied. It belongs to that remarkable group of sixteenth-century castles with rib vaults which includes Craig, Gight, Delgaty, Towie Barclay and Careston. The main tower is four storeys high with a garret. The stair wing rises a little higher and is now corbelled out to provide an elaborate square watch-room with crow-stepped gables, incorporating one of the angle turrets that once formed open rounds when the structure had a parapet prior to partial reconstruction of the upper works at some undated stage, probably in the seventeenth century. The watch-room is reached by a small corbelled-out turret stair in the re-entrant angle.

The basement of the castle was considerably altered when the later mansion was attached. The original door was in the re-entrant angle at the foot of the stair tower, and from this a straight stair, curving round the corner, led to the Hall. A turnpike stair carried up the ascent. This entrance has now been covered over with a late-eighteenth-century Venetian porch.

The vaulted basement contained the original kitchen and cellars. An unusual feature – a survival, MacGibbon and Ross suggest, from an earlier period – is that the first-floor hall is groined and vaulted in two bays as at Towie Barclay. The vault rests on grotesquely carved heads and carries shields on the angles. The spaces between the vaulting have painted armorial bearings of some of Scotland's best-known families. There is a private room in the wing. The second floor has four bedrooms, each with its garderobe. Angle turrets similar to those on the wing were obliterated when the main jamb lying north-west/south-east was rebuilt with a pitched roof and crow-stepped gables.

On the battlement, richly ornamented with medallion portraits as at Craigston, is the inscription I.WOD and E. IRVEIN, along with the date ANO 1569. The Woods were given the lands by James IV in 1488. John Wood, who succeeded to the estate in 1512, may have built the original castle. In 1687, the Woods sold Balbegno to Andrew Middleton, youngest brother of the notorious Earl. The castle next passed to the Ogilvies.

Balbithan House

Balbithan – anciently spelt Balbythan, Balbethane or Balbithen – lies in a secluded valley two miles north-east of Kintore.

Balbithan was once part of the estate of the Abbey of Lindores, but by 1490 was in the hands of the Chalmers family. The first House of Balbithan stood on high ground above the Don, opposite Kintore. No trace of it remains. The present house, built by the Chalmers, was probably an oblong keep with a round tower at the north-west corner, when it went up around 1560. The round tower was removed around 1600 and the house was extended to the north, a new stair tower being begun. Around 1630, a new wing at right angles reaching to the west was added; it was unusual in being the same length as the original building, and housed the unvaulted kitchen on the ground floor and the long Hall above it. On the next floor there was a long gallery or withdrawing-room and, above, bedrooms.

Early in the nineteenth century the top floor was removed and the second-storey ceiling raised, involving the blocking off of the gable turrets by roof beams, leaving the turret set too high in relation to the walls and causing the stair at the re-entrant angle turret to come to an abrupt end. Internal alterations were made between 1760 and 1860, large rooms being divided and a small addition, since removed, on the north side built to house a service stair. It is now very simple internally.

A metal sundial, now attached to the south turret of the west wing, carries the date 1679 and the initials of James Chalmers. Balbithan still has one of the finest gardens of any early Scottish house.

Montrose sought refuge in Balbithan during Covenanting times, and supporters of Prince Charles are supposed to have found shelter in it after Culloden. Sold by the Chalmers by 1696 to an Edinburgh merchant, James Balfour, it was in Hay ownership between 1699 and 1707, when it came to a branch of the Gordons, who held it until 1859. After passing through several hands, including the Earl of Kintore, it was bought in 1960 by Mrs M.M. McMurtrie, who has done much to restore it.

Balcomie Castle

In the East Neuk of Fife, late-sixteenth-century Balcomie Castle stands about two miles north-east of Crail. The estate belonged in 1375 to one John de Balcomie, though nothing of the surviving castle is that old. During the reign of James IV it passed to the Learmonts, though it is claimed that had James IV survived Flodden, he intended to make it a royal desmesne. Mary of Guise arrived at Balconie after landing, rather surprisingly, at Fifeness on her way to her marriage with James V. In 1705, Balcomie passed to William Hope, and then successively to Scott of Scotstarvit and the Earl of Kellie. It was then still a rectangular block lying east–west with a square wing projecting from each of its southern corners, a somewhat unusual design. The earl reduced its one-time sixteenth- and seventeenth-century courtyard splendour to the tall L-shaped form, tacking on what was left to the eastern extremity of a late eighteenth-century house.

The wing joins the main block at an angle, forming two re-entrants. In the southern angle a small stair-tower, complete with shot-hole, is corbelled out, linking the first and second floors. Two ashlar two-storey angle turrets, oversailed by the roof, perch at the top of the wing's gable, both also equipped with shot-holes.

The building, of fine coursed rubble, is five storeys high with a garret, the turnpike stair once being carried in a circular tower that projected from the north end of the main block. Most of the windows have been built in.

A later arched pend and gatehouse carries the arms of Learmonth and Myrton of Randerston, along with the mottoes SANS FEINTISE and ADVYSEDLIE, with the date 1602. The inscription above – UNLESS THE LORD BUILD THE HOUSE THEY LABOUR IN VAIN THAT BUILD IT – has an ironic ring in view of the castle's sad decline. It is now part of a farmhouse.

Balfluig Castle

Balfluig Castle, in the Howe of Alford a mile south of Alford village, is a tall, slim-jambed, L-plan tower house of the mid-sixteenth century. The wing projects eastwards from the main block in such a manner as to form two re-entrant angles, a semicircular stair tower rising in that facing the south-west. The main block has three storeys and a garret. The wing rises a storey higher, being topped with a watch-room. The outer angles of the rough rubble masonry are rounded, though corbelled square beneath roof level. There is a massive chimney stack on the south gable. The walls are liberally fitted with gun-loops.

The entrance, approached through a courtyard, is in the main re-entrant angle, through an arched doorway protected by gun-loops. There are two vaulted chambers in the basement of the main block; the kitchen, with the usual appurtenances, and the wine-cellar, linked by private stair to the Hall above (which, unusually, has a vaulted with drawing-room leading off it). A vaulted guardroom in the basement of the wing has a small prison fitted in beneath the turnpike stair.

Balfluig belonged originally to a branch of the Forbes family. 'Bydand tradition' avers that there was once another fortalice near enough to allow the rival lairds to shoot at each other from their watch-rooms, one eventually killing the other and then being filled with pointless remorse.

In 1753, Balfluig was sold to Farquharson of Haughton. By the time of MacGibbon and Ross, it was a farmhouse. By the 1960s it was deserted, its upper floors gone, its roof in danger. Bought by a new owner, Mark Tennant, it became one of the first near-ruined fortalices to be saved with the aid of grants from the Historic Buildings Council for Scotland, though not without argument as to its merit. Officials disagreed with the Council and disrecommended it as never having been an outstanding castle, and not having any outstanding history'. The redoubtable W. Douglas Simpson, author of many invaluable works including *The Ancient Stones of Scotland*, carried the day in a manner so trenchant that it is worth quoting his observations in full:

> I should like, however, to point out that Balfluig Castle is, in my opinion, in more than one respect a quite exceptional building. In the first place it bears on its door the date 1556, and therefore belongs to the period in Scottish domestic architecture which Mr Cruden has termed 'the Long Pause',[1] when little private building was going on in Scotland, and almost none in Aberdeenshire, where the brilliant effervescence of late Scottish Baronial architecture commenced only after the Reformation.
>
> In the second place, the plan is a highly unusual one, and the architectural details, in particular the rectangular gun-loop, strongly suggest that it was designed by the same master mason who built Abergeldie Castle on Deeside.
>
> In the third place, the castle is unique for its period in retaining the corbels, wall-plate, and two doors of access for a *bretasche* or timber hoarding on the entrance front – a feature more usually associated with the twelfth- and thirteenth-century castles than with a sixteenth-century house fortified for ground-level defence by firearms.
>
> In the fourth place, the open timbered roof over the main structure, though not original, is ancient. Probably it dates from the restoration of the castle after it was burned during the Battle of Alford, 2 July 1645.
>
> In the fifth place, the tall, high-shouldered tower is a conspicuous landmark all over the Howe of Alford and from the uplands enclosing it. Its disappearance would be widely regretted.
>
> At present the building is utterly neglected and in a deplorable state. Nevertheless it is still capable of restoration: but unless stitch-in-time repairs are promptly executed its collapse cannot long be delayed.

The reactions of the official are not recorded. Duly restored and open to the public by arrangement, Balfluig's main interest now is its exterior, although there are points of interest in the plan.

---

[1] *op. cit.* Second edition, 1968

Balgonie Castle

Balgonie Castle stands a mile south of Markinch, on a steep bank of the River Leven. It is a fifteenth-century tower of ashlar, rising to four storeys with a crenellated parapet and a garret above. It sits in a seventeenth-century enclosure which contains ruined buildings of some grandeur, one of which was the home of the Covenanting General Alexander Leslie, who died there on 19th April 1661. He had been created Lord Balgonie and first Earl of Leven in 1641.

The tower was restored by David Maxwell as part of Fife's contribution to European Architectural Heritage Year, 1975, though it is used only on the ground- and first-floor levels, both vaulted. They were originally entered by separate doors in the east front. The lower vault had no fireplaces and only slits for illumination, so may have been a prison. The first-floor Hall also lacks a fireplace, there once apparently having been a primitive open hearth by the gables.

The stair rises in the thickness of the wall at the north-east angle to the second floor, where there is a more comfortable room with a fireplace, window-seats and provision for an external-drop closet. A similar layout is to be found on the third floor.

The roof was probably originally of stone slabs, though it is now covered with Angus slates. The parapet walk is drained by cannon spouts.

The later sixteenth- and seventeenth-century additions include a building carrying the initials F.S.A.L. and D.A.R., for Field-Marshal (his ultimate rank) Sir Alexander Leslie and his wife, Dame Agnes Renton. The original link between the new buildings and the older tower seems to have been by means of a wooden bridge.

Sir John Sibbald first built Balgonie, leaving it to his daughter and heir. She married Sir Robert Lundie, ultimately Lord High Treasurer, their family holding it until it was bought by Leslie. Leslie's family retained it until 1824, when it was bought by James Balfour of Whittinghame, who intended to restore it but unfortunately never did so.

Ballindalloch Castle

Ballindalloch Castle, by the junction of the Rivers Avon and Spey, began as a Z-plan castle around 1546. The castle is supposed to have been burned by Montrose in 1545, though much seems to have survived. In 1717, the estate was bought by Colonel William Grant, who added a large two-storey wing to the north and made a new entrance in the re-entrant angle thus created. A parallel wing was added later in the eighteenth century thus forming a courtyard.

In the early nineteenth century Sir George MacPherson-Grant made some alterations, but after the great flood of 1829, the damage resulting from which included the flooding of the house and the destruction of the walled garden, Sir George commissioned W.H. Playfair to plan improvements. Sir George began to implement them, against the wishes of his son, John, who disapproved of the proposed destruction of the old castle. The father therefore turned his attention to the grounds until his death in 1846, after which the new Sir John brought in Thomas Mackenzie, who skilfully remodelled the south-west tower to match the 1602 remodelling of the north-east tower and added the gate-house.

The third baronet, whilst a minor, had his uncle commission Alexander Ross of Inverness to add a large extension southwards. This disfigurement was demolished in the mid-1960s, returning the castle to its Mackenzie appearance.

Internally, there has been a great deal of alteration to the old castle. At the head of the 1602 stair tower, which rises a storey higher than the original main block, there is a watch-room corbelled out square, with a re-entrant stair tower to give access, and the machicolated device to enable missiles to be dropped on unwanted visitors at the original re-entrant angle entrance beneath.

The lands originally belonged to Ballindallochs of that Ilk, but were in the hands of John and Barbara Gordon by the time the Z-plan castle was built, a stone with their names and the date, 1546, having been found behind panelling in 1818. In the eighteenth century, Ballindalloch was given to Colonel William Grant, second son of Grant of Rothiemurchus, whose heiress married George Macpherson of Invereshie, thus producing the Macpherson-Grants, one of whom was created a baronet in 1838, and whose descendants still live in the castle.

Ballone Castle

A rapidly decaying but once strong Z-planned castle. On a peninsula between the Cromarty and Dornoch firths, ten miles or so east of Tain, Ballone Castle dates from the late sixteenth century, was supposedly built by the Earls of Ross but last inhabited by the MacKenzie Earls of Cromarty. It has a square tower at the south-east containing the square main stair and a circular tower at the north-west, the latter with a circular stair tower corbelled out in the re-entrant to a square at the top. A remarkable feature is the use of stone-roofed angle turrets.

Balmanno Castle

Balmanno Castle stands on the northern slopes of the Ochil Hills, near the entrance to Glen Farg. Originally an L-plan house built in the late sixteenth century, it has a square tower in the re-entrant angle, and later lower additions to the north. A slim turret on corbels rises in the angle between the square tower and the wing and carries a stair up from the first floor. It also provides entry to the parapet platform, which has an open round.

Balmanno of that Ilk sold his lands to George Auchinleck about 1570, and the new laird built his castle soon after. By the latter part of the nineteenth century, after several changes of owner – including Sir Patrick Hepburn Murray in the eighteenth century – the castle had ended up being part-used as a farmhouse. It was, however, restored in 1916 by Sir Robert Lorimer. The original vaulted ground floor remains, though the old kitchen is now the dining-room. The stair wing in the west wall, which once led to the first-floor Hall, is also still in existence. Lorimer heightened the stair turret, crowning it with an ogee cap, and fitted up the interior with superb woodwork and plasterwork in the Scots seventeenth-century manner. He also added wings and an entirely new courtyard and gatehouse. The white harled castle as it now stands, complete with remade walled garden in which there is a sundial and an ogee-capped gazebo, both respects tradition in the broadest sense and yet at the same time provides a pleasing, modern, unmistakably Scottish ensemble.

Balmuto House

Balmuto Tower, three miles north-west of Burntisland, belonged to the Glens, whose line ended in an heiress. She married Sir James Boswell early in the fifteenth century. Balmuto was originally a square fifteenth-century keep, but was later incorporated in a nineteenth-century mansion. Three storeys high, it has a crenellated parapet resting on simply designed corbels. It has been extensively rebuilt, the large windows with ornamental heads surmounted by cherubs having been inserted as long ago as 1680. Still in Boswell hands, Ian Appleton's restoration for an American descendant has demolished the nineteenth century mansion.

Balnagown Castle

Near Kilday Station, Balnagown Castle, the ancient seat of the Ross family, apparently began as a tall gabled block of four storeys with towers at the north-west and south-west angles. It was at one stage probably an L-plan tower-house, but has been so altered and added to in the eighteenth and nineteenth centuries as now to be a mansion rather than a castle, albeit its inhabitants played their part in Scotland's turbulent history; not least by aiding the Earl of Bothwell when on the run after the rout of Queen Mary's army at the Battle of Langside, Glasgow.

Balquhain Castle

Balquhain Castle, a ruined quadrangular four-storey keep, stands about half a mile from the church of Chapel-of-Garioch. The castle was originally built in the fifteenth century, but was destroyed in 1526 during the feuding between its Leslie owners and the neighbouring Forbeses. Queen Mary lived in it the night before the Battle of Corrichie, in 1562. It stands even nearer the site of the more famous Battle of Harlaw, fought in 1411. It is said to have been 'deserted' in 1715, but was presumably reoccupied thereafter, for it was thought worth burning by the Duke of Cumberland in 1746, suffering further demolition in 1749. Today, of its six-feet-thick walls, originally battlemented (though later altered), only the south-eastern half remain. Traces of the wall enclosing the barmkin, including the foundations of a round tower, survive. The Bishop of Raphoe, John Leslie, who died in 1671, was born in Balquhain Castle.

Baltersan Castle

Baltersan Castle, built in the late sixteenth century on what were once the lands of Crossraguel Abbey, was probably put up by David Kennedy of Pennyglen, whose chief, the fourth Earl Cassillis, obtained them from the Commendator, Allan Stewart, by having him 'roasted in sop' in Dunure Castle until he signed them over. Though roofless and crumbling at wall-head level, this L-plan castle of weatherbeaten golden sandstone is still impressive. It rises to three storeys and has both an attic and a garret. The top of the square stair tower wing is finished in three-tiered corbelling, over which there is a watch-room with an unusual projecting square oriel window with shot-holes in the checks. There are ashlar angle turrets at the north-west and south-east corners, both equipped with shot-holes. The roof is drained by cannon spouts at the sides of the angle turrets, and there is a stone basin at the bottom to store the rainwater.

The entrance, in the wing at the re-entrant angle, leads to the vaulted basement containing the kitchen and cellars, and upwards to the well-lit first-floor Hall. Three of its windows have stone seats. There is generous provision of wall closets. A private stair in the south-west angle leads to the upper floors. The main stair rises to the second floor, after which access is by a turnpike stair.

The property passed to the Kennedys of Culzean in 1656, and by the end of the century was described as 'a fine house with garden, orchards, parks and woods about it'. It seems a pity that a restoring purchaser like those who have saved several castles in the north-east could not have been found for Baltersan.

Balvaird Castle

Four miles south of Abernethy, on high ground, stands ruined Balvaird Castle, built in the late fifteenth century by Sir Andrew Murray, a son of Sir William Murray of Tulliebardine, who married Margaret Barclay, the heiress of Balvaird. It consists of a strong stepped L-plan tower house with a corbelled parapet, the square stair tower being in the re-entrant angle.

The doorway is in the stair tower, and has the Murray and Barclay arms still just decipherable above it. There are three storeys and an attic in the main block, the wing having an extra storey. The stair tower is capped with a high two-storey crowstep-gabled watch-room with its own parapet. The tower house is complete and virtually unaltered, but the walled courtyard and gatehouse must have been less substantially constructed, for although dating from the sixteenth century they are much more ruinous.

A descendant of Sir Andrew's, the Reverend Andrew Murray, minister of Abdie, was created Lord Balvaird by Charles I for his persistence in holding moderate religious views at a time when such behaviour was unusual. Lord Balvaird heired the property of Sir David Murray of Gospetrie, first Viscount Stormont. His eldest son succeeded to both titles together with that of Lord Scone. All are now held by the Earl of Mansfield. Balvaird is still in the Earl of Mansfield's possession, but is now in the care of the State.

Balvenie Castle

Balvenie Castle stands on a rock in the valley of the River Fiddich, near its junction with the Dullan, half a mile north of Dufftown. It must once have been an impressive fortress, dating from the thirteenth, fifteenth and sixteenth centuries, for even in decline – a decline now arrested, since it has become an Ancient Monument – it gives an appearance of enormous strength.

It consists of a strong high wall of enceinte enclosing a large quadrangle one hundred and sixty by one hundred and thirty feet. The section of the castle most recently occupied – till about 1725, when it gave place to the 'new Castle of Balvenie', by James Gibbs, later part of a distillery and now alas demolished – is that to the south; basically, a sixteenth-century L-plan tower with a large projecting circular tower at the south-east angle. A tall stair turret is corbelled out in the re-entrant angle facing the courtyard.

Entry to the castle is through a vaulted pend, where there is still a double iron yett. A guardroom lies to the left. Above the entrance are the Royal Arms of Scotland and those of Stewart of Atholl, along with the motto, FURTH FORTUIN AND FIL THI FATRIS. This, too, is sixteenth-century work. The work to the left of the pend is the oldest portion of the castle, and contains a vaulted cellar and bakery with oven on the ground floor, and the old Great Hall, with a pointed vault, above. A higher storey and a garret above are roofless. The L-shaped castle has four storeys and two towers facing inwards to the courtyard. The larger of these, corbelled square above the third storey to provide a narrow gabled watch-room, contained the main stair. The upper works of the lower tower have gone. String courses and a better quality of finish to the stonework differentiate the older and later sections of the castle.

The L-shaped building has three barrel-vaulted rooms, and there is another in the base of the large external tower. On the first floor is the fourth Earl of Atholl's new Hall, projecting over the entrance pend and with lighter windows. Next to it is a private room, off which led a bedroom in the large external tower and another room, possibly the study, at an angle. There was a parallel arrangement on the floor above. The castle was well supplied with bedrooms upstairs.

There were lean-to buildings against various parts of the inner wall, the kitchen apparently being in one of them. In the centre of the courtyard is a well.

James Stewart of Balveny was the son of James Stewart, the Black Knight of Lorn, who married Joan Beaufort, the widow of the poet-King James I, thus becoming James II's half-brother. The younger Stewart of Balveny was presented with Balvenie on his marriage to Margaret, widow of the Earl of Douglas. He became Earl of Atholl in 1457. Their second daughter married John, Lord Forbes, whose coat of arms, together with that of Atholl, may be seen over the door of the central staircase. He probably built the newer part of the castle. It was sold in 1614 to Robert Innes, who was made a baronet in 1631 but ruined by the Civil Wars. In 1687, it was sold again to the Duffs, ancestors of the Duff Earls of Fife.

Barcaldine Castle

Barcaldine Castle stands four miles north of Connel Ferry, near the mouth of Loch Crerar. It is an L-shaped fortalice of three storeys and an attic with the two wings slightly offset so that the smaller can provide cover down both the front and the side of the castle. A circular stair tower rises in the re-entrant angle. Large conically-capped angle turrets adorn the four corners. There are several shot-holes and oblong gun-loops and three substantial chimney-stacks. The entrance is at the foot of the stair tower, and retains its iron yett. Above it is an heraldic panel with the arms of Sir Duncan Campbell, the seventh laird of Glenorchy, who built it in 1609. The panel also carries his initials and those of his first wife, Lady Jean Stewart, daughter of the fourth Earl of Atholl. She died in 1593, and Sir Duncan took a second wife, Elizabeth Sinclair, in 1597. How she viewed this posthumous commemoration of her predecessor is not recorded.

The vaulted ground floor contains kitchen and cellars, the most westerly being the wine-cellar with the usual private stair to the Hall, a handsome room. A Barcaldine Campbell became the first Earl of Breadalbane and built Kilchurn. When work there was nearly finished, Lord Breadalbane asked for an estimate in 1698 for repairs to Barcaldine, and was told by master mason Andrew Christie that the roof and much of the walls were 'totally failed', and that it would be best to build a new house. Breadalbane feued the old house to Alexander Campbell the following year, and this tenant paid for the repairs. When Barcaldine House was built in 1724 the castle was abandoned. After the sale of the estate in 1844 it became ruinous. It was bought back by Sir Duncan Campbell of Barcaldine in 1896 and by 1911 was well restored. It remains with his family.

Bardowie Castle

About two miles east of Milngavie, Bardowie Castle, an early-sixteenth-century structure originally a free-standing three-storey oblong tower with a parapet walk and a garret above, stands by the shore of Bardowie Loch. Later in the century, however, the upper storey was altered to provide a second Hall, the crenellations becoming the basis for the windows in the heightened portion. This later Hall has one of Scotland's rare open collar-beam timber ceilings, though it may once have been boarded in and covered with paintings. In the late seventeenth century the tower was extended westwards by a two-storey wing at a slight angle. This was remodelled in the eighteenth century with a Gibbsian door-piece and finally heightened to three storeys with a crenellated parapet in the nineteenth, when restorations to the original were carried through.

Entrance to the old building was by an arched doorway on the south front, giving access to a vaulted basement cellar and to a straight wall stair leading to the vaulted original first-floor Hall. A second straight mural stair leads upwards from the Hall. Two non-interconnecting small stairs, one straight, one turnpike, situated at diagonally opposite angles of this room, lead to the former but now covered section of the parapet forming the second Hall or gallery.

Bardowie was a seat of the Galbraith family, but in the fourteenth century it came through two heiresses to John de Hamilton, a scion of the Cadzow line, ancestor of the Dukes of Hamilton. Mary Hamilton, sister of John Hamilton of Bardowie, in 1707 married Gregor 'Black Knee' MacGregor, Rob Roy's nephew and chief of the clan.

Barholm Castle

Midway between Gatehouse of Fleet and Creetown, Barholm Castle stands imposingly above the road. It consists of an oblong tower, probably built in the sixteenth century, with a small stair tower at right angles added in the seventeenth century. The upper section of the stair tower carries a square watch-room on individual corbels, reached by a small turret stair from the top floor corbelled into the re-entrant angle.

The main block is three storeys and a garret high. The windows have moulded surrounds. The arched doorway, in the re-entrant angle, has unusually elaborate cable moulding, knotted at each end and straddled by a grotesque creature near the crown of the arch.

There is a poorly lit vaulted room on the ground floor. The main stair, a broad turnpike, rises up to the parapet. The first-floor Hall has a broad hooded fireplace, and is lit by four windows. The upper floors, formerly each of two rooms, have fallen in. The tower is roofless, having been replaced by a fine classical house by Robert Adam which, alas, disappeared after the Second World War.

Barholm was a McCulloch seat from the early sixteenth century. The McCullochs were Reformation supporters, and the young John Knox is said to have sheltered at Barholm on his way to the Continent – thus hiding only two miles or so away from Abbot Brown in Carsluith. John Brown the Younger of Carsluith killed McCulloch of Barholm in 1579, possibly over a religious quarrel. Presbyterian ardour made the McCullochs staunch Covenanters, and Major John McCulloch was executed in 1666 for his part in the Pentland Rising.

Barjarg Tower

A red rubble L-plan tower of four storeys and an attic four miles south-east of Penpont, Barjarg is now attached to a large nineteenth-century mansion. It has been modernised internally, and although it carries a crenellated parapet with conically capped angle turrets at two corners and an open round at another, the parapet may also be a later addition.

The tower seems to have been built in 1680 by John Grierson and his wife, Grizel Kilpatrick. The lands seem to have been gifted to the builder's father in 1587 by the Earl of Morton. The tower's owners have included Lord Tinwald, a judge, and Dr Hunter, Professor of Divinity at Edinburgh University.

Barncluith

Barncluith stands near the later house of the same name, the heating plant for which it accommodates, just under a mile south of Hamilton, near the River Avon. An oblong tower house, from which later accretions have been removed, it rises to three storeys, and has a garret within the steep pitch of its roof. It has crow-stepped gables, renewed chimney-stacks, but neither parapets nor rounds.

It was built in 1583 by John Hamilton, the ancestor of the Lords Belhaven, and was said to have been the house where Graham of Claverhouse spent the night before the Battle of Bothwell Bridge. It has a unique and delightful garden, consisting of six major terraces built out of the Avon gorge, below Barncluith House, and incorporating large pieces taken from demolished Hamilton Palace, as well as from a court house of 1698.

Barnes Castle

Standing on a dominant site on a slope of the Garleton Hills, midway between Longniddry and Haddington, is Barnes Castle, a monument to the forward-looking sense of symmetrical design and mighty ambition of Sir John Seton of Barnes. He died in 1594, having made 'ane great building at the Barnes, Vault height, before his death; intending that the building bound a court'. The idea was to have a great castle with six square towers projecting from the walls. The entrance gateway was in the centre of the south-west wall, facing which was the entrance doorway flanked on both sides by square towers in the re-entrant angle of the projecting wings.

Sir John spent much of his life as a diplomat at the court of Philip II of Spain. James VI recalled him and made him Treasurer of the Household and an Extraordinary Lord of Session.

Barns Tower

Barns Tower, once owned by the Burnets of Burntisland, who feature in John Buchan's early novel *John Burnet of Barns*, stands on the south bank of the Tweed, three miles west of and above Peebles. It is a rectangular keep three storeys in height, with an attic. The door lintel, at ground level, still with its iron yett – possibly the oldest in Scotland – carries the date 1498 (though the carving does not look so old) and leads through the lobby to a vaulted ground-floor room. On the lintel above the doorway are the initials w.b. and m.s., for William Burnet and his wife, Margaret Stewart of Traquair. A narrow wall stair rises to the first floor, from which, now at any rate, access above is by a modern wooden stair. The tower has lost its parapet. Though it has a comparatively modern roof and gables, it has probably not been occupied since the construction in 1773 of the nearby mansion.

Barr Castle

In the back streets of the little town of Galston stands Barr Castle, a massive fifteenth-century tower of five storeys. Unfortunately, the parapet above the corbelling has disappeared, the original roof being replaced with an inappropriate hipped one which reaches right down to the wallhead. The open rounds of the parapet have thus also disappeared, except for their corbelled-out bases.

Barr was a Lockhart seat. John Lockhart was a zealous Reformer and invited Knox to preach at Barr in 1556, as he had invited Wishart to do eleven years earlier. The ninth laird sold Barr to the Campbells of Cessnock in 1670. It is now a Masonic Hall.

Barr Castle

A rapidly deteriorating early-sixteenth-century square tower about one mile west of Lochwinnoch, Barr had four storeys and a garret within a plain, high parapet. It had two basement rooms, one of which was the kitchen, a turnpike stair leading up from the lobby, a first-floor Hall with a large fireplace and several wall cupboards, and a turnpike stair leading to the upper floors, each of which contained two rooms. It was once surrounded by a courtyard. The gables have collapsed within the past twenty years or so, except for a chimney-stack. The parapet, on triple continuous corbelling, had four open rounds. The walkway was drained by cannon spouts. The walls have slits for both arrows and guns.

Barr was built by the Glen family, but from the seventeenth century was owned by the Hamiltons of Ferguslie, who abandoned the tower in the eighteenth century in favour of a new mansion, itself replaced in the nineteenth century by a house on the same site.

Barra Castle

Barra Castle, one of the more unusual and attractive of Scotland's castles, stands about two miles south of Old Meldrum, on the slope above the Lochter Burn, occupying the site of Bruce's victory over the Comyn Earl of Buchan in 1307.

In design it is an intricate and singular variation of the L-plan type, the main block lying north/south with a circular tower at the south-west. At the south-east, a D-plan tower containing the main entrance and main stair, corbelled square at the top to provide a watch-room, links to a big square wing with a second circular tower at the south-eastern angle, answering that of the main jamb. A fourth tower at the north-west angle of the main block was labelled by MacGibbon and Ross as 'unfinished, probably an oven'.

An eighteenth-century addition runs eastward from the north end of the main block forming a square court, closed on the east side by a wall containing the entrance. The entrance to the castle itself is in the main re-entrant angle. The basement of the main block is vaulted, containing kitchen and cellars. The Hall has been a handsome apartment, but at an early date has been divided into dining-room and drawing-room, panelled and with a small ante-chamber. A bedroom at this level is in the wing, the rest of the bedroom accommodation being above and in the extension.

In its present form it is chiefly the work of George Seton, Chancellor of Aberdeen University, who was granted the estates in 1598. The rectangular main block and south-eastern wing are his, but the earlier castle of the Blackhalls of Barra may have been incorporated.

By the 1630s, the estate was in the hands of James Reid, and in 1703, his descendant, John Reid, received a baronetcy. His wife, Dame Mary Abercrombie, refitted parts of the house, perhaps being responsible for the fireplace now in the Great Hall.

In 1754 the castle was sold to John Ramsay of Melrose, whose successors still own it, a Ramsay heiress marrying Irvine of Drum early this century. Ramsay added the eighteenth-century north wing. He preferred his other estate, Straloch, however, and after his death in 1787 Barra sank to the status of a farmhouse but mercifully remained entire. It was tactfully restored in the first decade of the twentieth century (to plans by George Bennet Mitchell) as a dower house. Its comparative neglect throughout the landscape-gardening era has resulted in its entrance arrangements and walled garden enclosures remaining intact, with the result that externally it gives a more complete picture of how a great house of the seventeenth century looked in the mid-eighteenth century than almost any other.

Barscobe House

Three miles north-east of New Galloway, Barscobe House was built by William MacLellan of Bombie in 1648. It is a compact L-plan three-storey house with the door in the re-entrant angle and the stair in the wing rising a storey higher. The gables are no longer finished with crowsteps but with unusual ornamental skews, probably altered when the roof was at some stage lowered. The parapet has disappeared and the dormers have become attic windows. Internally, it has been much altered. The initials of MacLellan and his wife, Margaret Gordon, together with the year of construction, are on a dormer pediment. The MacLellan and Gordon arms are in a panel above the entrance.

The property passed out of MacLellan hands in 1779 and became a farmhouse. It has recently been restored.

Beldorney Castle

Beldorney, a Z-plan castle, stands in hilly country in the Deveron valley, two miles south of Glass. It consists of a main block, lying north/south, with a smaller square tower, containing the main stair, at the north-west angle, and a large drum tower with an unusual rounded gable at the south-east angle. Originally it was entered from the foot of the stair tower in the re-entrant angle. The vaulted basement contains a kitchen and two cellars, from one of which, the wine-cellar, there was a mural stair to the Hall above. The Hall had a painted ceiling, fragments of which survive to our own day. The second floor seems once to have had a second Hall and another tower room, reached by a second mural stair in a tiny turret in the re-entrant angle of the south gable, which also gave access to the third-floor watch-room.

George Gordon bought the lands from the Earl of Huntly in 1545; but, we are told, 'the said George builded the house of Beldorney and dyed'. Since his death occurred in 1575, Beldorney with Huntly Castle (1551-54) and Terpersie (1561), is one of the first examples of the Z-plan fortalice in the North East.

Two wings were built to the west in 1679, enclosing a courtyard entered through an arched gateway, which carries on its inner side the date and the initials of John Gordon and Anne, his wife. The original entrance was replaced with a new one in a moulded surround set in the centre of the west face. Above it is an ogee-headed panel containing a winged angel's head.

The castle passed to Alexander Gordon in 1713. He remodelled the principal rooms and the roofline, also building a new chimney gable on the west face of the main block. The first floor rooms, formed from the Hall, made one of the finest internal features of the castle, but have now been replanned again as a single apartment retaining and partly rearranging the panelling. During this restoration, more early wall paintings were discovered, including a highly interesting composition of a woman in early sixteenth century dress playing the lute.

Other floors were remodelled in 1890 under the supervision of Alexander Marshall Mackenzie, when a north wing, added in 1830, was altered. A further restoration took place in the early 1980s.

Bemersyde

The Haigs, descendants of the Norman Petrus de Haga, in obedience to the Act of Parliament of 1535 'for biggin of strengthis on the Borderis', built themselves a lofty rectangular peel tower on the left bank of the River Tweed, four miles or so east of Melrose. The remains of an earlier building may have been incorporated, since the family had been in these parts since the twelfth century, the first local reference to them occurring in 1120. They were the subject of a famous couplet ascribed to True Thomas of Ercildoune:

> Tide, tide, whate'er betide,
> There's aye the Haigs of Bemersyde

– a prophecy that has so far been fulfilled.

The original tower of local reddish rubble with walls ten feet thick rises to five storeys. A sixth storey was added by Anthony Haig in 1690. The parapets in the north and south faces end in open rounds supported at each corner by corbelling, but do not link with the north and east faces.

The main doorway on the south front has been enlarged, probably in the eighteenth century, when the adjoining mansion house wings were added. The tower door itself leads to a vaulted basement with an entresol at the spring of the vault. The Hall on the main first floor has three windows, one with a stone seat. Another window jamb contains an aumry with a wooden door, iron hinges and lock. A passage off the east end of the Hall leads to a garderobe and to a very small room with a fireplace and aumry. A turnpike stair in the south-east angle leads to the original upper floors, a wooden stair connecting the fifth and sixth floors.

In 1854 the twenty-fifth laird of Bemersyde died unmarried, and the house was left to a distant connection, Lieut.-Colonel Balfour

Haig. In 1921, however, it was bought back by the nation and presented to Field-Marshal Earl Haig as a token of gratitude for his part in bringing about victory in the 1914–18 war. His son, the second Earl, a distinguished painter, in due course heired it. The sale of the Field-Marshal's remarkable papers, chronicling a long life from school and military college days through his conduct of the 1914–18 war, having been bought for the National Library of Scotland, with the assistance of a grant from the National Heritage Memorial Fund, the future of Bemersyde is presumably now reasonably assured.

Benholm Tower

Benholm, a fifteenth-century square tower incorporated into a large plain Georgian mansion standing on high ground overlooking the sea a few miles north of Montrose, rises to four storeys and a garret within a crenellated parapet on individual corbels, and has open rounds at three angles. At the top of the stair in the south-east angle, is a square gabled watch-room.

The door in the south face leads to two vaults in the basement. Above, it has an interesting wall-chambered plan and some good details. The first-floor Hall has an ornamental fireplace and stone seats in the window recesses. The castle has shared the fate of the mansion, which fell into ruin after the Second World War, and the upper floors cannot now be reached. Restoration has been considered but presents formidable problems.

Benholm was built by an Ogilvy, but passed to the Keiths, kinsman to the Earls Marischal.

Birse Castle

Long a fragmented ruin in the centre of what was once the forest of Birse, Birse Castle now stands in a bare moorland landscape about six miles south of Aboyne. It was rebuilt in 1930 for Annie, Lady Cowdray, in an enlarged form by the Aberdeen scholar-architect Dr William Kelly, with the advice of his friend and biographer Dr W. Douglas Simpson. The original tower now has the appearance of being one jamb of a sizeable L-plan castle. Basically it dates from the end of the sixteenth century and was originally a simple, square three-storey tower with a round tower corbelled to the square at one angle; half way, so to say, to a Z-plan structure. The fretwork corbels of its angle turrets are similar to those at Knock Castle, near Ballater. Birse was owned by the Gordons of Cluny.

Blackhouse Castle

Two and a half miles from the south-east end of St Mary's Loch, on the left bank of the Douglas Burn, Blackhouse Castle, an oblong structure with a round stair-tower at the angle next to the door, is probably of late-sixteenth-century construction, but is now reduced to one storey. Tradition claims it to have been a Douglas house and the scene of the Douglas tragedy.

Blackness Castle

Three and a half miles east of Bo'ness, on the Forth, Blackness Castle, from its rocky promontory, once guarded the village of the same name when it was the seaport of Linlithgow. Originally, it was probably an oblong keep with a circular stair tower at the north-east angle. The keep – probably of fifteenth-century origin – survives, surrounded by a wall with embrasures for cannons. In the seventeenth century the keep was used as a prison for distinguished Covenanters and others thereafter till 1707.

In 1537, under Sir James Hamilton of Finnart, work began which was to include a thickening of the exposed walls with generous provision for defending guns, transforming the castle into one of the most effective artillery fortifications in Scotland. Cromwell besieged and damaged it. Charles II had it repaired. Following the Treaty of Union of 1707 it became an unimportant garrison, but in 1870–74 it was converted into an ammunition depot. Finally released from military use at the end of the First World War, it came into State care and has been restored. Except for the barracks, the pier and its drawbridge, all the buildings erected after 1870 were demolished, and in 1930–33 the upper parts of the tower were rebuilt to resemble the original appearance.

Blair Castle

Blair Castle stands on the banks of the River Bambo, in well-wooded and landscaped grounds two miles from Dalry. Despite the date 1203, engraved in Georgian lettering over the front entrance, there is nothing to suggest any surviving construction older than the sixteenth century.

The oldest section appears to be the remains of the tower built into the north-eastern range of the house when it was extended to form an L-plan structure, probably in the seventeenth century. A reset stone bears the date 1617 and the arms of Bryce Blair and Annabel Wallace Craigie. The long west wing is of later seventeenth-century construction, as is the square tower in the re-entrant angle. The present entrance is situated at the front of this tower, and the elaborate pediment contains the arms of William Blair and Lady Douglas Hamilton together with the date 1662.

A wing was added to the east in the eighteenth century, but altered in 1893 when Captain Fordyce Blair made other additions, using the architect Thomas Leadbetter. He designed a new northern wing, put a new front on the eastern range and raised part of the east wing, leaving the house in the shape of a slightly irregular T.

Little of the original internal work survives, except for the basement of the west wing, which contained the original kitchen, and the vaulted basement of the tower. Of the seventeenth-century work there survives the wide newel stair, with its boldly twisted balusters.

The family records go back to 1165, when William the Lion created the Barony of Blair. Sir Bryce Blair achieved the unusual literary distinction of being named both in Blind Harry's epic poem *The Wallace* and in John Barbour's greater epic *The Brus*, though admittedly only for the dubious honour of being hanged as a patriot at Ayr along with Sir William Wallace's uncle. In the seventeenth century William Blair raised a troop of horse to fight with the Covenanters, but was captured by Claverhouse. He escaped to become in 1707 one of the Commissioners to the Treaty of Union. He married the Duke of Hamilton's daughter, Lady Margaret. The castle is still in the family's hands.

Blair Castle

Blair Castle, the seat of the Dukes of Atholl since Celtic times, stands in an extensive estate entered from the village of Blair Atholl, through which the main road to the Highlands passes. The castle has had a long and chequered history. In 1269 David, the Crusader Earl of Atholl, complained to Alexander III that whilst he was in England John Comyn (or Cumming) of Badenoch (grandfather of the Comyn later killed by Bruce in Dumfries) had invaded Atholl territory and begun to build a castle at Blair. Traditionally, the main tower of the castle to the right of the entrance is stilll known as Cumming's tower.

The last of the Strathbogie earls (to whom the Celtic earldom had passed through the female line some time before 1211) had his title forfeited for opposing Bruce. Robert II and his son Walter held the lands until, in 1457, they were finally conferred by James II on his maternal half-brother, Sir John Stewart of Balvenie. When the new first earl was about to set out to deal with an insurrection by MacDonald of the Isles, he was told by James IV to gang 'Furth Fortune and Fill the Fetters', which means, in colloquial terms, 'to go forth bravely and put them all in irons', and has remained the family motto until this day. The Stewart line of earls ended in 1595, and until 1629 the earldom was held by the last earl's brother. In 1629, however, it went through marriage to John Murray, Master of Tullibardine, whose mother, Lady Dorothea Stewart, had been heiress to the fifth earl. It has remained with the Murray line ever since.

In all probability, only the foundations of Cumming's tower are as old as its legend suggests. Strathbogies, Stewarts and Murrays have all extended the castle. The parapeted flat-roofed and crenellated tower to the right of the entrance, with its irregularly spaced windows, may date from the fifteenth century. The Hall range was said to have been built in 1530 by the third Stewart earl.

In 1633, however, the castle was stormed and reputedly 'destroyed by powder' by Cromwell's commander Daniel. By 1684 it must have been partly rebuilt, for Claverhouse garrisoned it in 1689, and it was to Blair that his body was brought after his last Royalist stand against General Mackay at the Battle of Killiecrankie in 1689. Shortly after the death of the first Marquis of Atholl, his son was made Duke of Atholl in 1703 by Queen Anne. The new Duke protested so vigorously over the massacre of Glencoe that he

Blair Castle: the central block as re-baronialised by Bryce.

found himself appointed a Commissioner to inquire into the outrage. He also held out for a time against the Union of 1707 until he considered that better terms had been offered to Scotland.

The Jacobite risings divided the house. The Duke and his second surviving son remained loyal to the government in 1715. His elder brother, William, Marquis of Tullibardine, and his younger brothers, Lord Charles and Lord George, were Jacobites, the latter becoming Prince Charles' aide-de-camp.

Lord James, who in the event succeeded his father as second Duke, commissioned schemes from John Douglas and James Winter to Palladianise the castle and apparently began to extend it, but it was attacked by Lord George's Jacobites, since it was then occupied by government troops, and severely damaged.

Peace again restored, the castle was 'Georgianised', having its two top storeys docked, its parapets and turrets removed and its façade remodelled in plain vernacular style by James Winter in 1747–58. It was even renamed Atholl House. Queen Victoria, who came to Blair in 1844, therefore saw it as merely 'a large plain white building'. The taste for the Georgian style waned, however, and in 1869 the seventh Duke engaged David and John Bryce to recastellate the building, adding the present Fyvie-inspired entrance and a ballroom to the south. Turrets, bartisans and crow-steps reappeared, and Blair Castle is now thus a splendid and tasteful monument to neo-Scottish Baronialism. Some old vaulting remains. Internally, the castle is now memorable mainly for the superb Rococo interiors created by the great plasterer Thomas Clayton and for the work of the English carpenter Abraham Swan concurrently both engaged while Winter was remodelling the exterior.

Blairfindy Castle

A hunting seat of the Earls of Huntly, Blairfindy stands on high ground above the River Liver, five miles south of Ballindalloch. It is a ruinous late-sixteenth-century tower house of the L-plan variety, though the wing projects slightly so as to command two sides of the main block. The defence of the other side was by an angle turret on label corbelling.

The arched entrance doorway is in the re-entrant angle of the wing. It is defended by a shot-hole in the wall, and above by a heavily corbelled and machicolated projection at eaves level for the dropping of missiles. Above the door a panel bears the quartered arms of the Gordons, the initials I.G. and H.G. and the date 1586. A thin semi-circular stair turret on corbelling rises in the re-entrant angle above the door.

The basement is vaulted. A passage leads to the kitchen, which has a large fireplace, oven and water drain, at the north end of the block. There is a wine-cellar to the south of the mural stair up to the Hall. The Hall occupied the whole of the first floor, and was clearly a fine room, with a carved fireplace and the remains of panelling. The bedroom accommodation above cannot now be reached.

A castle here was originally owned by the Grants, but the present structure is Gordon work. Nearby is the site of the Battle of Glenlivet when the Earls of Huntly and Erroll defeated a much larger Protestant army under the young Earl of Argyll in what, however, was destined to be a short-lived victory for the Catholic cause.

Blervie Castle

Blervie Castle, all that remains of a Z-plan fortalice four miles south of Forres – and not far from Burgie Castle, which in some respects it resembles – is a five-storey angle tower attached to a fragment of the now fallen main block. There is a circular stair-tower corbelled out in what would have been a re-entrant angle, once finished with a caphouse.

Blervie must have been an important stronghold. Now, all that remains of the Hall is the large fireplace, on the east wall of the tower, a lintel of which carries the date 1398; a mistake, presumably, for 1598. The castle was built by the Dunbar family, who sold it to the first Earl of Fife. There was an earlier castle on the site, garrisoned by the Earl of Buchan when Norse invasion threatened.

Bonshaw Tower

Bonshaw stands above the Kirtle Water a mile south of Kirtle-bridge. Unlike Robgill and Wardhouse, the other two towers in this beautiful valley, Bonshaw is entire and habitable, though now really a free-standing adjunct to the adjacent early-nineteenth-century mansion. It has a splayed base, is oblong and rises to three storeys with a garret inside the parapet. The entrance door, within a modern porch, has over it the motto SOLI DEO HONOR ET GLORIA, and a flat gun-loop above at each floor level.

The entrance passage in the thickness of the wall is vaulted, as is the basement it leads to. This has four splayed shot-holes, one on each wall. There is a dungeon with a ventilation flue but no window within the thickness of the south-west mural angle. A hatch in the vaulting opens to the Hall above. A turnpike stair rises to all floors from the north-east angle of the cellar.

The Hall is a handsome apartment, with a wide fireplace and four windows, two having aumbries in the jambs. Another aumbry has an ogival-arched Gothic-style lintel. The second-floor bedroom also has four windows, one high in the wall, as well as a wall press and a garderobe, but no fireplace.

The individual corbelling of the parapet, drained by gargoyled cannon-spouts, has, unusually, a machicolated opening above each gun-loop. Unfortunately, early in the nineteenth century the flagstone roof was removed to floor a farmhouse and was replaced with a lower-pitched slate roof.

Bonshaw was an Irving stronghold, though in recent years it has had several other owners.

Borthwick

Borthwick, the highest tower house in Scotland and in many respects one of the best-preserved and most impressive of our medieval buildings, stands just to the east of the hamlet of Middleton, thirteen miles or so from Edinburgh, near the Galashiels road. It was built in 1420 by Sir William (later Lord) Borthwick on the site of a motte castle known as Lochorwart, granted to him by James I.

The building of dressed ashlar rises to a height of one hundred and ten feet, has walls fourteen feet thick at the base, and is a U-shaped castle, the tower wings projecting to the west, separated by a deep narrow recess.

The main entrance is on the first floor, through the north gable end of the main block, reached by the gate-house circuitously, round two sides of the tower, and accessible by a high bridge from the curtain wall. A guardroom opens off one side of the entrance. The basement has a separate entrance at ground level, but a wheel stair to the first floor enters through the guardroom, a useful security precaution.

The Hall, fifty feet long and with a minstrel gallery reached by a small stair, is covered by a stone vault thirty-seven feet high, and occupies the entire length of the main block. On the rear wall there are two deeply recessed windows, and at the end where the high table would once have been situated there is a massive hooded fireplace. Close by is a buffet recess in the side wall decorated with heraldic shields. On the same floor, but *en suite* with the wings, are the kitchen, once entered through a doorway and still having a huge fireplace, and, off the fireplace end of the Hall, a solar or private apartment. Next to the solar is a garderobe of superior

Borthwick Castle: the entrance gateway to a well-preserved tower house.

design. Instead of discharging its contents straight to the ground, or into a stone chamber within the walls covered by a movable 'grund-waa-stane', this garderobe had a system of movable containers.

Beneath the main block is a vaulted basement bearing evidence that there was once a timber entresol floor. Above the Hall are three further storeys, one of the rooms on the second floor, with an unvaulted ceiling, containing an oratory with piscine and aumry.

The wings house bedrooms and servants' quarters, appropriately reached by separate stairs in the thickness of the walls. The floors in the wings are at somewhat different levels from those in the main block. The north tower has eight storeys and the south seven, though both sit beneath a common roof level.

Bothwell and Mary, Queen of Scots, came here a month after their marriage. The approach of the Confederate Lords, however, forced them to flee to Dunbar, Bothwell riding off first and Mary following two days later, booted and spurred like a man.

Cromwell also visited Borthwick, having previously sent a letter dated 18 March, 1650, to John, tenth Lord Borthwick, a Royalist.

'I thought fitt to send this trumpett to you, to lett you know that, if you please to walk away with your company, and deliver the house to such as I shall send to receive it, you shall have libertie to carry off your armes and goods, and such other necessaries as you have. You harboured such parties in your house as have basely unhumanely murdered our men: if you necessitate me to bend my cannons against you, you must expect what I doubt you will not be pleased with.'

Cromwell did bend his cannon, knocking a piece off the eastern parapet of Borthwick, before Lord Borthwick honourably capitulated. That damage was repaired, though the parapet was not replaced. The walls are crowned with an otherwise continuous parapet supported on heavy machicolated corbelling. Each corner has an open round. There is a pitched flagstone roof.

The tower itself has no gun-loops, relying for initial defence on curtain walls round three sides and circular flanking towers, only one of which, that of the south-west and now a gatehouse, survives. There are some remains of the other towers of the curtain, which eighteenth-century views show as being of enormous strength. A moat protected the fourth side. The castle was recently leased as a conference centre, but has again changed hands.

Bothwell Castle

Bothwell, the finest of Scotland's thirteenth-century castles, stands on a rocky promontary above the River Clyde, near the village of Bothwell. It is similar to those built during the same period in France and England, and consists of a bailey, or great courtyard, surrounded by high enclosing walls. The corners are protected by round or square towers, and a powerful-looking round donjon dominates the whole. The donjon, which stands on the enceinte, is separated from the courtyard by its own ditch and parapet, and is built of carefully dressed red freestone, as is some of the masonry in the south curtain and towers, all dating from the later thirteenth century. It has walls fifteen feet thick and a tower sixty-five feet in diameter rising to a height of ninety feet to the top of the parapet. When complete, the cylindrical donjon would have been surpassed in Britain only by that at Conisborough, in Yorkshire. Internally, however, the Bothwell donjon has been octagonal in shape, though only four walls of the octagon still remain, the western enclosing wall being of a more recent date.

The basement floor of the donjon is entered by a newel stair from above. This room was no doubt a store, and it also has a well half sunk into the wall. The floor above houses the Hall, once thirty-seven feet in diameter and twenty-two feet high to the apex of its vault, which was probably of timber. It was supported by moulded ribs resting upon corbels in the angles of the octagon. The window overlooking the court is embellished with tracery.

The entrance, three feet above floor level, is on the Hall floor, the entrance passage being cunningly zig-zagged to facilitate additional defence. A portcullis is worked from a room above, which also controlled the workings of the drawbridge. There are large stone corbels near the parapet, as at Coucy, in France, apparently designed further to protect the spur containing the doorway.

The newel stair, which enters not from the door passage but from the Hall, also provides access to the floors above and once led to the parapet, which has now gone. The floors of the upper storeys appear not to have been vaulted. The intermediate floors were thought by MacGibbon and Ross to have housed the defensive garrison. The solar, or private apartment of the lord and his family, was probably located on the top storey, where there is a decorated pointed window facing the courtyard. There was almost certainly a watch-room at the top of the stair, higher than the parapet. A mural

Bothwell Castle: the strong surviving donjon tower.

door from the donjon led to garderobes in the south curtain. The chutes from the garderobes lead down the walls to a cunningly protected opening which would make it possible for water from the moat to be used to wash them out, yet did not permit a hostile intruder to squeeze past its protecting pillar.

Strongly defended doors on narrow passages link the donjon from its two upper floors to the south curtain wall parapet, connecting with the adjoining tower and eventually with a postern escape gate in the south wall, itself defended by a portcullis.

The castle was built by the De Moravia or Murray family, taken by Edward I during the Wars of Independence and given to the Earl of Pembroke, but retaken by its original owner in 1337, and 'slighted'. It passed to the Douglases by marriage and remained with them until forfeited to the crown on the downfall of that family at the hands of James II in 1445. It eventually became the property of the Earls of Home before passing into care as an Ancient Monument.

The Douglases rebuilt the castle on more spacious lines – the sketch of a possible reconstruction by MacGibbon and Ross is of interest – providing halls and other accommodation against the southern enceinte, including a Great Hall and a chapel, probably once roofed with groined vaulting. Its French character led W. Douglas Simpson[1] to suppose it to be the work of Archibald, the fourth Earl, who was also Duke of Touraine. The upper portion of the Hall, with its row of ten windows, dates, in all probability, however, from around 1500.

No trace survives of the main gateway, though it is believed to have stood at the gap in the north curtain, and was probably defended by towers. A large collection of medieval pottery has been excavated at Bothwell.

Braemar Castle

Braemar Castle, on the upper River Dee, just outside the village of Braemar, is an L-plan structure built in the early seventeenth century. It then had angle turrets on the corners and a circular stair tower in the re-entrant angle, and was the work of the seventh Erskine Earl of Mar, who held it for the Government in 1689 during the early Jacobite campaign of Viscount Dundee. The Earl, however, died during the investment and the garrison was captured by the Jacobites of Farquharson of Invermey.

Twenty-five years later the next Earl of Mar, 'Bobbing John', raised the Jacobite standard on the Braes of Mar, thus beginning the 1715 Rising. In 1748, after the defeat of the Rising of 1745, the Government leased the castle, then semi-ruinous, from the Farquharsons of Invercauld (still its owners), who had bought it from the disgraced Mar. It was then turned into a fortress and barracks as part of the plan to subdue the Highlanders. At this time the upper works were altered, crenellations replacing the conical roofs of the turrets, leading many now to regard it as a 'sham', though they were for the practical purposes of outlook and musket fire. As at Corgarff, the original outbuildings were cleared away and replaced by an elongated star-shaped curtain with créneaux according to Renaissance theories of fortification. In that form, it carried the purpose of the fortalice well into the second half of a century when almost all its contemporaries had settled into the role

[1] *op. cit.*

stronghold, as its place in balladry and Scott's reference in *The Lay of the Last Minstrel* would suggest:

Nine-and-twenty knights of fame
Hung their shields in Branxholme Hall.

The Earl of Northumberland burned Branxholme in 1532, and the Earl of Sussex in 1570. Inscribed dates show that the restoration after the destruction by Sussex was completed by Sir Walter Scott between 1571 and 1576, but the house was subsequently largely remodelled by William Burn in 1837 for the 5th Duke.

Breachecha Castle

Early-fifteenth-century Breachecha Castle, on a promontory three miles from the south-west tip of Coll – not to be confused with nearby Breachecha 'new' Castle, an unprepossessing eighteenth-century Georgian mansion – consists of a square keep in the north-west corner of a wall of enceinte, the wall partly incorporated in a sixteenth-century house, and a flanking round tower at the south-east angle. It is one of a series of keeps built to defend the western seaboard.

The keep, c.1430–50, about forty-four feet high, rises to four storeys and a gabled garret within a flush parapet. The later turnpike stair finishes in a cap-house, and is in the south-east angle. There is one open round on the simplest of corbelling. The round tower rose a storey higher and was vaulted to support a platform roof. On the linking house there is a machicolated device for dropping missiles on unwelcome visitors. Prior to its recent restoration, the keep had neither fireplaces nor chimneys. The Hall, on the first floor, was superseded in the seventeenth century by the three-storey house alongside the round tower. There is a garderobe chute on the west wall. In recent years the keep has been re-roofed, and the timber floors replaced.

Breachecha was given by Bruce to Angus Og of the Isles, but frequently changed ownership, until in 1631 it became a seat of the Macleans, who probably built the keep.

Hector Maclean, thirteenth of Coll, built the neighbouring mansion about 1750, in which he entertained Boswell and Johnson in 1773. Boswell thought it 'a neat new-built gentleman's house',

Breachecha Castle: bought by a descendant of its Maclean builders in 1965 and restored.

though the more discerning Johnson considered it 'quite a tradesman's box'. The estate passed to John Stewart of Glenbuchie and Lorn in 1856. In 1965, Breachecha Castle was bought and restored by Major N.V. MacLean Bristol, a descendant of the family of MacLean of Coll.

Breckonside Tower

A small, much-altered tower house in a valley three miles south-east of Moffat, Breckonside is probably of late-sixteenth-century construction with seventeenth-century alterations and additions. Originally, it was an oblong tower of three storeys and a garret. The north and east sides remain more or less unaltered, though the crow-stepping has been added to the west side and the windows have been enlarged.

The original door was no doubt by the south-west angle, leading to the turnpike stair, now replaced. The basement contains two linked vaulted rooms. The first-floor Hall is now subdivided. The second floor has two rooms, one with two garderobes. Some seventeenth-century panelling still survives.

Once a seat of the Annandale Johnstones, Breckonside is now a farmhouse.

Bridge Castle

Bridge Castle, formerly Little Brighouse, internally altered and enlarged by James Maitland Wardrop in 1871 as a Victorian mansion, stands on a rocky site three miles north-west of Bathgate. Originally a rectangular tower house of three storeys with an attic storey above the parapet, it was sold to William, Lord Livingston in 1588 by Alexander Stewart. He appears to have added the crow-step-gabled wing, forming it into an L-plan, the parapet of the original tower being very unusually bridged across a recessed lintel to join up with the new wing. The Livingstons became Earls of Linlithgow, but forfeited their lands and titles in the Jacobite Rising of 1715, giving place to the Hopes, who have held the title ever since.

Brims Castle

Standing on Brims Ness, a promontory in the Pentland Firth, Brims Castle is a late-sixteenth-century L-plan fortalice of three storeys and a garret. The square stair-wing once had a watch-room at its top in earlier times, but this has been replaced with a pitched and pended roof for many decades. The plan is unusual, with a semi-circular open turret near the centre of the east front over the entrance at the junction of the main block and the stair jamb. A courtyard to the north has been filled up with later buildings, but once had a sea-gate.

The doorway was at first-floor level, approached by movable timber stairs, though the modern entrance is by forestair. There is a vaulted basement connected by private stair to the first-floor Hall. There was also an access hatch in the Hall floor. There were bedrooms above, apparently one on each floor, though doubtless lean-to accommodation provided more bedrooms as well as the kitchen in the courtyard.

The castle was owned by the Sinclairs of Brims. It is now used in connection with the work of a farm, but is not in an encouraging condition. Some demolition took place recently.

Brodick Castle

Although at first sight a nineteenth-century castle, Brodick incorporates at its eastern end an ancient tower house, some of the stones in the lower storeys of which are believed to date from Bruce's time. Certainly, its history goes back to the fourteenth century, when the historian John of Fordon records that in Arran there are 'two royal castles, Brethurgh and Lochrancie'. Brodick was apparently stormed by the Earl of Rothesay in 1455 and levelled, then attacked again in 1544 by the Earl of Lennox on behalf of Henry VIII, when once again it was supposed to have been demolished. Great stone castles, however, were not so easily destroyed in those distant days before planners and bulldozers provided a more serious menace. MacGibbon and Ross believe that nothing older than around 1500 survives, The National Trust for Scotland[1] think the oldest part to be the east tower, giving 1568 as its date of construction.

The old castle consists of a long main block lying east/west. The join with the nineteenth-century building is visible on the main south front, where the longer first-floor windows begin. The old block comprises three storeys and an attic, with a crenellated parapet and walk projected on three courses of continuous corbelling. To the north are joined, unusually, two stair towers. One is similar at its base but corbelled out to the square above second-floor level, and has the parapet continuing round it. It is topped with a cap-house. The other is square, and has joined to it a slightly taller, gabled square tower. Still further extending to the north is a low battery erected for Cromwell's cannon and approached by a stone forestair that once led to the original entrance to the castle – probably replacing an older movable timber stair. The entrance is now by means of the nineteenth-century building.

The basement rooms are vaulted, the original kitchen being higher than usual because of the falling-away of the sloping

---

[1] *Brodick Castle Guide*, Edinburgh, 1981

remodelled the ground floor, providing the massive crypt-like entrance hall and neo-classical library. The stencilled decorative work was added to the drawing-room which has recently been restored.

Brodie Castle is thus now a country house rather than a fortalice, albeit of unusual interest as the home of a family whose occupation, at least of the site, stretches from Malcolm, Thane of Brodie, in Alexander III's time to the Brodie of today, who retains a family flat. In between came that pious diarist Alexander, the eleventh laird, later Lord Brodie, a Session Judge, and one of the Commissioners sent to the Hague to arrange for the return of Charles II from Holland. The line has zigzagged somewhat as a result of the failure of male heirs. A Brodie was Lord Lyon King of Arms in 1727.

Broughty Castle

Jutting into the Tay estuary three miles east of Dundee, Broughty Castle, now a museum, was latterly a War Office gun battery, yet in spite of inevitable military additions is still dominated by the tall keep built by the Lords Gray in the fifteenth and early sixteenth centuries. It was originally a free-standing oblong tower of five storeys, and still has a parapet with an altered and rebuilt garret storey above. The stairway rises in the walls of the south-west angle and ends in a gabled cap-house. The wing dates from the military conversion. The parapet is well equipped with facilities for dropping liquids or missiles from various standpoints.

In June 1490, Lord Gray of Foulis and Castle Huntly received a Crown charter of the rock and fishings of Broughty, and licence to erect a fortalice. In 1514, the Earl of Crawford refers to it as 'the new fortalice of Broughty'. During Somerset's invasion of Scotland, when Mary of Guise was Regent, the treacherous Patrick, fourth Lord Gray, secretly agreed to deliver up Broughty Castle to the enemy, for which treachery he was eventually briefly imprisoned in Edinburgh. It was, of course, a useful base for Somerset's men to harass Dundee. The Scots raised an army of a hundred hagbutters, a hundred spearmen and a hundred horsemen, but it took two years to drive out the English, after which Broughty was partly demolished. Once again it was attacked and taken in 1565 by the Lords of the Congregation, and held until 1571, when the Popish faction took it back.

By 1821 it was a roofless ruin and was offered for sale in the *Dundee, Perth and Coupar Advertiser* on 21 December as a potentially 'delightful residence' capable of restoration at small expense, or which 'would make an excellent situation for an inn'. There were no takers. The ruinous building was eventually bought by the War Office in 1855, radically enlarged and altered internally, and provided with a completely new gun battery enceinte. The original structure had a second circular tower, as at Loch Leven.

Brunstane Castle

Brunstane Castle, two and a half miles south-west of Penicuik, on the banks of the North Esk, is now a ruined L-shaped structure, once standing in a courtyard.

The main block rises to three storeys and no doubt once had a garret. There are oval gun-loops under the windows. The square stair-tower wing has its upper storeys corbelled out. The moulded entrance door has over the cornice the Crichton arms and the date 1568. The kitchen, at the north end of the basement, has a large fireplace, as has the Hall on the first floor.

Brunstane sheltered George Wishart, and its laird was with the reformer when Cardinal Beaton's men seized him to carry him to St Andrews for trial and death by burning. The laird of Brunstane was subsequently found guilty of plotting treasonably with the English, and his castle was burned.

Brunstane House

Brunstane House, in Brunstane Road South, Edinburgh, was probably originally a square fortified tower owned by the Crichtons of Brunstane but destroyed after the Battle of Pinkie, fought nearby, in 1547. The incorporated gable end of the north-east wing may survive from this structure. The Crichtons first intended to pull down the remains, but instead built a new L-plan tower house on the site, *c.* 1563.

In 1632, this came into the possession of John, Lord Maitland, later second Earl and first Duke of Lauderdale, the possessor of Thirlstane Castle and regarded by many as the 'uncrowned King of Scotland'. By 1639, Lauderdale had remodelled the house, extending it to the west and adding a tower to the north-east corner. In 1672, Lauderdale brought in Sir William Bruce with a view to doubling the size of his tower house, but in the end, contented himself with adding a shorter east range than he had originally envisaged and erecting a new office wing to the south.

The judge Lord Milton bought Brunstane in 1733, and employed William Adam to rebuild the south range and make a new office court between 1735–64. Adam contrived an effect of symmetry, although the projecting wings have octagonal stair towers differently roofed, that to the north having an octagonal roof, that to the south a flattened ogee. Adam also added a single storey corridor across the east range. There are also two corner towers on the east front, to the garden, again, differently roofed.

The 1639 kitchen, with a huge arched fireplace, is in the north-west corner. The ceiling is by Adam, whose panelled octagonal parlour also survives at the south-east corner of the ground floor. The fireplace in this room has a stucco overmantel, richly ornate and possibly by Thomas Clayton.

The dining room on the first floor is now divided, though it retains a mid-eighteenth century marble chimneypiece. The drawing room to the west has a characteristic William Adam basket-arched chimneypiece, and there is further decorative work, also possibly by Clayton elsewhere, though plainly room for tapestries was allowed for. Lord Milton's dressing room has an overmantel depicting a naval battle.

There are two coomb ceilings done in a square north-east room on the second floor and the other in an adjacent closet.

The single storey south range of offices by Adam also has Clayton decorative work. The house is now two separate dwellings.

Buckholm Tower

Remote Buckholm Tower stands high above the Gala Water a mile or so north of Galashiels. Dating from about 1582, it is an L-plan tower rising to three storeys. A small stair tower projects from the main block. The castle was once enclosed by a barmkin, a small section of the wall remaining.

The vaulted ground floor has had a door in the east wall which did not, however, connect with the Hall on the first floor. The Hall was entered through the stair tower by a removable wooden stair or gangway from the slope behind the building. Each floor originally had one room, although these were later subdivided.

The lands of Buckholm were owned by Melrose Abbey, but were given in life rent by the Commendator to James Hoppringle of Tynns, whose son probably built this tower, still in Pringle hands.

In recent years the roof of Buckholm has fallen in, and at the time of writing the tower awaits a restorer.

Burgie Castle

Burgie Castle, like nearby Blervie, is a square tower, all that remains of a once-powerful Z-plan fortalice, four miles east of Forres. Here the north-west tower survives, with attached to it the circular stair tower and a fragment of the main block. The Hall fireplace lintel, facing now not a great room but empty air, carries initials, a weathered motto and the date '1602 ZEIR'.

Six storeys high, this tower still has its parapet with open rounds. As at Blervie, Burgie is well provided with gun-loops and shot-holes; and, like it, it was a property of the Dunbar family, obtained by dubious means from the Abbey of Kinloss at the Reformation.

One Dunbar owner defied Montrose in 1645 and Lord Lewis Gordon a year later. Four years later, he bankrupted himself supplying food to Charles II's army. Burgie House was destroyed in 1800 to provide stones for the building of a nearby mansion. A sketch by John Claude Nattes, done the year before, illustrates just what an act of vandalism this 'replacement' was.

Burleigh Castle

Just outside Milnathort, Burleigh Castle, the seat of Balfour of Burleigh, was once a much more imposing edifice than what is left of it might suggest. The original early-sixteenth-century tower, which survives to the level of the parapet, was adjoined by a curtain wall with a defensive barmkin, only one side of which remains, and by a moat. Connected to the ruined tower by the surviving section of barmkin wall is a small angle tower, circular at the base but corbelled so as to provide a square watch-room at the top. The stair is encased in a curious bulge to the back, as if the designer had originally forgotten to make provision for it. Splayed shot-holes survive at ground level, as do shot-holes under several of the windows, and there is a wooden sill with a hole to house the prong of a harquebus, or hakbut, a weapon first used in 1513. The small tower retains its roof. 1582 is the date shown at the front of the north crow-stepped gable, together with the initials I.B. and M.B. and the Balfour arms.

The red rubble rectangular main tower, its walls five feet thick and four storeys high to parapet level, once also had an attic storey above its parapet, which was carried on three tiers of corbelling. The parapet has gone, but the remains of open rounds survive, except at the north-east angle, where once the turnpike stair would have ended in a cap-house. The entrance was on the east front, giving access to a lobby. There is a vaulted ground floor beneath the Hall, as usual, on the first floor.

The Balfours were granted their land by James II, and Sir John Balfour of Balgarvie built the older part of the castle. The family was raised to the peerage in 1606, but the fifth Baron had his lands attainted for his involvement in the 1715 Rising. It was he who, in 1707, when Master of Burleigh, fell in love with a young servant of his father's household. The Master was sent abroad to forget her and improve his mind. On the evening before his departure, he swore to the girl that should she marry during his absence, he would return and kill her husband. She married the schoolmaster of Inverkeithing. The Master duly returned and shot the schoolmaster, fatally wounding him. Burleigh fled, but was captured, and two years later was tried and on 29 November 1700 sentenced to death by the axe, the date of the execution being fixed for 6 January the following year, an interval which allowed his family adequate time to organise his escape from Edinburgh Tolbooth disguised in his sister's clothing. Back on the continent, however, he remained a Jacobite, and at the Cross of Lochmaben proclaimed the Pretender, James VIII. The title remained in abeyance until 1868, when the House of Lords proclaimed Alexander Hugh Bruce the rightful heir, and there was once again a Balfour of Burleigh.

Burnhead Tower

A late-sixteenth-century oblong keep on high ground a mile north-east of Hawick, once of three storeys in height with a garret floor and an incomplete parapet, but now attached to a modern house. It was originally owned by a branch of the Scott family.

Busby Peel

Standing above the Kittock Water, the Peel began as a small sixteenth-century tower four storeys high with a parapet on elaborate chequered corbelling. Attached to it is a tall stair tower of the early seventeenth century with a crow-step gable roof. The ensemble now forms the north-east corner of a mainly Georgian house.

The Peill, as it was once written, seems to have belonged to James Hamilton in 1607. Ten years later he signed himself Hamilton of the Peill. Andrew Houston of Jordanhill, one of its many subsequent users, had it in 1793.

Cadboll Castle

Much-ruined Cadboll Castle stands in a farm steading ten miles south-east of Tain. It was originally a Z-plan tower house with a wing to the east and a circular tower at the north-west angle. There is an angle turret at the south-east corner. The walls are well provided with shot-holes and there is a gun-loop to guard the door in the re-entrant angle, which gave access to a movable forestair direct to the first floor.

It had associations with the Abbacy of Fearn, and the nephew of the last Abbot, a Cadboll – the name is usually taken to be a variant of Campbell – got possession at the Reformation. The castle was abandoned in favour of a neighbouring house in the eighteenth century.

Lord Maxwell, but was recovered a few months later. The English took it again in 1572, partly destroying it.

It was probably when repairing the damage done from this siege that the Earl of Nithsdale added his splended domestic range. Two years later the Covenanters, under Lieutenant Colonel Home, besieged it again. The Earl insisted on an inventory of the contents being signed before handing it over. The Maxwells then moved their seat to Terregles, on the west side of Dumfries, later moving on to Traquair House, Peebleshire, where the present laird is their lineal successor, and Caerlaverock fell into ruin. It is now an Ancient Monument.

Cairnbulg Castle

Cairnbulg Castle, a large fortalice incorporating work from many centuries, stands near the sea two miles south-east of Fraserburgh. Basically, it is a massive tall oblong fifteenth-century keep of four storeys with a garret storey above the parapet, attached to later work a storey lower, and given an enormous Z-plan structure by a sixteenth-century flanking tower joined on to the lower extension.

Cairnbulg Castle had become ruinous by the end of the eighteenth century, but was restored in 1896 by the Aberdeen firm of Jenkins and Marr. The parapet, on individual corbels, and a substantial section of the walls and upper works of the main block had to be renewed during the restoration. There are open rounds at three angles, the south-east angle being taken up by a crowstep-gabled cap-house. The door in the east front has a defensive projection above it at parapet level.

Basement and Hall are both vaulted, the latter having stone seats, garderobes and aumries.

The second floor has, in the south-west angle, a mural chamber with a small turnpike stair leading down to a prison; presumably so that the laird could view his victims from his bedroom without too much inconvenience.

The round flanking tower has a dome-vaulted basement and gun-loops. The cylindrical machicolated turret within the machicolated tower-head is reputed to be a copy of the original. The linking lower house is a reconstructed copy of the sixteenth century original.

Sir Alexander Fraser, ancestor of the Lords Saltoun, probably began the keep soon after he came to Scotland in 1375. He married a daughter of the fifth Earl of Ross and was granted the barony of Philorth. The laird of 1666 had to sell his castle, doubtless to pay his Civil War debts, and so built himself the house of Philorth, two years later becoming the tenth Lord Saltoun. The restoration of Cairnbulg was the work of its then owner, John Duthie. After Philorth House was burned down in 1915, the nineteenth Lord Saltoun bought back Cairnbulg, the ancient family seat.

Cakemuir Castle

A mid-sixteenth-century square tower about four miles south-east of Pathhead, by Cakemuir Water, in dreary countryside, Cakemuir was built by Adam Wauchope, fifth son of Gilbert Wauchope of Niddrie Marischal (now virtually demolished). Wauchope, an advocate, defended the Earl of Bothwell against the charge of murdering Darnley.

The thick walls of Cakemuir now rise to four storeys, with a parapet walk and garret above. The details of the parapet are unusual, containing two covered recesses for guards, one of which is still more or less intact. The parapet walk is paved with thick slabs. None of the floors is vaulted. The upper floors are liberally provided with shot-holes. The projecting square-capped tower carries a wide turnpike stair. The Hall, panelled, is known as Queen Mary's room, since it is here she is supposed to have arrived exhausted, dressed as a page, from Borthwick in 1567. Reunited with Bothwell, she rode with him from Cakemuir through the night to Dunbar.

Large additions adjoining the tower to the west were made in 1701 by Henry Wauchope. The last Wauchope to own Cakemuir died in 1794.

Carberry Tower

The small square tower of Carberry, about three miles from Musselburgh, was built around 1577, by the advocate Hugh Rigg on the western slope of the hill where, after the battle of Carberry, Mary, Queen of Scots, defeated by the Confederate Lords, bade farewell to her third husband, the Earl of Bothwell. The tower is now attached to a sizeable mansion dating from 1819, with later additions by Bryce, Lorimer and by Thomas Ross and Frederick MacGibbon.

The walls of the four-storey tower are over seven feet thick. The massive parapet projects from the wall-face on corbelling decorated with French or Italian style *putti*, similar to those erected at Stirling at about the same date. The flat roof is drained by spouting gargoyles. In the centre of the north, west and east sides are rounded wide-mouthed gun-loops of a style otherwise only to be seen at Mains Castle, Dundee. The turret capping the stair in the south-west angle is a later addition, perhaps contemporary with the late-sixteenth-century southern extension.

Hugh Rigg's son added an extension to the tower itself. After being for some years in the hands of Sir Robert Dickson and his family, the tower and the house came by marriage to the Elphinstone family.

Cardrona Tower

Cardrona Tower, overlooking the Tweed, three miles from Peebles, on the shoulder of Cardrona Hill, is a small L-plan castle which was once three storeys high, with a parapet walk on the south-west wall of the main block. This was reached from the staircase that rose over the main well-head. There was probably also a garret in the roof-space.

The entrance is at the foot of the small wing, leading to the turnpike stair which, unusually, rises anti-clockwise. A door to the right leads to the vaulted basement, a single storeroom lit by slits at both ends. The first-floor Hall has a fireplace at the south end, and was lit by four windows. The fireplace on the second floor is in the south-east gable. The third floor has gone.

The Govans held the lands of Cardrona from the fourteenth century until 1685, when the castle passed to the Williamsons. Though abandoned by 1794, it was then 'still almost entire', according to the *Statistical Account*. MacGibbon and Ross, more than three-quarters of a century later, still found traces of courtyard wall and the remains of a pond, both now gone.

Cardross House

Cardross stands on the River Forth two miles south-west of the Lake of Menteith (Scotland's only natural lake so called). Cardross began as a small L-plan tower in the early sixteenth century, with a circular stair tower in the re-entrant angle. A long three-storey extension to the east was added on to the wing of the original building later in the century, the original tower being remodelled to match the new work with corner turrets. In the eighteenth century a new north front was added, together with further domestic extensions to the west.

The original entrance was in the stair tower, the circular stair, unusually, being taken up to the Hall on the first floor, and then in a narrowed form, continuing upwards to serve the bedrooms. The first extension contains some fine plaster ceilings, one said to date from the sixteenth century, but almost certainly from the early seventeenth. Further high quality plasterwork was added in the mid-eighteenth century.

Cardross was owned by a branch of the Erskine family, one of whom died there in 1611 while Commendator of Inchmahome, the Priory on the lake's island. Cromwell is said to have garrisoned troops in the castle, though it is now, happily, in gentler occupancy.

The basement is vaulted. The kitchen was in the wing. There is an entresol floor in the basement of the main block, and a prison within the walling. The first-floor Hall has a good fireplace and windows with stone seats. Garderobes in the walls have flues which meet in one vent, the waste material from which fell into a specially constructed chamber at ground level, where access for cleaning purposes was a movable stone; advanced sanitary arrangements for the time. Even more forward-looking was the use of rainwater collected by stone roof spouts to flush the whole system.

Cardoness Castle

Cardoness Castle stands on a rocky mound a mile south-west of Gatehouse of Fleet. It is an oblong fortalice of the late fifteenth century, with a courtyard to the south, rising to four storeys beneath a parapet that is flush with the walling. Gables show that there was once an attic.

The entrance in the south wall leads to a mural lobby, from

Cardoness Castle: the gable of this 15th century tower house on a rocky mound.

which there is access both to a guardroom and to the turnpike stair rising in the south-east angle.

There is a vaulted basement of two rooms. Once, there was an entresol floor. There are the remains of a hatch for hoisting provisions, and also a prison once reached through a trapdoor.

The Hall on the first floor has high windows, though two at

normal level have stone seats. There is a wide fireplace with moulded jambs, four mural chambers and an ogee-topped aumbry.

A flight of straight steps from the turnpike stair leads to the second floor, which has two rooms with fine fireplaces similar to that of the Hall, and garderobes with drains. There are also the remains of outbuildings.

Cardoness came to the MacCullochs by marriage around 1450. They were an unruly family, feuding with and plundering their neighbours. Thomas MacCulloch died at Flodden, having previously besieged the Adairs of Dunskey in 1489 and, soon after, gutted the castle of MacCulloch of Ardair. The line ended with Sir Gordon MacCulloch, who shot Gordon of Buck o'Bield in 1690, fled abroad, sneaked secretly back to Edinburgh, was detected in church, arrested, tried and executed by the Maiden, a Scottish form of guillotine.

Careston Castle

Careston, or Carvaldstan Castle, stands on the Noran Water four miles west of Brechin. Originally a Z-plan house four storeys and a garret high, it has been much added to and altered.

The remains of an earlier fifteenth-century castle are said to be incorporated in the main block. The corbelled keep has a stair turret, now engulfed in later additions – a two-storey range with a crow-step gable extension tacked on at right angles – and, like the angle turrets, has had its conical caps replaced with crenellations. There is now a handsome symmetrical eighteenth-century front on the other side, with tall gabled corner towers and other ornamentation, including an arcaded basement storey. The richness of Careston's chimney-pieces is unique, and its rib vaulting is of the highest order.

The Dempster, or Adjudicator of the Scots parliament appointed by Robert II in 1369, was Andrew Dempster of Careston, and his became a heritable office. The fifth of the line turned out to be a cattle thief and a most violent man. His son was the last of the line, after whom the property came to the Lindsays, who added to the earlier Dempster work. From the Lindsays, Careston went to the first Earl of Southesk's brother, Sir Alexander Carnegie, and from him to Sir John Stewart of Grandtully, who bought the estate in 1707 and built the new façade in 1714.

Carnasserie Castle: the base of a corner round survives on the upper string course.

Carnasserie Castle

Ruined Carnasserie stands above the main road from Oban to Lochgilphead, about a mile from Kilmartin village. It was built by John Carsewell, Bishop of the Isles, after the Reformation of 1560. It consists of a tower attached to which is a contemporary hall wing. In this it resembles the earlier castle of Melgund, in Angus.

The tower itself is of four storeys, with a narrow roofless gabled garret above. The west wing is a storey lower, decorated with string courses and with a corbelled turret on the west front. There is liberal provision of gun-loops and shot-holes.

The entrance is at the north-west corner of the wing. Over the door is a two-tiered Renaissance panel and the remains of a Gaelic inscription urging faith in God. The door leads through a long narrow passage to the cellar of the keep, probably the wine-cellar, and to three intermediate cellars in the wing, the first of which is the kitchen with arched fireplace, with oven, water supply ducts and stone sink. The door through to the keep cellar is narrow, and could be easily defended. The entire basement is vaulted.

The first floor contains the Hall, which has an ornamental fireplace, with the view chamber for the owner in the tower. Above would be the usual bedroom accommodation. It is uncertain what there was above the Hall, though the remains of an elaborately corbelled window suggests it must have been of some importance.

The parapet of the tower has open rounds at three angles, the fourth having carried the stair cap-house. The parapet walk was drained by cannon spouts.

There was a courtyard to the south, but the walls and outbuildings have mostly gone, the surviving gateway having an arch with on it the initials of Sir Duncan Campbell and his wife, Lady Henrietta Lindsay, and the date, 1685.

Carsewell, whose father had been Constable to the Earl of Argyll, published the first book ever to be printed in Gaelic, John Knox's *Liturgy*, which appeared in 1567. He was Rector of Kilmartin and Chancellor of the Chapel Royal at Stirling in pre-Reformation days. Made Superintendant of the Isles by the Reformers, he was appointed Bishop by Queen Mary – an appointment which annoyed his Presbyterian masters – but was never actually consecrated, though he used the title for the rest of his life.

He died in 1572 and the castle passed to the Campbells of Auchinleck. The castle was blown up during Argyll's Rising of 1685.

Carnell, or Cairnhill Castle

Carnell, on the outskirts of Hurlford, is a small, rectangular early-sixteenth-century tower originally linked on the north and east to a lower L-plan block of buildings of two and three storeys added at various times between the late sixteenth and early eighteenth centuries, the courtyard thus formed being closed by a wall with an arched gateway in it. The tower, with its corbelled parapet, crow stepped cap-house and staircase projection, survives, as does the stair tower of the later buildings, semi-circular but corbelled square at the top.

In 1843, Colonel John Ferrier Hamilton invited William Burn to turn the older buildings into a more convenient house. Burn built an L-plan neo-Jacobean house with two storeys and an attic to the south-east and east of the original tower, making use of the earlier stair tower. He also renewed the parapet and chimneyheads. It is the home of the Findlay family.

Carnousie Castle

This sizeable late-sixteenth-century Z-plan castle stands four miles south of Aberchirder. From its main block there projects a square gabled tower on the north-west corner and a round conically capped tower on the south-east one. The principal stair turret is in the main re-entrant angle. There is a very small turret corbelled out in the southern re-entrant angle above the second-floor level to give access to the watch-room at the top of the taller square tower. In 1740 William Adam added a long wing, tactfully adopting the style of the original building, but in recent years this was removed to bring the task of restoring the original tower to manageable proportions.

The main building rises to three storeys and a garret. Entrance is by a door at the foot of the square tower, a scale-and-platt stair rising only to the first floor. There is a vaulted basement containing the kitchen.

It seems likely that Carnousie was built by Walter Ogilvy shortly before 1583, when he sold the lands and his new fortalice to his brother, Sir George Ogilvy. Like so many who adhered to the Royalist cause, Sir George was ruined for his loyalty and Sir George Gordon, son of the laird of Park, bought it. Changing hands several times more, it was occupied into our own century. It deteriorated disastrously after the Second World War, its fine Adam interiors being slowly lost and the finials of its roofs removed as garden ornaments. Restoration of the original tower was begun but has never quite been fully completed.

Carrick Castle

Carrick Castle stands on a low-lying rock jutting out into the sea near the lower end of the west side of Loch Goil. It is an oblong tower house of three storeys, simple but very finely detailed. The parapet was flush with the wallhead. Gargoyles, all damaged, abound. Unusually in a fifteenth-century castle, none of the floors are vaulted. It has two doors, both opening from the small polygonal walled courtyard, on the east side, which follows the contours of the rocky site. The ground-floor door is now destroyed. The other, above, was the first-floor entrance, connected by movable stair. There was also a postern gate and access to the sea. There are two garderobe flues on the ground floor at the south front. The Hall must have been a fine room, though its fireplace has been taken out. Of its three windows two have seats and all have barhole sockets, as has the door. There are two garderobes. Two straight mural stairs rise on either side of the doorway in the east wall, one leading to the second floor, the left-hand stair rising to the other portion of the subdivided floor and going up to the battlements. Many of the window arches are pointed and moulded, giving the building a somewhat ecclesiastical character.

Carrick Castle was originally a Lamont stronghold which passed, early in the sixteenth century, to the Campbells of Ardkinglas. Tradition avers that it was used as a hunting lodge by the Scots kings. In 1685, the year of the Earl of Argyll's rebellion, John Campbell of Carrick was summoned to Edinburgh to explain his position in the affair, during which time his lands were harried. In 1715, Sir John Campbell of Carrick pledged support for King George, the family lesson perhaps learned. Later in the century Carrick passed to the Murrays, Earls of Dunmore, but was probably deserted by 1800. A sympathetic scheme for restoration as a residence is currently under consideration.

Carsluith Castle

Four miles south of Creetown, Carsluith Castle stands on a slope above Wigtown Bay. It began as a rectangular tower early in the fifteenth century. A smaller but taller wing to the north was added in 1568, doubtless replacing an earlier stair tower. The 1568 addition carried a broader stair and ended in a watch-room, reached by a corbelled-out semi-circular stair turret from second-floor level.

The main block rose to three storeys, to parapet level. The parapet and parapet walk now top only the east and west walls. Corbels of an earlier pattern on the north wall suggest that there might once have been a walkway completely round the original tower. The north-west angle would have been crowned by a cap-house over the stair. The other angles have open rounds. The walls have numerous gun-loops and shot-holes.

Over the doorway, in the re-entrant angle, are the Brown arms, the letter B and the date, 1586. There are two vaulted basements, one with a mural chamber. A turnpike stair rises by the door to the fine first-floor Hall, which has a moulded fireplace, five windows, a garderobe and an aumbry. There are two rooms on the second floor, the turret stair leading to a two-roomed attic.

Carsluith was Cairns property, but in 1460 passed to James Lindsay, Chamberlain of Galloway, who probably built the rectangular tower. He lost his son at Flodden so the property went through his daughter to her husband, Richard Brown, the builder of the 1568 addition. Gilbert Brown of Carsluith, a member of the family, was the last abbot of Sweetheart Abbey. Richard's son, John, was heavily fined when his own son, also John, broke surety by failing to answer the charge of murdering McCulloch of Barholm. The Brown family emigrated to India in 1748, and Carsluith fell into ruin. It is now an Ancient Monument.

Cassillis House

The seat of the Marquess of Ailsa, to which state the twelfth Earl of Cassillis was raised by William IV, Cassillis House stands above the River Doon, about four miles north-east of Maybole, where the family town house, Maybole Castle, is now the Cassillis estate office.

Cassillis House, a mansion designed to impress, dates from three periods. A massive thick walled oblong tower may be of fourteenth-century origin. It was greatly altered in the seventeenth century. A square stair tower was added to the south-east and everything above parapet level on the existing buildings was remodelled. Large extensions in the manner of William Burn were added in 1830, though in such a way as not wholly to detract from the character of the older parts.

Only a few features survive internally. These include the vaulted basement and the prison, built into the sixteen-foot-thick north wall. There is a very wide hollow centre post or newel to the seventeenth-century turnpike stair.

The Kennedy family acquired Cassillis in 1373 when its heiress, Marjory de Montgomerie, married Sir John Kennedy. Sir Gilbert Kennedy was one of the six Regents during the reign of James III, and in 1452 was made Lord Kennedy. The third Lord Kennedy was elevated to Earl in 1509. The fourth, another Gilbert, and the so-called 'King of Carrick', successfully roasted the Commendator of Crossraguel in order to wrest the Abbey lands from him. The fifth, in 1601, at the head of two hundred men, waylaid Mure of Bargany, mortally wounded him in an unequal contest and carried him to Maybole where, had he recovered from his injuries, arrangements were made for him to be dispatched by Cassillis in his role of Judge Ordinary of the area. Not only did Cassillis, by dishonest diplomacy, escape punishment for this outrage, but he actually persuaded the King that he had done the monarch a service. The murdered man's son-in-law, now the new Lord of Auchendrane, took his revenge by waylaying and killing one of the Earl's closest kinsmen, Sir Thomas Kennedy of Culzean. As accomplice, Mure used a student, Dalrymple, who then had to be got rid of. Mure and his son, less influential than Cassillis, were caught, tried and executed. All this, and the minor details, inspired Sir Walter Scott's play *Auchendrane, or The Ayrshire Tragedy*.

Castle Campbell

On a spur of the Ochil Hills, high above the town of Dollar, Castle Campbell stands where the Burns of Care and Sorrow join. When the original rectangular fifteenth-century tower house was first built, it seems to have been known as Castle Gloume. The only explanation for so much verbal depression is Nigel Tranter's suggestion[1] that our forebears 'did tend to equate the grandeur of mountain and rock scenery with sorrow and foreboding', a characteristic certainly true so far as the English were concerned up to the end of the Romantic period. Perhaps it was also a Lowland Scottish characteristic.

[1] Nigel Tranter: *The Fortified House in Scotland,*

Castle Campbell: the tower and later stair tower.

No one knows who built the Castle Gloume, but it was acquired by Colin Campbell, first Earl of Argyll and Chancellor of Scotland, who no doubt wished to have a residence nearer to James IV's Stirling Castle than his Highland seat provided. The Earl had the name changed to Castle Campbell by Act of Parliament in 1489, and may have subsequently added the spacious hall range on the north side of the courtyard. Further additions were made in the late sixteenth or early seventeenth century, on the east side of the courtyard, with an elegant loggia at their base.

The courtyard is entered by an arched pend to the north, which once rose into a gate-house. The tower itself rises to four storeys, with a parapet which has open rounds at each corner. The roof is flat, the ceiling of the top floor having been vaulted in the sixteenth century. It is, unusually, ribbed.

The original door of the tower was that in the west wall, at basement level, leading to the vaulted ground-floor room and a straight stair in the thickness of the wall up to the first floor. The other door, at first floor level, would once have been entered by a movable forestair. Nowadays, the first floor is reached through the later stair tower, late sixteenth or early seventeenth century in date, built against the south-east of the structure. The original stair, unused for many years, was in the opposite wall in the thickness of the south-west angle.

The first floor Hall is vaulted. In the thickness of the east wall there is a thoroughly unpleasant prison, reached through a hatch in the stone floor.

The second floor is not vaulted. The castle is well provided with garderobes and mural chambers built into its very thick walls.

Much of the later work, including the arched loggia joining the bottom storeys at the foot of the new stair, is of a high order. The later curtain wall is not dissimilar in corbelling and machicolation and in the nature of its corner tower to that put up around Craigmillar in 1427.

John Knox stayed in Castle Campbell in 1566, when its laird was the Protestant fourth Earl of Argyll. In 1645, the castle was taken and burned by the Marquis of Montrose. Six years later its then owner, the eight Earl, was responsible for hanging, drawing and quartering Montrose, though Argyll himself also died at the executioner's hands in due course for supporting the Duke of Monmouth's rising against James VII and II. It is now in State care.

Castlecary

Castlecary stands about six miles south-east of Falkirk and half a mile south of the viaduct that carries the Edinburgh/Glasgow railway. The older part of the building is an oblong late-fifteenth-century rubble tower (though incorporating some diamond or feather-broached blocks from the Roman fort nearby). An L-shaped wing two storeys high with an attic, the small wing of which houses another turnpike stair, was added in the seventeenth or eighteenth century. Both structures have a pitched roof with crow-stepped gables. The main tower has a rebuilt crenellated parapet, without rounds, the walk drained by cannon spouts. At the east end of the north wall, at parapet level, there is a curious machicolated projection apparently intended for the dropping of missiles or offensive liquids on unwelcome guests underneath, though it seems odd that this defensive device should not have been placed directly above the entrance.

There is a theory that the tower was meant to be L-shaped with a north wing. This may never have been built, or, if it was, then it may subsequently have been demolished, possibly because of the proximity of the Red Burn, which might have rendered it unstable.

The entrance on the north front gives access to a turnpike stair rising to the parapet, where there is a cap-house with an unusual lean-to roof. Access to the attic is by means of the cap-house. The ground-floor cellar is barrel-vaulted. The Hall, which has the moulded jambs and bases of the original fireplace, also has the remains of some post-Union eighteenth-century wall painting. The rest of the interior has been altered, although an iron yett or grille that must have been part of the defences of the original door is preserved inside the building.

The tower appears to have been built to replace an earlier castle by Henry Livingstone of Myddillbynning shortly before 1485. The castle was held by the Livingstones of Dunipace in the sixteenth century and for the first half of the seventeenth, after which it went to the Baillies. The antiquary Alexander Baillie is presumed to have been born at Castlecary. His sister, Lizzie, eloped by leaping into the plaid of a Highland farmer, Donald Graham, to the annoyance of her brother, producing the contemporary rhyme:

Shame licht on the loggerheids
That live at Castlecary,

To let awa' the bonnie lass
The Highlandman to marry.

In 1730, Castlecary passed by the marriage of Bethia Baillie to
Thomas Dunbar of Fingask, whose descendent, the Marquess of
Zetland, still owns it.

Castle Fraser

Castle Fraser – considered by some the finest of all the great
seventeenth-century castles of the north-east, a group that includes
Fyvie, Midmar, Crathes and Craigievar, all but Midmar now in the
care of the National Trust for Scotland – stands three miles south of
Kenmay. It is a tall, substantial Z-plan tower house, the central
block of which is a double-width sixteenth-century tower
incorpating an earlier keep. A square tower projects to the north-
west and a circular tower to the south-east; both were added in
1592. Even although the walled gardens which must once have
surrounded it have been landscaped away, Fraser has been lucky in
having preserved its subsidiary buildings almost intact. Two long
lower wings, probably the work of James Leiper in 1614, form an
approach courtyard to the north, the arched gateway, an enlarged
replacement of the original, flanked by two crow-stepped gabled
lodges, guarding the end of the courtyard.

The main block rises to four storeys and an attic in height. The
round tower reaches two storeys higher and is crowned with a
balustraded parapet. This is reached by a little stair that has an ogee-
roofed and arcaded cap-house. The other angles of both the main
block and the square tower have two-storeyed conically capped
angle turrets resting on highly decorative corbelling. The number
of shot-holes they carry remind us that Highland raiders could still
be a very real threat when this castle was built.

The upper storeys are also carried on elaborate corbelling and
have dormer windows with decorated pediments and imitation
cannon-spouts. The walls, too, are liberally provided with gun-
loops, arrow-slits and shot-holes.

The original doorway was in the north-west re-entrant angle of
the square tower. Today, the doorway is in the south front, a new
entrance having been formed and the old forecourt turned into a
service court by Eliza Fraser. Above it, between the level of the

Castle Fraser: the main block with its balustrade tower.

windows of the second and third storeys, are panels bearing the Royal Arms of Scotland and the date 1576; another carrying the date 1683; and one reading Eliza Fraser 1795, the date of her alterations.

The basement of the main block has a vaulted kitchen and cellars. A turnpike stair near the original entrance rises to the first floor. Access thereafter is by turret stairs.

The Great Hall paved by James Leiper in 1614, and other main apartments, are on the first floor. Two stairs lead to the domestic quarters below. In one of the windows a secret listening device known as a 'Laird's lug' communicates with a mural chamber in the bedroom above, though the bottom end of this was destroyed during alterations made about 1820 by William Burn, whose redecoration of the Hall was swept away in the 1920s.

The northern wings are each of two storeys, and end with a three-storey conical tower. The embellishment of the upper works in the earlier parts of the main castle has a panel bearing the date 1617 and carrying the inscription I.Bell, a member of the family of master masons who built much in the North East.

The Frasers – descended from a French family called Frisell, from the French *fraise*, strawberry – probably came over to England with William the Conqueror, and reached Scotland in the late thirteenth century. Thomas Fraser, by charter of James II, exchanged his lands of Cornton, Stirlingshire, for Muchal-in-Mar, Aberdeenshire, within which Castle Fraser now stands; some think incorporating the core of an older structure.[1] The first builder of the present structure was probably the fifth laird, Michael Fraser. His son, Andrew, completed the Z-plan design. The sixth laird, another Andrew, was created Lord Fraser in 1633. The second Lord Fraser was described as 'a pryme Covenanter', and suffered accordingly. Montrose destroyed his crops, but fortunately not his castle. The fourth Lord Fraser, a Jacobite, fell off cliffs near Pennan while on the run from Government troops in 1716.

Being childless, his heir was William Fraser of Inverallochy, to whom the castle had already been 'disponed' because of the last Lord's Jacobite proclivities. Five years later, in spite of William having produced three sons, two were killed in battle and the third predeceased him. The castle then went to Eliza Fraser, a daughter, whose portrait by Raeburn is still to be seen. She left the property to Major-General Alexander Mackenzie, who took the name Fraser, but died before Eliza. His great-nephew, Charles Mackenzie Fraser, heired, and carried through drastic alterations internally.

Thereafter, the family history was unlucky; the last Fraser dying childless in 1897. The building remained empty until 1922, when it was bought by Viscount Cowdray (whose wife, Annie, stabilised and partly restored Dunottar). Viscount Cowdray's second son, the Honourable Clive Pearson, had Castle Fraser repaired and partially restored by Dr William Kelly. In 1947, the castle was made over to his second daughter, who married Major Michael Smiley. They removed the Georgian staircase from the forecourt and, as far as possible, restored the original concept. In 1976 they donated the castle, along with twenty-six acres, to the National Trust for Scotland.

[1] H.G. Slade: *Proceedings of the Society of Antiquaries of Scotland,* Volume 109

Castle Grant

A mile north of Grantown, in Strathspey, stands Castle Grant, an E-shaped fortalice which evolved from an L-plan structure of the fifteenth and sixteenth century. There were major additions in 1765 designed by John Adam.

Originally, the oblong block of the L lay east/west. In this there was a vaulted basement with a Hall above. The original door would be in the re-entrant angle. A wide staircase in the wing led to the first floor, and a turret stair continued the access to the rooms above. There was doubtless also a parapet walk, though this has been heightened into a two-storey watch-tower-style addition reached by an extension of the circular turret, crowned, when this work was done in the sixteenth century, with a conically roofed cap-house. Richard Waitt's portrait of the Piper of Grant shows that the courtyard to the south, with its formal approach, had been put up by 1714, though the castle itself never achieved the symmetrical turreted form evidently then planned.

Sir Ludovic Grant (1743–73), who designed the town of Grantown, commissioned Adam to envelop the old castle in new building on its northern face and rebuild the east wing in an enlarged form. He also erected the raised terrace within the forecourt. Plain but tall in proportion, Adam's work has a simple dour grandeur with a very low proportion of window to wall.

Freuchie was the original name of the castle, changed, however, when in 1693 it became the principal residence of the Grants and the eighth laird had the lands made into the Regality of Grant.

Burns visited Castle Grant in 1787 during his Highland tour, the then laird, Sir Ludovic's son, Sir John, being the brother-in-law of the poet's friend Henry Mackenzie, author of *The Man of Feeling*. The grandson of the builder Ludovic heired the title of fifth Earl of Seafield, and the house was until recently a Seafield possession.

Castlehill Tower

Castlehill Tower, a mile and a half from Kirkton Manor, stands on a rocky knoll commanding the old road to Hundleshope. Dating from the end of the fifteenth century, it is oblong and may have had three storeys and a garret, though only two now survive. The basement walls are six, sometimes more than seven, feet thick.

The tower was entered at ground level, in the east wall. The yett of the door and the arch now lie nearby. The door leads to a small lobby to the north, from which a stair ascends to the first-floor Hall. The basement has two barrel-vaulted cellars, one lit by two narrow slit windows, the other by a single slit. The rock on which the castle stands has been incorporated into the foundations of the structure.

The stair to the first floor makes a quarter turn near the foot, then runs straight up inside the north wall to a passage which gives access both to the Hall, once barrel-vaulted, and to a turnpike stair in the north-west angle of the tower. There is evidence at ground level of latrine chutes, descending from garderobes on the upper floor. Attempts were made to consolidate the ruin in 1889, not altogether successfully.

Castlehill was built by the Lowis of Manor family. In 1555, its furnishings included 'ane set burd, twa furmes (forms) hingand durres (hinged doors) four without lokkis' and 'ane hart horn hingand in the hall': hardly accoutrements which suggest great comfort. John Lowis sold the castle to Alexander Veitch, from whom it passed to George Maillie of Jerviswood in 1672. In 1703 it was disponed to William, first Earl of March, who sold it to James Burnet of Barns in 1729. In 1838, William Tweedie of Quater apparently owned it, but abandoned it soon after.

Castle Huntly

A huge L-plan tower built on a rocky volcanic upthrust seven miles west of Dundee, Castle Huntly is basically a fifteenth-century tower much altered in the seventeenth century and Georgianised at the end of the eighteenth.

Andrew, the first Lord Gray of Fowlis, built the tall tower in 1452. The Grays held Castle Huntly till 1614, when it was sold to Patrick Lyon, eleventh Lord Glamis, first Earl of Kinghorne.

Its red sandstone walls are ten feet thick, and it gives the appearance of being almost bonded to the rock; besides having a singularly unpleasant prison cut out of the rock, it rose to three storeys, the fourth being fitted in two hundred or so years after the original building.

Once, the only approach to the living-rooms was by a remarkable internal ladder, which did duty in place of a stair. There was a first-floor barrel-vaulted Hall until the seventeenth century, when the third Earl of Kinghorne removed the vaulting to make way for an extra floor, at the same time renaming the place Castle Lyon. In 1777 it was bought by George Paterson, who restored the original name, but worked his fancy on it. To the top storey he added imitation angle turrets and other defensive features, at the same time Georgianising the interior. A large two-storey extension with bow windows, in which the main entrance is now located, was added to the east. An appalling two-storey brick erection was added onto the western terrace when the building was institutionalised, and within the last few years the superb turreted doocot has been allowed to collapse.

Castle Kennedy

Castle Kennedy stands on a peninsula of the White Loch in the grounds of Lochinch, the 1867 Scottish baronial-style home of the Earl of Stair, four miles east of Stranraer.

As the name suggests, the lands belonged to the Kennedys, who 'acquired' them from the Church in 1482. The old castle was begun in 1607 by John, fifth Earl of Cassillis, but, because of the expenses he incurred supporting the Covenanting cause, was left unfinished. The estate was acquired in 1677 by Sir John Dalrymple, Lord President of the Court of Session and later Viscount Stair, who completed the castle.

It is of unusual design, having a main block four storeys high which once had an attic, and two square wings projecting at the north-east and south-east corners. Within the re-entrant angles thus created there were a further two still higher square towers, the one to the south containing the main turnpike stair. Later still, though not much, three-storey gabled wings were added to the north-west.

Unfortunately, this grand structure accidentally caught fire in 1716 and was never rebuilt. It now forms a roofless ivy-clad folly-like feature in the beautiful French-style garden[1] laid out by Field-Marshal the second Earl of Stair early in the eighteenth century. Allowed to revert to a wilderness after his death, the garden was recreated just over a hundred years ago from the original plans, found in a gardener's cottage.

[1] A.A. Tait, *The Landscape Garden in Scotland, 1735-1835*, 1980

Castle Leod

Castle Leod, seat of the Earl of Cromartie, built near Strathpeffer in
1600 by his ancestor, Sir Roderick Mackenzie, the Tutor of Kintail,
is a variant of the L-plan fortalice. Two decades later it was
extended by the filling-in of most of the arm of that letter with a
higher extension fronting the main block. Part of the purpose of
this extension was to provide a wide staircase, scale and platt as far
as first-floor level, and part to allow for extra accommodation.

The original castle of four storeys and a garret had a parapet walk
with open rounds on the south, east and west sides, the north side
having a dormered wallhead between conically roofed turrets.
Such extensive parapets were rare by 1600, an indication of the
troubled state of the area. The extension has a conical angle turret
and dormers on the south face, one of which contains the builder's
initials, those of his wife and the date 1616. The effect of the
extension, looked at from the south-west, is of a double pile house,
with its two gables. Sections are liberally supplied with shot-holes
and gun-loops.

The ornamental entrance door is in the south front, from a
terrace. The basement houses the old kitchen in the wing and
vaulted cellars in the main block. The Hall on the first floor has a
fine fireplace. The private room off it is now the dining-room.

Castle Levan

High above the Clyde some three miles south-west of Gourock,
Castle Levan (or Leven) stands in the grounds of the house that
succeeded it. It is an L-shaped castle, but with the wings joined by
their corners. The northern tower is probably of late fourteenth or
early fifteenth century origin, the larger south-east wing dating
from the early sixteenth century.

The building rises to three storeys and a garret, has a parapet and
walk carried on chequered corbelling, and open rounds at the
angles. The thick walls have several keyhole type arrow-slits.

The re-entrant angle carries three entrances, one of them
modern. Both basements are vaulted, housing kitchen, wine-cellar
and store. Narrow stairs in the walls rise to the Hall on the first floor
of the southern tower. There was once a turnpike stair in the corner
where the wings joined. The upper floors have collapsed, as has the

north-west corner of the north tower, but rebuilding is now in hand, a brave enterprise with a castle so incompletely preserved. Until 1547, Castle Levan was a Morton stronghold, but it was then sold to the prominent Renfrewshire family of Semphill, who held it until 1649, when it passed to the Stewarts, now Shaw-Stewarts of Inverkip.

Castle Menzies

Castle Menzies, one of the finest examples of an extended Z-plan castle, stands at the foot of Weem Hill, a mile or so west of Aberfeldy, and was the seat of the chiefs of the Clan Menzies. Comrie Castle, the family's older seat, had been destroyed by fire in 1487. The then laird, Sir Robert Menzies, built himself a new house known as The Place of Weem on the site of the present castle. This was destroyed by his feuding enemy Stewart of Garth. Sir Robert got a promise of compensation from James IV, but no money.

The present castle was built by Sir Robert's great-grandson, Sir James Menzies, in the 1570s, and consists of a main block of three storeys and an attic with square towers of five storeys, each projecting on opposite corners. Circular turrets adorn most of the angles. The walling has gun-loops and heraldic decorations. The original entrance, that in the re-entrant angle at the front of the south-west tower and guarded by a gun-loop, has above it the arms of James Menzies and his wife, Lady Barbara Stewart, daughter of the Earl of Atholl; a marriage which would certainly attract money for further building. The porched entrance in the centre of the main block was part of William Burn's additions of 1839. A dormer pediment carries the date 1577, the initials I.M.B. and the motto IN OWR TYME, and on the lintel PRYSIT BE GOD FOREVER.

The ground floor is vaulted. The first floor contains the Hall and a room to the east. The stair, in the south-west tower, leads to generous domestic accommodation above.

Nevertheless, in 1839 40 the sixth baronet, Sir Niall – the family had obtained a Nova Scotia baronetcy in 1665 – had the architect William Burn add a huge west wing. On the death of the last Menzies in 1918 the castle changed hands several times, becoming dangerously neglected before it came into the possession of the Clan Menzies Society in 1957. Since then, with the assistance of grants from the Historic Buildings Council for Scotland, the main block has been well restored, the eighteenth-century main stair and offices to the rear, which were beyond repair, demolished and the restoration of the 1840 wing begun.

Castle of Mey

Looking over the Pentland Firth fifteen miles from Thurso, the Castle of Mey, or Barrogil as it was once called, was the seat of the Sinclairs, Earls of Caithness. Originally, it was a late-sixteenth-century Z-plan tower, probably c.1566–72, with eighteenth-century additions, further added to in the nineteenth century. It has a large square wing at the south-west and a smaller square stair tower to the north-east. The main block rises to three storeys and an attic, the wings a storey higher. The angle turrets, mostly two-storeyed and originally conical-roofed, rest on chequered corbelling. Their Braemar-type crenellated parapets date from a partial remodelling by William Burn in 1819. A huge chimney-stack, which rises at the east end of the main block, somewhat resembles another tower. The porch is Burn's. The building was begun by George Sinclair, fourth Earl of Caithness. (He, incidentally, was chairman of the jury that acquitted Bothwell of Darnley's murder.) His grandson, the 'wicked' fifth Earl, completed the building. The sixth Earl died in financial difficulty, and his Campbell widow married the main creditor, Sir John Campbell of Glenorchy, an unsavoury character who got himself granted the Caithness Earldom, though he lost it to the second son of the fifth Earl after a legal wrangle, the displaced Campbell being made Earl of Breadalbane as consolation.

After falling into some neglect in the present century, the castle was bought and repaired by Queen Elizabeth, the Queen Mother, some of Burn's alterations being retained.

Castlemilk

Of Castlemilk, a late-fifteenth-century oblong tower, only the stump remains surrounded by the Glasgow housing scheme of the same name. Formerly, it rose to three storeys with a romantically modernised parapet and garret. Internally, it had been much altered, providing the main entrance to a large Georgian castellated mansion which achieved final form in 1891. The Hall on the first floor was still known as Queen Mary's room on the strength of the possibility that she lodged there rather than at Craignethan the night before the Battle of Langside, fatal to her cause, in 1568. Bought by Glasgow Corporation in 1938, the mansion was occupied as a children's home until 1969. It was thereafter reduced to its present state.

Castle of Park

Park Castle, which stands high on a ridge overlooking the Luce valley a mile south-west of the village of Glenluce, is a noble example of a late-sixteenth-century laird's house. A lofty L-shaped building of harled rubble, the main block rises to four storeys, while the wing which houses the stair rises a storey higher and is crowned by a watch-room reached by a tiny stair in a turret in the re-entrant angle corbelled out at fourth-floor level. The steeply pitched roof has crow-stepped gables, and a massive chimney-stack dominates the upper part of the east wall.

The door is at the foot of the stair tower in the re-entrant angle, and has a shot-hole beside it to ensure defence. Above the doorway is the inscription BLESSIT BE THE NAME OF THE LORD THIS VERK VAS BLVIIT [sic built] THE FIRST DAY OF MARCH 1590 BY THOMAS HAY OF PARK AND IONET MAKDOVEL HIS SPOUS. Above this is an empty panel space.

The door opens on a vaulted corridor leading to three vaulted rooms in the main basement, that to the north being a kitchen with a huge arched fireplace, a room singularly well lit for its kind. The lobby also gives access to a turnpike stair, leading to the first-floor Hall, a splendid room with a fine moulded fireplace, well lit by six windows one of which has a stone seat. The north-east angle contains a garderobe, the north-west angle a service stair down to the kitchen and the laird's wine-cellar. This private stair also leads up to the bedrooms. The two upper floors each have two bedrooms with fireplaces and mural chambers.

Two wings, added during the eighteenth century, have recently been demolished.

Park was Church land. At the Reformation, Thomas Hay got himself made Commendator of Glenluce Abbey, and proceeded to pull it down to build his fine House of Park. Despite trouble with the fourth Earl of Casillis, the Hays hung on to Park until the nineteenth century. In 1830, its Cunninghame owner deserted it for his new home of Dunragit, using Park to house farm labourers. It is now happily an Ancient Monument, and so in good hands.

Castle Stalker

Castle Stalker stands dramatically on an islet in Loch Linne, off Portnacroish. What remains comprises a tall, massive, rectangular keep of mid-sixteenth-century construction, with upper works remodelled about a century later and traces of an associated barmkin.

The approach is from the east, where the islet on which the castle stands is separated from the mainland by a stretch of shallow water. It must therefore usually have been necessary to arrive or depart by boat. There was an ascent from the landing-place to the barmkin by a stone stair.

The castle itself has two entrances. There is a moulded doorway in the vaulted basement on the east front, with machicolation above it at parapet level. The main entrance is on the north face at first-floor level, originally reached, no doubt, by a movable wooden stair but now by a stone forestair which is joined to the building though there was once a gap that would have been covered by a wooden platform.

The castle rises to four storeys and has an open parapet at wallhead level. There is a crow-stepped-gabled garret storey within the parapet walk and a similarly gabled watch-room at the head of the turnpike stair in the north-west angle. These works were added in 1631, along with the open round, equipped with shot-holes, at the south-west angle.

The ground floor has four rooms, barrel-vaulted, from the largest of which the turnpike stair ascends to the top of the building. This room was probably the kitchen. The fourth room is a prison in the thickness of the wall which, though it is furnished with a garderobe, is accessible only by means of a hatch from above.

The first-floor Hall has a fireplace, garderobe and, in one of its three windows, stone window seats. The second floor was perhaps originally an upper hall but was subdivided by timber walls early in the eighteenth century.

Castle Stalker was possibly begun by Duncan Stewart, second of

Castle Stalker: recently restored. It is islanded at high tide.

Appin, and finished by his son Alan, who died about 1562. It is said to have been paid for, however, by James V, as part of his campaign to suppress the unruly Highlands. Since his island expedition took place in 1540, two years before his death, this, if true, would seem to date the foundation of the castle. In the third decade of the seventeenth century, the castle passed into the hands of Sir Donald Campbell of Ardnamurchan and Airds, though whether by legal action or purchase is uncertain. He was probably responsible for the 1631 alterations. It remained in Campbell hands till the fall of the ninth Earl of Argyll in 1681 when, after a legal action and a violent refusal of the Campbells to submit to the decision of the Courts, it came back to the Stewarts in 1686. The eighth Stewart of Appin fought at Sheriffmuir on the Jacobite side, and the ninth was 'out' in 1745, the resulting forfeiture forcing him to sell his estate. The castle was garrisoned with Hanoverian troops at that time. Pococke, in his *Tours*, found it occupied in 1760, but it was abandoned and roofless early in the nineteenth century. An extensive scheme of restoration was begun in 1965 by its present owners.

Castle Stewart

Castle Stewart, five miles north-east of Inverness, stands at the head of a sandy bay by the Moray Firth. It is a U-plan tower house replacing an earlier structure. The central block has square towers projecting southward at each end in such a manner as to protect both the front and side faces, thus forming two re-entrant angles for each tower. The main block has four storeys, the western tower six and the eastern five. The tower to the west has a flat roof and a parapet with nineteenth-century crenellations and is drained by cannon spouts. The east has crow-stepped gables and three conically roofed angle turrets. The north-east and north-west angles of the main block have square two-storey turrets with crow-stepped gables corbelled out on the diagonal at second-floor level, at an angle. Two stair turrets are corbelled out from first-floor level in the northern re-entrant angles. The western stair tower is topped with a later open crown. There are numerous shot-holes and gun-loops.

The original entrance is in the re-entrant angle in the south-west tower, which houses a large scale-and-platt main stair to the first floor, after which access is by the two turret stairs. The main entrance is now a later door in the south front.

The basement has four vaulted rooms; a kitchen with fireplace and oven; a wine-cellar with private stair to the Hall above and another cellar and store.

The Hall occupies most of the first floor, though there is a withdrawing-room adjacent. The second floor also has a Hall and withdrawing-room with a bedroom attached. There are bedrooms on this floor in both towers, and on the floor below another bedroom in the tower that does not carry the first-floor stair. There are still more bedrooms above. It was internally dismantled in late Georgian times but reinstated with minimal alterations under the supervision of James Maitland Wardrop in 1869. The present Earl of Moray still owns it, though it is lived in by a tenant.

Castle Sween

Castle Sween stands high upon a rock on the eastern shore about two miles from the mouth of the sea loch Loch Sween. The castle consists of four curtain-walls, almost rectangular in shape, origin-

Castle Sween: the added square corner tower and a section of the original curtain wall with no apertures.

ally without towers, although a round and a square corner tower were added against the two northern corners some time after the construction of the seven-foot-thick curtain walls. These rise to a height of some forty feet. Within the open courtyard only fragmentary foundations remain. There is also a well.

The curtain of the castle has no apertures, except for the main entrance in the middle of the south front, and a sea-gate, now broken, in the west. The only features on the walling are the flat clasping buttresses which strengthen each corner, and a flat pilaster buttress projecting midway along each side. Such buttresses, Cruden states,[1] are 'characteristic of early Norman work'.

The entrance is a round-headed opening, and the jambs are checked for a door, evidently once secured by a drawbridge for which the slots survive. The entrance passage is barrel-vaulted. To the right of the entrance, a stone stair rises against the inner face of

[1] *op. cit.*

the wall to the walkway above it. It finished in a small square cap-house, now badly ruined. A projecting bretasche probably hung over the entrance, as at Tioram, Mingarry and Kisimull.

The wall-walk had an inner and outer parapet. In the north-east corner there is a small room entered by a lintelled doorway and lit by two windows.

Round the inside of all three walls, other than that containing the stairway, there is a deep mural channel, apparently constructed to carry timber flooring for the keep that must once have stood within the walls.

Tradition avers that the oldest part was built by Sueno, Prince of Denmark: but Cruden points out that the name Sween is a corruption of the Gaelic *Suibhne*. There was such a noble in the *Annals of Ulster* of 1034. During the thirteenth century Knapdale was controlled by MacSweens, who sided with the English during the War of Independence.

Castle Sween was besieged, captured and burned by Montrose's lieutenant, Macdonald of Colkitto.

Castle Tioram

Castle Tioram stands on a rocky platform of a tidal island in the mouth of Loch Moidart, three miles or so south of Acharacle. It began as a crenellated wall of enceinte shaped to the contours of the rock in the thirteenth century, with lean-to accommodation inside, as at Kisimull, Mingary and elsewhere. Tioram was taken over in the fourteenth century by Amy MacRuary, the first wife of John, seventh Lord of the Isles, after she was cast aside by her husband so that he could marry Margaret, the daughter of Robert II. From her family sprang the Calanranald division of the MacDonalds.

The wall of enceinte is thinner in the north-eastern section than elsewhere. This section may therefore be of a later date. The narrow entrance doorway is in the north wall. An outside stair on the inner side of the wall led to the parapet, drained by spouts in the form of gargoyles.

Later buildings were added within the enclosure, the most prominent feature being the keep in the north-west angle. It is square with a vaulted basement, and now inaccessible upper floors. There are open turrets at the angles. There is another similar tower dating from about 1600. The room in the south-east is thought to

Castle Tioram: the wall of enceinte shaped to the contour of the rock.

have been the kitchen, since the remains of what looks like an oven are in the angle, and those of an arched fireplace are still to be seen. The Hall may well have been to the north, at a higher level.

Tioram was attacked by the Earls of Huntly and Argyll in 1554 on the orders of Mary of Guise, and again by Cromwell, who took it and occupied it. Its Clanranald owner of the time set it on fire during the 1715 rising to prevent it falling into government hands. Today, it is an interesting consolidated ruin.

Cavers House

Three miles east of Hawick, above the Teviot valley, the shell of Cavers House – radically altered in 1887–90 when its vault was taken out, then unroofed and stripped in the 1960s by its Palmer-Dougals owners – is a sorry reminder of the fate that too often overtakes all but the best of our stone and mortar heritage. The

Balliols had a castle on the site in the twelfth and thirteenth centuries. The oldest portion, a lofty square tower of five storeys and an attic, is said to have been built by Sir Archibald Douglas, youngest son of the Earl of Douglas who fell at Otterburn in 1388, but from the scale of the building it seems unlikely to be older than the fifteenth century. Sir Archibald's descendants were the Hereditary Sheriffs of Teviotdale. Much of the added house was sixteenth-century, but had many later additions and modernisations, including many castellated features in the Scottish Baronial style.

Cawdor Castle

Six miles south-west of Nairn stands Cawdor Castle. This substantial building developed around an oblong keep, supposed to date from 1396, although upper works are now dated 1454, in which year royal licence to build a defensive castle was granted. The ground floor is vaulted, and contains the preserved remains of a yew tree associated with the legend of the Thane of Calder (as the original spelling had the name). Having to build a new castle, he was supernaturally directed to load a donkey and follow where it led. It would bring him to an area of three thorn trees, under the third of which it would lie, and there the building should be erected. The donkey lay down and the castle was duly built, surrounded by a deep dry ditch and approached, as it still is, by a drawbridge.

Once over this, a substantial iron yett, under the belfry, provides further protection. This came from Lochindorb Castle, after the fall of the Douglases in 1455, when James II entrusted the destruction of his fallen enemy's stronghold to the Thane of Cawdor.

The keep is four storeys high and has a garret. There is a crenellated parapet level with the walling. It is drained by cannon spouts, and has machicolated projections for the tossing down of missiles. The original open rounds were raised in the seventeenth century and provided with conical roofs.

The original entrance was at first-floor level, by movable timber stair. Now, the entrance is at basement level, which is vaulted, as is the third floor of the keep. A straight stair in the north wall connects basement and Hall, which had mural chambers that now connect it with later work.

Cawdor Castle: a view of the original keep and drawbridge entrance.

The first extension, erected on the walls of enceinte, suggest that the lower portions on the north and west, with their gun-loops and cellars, are the oldest. The long three-storey ranges to the north and west which provide additional accommodation were the work of Sir Hugh Campbell, the fifteenth Thane, and date from 1672. They formed a courtyard on the north side of the keep. Stables and domestic offices occupied the south side.

In the sixteenth century the estate had come by the marriage of an heiress to Sir John Campbell, third son of the second Earl of Argyll, and ancestor of the present Earl of Cawdor. Between 1660 and 1670, major additions and improvements were made by Sir Hugh Campbell, who built a central block abutting the keep and linking it with the north and west sides of the courtyard. This block contained a wide staircase which, so to say, drew the whole edifice together by providing a central entrance doorway and focal point. A panel over the entrance to the central block carries the date 1672, with the initials of Sir Hugh and his wife, Lady Henrietta Stewart.

There are several splendid seventeenth-century Renaissance fireplaces, including one in which a monkey blows a horn, a cat plays a fiddle and a mermaid a harp. A fox also smokes a pipe, though the date – 1511 – if accurate, suggests that somehow it anticipated the introduction of tobacco to England! This particular fireplace commemorates the marriage of Muriel, Heiress of Cawdor, whose kidnapping from the guardianship of Lady Kilravock in 1499 by Campbell of Inverliver on the instructions of the Earl of Argyll led to the death of all six of Inverliver's sons.

To-day, though there have been later restorations and alterations, mainly by Thomas Mackenzie, the great keep still dominates the castle, now open to the public and with its contents and treasures presented in an exemplary manner to its visitors.

Cessnock Castle

Cessnock, which stands upon a ravine through which the Craufurdland Water flows near Galston, is now a large U-plan house, the oldest feature of which is the massive rectangular keep at the south-west. It was probably built by John Campbell of Loudon in the fifteenth century. It is three storeys high with an attic, and has immensely thick walls and a rather squat appearance. Presumably it once had parapets, but it now has a crow-stepped gable roof containing a garret, though the open rounds at the angles survive. Of the three windows on the west wall, the south window at second-floor level is higher than its fellow, causing the three-tiered corbelling to be shaped round the top of it. There is a wide gun-loop at ground level on the west wall.

Internally, the tower house still has its two vaults, and would once have had the usual arrangement of its Hall on the first floor with the bedrooms above. The castle, however, has experienced a succession of enlargements. At the end of the sixteenth century, Sir George Campbell added an L-shaped mansion of three storeys on the north-eastern face. From 1630 onwards his grandson, Sir Hew Campbell, enlarged the newer part, forming the present Great Hall. The U-shape was achieved through further additions before 1675, the circular stair in the re-entrant angle of the late-sixteenth-century house being constructed in 1666.

By 1890 the house was in poor condition, part of it being used for agricultural purposes. After being owned by Wallaces and Scotts, Cessnock came to the Duke of Portland, who commissioned Thomas Leadbetter to restore it and build a modern mansion on to the old structures. Once, the house had panelled seventeenth-century ceilings, according to McGibbon and Ross, but the present ceilings are now Leadbetter's, only the Great Hall still carrying a late-sixteenth-century painted ceiling. There is still one seventeenth-century ceiling and some contemporary plasterwork at second-floor level.

In 1946 the house was bought by the Baron Robert and Lady Fiona de Fresnes, she being a Campbell of Loudon. They enclosed the court with a stone archway. The ground floor was sold off as a self-contained flat in 1981.

Mary, Queen of Scots came to Cessnock after her defeat at Langside, when one of her ladies died there and is said to haunt the castle. The Reformers Wishart and Knox visited it. Sir Hew Campbell was a strong Covenanter, for which he was persecuted. Appointed Lord Justice Clerk in 1649, he declined to act, and was consequently excluded from the Act of Indemnity and imprisoned. His son was reinstated, also became Lord Justice Clerk, but did act. His heiress married Sir Alexander Home who in 1704 was raised to the bench as Lord Cessnock. Burns visited the Castle.

Clackmannan Tower

Clackmannan Tower, which stands at the top of the hill by the old town of Clackmannan, was a possession of the Bruces. The rumour that King Robert himself built it as a hunting lodge cannot be substantiated. In 1359, David II gave it to another Robert Bruce, of a bastard line related to the Royal House. These Bruces remained in possession until the death in 1796 of the widow of the last laird, like her husband a zealous Jacobite. On 26 August, 1787, in the adjoining mansion, now vanished, she knighted the poet Robert Burns with the sword of King Robert the Bruce.

The lower half of the original tower, built of grey coursed rubble, does indeed date from the fourteenth century. The higher portion is taken in slightly, at a small set-off rising to a further two storeys with a partial parapet on corbelling. In the late fifteenth century, however, a still taller tower in a warmer coloured dress stone rising to four storeys with a machicolated parapet on corbelling was added, making the house into an L-plan structure.

The original entrance to the old tower was at first-floor level, by movable timber staircase. When the new tower was added, a turnpike stair was inserted into the re-entrant angle, entered by a door at ground level. Only the top of this stair survives, the lower part having been removed to construct a more generously proportioned scale and platt stair to first-floor level in the late seventeenth century. The fine Renaissance arch and pedimented doorway on the east front is also of that date.

Both ground floors are vaulted, and once had timber entresol floors. Both first floors are also vaulted, the Hall being in the main block and having a handsome sixteenth-century fireplace with a decorated surround. There is an unusual long narrow gallery within the walls of the third floor, entered through one of the window embrasures.

As at several other Bruce castles, Clackmannan Tower is equipped with a brazier for containing a warning beacon fire. It is now in State care.

Claypotts Castle

Although it may not seem so at first sight, the plan of Claypotts, one mile west of Broughty Ferry but now engulfed by the hinterland of Dundee, is very similar to that of Z-plan Terpersie. The centrepiece is an oblong block with two large circular towers diagonally opposite each other at the north-east and south-west corners. There are two much smaller stair towers with turnpike stairs in two of the angles between the main block, one on each side. The larger stair is that by the entrance.

The main block is three storeys high and has a garret. The walls are well provided with gun-loops and shot-holes. The two squared-off and corbelled watch-rooms which top the large tower look

Claypotts Castle: a good example of how to gain extra
accommodation upwards.

similar, but are of slightly different dimensions, the one built a
generation later than the other.

The basement has a kitchen and three cellars or store-rooms.
Each of the floors in the main block has a large public room, that on
the first floor being the Hall, at one time divided by a screen so as
not to be directly entered off the stair. There are no fewer than eight
bedrooms in the towers. One fine dormer window survives. Two
dates are carved on skews in the gables. The southern tower carries
the date 1588, the northern tower 1569 (though the five has been
cut upside down).

Thus, Claypotts in the form it has come down to us dates from the late sixteenth century. The Abbey of Lindores received the lands from Alexander II. By 1511, they were apparently in the hands of the Strachans (probably leased), Gilbert Strathauchtyne, Strathachin or Strachan (as the name, not surprisingly, contracted to) of Claypotts' being involved in the theft of seven horses and carts owned by the clerics of Dunkeld.[1]

At the beginning of the seventeenth century, the superiority of the Abbey of Lindores was transferred by the Commendator, Patrick Leslie, about the time the Strachans transferred their interest in Claypotts to William Graham. His eldest son sold the lands to the Grahams of Claverhouse in 1619, whose great-grandson was 'Bloody Clavers', Viscount Dundee. His lands being forfeited, in 1694 Claypotts went to the Earls of Angus and Douglas, through whose descendants it came to the Earls of Home. In the nineteenth century it was used to house farm labourers. It is now an Ancient Monument.

Cleish Castle

An L-plan fortalice a mile west of the village of Cleish, Cleish Castle stands on the northern slopes of the Cleish Hills about four miles south-west of Kinross. By 1840 it had become ruinous, but in the 1840s its owner, Harry Young, had it restored. His architect was John Lessels. The massive walls are of good quality ashlar and carry the building to five storeys in height. An older edifice is possibly incorporated, but as it now comes down to us the building is basically of sixteenth-century origin with changes in the upper works made a century later.

The main block, running north to south, has an attic and a garret. The wing to the east is narrower and, because of the falling away of the ground, taller, which necessitates buttress-like support at the base of the gable. This wing contains an extra storey. There is a stair turret on the north side above first-floor level, which has a former window pediment with the arms of Robert Colville and Beatrix Haldane and the date 1600.

The original entrance was in the re-entrant angle, but at the restoration, when the interior was much altered, this was closed up

[1] M.R. Apted, *Proceedings of the Society of Antiquaries of Scotland*, 1954/6

in favour of an entrance at first-floor level reached by a forestair. In the late 1960s the castle was de-Victorianised by the architect Michael Spens, who removed the porch and forestair and replaced the Victorian sash windows with modern ones based on the sixteenth-century window divide.

The Colvilles were for long the owners of Cleish, the arms being amongst those of the ancient Fife families displayed on the ceiling at Collairnie Castle. In 1530, Sir James Colville exchanged his lands of Ochiltree for lands in Fife which included Cleish, bestowing them on his son, Robert, the original builder. The date 1600 and the initials of his grandson, another Robert, suggest that the younger Robert was responsible for the seventeenth-century alterations.

When Mary, Queen of Scots escaped from Loch Leven Castle in 1568, it was to Cleish that she first fled.

The earlier castle on the site was the birthplace in 1493 of Squire Meldrum, the hero of Sir David Lyndsay's poem *The True History of Squire Meldrum*.

Closeburn Castle

Closeburn Castle vies with Traquair House, in Peebleshire, for the distinction of being the oldest continually inhabited house in Scotland. Closeburn, a mile to the east of the village of the same name, is a plain oblong fourteenth-century tower with walls ten feet thick culminating in a crenellated parapet flush with the wallhead. It is vaulted at the basement, Hall and roof. Both the crenellations and the square cap-house have been altered in late Georgian times, as has much of the interior; the Hall for example, having been subdivided. There is a nineteenth-century extension.

The Kirkpatricks built Closeburn, one of their ancestors, Roger de Kirkpatrick, along with Lindsay of Dunrod, having 'made siccar' by administering the *coup de grâce* with their daggers after Bruce had stabbed the Red Comyn at Dumfries. A baronetcy was conferred on the family for loyalty to Charles I in 1685, and from them the Empress Eugénie, wife of Napoleon III, was descended. The estate was sold by the Kirkpatricks in 1783.

Cockburnspath Tower

This much-ruined stronghold, a square keep which had out-buildings in its courtyard, stands about one and a half miles south of Cockburnspath railway station. The north and west walls survive in a reduced state, and there is a good seventeenth-century doorway. Late fourteenth or early fifteenth century in date, the tower was given to the Earls of March in return for an undertaking to purge the Merse and Lothians of thieves and robbers. It passed to the Earls of Dunbar, but to the Crown on their forfeiture in 1435.

Colinton Castle

The ruins of the L-plan Colinton Castle, Edinburgh, stand in the grounds of Colinton House. There is mention of it in 1545, and it could be of that date, with the second stair tower to the south added early in the seventeenth century. The entrance was in this later tower.

The lands of Colinton belonged to the Foulis family. There was a fire in the castle in 1650, after which it was repaired. It was abandoned, however, when the barrister Sir William Forbes of Pitsligo bought the estate from the Foulises in 1800 and finished the building of Colinton House in 1806. By that time the painter Alexander Naysmith had advised Sir William to unroof and partly demolish the old castle to make a picturesque ruin, in keeping with late-eighteenth-century classical taste!

Collairnie Castle

Collairnie Castle, once an L-plan structure, the smaller wing being five storeys high and the larger four storeys, now stands in the farm steading of the same name four miles or so east of Newburgh. Although the main block has been reduced to a single storey and the tower roof altered to oversail the turrets, it still contains two fine panelled *tempera* ceilings in the second- and third-floor rooms. Here, precariously preserved, are the armorial bearings of the Barclays, who built Collairnie in the sixteenth century, as well as those of almost fifty other families, mostly of Fife origin.

Mary, Queen of Scots is said to have spent three days at

Collairnie on her way to St Andrews to meet Darnley. The Barclays held Collairnie until 1717. The husband of the heiress with whom the line ended married a Stewart, who added Barclay to his name. Later intermarriage with the Balfours and the selling of the property in 1789 to Balfour of Fernie preceded the castle's demotion to its present somewhat sorry agricultural role.

Colliston Castle

A Z-plan castle, Colliston is situated on the Brothock Water four miles north-west of Arbroath. Both its towers were once corbelled square at the top, but only the larger one still is.

There were alterations in the seventeenth century and, clearly, further extensive alterations in 1894–5, when George Henderson, for the then owner, J. Peebles Chaplin, raised and redesigned the upper works.

The original door has been reinstated at the foot of the main tower. The seventeenth-century door, now again a window in the centre of the main block, has over it the date 1621, together with the royal arms of Scotland and the initials I.R., for James VI, with the motto LAUS DEO.

The original builder was probably John Guthrie, who, with his wife Isabella Ogilvie, received the lands from Cardinal Beaton, then Abbot of Arbroath, in 1545, possibly because the lady was his own daughter! Sir John's initials survive on a panel with the date 1553. Another panel, with H.G. inscribed on it, probably refers to Sir Henry Guthrie, Coroner of Arbroath, who no doubt built the seventeenth-century additions.

The ground floor is vaulted, with the kitchen beneath the main room. The original turnpike stair to the first floor has been replaced by a squared scale-and-platt stair in a projection to the rear.

The fine Hall has the customary mural private stair to the wine-cellar, but has had its windows enlarged in the seventeenth century.

Sir Henry Guthrie sold Colliston to a Dr Gordon in 1670. In 1721 it was bought by George Chaplin, with whose descendants it remained until our own time.

Comlongan Castle

Comlongan Castle is a massive fifteenth-century tower, rather similar to its now vanished contemporary, Elphinstone, and standing adjacent to a large Victorian mansion. Comlongan stands eight miles south east of Dumfries. It has a plinth base – a kind of primitive damp-course as well as a strengthener on what was once marshy ground – and is constructed of coursed rubble. Oblong in shape, it rises to five storeys beneath the parapet. Its thirteen-foot-thick walls are a complex warren, containing a ramification of mural chambers, closets and stairs. Only the ground floor is of solid-wall construction, and even that contains an oblong, windowless dungeon.

Comlongan differs from Elphinstone and Borthwick, with which it also has resemblances, in that each of its floors is systematically planned to make the best use of the entire area. The upper section thus does not degenerate into randomly placed small rooms.

The northern entrance is reached by a short upward flight of stone steps. The doorway still has its iron yett. In the lobby there is a recessed porter's seat, the entrance to the vaulted basement, which once contained an entresol floor, and the foot of the turnpike stair in the south-east angle, leading to the Hall above.

The impressive Hall has stone flags, a fine fireplace with elevated flanking windows such as also occur at Borthwick and at Castle Campbell, a cusped aumbry, three windows with seats and, at the other end of the Hall, a second fireplace within a deep arched recess. This would have been the kitchen, separated from the main room by a screen. At a later date it was enclosed by a wall.

There are also two walled chambers. The one to the north, reached by a descending stair of ten steps encased in the wall, leads to a guardroom and prison. From the guardroom a hatch gives the only access to an unventilated and unlit cell at ground level.

The floors above are of timber. Each room on the second floor has a fireplace and garderobe, and the third floor is similarly laid out. There is a garret storey within the corbelled parapet. On the west side, the parapet walk is roofed in to form a small crow-stepped-gabled room with fireplace, lamp recess and drain. A similar enclosure was also added to the south-east angle. The main turnpike stair is topped with a cap-house.

Comlongan was built by Murray of Cockpool. James IV made

the Murrays Earls of Annandale, some of whom were Wardens of the West March. From them are descended the Earls of Mansfield, who in 1984 sold it to Mr Tony Ptolmey, who is currently repairing it.

Comrie Castle

Comrie Castle is a small L-plan keep on the River Lyon, about three miles from Kenmore. The main block has a square stair tower at the south-west angle. It has had three stories and an attic, but is now ruined. There is a vaulted basement. The doorway, in the re-entrant angle, is of the roll-moulded variety. Above is a corbelled stair turret, only the base of which survives.

Comrie Castle was the original seat of the Menzies family, though when the previous castle on this site was burned, they built and then moved into Castle Menzies. Comrie was rebuilt around 1600 for the use of younger branches of the family. It had been abandoned by the beginning of the nineteenth century.

Corbet Tower

Odd-looking Corbet Tower, remote in the Cheviot Hills a mile south of Morebattle, on the top of the steep bank that bounds the Kale Water, was probably once part of a much larger castle, possibly a possession of the Abbey of Melrose. It has four storeys and a garret, each floor containing a single small apartment. Above second-floor level, the corbelling stands out like a string course. The tower still has a surprising number of strategically placed splayed gun-loops. A Ker stronghold, it was burned by the English in 1522, and again by Hertford in 1544. The parapet has been removed and the roofline altered. Crosses now top both gables, with the engraved date 1572. The structure was 'done up' by Sir Charles Ker in the latter part of the nineteenth century.

Corgarff

Corgarff stands on a height near the head of Strathdon, on the Lecht road – so frequently blocked by snow in the winter – that leads to Scotland's highest village, Tomintoull. Corgarff is a tall tower, four storeys high, oblong in plan, with its original staircase carried a storey higher to provide a cap-house on the south-east angle. It replaced the structure, destroyed in 1581, which had been a hunting-lodge for the Earls of Mar and in which the tragic events recounted in the well-known ballad 'Edom o' Gordon' are said to have occurred. Annexed by the Crown in 1435, the lands were given by James IV to the Elphinstones, who were probably the builders of the present tower. The Mars recovered it in 1626, but after the family disaster resulting from the rising of 1715, it passed to the Forbes family.

Corgarff was burnt by the Jacobites in 1689 to deny it to the government troops, and again in 1716 by the government to punish Mar. The Jacobites nevertheless repossessed it during the '45. The government then took over Corgarff and turned it into a garrison outpost to help subdue the highlanders. Extended alterations were made to it, a single-storey wing being added to house the service offices. An enclosing oblong wall, with salients projecting from each face and well provided with loopholes, was also added. It is now in State care.

Corse Castle

Ruined Corse Castle stands three miles north-west of Lumphannan, a Z-plan tower with a rectangular main block, a square tower to the north-east and a circular tower, which has now virtually collapsed, to the south-east. Another, but smaller, circular tower projecting to the south carried a stair above the wallhead to end in a watch-room, now fallen, resting on corbels.

Above the main entrance in the re-entrant angle, at the foot of the square tower, is a lintel with the initials W.F. and E.S. and the date 1581. There is a corbelled-out triangular projection in the re-entrant angle from first-floor level which would have carried a stair. Three open rounds survive, though doubtless there once were four.

The lands of Corse formed part of the barony of Coull – the castle of which is little more than a heap of stones – and O'Neill, which was bestowed in 1476 by James III on his armour-bearer, Patrick Forbes, youngest son of the second Lord Forbes. The builder of the castle was William Forbes, who married Elizabeth Strachan, and whose descendants included the Patrick Forbes who, in 1618, became Bishop of Aberdeen, ten years after his brother, John, had been Moderator of the General Assembly of the Church of Scotland. Corse was raided by Highland freebooters in 1638. It was abandoned in the nineteenth century in favour of the nearby mansion, but a descendant of the original builder has plans to restore the castle.

Cortachy Castle

This seat of the Earls of Airlie stands by the River South Esk, near the Grampian foothills, four miles north of Kirriemuir. A Z-plan castle with an additional large round tower at one of the angles, it may date from the fifteenth century, but is sixteenth-century in its present form. On the smaller circular tower of the original Z, the gabled watch-room is supported on corbelling shaped like a W, an unusual feature.

The castle has suffered many vicissitudes, and is consequently much altered. The Covenanting Earl of Argyll destroyed the place in 1641. Restored, it was again destroyed by fire as part of Cromwell's revenge for its owner's having given hospitality to Charles II for one night in 1650.

Though there was a castle here in the fourteenth century, owned by the Earls of Strathearn, the nucleus of the present structure is probably the work of Sir Walter Ogilvy of Oures, who was granted Cortachy by James III. No evidence of the previous building survives. As it now stands much of the detail of Cortachy is the work of David Bryce, whose palatial new wing of 1870 – remodelling R. and R. Dickson's Georgian Gothic wing and extending it to the north – was completely removed after the Second World War. The fine Jacobean pendant ceiling on the first floor was reproduced from Auchterhouse, then an Airlie possession. Cortachy is the home of Lord Ogilvy, the Airlie heir.

Couston Castle

Couston, a few hundred yards from the remains of Otterston Castle, stands on the edge of Otterston Loch, two miles south-east of Inverkeithing.

The lands of Couston figure in late-twelfth-century charters. What survives of the castle – basically, L-plan, with a circular stair tower in the angle, together with a lower wing – date from the late sixteenth or early seventeenth century, but are based on a much earlier structure, the present north wing having an in-filled post-medieval arch.

The tower is roofless and has suffered the loss of the greater part of its south end, which was demolished in the 1830s to provide stones for the building of the nearby farm steading. The north gable of the tower is complete to the chimney head. The roofless north wing probably dates from the eighteenth century.

Couston's most famous occupant was a former tutor of Charles I, the Reverend Robert Blair, the bigoted seventeenth-century Presbyterian clergyman who opposed prelacy with such vigour that after the Restoration he was required in 1666 to present himself in Edinburgh to face a charge of high treason; a fate he escaped by being called on the same day to face his Maker. He was in all probability one of the collaborators involved in the murder of Archbishop Sharp on Magus Muir.

The castle, reasonably entire until the 1830s, was Moray property. It has been bought by a restoring purchaser, Alistair Harper, who is, however, at the moment of writing about to rebuild it to designs by Ian Begg.

Cowdenknowes

Cowdenknowes, on the left bank of the Leader Water, a mile south of the village of Earlston, was once a powerful fortalice, seat of the Earls of Home, whose cruelties in feudal times produced the rhyming maladiction:

> 'Vengeance! vengeance! when and where?
> Upon the house of Cowdenknowes, now and evermair.

All that survives of the original castle is the sixteenth-century tower, although the mansion to which it is attached goes back in part to the same century. The oblong tower, which carries the date 1554, rises to four storeys, its basement chamber partly below ground level. The walls, more than three feet thick, are of rubble with dressed quoins. A parapet of dressed stone added a little later, as may be seen from the style of the corbelling, carries the north and south walls only. Quatrefoil-shaped gun-loops are provided. A ruined old tower to the south still retains its basement and sunken chambers, presumably once dungeons, reachable only by a trapdoor in the floor.

The mansion, though much altered – for example, the ground floor of the tower has been gutted to provide it with an entrance hall – and added to over the centuries, carries the date 1574, with the initials SIH and VKH over the small south-east-wing stair tower, along with the inscribed motto FEIR GOD. FLEE. FROM. SYNNE. AND. MAK. FOR. YE. LYFE. EVERLAST-ING. The initials were those of Sir John Home and his wife. The pilastered windows and the upperworks of the tower are ornate for the period.

Home of Cowdenknowes was prominent as a supporter of the Protestant Lords at the time of the Reformation, and in 1582 was involved in the Raid of Ruthven, when James VI was imprisoned in Ruthven Castle for six months.

Cowdenknowes had pleasanter associations, however, one of several versions of the sung ballad commemorating its surroundings containing the lines:

> Oh the broom, and the bonny bonny broom,
>   and the broom of the Cowdenknowes,
> And aye sae sweet as the lassie sang
>   I' the bught, milken the yows.

A severe frost in the winter of 1861–2 destroyed what the advance of agriculture had left of the broom, described by a nineteenth-century writer as 'golden adornments'.

Coxton Castle: only one room to each floor.

Coxton Castle

Coxton, three miles east of Elgin, is a remarkable tower house, square with walls five feet thick and rising to four storeys.

All the ceilings except those on the top floor are vaulted, and the vaults are at right angles, one above the other. An open bartisan, drained by a cannon spout, is corbelled out. Iron grilles still cover some of the windows.

The original entrance was on the first floor, approached, as usual, by means of a movable ladder. The ground floor had a doorway to what would be a shelter for cattle. The first-floor entrance, however, was provided with a stone forestair at some later date. Above it are the initials R.I. and A.I., for Alexander Innes and his wife, together with the date 1644.

There are two mural stairs, the main one in the north-east angle, that from the third floor leading the bartisan. There is also a stair to the basement cellar. Like Scotstarvit and Hallbar, Coxton has only one room on each floor. It came into the hands of the Earls of Fife and was used as a gardener's house in the nineteenth century. Now empty, it is still restorable.

Craigcaffie Tower

Three miles north-east of Stranraer, overlooking ground believed once to have been occupied by the Roman base of *Rericonium,* stands Craigcaffie Tower, once called Kellechaffe, an oblong castle built in the second half of the sixteenth century. Its rubble walls, roughcast, rise to three storeys and a garret in height. It has crenellated parapets on the east and west walls, but open rounds at all four angles. There is a broad chimney-stack rising on the north wallhead almost to the height of the crow-step-gabled steeply pitched roof.

A turnpike stair from the doorway on the north front provides access to each floor. At parapet level, a projection above the door allows the dropping of missiles or suitable liquids on unacceptable would-be entrants. The canon-spouts draining the parapet walk are individually decorated.

The vaulted basement has had its kitchen fireplace filled in. There is a hatch for serving the Hall above, through a small adjacent first-floor pantry. The Hall has a moulded fireplace, but is poorly lit by only two windows. The rooms above have been subdivided at some later date.

Halfway between the door and the missile-dropping facility, a panel carries the initials I.N. and M.S. and the arms of the Neilsons and the Strangs.

The Neilsons held Craigcaffie from the 1470s until 1791, when it came into the possession of the Earl of Stair. Having been unoccupied for some years, it has recently been sold by the Stairs to enable restoration to take place.

Craig Castle

The castle of Craig of Auchindoir stands on a dramatic ravine site two miles north of Lumsden, linked to the early-eighteenth-century mansion which superseded it. It is a huge L-plan tower-house castle rising to four storeys and well supplied with gun-loops. It was probably built in 1510 by the first Gordon of Craig, who died at Flodden, and is the most completely preserved of that group of castles distinguished by high-quality late-medieval rib vaults, being complete to the corbelled parapet, which has been enclosed with an oversailing roof, turning the walk into a gallery. The gables, very unusually, have gabletted crow-steps.

The entrance, in the re-entrant angle, has a moulded arched doorway. Above it are heraldic panels. The centre one carries the arms of Patrick Gordon, the first laird, and his wife, Elizabeth Stewart of Laithers. On either side are the arms of the second and third lairds, the latter carrying the date 1548. Above the panels is a Hall window still with its original grille. The eastern angle at parapet level has a conically roofed turret.

The tower is entered by a vestibule, smaller than those at Gight and Delgaty. There are two vaulted cellars in the main block, and another, the kitchen, in the jamb. A small guardroom leads to a prison in the walling. A stair connects the wine-cellar with the Hall above.

The main turnpike stair leads to the Hall, subdivided by late-seventeenth-century partitions, as is the Upper Hall on the second floor. An ornate gateway to the east, leading into the courtyard, between the castle and the later mansion, carries the date 1726 along with the arms of the eighth laird and the initials of his three wives.

The family had an unfortunate history. The grandson of the Gordon killed at Flodden died at Pinkie. His son suffered for his share in the murder of the Bonnie Earl o' Moray. The line ended in 1812, when the heiress and her daughter were burned to death in an hotel fire at Nice. The castle is still occupied.

Craig Castle

Craig Castle, overlooking the tidal Montrose Basin, has been quadrangular, but only two of its four sides remain. Its main features are two small square towers with parapets, probably of fifteenth-century construction, linked by the surviving outer wall of the demolished south range. The west and north sides are made up of buildings of a later date, probably seventeenth-century, though constructed on older foundations. The east side has gone altogether, and the courtyard now opens into the much larger outer court, which has two circular towers flanking the gateway in its south wall.

The two towers differ slightly. Both are of three storeys and a garret in height, but the eastern one has a plain parapet with open rounds while the western is crenellated. Both have garret rooms with crow-stepped gables inside the parapet. Once, in all probability, there would have been matching towers on the other corners of the inner court. The towers have vaulted basements, the east one preserving evidence of an arched inner gateway to the courtyard. The main house, probably dating from 1637, is plain and has more modern additions.

The De Bocos, later Woods, built the original castle in 1617. Within a decade, however, it was bought by David Carnegie, first Earl of Southesk, who settled it on his second son, Sir James. When Sir James succeeded to the title, Craig went to his younger brother, who married Jane, daughter of the Constable of Dundee, Sir John Scrymgeour of Dudhope. Their sister, Lady Magdalene Carnegie, married the great Montrose.

Craigcrook Castle

Craigcrook nestles at the foot of the north-eastern slope of Corstorphine Hill, Edinburgh. It was probably built in the late sixteenth century by one Adamson, an Edinburgh burgess, as a Z-plan castle with a round tower projecting to the south-west, a central block of three storeys and a square tower projecting to the south-east, though the latter has long since been encased in later additional construction work. Its main claim to fame is that its distinguished owners have included Sir John Hall, Lord Provost of Edinburgh in 1689, and Archibald Constable, the famous publisher who lived in it from 1802– 14. He was followed by the critic and lawyer Francis (later Lord) Jeffrey, who described it as 'an old narrow house . . . with irregular projections of all sorts'. During the thirty-five years he spent his summers there, he had W.H. Playfair add to the house and remodel the gardens, supposed to be the prototype of the garden at Tully-Veolan in Scott's *Waverley*. Scott himself was often a guest at Craigcrook. Later enlarged again by Leadbetter and Fairley, it now provides offices for a firm of architects.

Craigentinny

Craigentinny, an L-shaped tower of the late sixteenth century, stands near the ancient village but now industrialised area of Restalrig, a suburb of Edinburgh. The building rises to three storeys with an attic. It has been much altered since the Nisbets erected it. Though the 1852 wing, by David Rhind, has been demolished, his alterations to the original house remain.

The original doorway is in the ground floor of the wing. A broad stair rises to the first floor, and in the usual fashion the access thereafter is by a turnpike stair in the turret at the re-entrant angle. Amongst the many later alterations are the grotesquely exaggerated cannon water spouts which drain the roof.

Craigievar Castle

Craigievar Castle stands on a hillside twenty-six miles west of Aberdeen and five miles north of Lumphanan. It is the finest tower house of its kind to be built in Scotland, combining the full flowering of the vernacular tradition with French influence, and so 'claiming a Scottish place in the front ranks of European architecture'. An L-plan castle, it has been called by W. Douglas Simpson[1] a medieval hall-house built vertically instead of horizontally, the spiral stairs which lead from storey to storey being, so to say, inverted corridors.

Be that as it may, all the ornamental elaboration is exercised upon the upper storeys, the lower walling of this warm peach-shaded structure being plain. The square tower in the re-entrant angle contains the door, giving access to three vaulted basement rooms and to a straight stair rising to the first floor. The tower has a balustrated parapet within which is the ogee roof of the cap-house.

The first-floor Hall, practically unchanged since it was constructed, apart from minor alterations in 1825, is a magnificent room, its attractions including a stucco representation of the arms of the United Kingdom above the handsome fireplace and a splendid ceiling of raised panels, heraldry, foliage and decorative pendants, the focusing features of which are the medallions of Joshua and David, Hector of Troy, Tarquin, Lucretia, Alexander

---

[1] *Guide to Craigievar Castle*

Craigievar Castle: a prosperous merchant's tower house.

the Great, and other Biblical and classical heroes of antiquity. The ceiling also carries the coat of arms of the builder, William Forbes – known as Danzig Willie because of the fact that he made his fortune exporting fish and woollen goods to the Baltic and importing Swedish memel pine – and of his wife, Margaret Woodward, together with the date 1626. The Hall still retains its oak-panelled screens at the east, providing a service lobby. A small pantry and a stair to the wine-cellar are behind the screen, as well as access to the minstrels' gallery to the east.

Five turret stairways lead to the private rooms on the upper floors, most of them panelled. The Queen's Room, on the third floor, is so named, it seems, because Danzig Willie hoped that James VI and his consort would visit the castle, though there is no evidence that they ever did so. Portraits by Raeburn and others, and family related *objets d'art* too numerous to detail here, abound.

The upper works feature a well-balanced cluster of two-storey conically-capped angle turrets, small gables, chimney-stacks and a variety of inventive corbelling. Once, the castle stood inside a barmkin only one of the round towers of which remains, together with the arched gateway.

In 1630, Danzig Willie's eldest son, a zealous Covenanter and Member of Parliament, was created a Nova Scotia baronet by Charles I. His portrait by the first identifiable Scottish portrait painter, George Jamesone, is on display. In Sir William's day Craigievar, like Corse, was attacked by Highland freebooters. Many of them were caught and executed, including the notorious Gilderoy of ballad fame.

The fifth baronet married Sarah, daughter of the twelfth Lord Sempill, and their grandson succeeded as the seventeenth Baron. Thus the Sempills became associated with Craigievar. William Francis Forbes, tenth Baronet of Craigievar and nineteenth Baron Sempill, succeeded to the title in 1934. In 1963, the eighteenth Baron Sempill, shortly before his death, allowed a local conservation group to buy Craigievar Castle together with thirty acres of land on condition that it should be presented to the National Trust for Scotland, in whose care it now rests.

Craigmillar Castle

The imposing ruins of Craigmillar Castle stand on an irregular rocky ridge three miles south of Edinburgh, the suburbs of which have now all but engulfed it, though the new buildings at least keep a decent distance, as befits so dignified and historic a ruin.

Although apparently an elaborate structure, basically it is an L-shaped tower, built about 1374. In that year Sir Simon Preston of Garton purchased the previous structure on the site – itself then probably about two centuries old – from one John de Capella. In 1427, a thirty-foot machicolated curtain wall – the best-preserved example of its kind in Scotland – with circular angle towers was thrown round the tower house. Early in the sixteenth century an additional walled enclosure protected by a moat was constructed. Within the resulting courtyard various domestic lean-to buildings and a pleasaunce were added to match the sixteenth-century structure. The western range was reconstructed in 1661.

The building is entered through a wide arched doorway in the corner of the wing, over which is the heraldic device of the Prestons.

The vaulted lobby leads to a turnpike stair, and also gives access to the poorly lit cellars, now reached by doors from later additions. There is a timber entresol floor. The Hall is thirty-five feet by twenty-one. On the gable opposite the entrance end there is a fine hooded fireplace with lintels supported at each side upon richly modelled shafts. The capitals and bosses are reminiscent of those to be found in the Laird's Hall at Doune, and clearly of late-fourteenth-century ecclesiastical inspiration. The vaulted chamber in a wing is known as Queen Mary's room, though it was once the original kitchen.

Another turnpike stair leads to the main second floor, a vaulted entresol without a fireplace, though the vaulted wing apartment has both a fireplace and a garderobe with a chute.

The main block is topped with a low-pitched stone slab roof inside the parapet walk. At the top of the stairhead is a guardroom having a fireplace and garderobe.

The later buildings inside the courtyard have several basement cellars in the four-storey range, three of them vaulted and reached through a vaulted passage. At one time they probably provided a kitchen and a service store. A turnpike stair, built partly within the keep's wall, leads to the next floor, which also has four apartments, two of them vaulted. The middle room is yet another kitchen with a large fireplace and chimney-stack to carry the flue. Above it there was one long apartment, presumably providing accommodation for the guards.

The west range has three rooms in each storey over the older vaulted cellarage. The crow-stepped chapel was in the outer court. A round tower in the north-east angle of the outer curtain wall was a dovecote.

Craigmillar was much used by royalty. James III imprisoned his awkward brother, the Earl of Mar, in one of its cellars. The boy James V came to Craigmillar with his tutor, the poet and future Bishop of Dunkeld, Gavin Douglas. Mary, Queen of Scots used it so regularly that the nearby hamlet accommodating her French ladies was, and indeed still is, known as Little France.

It was at the so-called Conference of Craigmillar that the Queen's half-brother, the Regent Murray, conspiring with Borthwick and

Lethington, is supposed to have tried to persuade the Queen to divorce Darnley, her second husband. When she refused, they then laid the plans for Darnley's murder. The ambitious Moray was himself assassinated soon afterwards at Linlithgow, his place in the plot being taken by Morton, whose motive was fear of a Popish plot in which Darnley was supposed to be a leading figure. Bothwell, of course, wanted to marry the Queen, an ambition he disastrously achieved. Party to the murder or no, amongst all the scheming and treacherous nobles who surrounded Mary, Bothwell was virtually the only one who was at no time ever disloyal to her.

In 1660 Sir John Gilmour, Lord president of the Court of Session, bought Craigmillar, and it remains with his descendants, though now in State care.

Craignethan Castle

Craignethan Castle, formerly called Draffone, but better known locally now as Tillietudlem, the name bestowed upon it by Scott in *Old Mortality*, stands on a promontory above a deep ravine of the Nethan Water shortly before it joins the Clyde at Crossford. A steep fall-away of the ground provides a strong defence on three sides, while the fourth side has the protection of a thirty-foot-deep ditch.

The original keep, begun about 1530 by Sir James Hamilton of Finnart within a barmkin, is oblong. The vaulted basement of the keep is below ground level, and there are three floors above it. The building is roofless and whatever stood above the parapet has now gone. The parapet rests on chequered corbelling. There are open rounds in the angles and a bartisan above the west door, which carries over it the Hamilton arms.

The door leads to the first floor, where there is a large lobby. The Great Hall lies to the north and a turnpike stair rises to the south. There is also a guardroom. To the north of a thick internal wall is the vaulted kitchen with its fireplace, and another room. The subterranean basement is also vaulted. The upper floors have long since gone.

A sizeable flanking tower, also of the fifteenth century, stands to the south-east, but only the base of another to the north-east has survived.

When the later-sixteenth-century expansion work was carried out, the only direction in which to build was westwards over the dry ditch, where an outer courtyard was formed, probably the work of the second Earl of Arran, Duke of Châtelhérault and Sir James's half-brother. Although the extension is less intact, clearly it was of some magnitude. There is an impressive range of curtain walling to the west with a gate-house at the centre and a northern corner tower surmounted by a dovecot. The southern tower was incorporated in a further seventeenth-century range, which happily survives.

The main block of this range joins at right angles to the older tower. It has an attached circular stair tower containing the door, over which are the arms of the Hays. It has three storeys and crow-stepped gables, and was obviously built after the period when defence was a domestic consideration.

The castle came to James, Lord Hamilton, after the Earl of Douglas had forfeited it in 1455. The first Hamilton Earl of Arran in 1529 settled it on his bastard son, Sir James Hamilton of Finnart, a talented architect and the King's Superintendent of Palaces, who, though he was probably responsible for much of the Palace Block at Stirling and the Renaissance façade at Falkland, nevertheless ended his days at the hands of the executioner, found guilty of treason. Hamilton added the sixteenth-century range, strengthening the castle. The castle was sold in 1665 by Ann, Duchess of Hamilton, to Andrew Hay, who built the south-west range, the house which is now occupied by the Custodian.

Mary, Queen of Scots is said to have spent the night before the Battle of Langside at Craignethan, a supposition that vies with the topographically more probable claims of Castlemilk. Scott not only used Craignethan as the prototype of Tillietudlem, but seriously considered restoring it in part and living in the seventeenth-century house as an alternative to building Abbotsford. In the event, preservation was carried out by the twelfth Earl of Home at the end of the nineteenth century. The fourteenth Earl gave Craignethan into State care. The Ancient Monuments section of the Ministry of Works, now the Historic Buildings and Monuments Directorate, discovered in recent years a *caponier*, or tunnel, with low-level gun-loops guarding the deep ditch which, in the days of the old castle, would have brought a besieger under a devastating range of fire.

Craigston Castle

About four and a half miles north-east of Turriff stands Craigston Castle, a U-shaped structure, harled, but with long picked-out quoins. Except for a relatively brief period – from 1657 to 1746 – it has been in the hands of the Urquhart family. A main block lies north/south, in front of which are two wings projecting westwards. These are linked by a great arch with a highly ornate sculptured balcony at fourth-floor level. Each of the outer angles has elaborate corbelling for angle turrets, but in all probability these were never built. The roof is gabled, and has an unusual flat-topped and balustraded cap-house rising above the fifth storey. An 1834 porch by John Smith fills the bottom of the recess at the foot of the arch, providing an outer door in front of the original. The high arch may have been copied from Fyvie, and was certainly built about the same time; or Craigston may even have been designed by whoever built Fyvie, since both buildings appear contemporaneous. Inside the planning is spacious.

Of the several heraldic and decorative panels which grace the wings, the one on the left bears the arms of the builder of the house, Captain John Urquhart – great-grandson of the Tutor of Cromarty, whose father, Alexander Urquhart, had acquired the estate in the mid-sixteenth century. The panel on the right states: THIS VARK FOUNDIT YE FOURTINE OF MARCH ANE THOUSAND SEX HOUNDER FOUR YEARIS AND ENDIT YE 8 OF DECEMBR 1607. The builder Urquhart, a Jacobite Captain who survived Sherrifmuir, found himself unable to pursue a normal calling because of his political convictions. He therefore became a privateer, in which capacity he made enough money to buy not only Craigston, but also Cromarty, the latter eventually passing to the author of *The Jewel* and the translator of Rabelais, Sir Thomas Urquhart of Cromarty. Craigston has a fine interior, with carved woodwork and panelling. It has a vaulted basement. The large Hall has much eighteenth-century woodwork, as well as a series of oak panels from the seventeenth century representing Biblical figures. The long gallery, on the fourth floor, subdivided in the later nineteenth century, now houses a splendid library in the major part. There is a seventeenth-century dovecote in the garden.

In the eighteenth century, small flanking courtyards were formed by the addition of low two-storey ranges extending north and south, at which time extensive repairs to the main block and some repanelling were carried out by Smith. The drawing-room and ante-room were provided with compartmented ceilings, new chimney-pieces and elegant door-frames.

Cramond Tower

Standing in the policies of its successor, Cramond House, overlooking the meeting-place of the River Almond and the Forth, Cramond Tower was once part of a residence of the bishops of Dunkeld, who held the estate then called Bishop's Cramond. All that survives is the fifteenth-century four-storey tower, the first-floor Hall and the fourth floor. The door, a few feet above ground level, leads to the steeply pointed vault of the basement. Cramond Tower was acquired in 1622 by an English merchant, John Inglis, whose grandson received a baronetcy, and abandoned the tower towards the end of the century in favour of nearby Cramond House. During the present century, ivy and saplings reduced it to a dangerously damaged condition, but mistakenly believing themselves to be the owners, Edinburgh Corporation consolidated it, capping the wallhead with concrete. It has recently been restored and reoccupied, a pitched roof having once again been erected.

Cranshaws Castle

Cranshaws Castle, in the Lammermuir Hills a mile west of Cranshaws Church, is a rectangular harled tower house of four storeys with a crow-stepped garret above, within a corbelled and crenellated parapet drained by octagonal stone spouts. It is of uncertain age, though various analogies suggest late-fourteenth-century origin. Today, it stands on its own, though it must have been surrounded by a barmkin and had ancillary buildings, since the original tower appears not to have had a kitchen. It has rounded corners, like Neidpath or Drum.

The entrance would originally have been in the west front, adjoining the turnpike stair, which still rises in the south-west angle. A little room on each floor above occupied the equivalent space over the entrance.

The lands of Cranshaws were in Douglas hands by 1362, passing to the Douglas Earls of Morton, who made numerous internal changes in the eighteenth and nineteenth centuries. The thirteenth Earl of Morton possibly removed the ground-floor vault in the mid-eighteenth century to created two low storeys. He may also have demolished the ancillary structures. There were further alterations internally, and to the parapet, in 1895.

In 1978, the present owner had Robert Hurd and Partners improve the by then somewhat haphazard internal arrangements, making a dining-room and kitchen on the ground floor and removing partitions on the second floor to form a 'Great Hall'.

In pre-Trade Union Douglas days, the castle was reputedly the haunt of an obliging 'drudging brownie'.

Crathes Castle

Crathes Castle, three miles east of Banchory, is, after Craigievar, perhaps the finest surviving continuously occupied late-sixteenth-century tower house in Scotland. The Burnards, who later changed their name to Burnett, came to Scotland in the reign of David I. For generations, their home was a wooden stronghold on an island in the now drained Loch of Leys. For assisting the Bruce against Edward I, they received part of the royal forest of Drum, on Deeside – as well as the famous Horn of Ley, according to family tradition – and the ninth laird, Alexander Burnet of Leys, the name already changed though without the later second *t*, began in 1553 to build his L-plan stronghold of Crathes, raising it to four storeys and an attic. For some reason the castle took more than forty years to finish, so was completed by his great-grandson, the twelfth laird, in 1596. The beginnings are commemorated in the east wall by two shields over the doorway, one containing the Burnett arms impaled with those of Hamilton and the date of commencement, the other the monograms of Alexander Burnett and Jean Gordon, and the date of completion. It is possible that George Bell, a member of the well-known north-east family of master masons, was responsible for the final construction. The plan is most unusual, the main block being made double pile by the incorporation of the stair, its great width being spanned by a double ridged roof the valley of which is marked on the south by a stair turret corbelled out at second-floor level.

The lower storeys are plain, except for perhaps an obviously late Victorian Renaissance window at first-floor level. The upper

Crathes Castle: the decorative capping of a tower house that took forty years to build.

works incorporate a rich variety of corbelling, string courses, angle turrets, stair turrets, gargoyles and gabling which challenges comparison with Craigievar and Fraser. An unusual feature is that the main south gable has circular turrets whereas the other angles have square gabled ones.

Externally, the tower has a defensive appearance. It has rounded corners, the idea in older times being that this made it more difficult for an enemy to knock out corner stones and so weaken the structure. The castle also tapers towards the top, following the original theory that this made it more difficult for an enemy to shelter under the battlements while attempting to tunnel beneath the foundations or throw fireballs through the lower shot-holes, though by this time adopted for structural or aesthetic reasons. There was, however, the traditional iron yett, and a device known as a tripping-stone on the turnpike stair, which rises to the third

Crathes Castle: The Nine Nobles Ceiling.

Crathes Castle: Ceiling musicians on one of several fine painted ceilings.

floor. An enemy running up the stair would find the eleventh step so adjusted that he would almost certainly take a clattering fall.

The basement of Crathes is vaulted and contained the usual kitchen and cellars, the wine-cellar having the normal service stair to the Hall above. The Hall stands over the western cellars, which have a plastered semi-circular vault with painted decoration at the arched recess and soffits of the window embrasures. The bold caryatid chimney-piece is 16th century Italian, imported in the 1870s. There was a withdrawing-room on the first floor over the kitchen.

The upper floors provide for an unusually large number of bedrooms, one with a painted ceiling of colourful representations of the nine nobles, or military heroes of antiquity. An original four-poster bed of 1594 and other contemporary furniture survive. The top floor has an oak-ceilinged long gallery, the ceiling sloping to fit the eaves of the roof. It lies along the north side of the castle, its axis at right angles to the hall extending into the jamb.

The eleventh baronet added an alien late-Victorian wing overlooking the upper garden, but this was destroyed by fire in 1966, and not rebuilt by the present owners, the National Trust for Scotland. Instead, the original 'laigh biggins', or low buildings incorporated in the addition, were restored, leaving the wing reduced to its original two storey height, returning the castle to its pre-nineteenth-century profile.

Craufurdland Castle

Craufurdland Castle stands on a bank above the Craufurdland Water, some three miles north-west of Kilmarnock. The oldest part is a mid-sixteenth-century tower at the west end, with eighteenth-century sashed windows. The eastern half of the house dates from various years of the seventeenth century. The interior has been much altered to connect with the house, added in the eighteenth century and remodelled with further additions in the nineteenth. The King's Room has a fine plaster ceiling dotted with lions and unicorns, its centrepiece the arms of Charles I, and carrying the date, no doubt added after, of 1668.

The Craufurds of Craufurdland were one of the oldest Ayrshire families, going back to Sir Reginald de Craufurd, Sheriff of Ayr in the early thirteenth century, the line coming to an end only in 1793. Colonel J.W. Craufurd, though an officer in the King's army, felt such loyalty to his old friend and neighbour the Earl of Kilmarnock, of nearby Dean Castle, that he held one corner of the cloth which received that unfortunate nobleman's head on his execution for his part in the Forty-Five. For this, Craufurd was demoted, though he was again to rise to the rank of Lieutenant-Colonel.

He left his estate to Thomas Coutts, the banker, but following litigation, the Craufurd lands were settled on his aunt, the wife of John Houison, one of whose ancestors reputedly rescued James V when he was attacked by vagrants at Cramond Bridge whilst wandering around in his disguise as 'the guid man of Ballengeich.' The king bestowed the Crown property of Braehead on the Houisons in exchange for a basin, ewer and towel when required for the royal use. The family still survives as the Houison-Craufurds.

Crichton Castle: The entrance.

Crichton Castle

Crichton Castle stands on a hillock on the right bank and almost at the head of the Scottish River Tyne, two miles south of Pathhead. It has long been ruinous, although it is fairly intact up to the wallhead, and is now consolidated and in the care of the State. In some respects it compares with Craigmillar, on the outskirts of Edinburgh, being an early tower house enlarged into a major castle by stages.

The building began as a rectangular fourteenth-century three-storey square ashlar tower, its walls seven feet thick. It had a vaulted basement with an entresol timber floor at the level of the springing. Above this was a vaulted Hall with the usual wooden screen at the north end, and a second storey. A tiny kitchen and, beneath it, a small but unpleasant Saracen-style prison – known as Massie More, a corruption of Mazmarra – were fitted into the north-east corner. The barmkin or fortified courtyard, on the western side, screened the outbuildings. This tower was partly destroyed in 1445, but reconstructed.

Crichton Castle: The courtyard diamond facade, as drawn by Thomas Ross.

An oblong keep-gatehouse of three storeys was added on the south side of the barmkin in the early fifteenth century by Lord Chancellor Crichton. Entry was through a vaulted pend in the south wing, now built in. There were vaulted cellars on either side of the entrance pend. On the first floor was a large well-lit Great Hall, later subdivided, with a hooded fireplace and a pantry and buttery. Above this was a second Hall, or withdrawing-room, with a fireplace midway in the south wall. Both the Great and the Upper Halls were considerably altered in the sixteenth century.

In the second half of the fifteenth century, a mainly three-storey west wing was added, but with a tall unvaulted six-storey tower at the south-west angle. Above the basement there were living-rooms

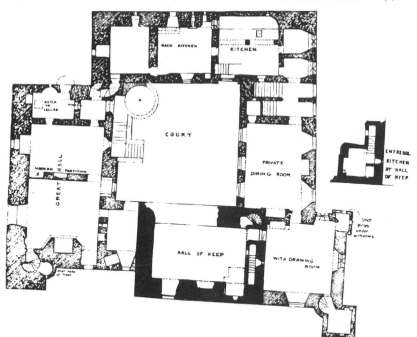

Crichton Castle: plans of the first and second floors.

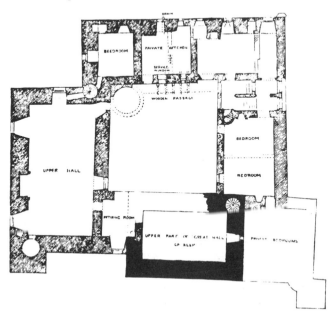

with privies. Doors were cut to connect with the newel stair in the keep-house.

The lower part of the north wing, completing the courtyard extension, and providing services, dates from the fifteenth century. It was much extended and rebuilt in the late sixteenth century. As it now exists it has the elaborate gables, angle turrets, gun-loops and corbelled courses of this period.

This reconstruction was carried out by Francis Stewart, Earl of Bothwell, and his countess, Margaret Douglas, as their carved initials and an anchor confirm, probably between 1581 and 1593, while Bothwell was Lord High Admiral of Scotland. They were responsible for the castle's great glory, the piazza and embellished courtyard in the diamond-studded manner of the Palazzo dei Diamante at Ferrara, built in 1582.

Internally, they rearranged the cellars in the ground floor of the north wing and improved the kitchen facilities. East of the kitchen they provided a well-lit dining-room, with a handsome fireplace and buffet, and beyond, in a new building added to the north end of the ancient tower, a withdrawing-room. Above were bedrooms and a third kitchen (in addition to the kitchen in the fifteenth century wing and one in the old tower). The parlour wing has a bakehouse basement with wide-mouthed gun-loops.

Lord Chancellor Crichton, who built the old tower, died in 1454. His son, Sir William Crichton, was Chancellor to James I and again to James II, on whose instructions Lord Crichton – as he became in 1445 – arranged the episode known as the Black Dinner. For this unusual meal the sixth Earl Douglas and his younger brother were lured to Edinburgh Castle to dine with the king, seized at table and summarily beheaded. The Chancellor himself probably built the fifteenth-century extensions. The third Lord Crichton supported Albany against James III, so in 1483 had his estates forfeited. They were given in 1488 to Patrick Hepburn, Lord Hailes, who was created Earl of Bothwell, but who died with his king at Flodden.

The estates were again to be forfeited, this time by the third Earl of Bothwell in 1567 for his share in the murder of Darnley. Nine years later they were bestowed by James VI on Francis Stewart, a bastard grandson of James V. Stewart had lived much in Italy, and though undoubtedly a Renaissance ruffian had outstandingly good taste.

Mary, Queen of Scots is said to have visited Crichton for the wedding of one of her many illegitimate half-brothers in 1562, and again perhaps in 1565 (if, as is sometimes claimed, she did, indeed, spend part of her honeymoon with Darnley there). The initials M.S.D. are cut into the stone above the two central pillars on the east side of the courtyard.

Sir Walter Scott greatly admired Crichton, fortunately a more complete ruin in his days than it is now, and celebrated it in his poem *Marmion*:

> The courtyard's graceful portico;
> Above its cornice, row and row,
> Of fair hewn facets, richly show
> Their pointed diamond form.

A little to the south of the castle is a roofless stable block with massive buttresses. There is a horseshoe window above the door. The grooms' quarters were above the ground floor.

Crichton Castle was handed over to State care by its final owner, Henry Callander of Prestonhall, in 1956.

Crombie Castle

Crombie Castle, two miles west of Aberchirder, is a small much-altered L-plan fortalice built about 1543 probably by James Innes of Crombie, who was killed at the Battle of Pinkie. A former Lord Lyon of our own century, Sir Thomas Innes of Learney, bought it back to the family after several centuries in other hands, and kept it in repair. It is now attached to a farmhouse.

Crookston Castle

Crookston Castle, which stands on a knoll, still surrounded by a great ditch, a little to the south of Paisley, is thought to date from the thirteenth century, though it may have replaced an earlier castle on the site. It has a unique place in Scottish castle-building, as Cruden[1] points out, being, like Hermitage (the original manor-house of the Drews) a central block strengthened with irregularly placed towers at each corner.

[1] *op. cit.*

The basement is a stone barrel-vault reinforced by broad splayed ribs in the thirteenth-century manner. Yet there is no wall of enceinte and no donjon; even a surprising absence of defensive loops. The main block is a parallelogram with a vaulted Great Hall on the first floor, having a large fireplace and windows with stone seats. The surviving stone tower is at the north-east corner. There are also the remains of a similar tower at the south-east corner. The entrance adjoins the north-east tower, and has been defended by two doors and a portcullis, the inner door strengthened with a sliding bar which, when drawn back, would have crossed the staircase of the north-east tower, barring access to it. A small stair in the tower wall leads to a guardroom, under which, through a trapdoor, is a dungeon. The south-east tower has a cellar rib-vaulted in the manner of the central block basement hall. Access to the upper floors of both towers was by a newel stair at the south-east corner of the Great Hall, which also led to the rooms above in the central block.

The estate belonged in the twelfth century to Robert de Croc, passing by marriage in the thirteenth century to the Stewarts. Queen Mary's husband Henry, Lord Darnley, had it, but in 1572 it was granted to his younger brother, the fifth Earl of Lennox. Afterwards it had many owners, including the Duke of Montrose who, in 1757, sold it to Sir John Maxwell of Pollok, who restored the north-east tower and carried out other repairs in 1847, to commemorate Queen Victoria's first visit to Glasgow.

Burns, Tannahill, Motherwell and earlier, John Wilson (author of *The Clyde*) have celebrated Crookston in verse. In *The Abbot*, Sir Walter Scott alleges that Queen Mary watched the Battle of Langside from its towers, a physical impossibility, however, because of the intervening folds of land.

It is now in care as an Ancient Monument.

Crosbie Tower

Crosbie Tower stands a mile west of West Kilbride, a typical early-seventeenth-century T-plan house. It has a two-storey main block with attic, and an off-centre stair wing on the south which rises a storey higher. Dates above the door in the re-entrant angle record the years 1676 and 1896, the date of its restoration by MacGibbon and Ross. A large modern mansion adjoins the old castle. Crosbie was a possession of the Craufurds of Auchenames, and replaced an earlier tower on the site seen and described by Timothy Pont. Service at the Battle of Largs in 1263 earned the Craufurds their favour and fortune. Wallace is said to have hidden in the older tower when the laird was his uncle, Reginald de Craufurd. The entire property is now a Youth Hostel.

Culcreuch Castle

Culcreuch stands at the foot of the southern slopes of the Fintry Hills a mile from Fintry village. An oblong tower of coursed rubble, it is late fifteenth century in origin, but was extended in the eighteenth century. It has three storeys, a crenellated parapet on chequered corbelling and a garret storcy above. The parapet walk is drained by an exceptionally large number of water-spouts. There are no rounds.

The original entrance, over which later work has been built, gave access to the vaulted basement and the stair wing. Originally, there would be the normal arrangement of the Hall on the first floor and bedroom accommodation above. Over the present doorway there is a heraldic carving, the initials M.L. and the date 1721, when the extension was presumably added and the windows of the original tower enlarged.

Culcreuch, still inhabited, passed through the hands of the Galbraith and Napier families. In 1796 it came into the hands of Alexander Speirs, who built a large and prosperous cotton mill on his estate. A Speirs heiress married Sir George Hume in the mid-nineteenth century.

Cullen Castle

Cullen House, as the one-time home of the Earls of Seafield is most commonly called, on the Deskford Burn just south of Cullen, began as an L-plan fortalice in the mid-sixteenth century. From March 1600 those portions were added which still form the angle of the present building. In 1711 further extensions were put on, in 1767 James Adam remodelled the interior and in 1858 the castle was remodelled by David Bryce, who renewed completely the much-altered east front. The original architecture is much more in evidence on the courtyard side. Internally, so great are the alterations that beyond observing that the usual arrangements of vaulted basements and cellarage with the Hall on the first floor above originally applied, there is no point in entering into a detailed description, although a major coved painted ceiling survives. Its cove is painted with the Siege of Troy, the central panel depicting Neptune, Mercury, Flora and Luna in swirling cloud.

During the 1970s the Seafield family put the house up for sale, intending to strip some of the fittings including the ceiling, a plan fortunately thwarted because of the building's listed status. It has now been sympathetically converted to flatted accommodation. It once housed a fine collection of pictures, including one of Mary Beaton, one of the 'Queen's Maries', who married a local laird, Ogilvie of Boyne.

Sir William Ogilvie, the seventh in his line to own Cullen, married Mary Douglas, and their arms, together with the date 1603, appear on the west front. He became the first Earl of Findlater and first of Seafield and helped to facilitate the unpopular Union with England in 1707, commenting on the dead with the famously cynical remark, 'There's an end to an auld sang!'

Dalcross Castle

This impressive castle stands on a ridge about eight miles east of Inverness, near Culloden, for which battle it was the mustering point of the Government forces prior to their attack.

An L-plan castle, its two wings are joined together by means of a stair tower, though in such a way at the back as to provide two large re-entrant angles; or, as MacGibbon and Ross so picturesquely put it, as if 'a large notch is cut out of the heel of the L'.

The south has four storeys, an attic and a garret, the north wing three and an attic. A low two-storey eighteenth-century addition to the north gable has still later stabling added to it.

The square stair tower in the eastern re-entrant angle rises a storey higher, topped by a square gabled watch-room with a conically capped angle turret, similar to that on three other gables. There is a massive chimney-stack at the head of the east wall of the northern wing.

Through the courtyard the entrance to the castle is by a door at the foot of the stair tower, still having its iron yett and draw-bar. Splayed gun-loops cover it.

The basement contains a vaulted passage and several cellars as well as the kitchen. The wine-cellar has a private stair to the Hall above in the south wing, also reached by the main staircase which then continues upwards. A small turnpike stair also leads to upper bedroom quarters.

Dalcross was built by the eighth Lord Lovat in 1621. A shield over the entrance records the date 1720, and the Mackintosh arms, the chief of that clan becoming its laird at the end of the seventeenth century. The initials of Lachlan Mackintosh, the nineteenth chief adorn another panel.

Dalcross was deserted by the early nineteenth century and lost its roof and upper floors. From the late nineteenth century onwards it has been admirably restored by descendants of the earlier Mackintosh lairds, mainly under the direction of W.L. Carruthers, an Inverness arts and crafts architect who had been a pupil of Sir Ernest George.

Dalhousie Castle

Dalhousie Castle stands on a wooded promontory above the South Esk, about two and a half miles south west of Dalkeith. Simon de Ramsay received a grant of the land from David I, and in 1296 and 1304 his descendant, William de Ramsay, swore fealty to Edward I for 'the lands of Dalwolzic'. His son, Sir Alexander, was, however, a leader of the Scots side during the War of Independence, and in 1400 his namesake, the fourth descendant, held a castle on the site against Henry IV. More peaceably, Queen Victoria descended on Dalhousie in 1842.

The oldest parts of the present castle – a tower, once L-shaped but with the re-entrant angle partially built in to provide a new stair c.1600 – and a wall of enceinte with a triangular projection at the south-east corner, are in hard reddish-pink sandstone and date from about 1450. The curtain wall was surrounded by a dry moat, traces of which remain.

The castle consists of three main elements; the tower block, much altered internally; the portcullis main entrance, recessed in a tall arch, topped by two machicolated bartisans, and with the corbels for the drawbridge mountings and the Ramsay crest, an eagle, framed beneath; and a huge drum tower at the north-east corner of the enceinte. The basement floor of the tower contains a well. A mural stair led to the floor above, though the inner portion of this wall was later removed to enlarge the tower rooms.

In 1633, William, created first Earl of Dalhousie by Charles I, built out into the curtain from the old tower, putting his initials and those of his wife in pediments on the two windows of the north front nearest the portcullis gateway.

Substantial internal alterations, and some external, were made in the 1820s by William Burn. The ninth Earl was raised to the United Kingdom peerage in 1815 for services in the Peninsular War, as Baron Dalhousie. His third son and heir became Governor-General of India, and Marquis of Dalhousie. As such, he died without an heir in Dalhousie Castle in 1860 and the earldom passed to his cousin, Lord Panmure.

In 1972, Dalhousie became an hotel and the architects – Mottram, Patrick, Whitehorm, Dalgleish and Partners – uncovered some antiquarian detail, at the same time respecting Burn's work.

His double-square entrance hall, with its miniature imperial staircase in one half, elaborate plaster-work, ribbed-roofed lanterns and other details, is remarkable. His dining-room has a Gothic timber ceiling. There is a Jacobean ribbed-style ceiling and two white marble chimney-pieces at each end of the Long Room, on the first floor of the south side of the original tower. The Library and Armoury also bear the stamp of Burn's energetic imagination.

Dalquharran Castle

Yet another seat of the Kennedy family, Dalquharran is a large, ruinous, rectangular fortalice with a circular tower at the south-east angle. It stands about six miles up the Girvan Water, near the village of Dailly. In all probability it was a fifteenth-century tower, doubled in size to an L-plan arrangement and embellished on the north in 1679. Of red sandstone, it rises to three storeys. The garret storey within the crenellated parapet on heavy individual but unusual corbels, shown in MacGibbon and Ross, has unfortunately gone.

It has vaulted cellarage, and was entered by movable stairs leading to first-floor level, which contained the Hall and a small room. Each floor had an additional room in the circular tower. The usual bedroom accommodation occupied the upper floors.

The 1679 work was of advanced Renaissance design with rusticated quoins and a generously proportioned stair in the re-entrant angle, but answered the plan of the old tower house in having a circular tower at the north-east angle. It was by far the best house in Carrick at the end of the seventeenth century.

Dalquharran was owned in turn by the Kennedys of Bog, Culzean, and Girvanmaing before coming into the hands of Sir Thomas Kennedy of Kirkhill, Lord Provost of Edinburgh. In 1786–90, one of his descendants, Thomas Francis Kennedy, Member of Parliament for the Ayr burghs from 1813 until 1834, built an impressive new castle nearby to the designs of his brother-in-law, Robert Adam, thereafter abandoning the old castle.

Dalyell House

Dalyell House, or Castle, stands on the bank of a rocky ravine in a park on the outskirts of Motherwell. It once had steeply falling sloping ground by way of defence on two sides and a moat round the other two, later developed as superb terraced gardens.

It is built around three sides of a court, the earliest part of which, in the centre of the east side, is an oblong tower house of coursed rubble rising to three storeys beneath the parapet and with a garret above. The parapet rests on a double course of chequered corbelling. There is a parapet walk with three open rounds, a later circular cap-house crowning the stairhead in the south-east corner.

The original doorway was situated in a projection to the south-west constructed to hold a portcullis, the chain-grooves of which remain. The present wide doorway in the west front leads to a large entrance hall occupying the whole of the gound floor. A straight mural stair in the east wall rises to the first floor, after which ascent is by a turnpike stair.

The first-floor Hall, which once had its own direct entrance by movable timber stair, is vaulted, and had at one time an *entresol*. There are two angle garderobes.

In the early seventeenth century there was added a north wing, its upper parts twice rebuilt, linked to the original tower by a passage cut through its wall, with a square north-east tower, and a circular south-east tower. There is a larger wing on the south side of the court. A strong defensive wall enclosing the court on the north and west was added at this time, but the northern section has made way for later buildings. A vaulted kitchen in the basement of the addition was located behind the north-east tower and another at the west end of the south wing. Both kitchens have vaulted cellars beneath. In the seventeenth-century south wing, above first-floor level on the courtyard side, was a large circular stairway, corbelled out and rising the full height of the building. It is conically capped. There are seventeenth-century shot-holes and decorative window pediments, one of which carries the initials of James Hamilton of Boggs and the date 1649, in which year Hamilton bought the estate from the Dalyells, Earls of Carnforth. The Hamiltons eventually became the Lords Hamilton of Dalyell.

During the 1850s, the Lord Hamilton of the day had James Maitland Wardrop reconstruct the gables, the staircase cap-house of the tower house and the battlements. In 1856, Robert William Billings was called in to modernise and extend the house to the standards then acceptable to the Victorian gentry. Billings constructed a new wing to the north-west and remodelled the old north wing in conformity with it. He was also responsible for the modern doorway, the arched entrance and exit in the courtyard wall, and the huge canted bay in the centre of the south-west front.

Dalyell House has been in the hands of the local authority for some years, unfortunately without sufficiently energetic effort being made to find a new use for it, although extensively repaired in the 1970s. Its interior has been recently vandalised, but its repair as flats is now in hand.

Dargarvel Castle

Now enclosed, so to say, in the Royal Ordnance Factory premises at Bishopton, and therefore inaccessible, Dargarvel is a large late-sixteenth-century Z-plan castle built in 1584, added to in 1670, according to the date on a sundial above a window, and again in 1857 by David Bryce. Early this century it was remodelled yet again by Dr Peter MacGregor Chalmers, in whose hands it lost much of its original character.

The main block has circular conically capped towers projecting at the north-east and south-west angles and rises to three storeys and an attic. The towers become slightly thinner above first-floor level, at which there is a projecting garderobe. The arrangements were traditional, with three vaulted rooms on the ground floor, one being the kitchen, and a Hall on the first floor. The main stair ran from the now built-over door on the south front as far as the second floor, ascent thereafter being by two turnpike stairs. The stair tower with the crenellated top is a nineteenth-century addition.

Patrick Maxwell, son of George Maxwell of Newark, acquired the lands of Dargarvel around 1576; by which time the Dumfriesshire family were firmly ensconced in Renfrewshire.

Darnaway Castle

Darnaway Castle, the seat of the Earls of Moray, in the Findhorn valley was founded by Randolph, Earl of Moray, Regent during the minority of David II. The oldest, and only, surviving part of an early castle is the Hall, thought to have been begun by Archibald Douglas, Earl of Moray, around 1450. It was encased by Alexander Laing's Gothic style house in polished freestone built for the Earl of Moray between 1802 and 1812. The Hall still has its fourteenth-century open-timber oak roof of arch-braced collar-beam truss construction with carved bosses at the hammer beams, one of the finest to survive in Scotland, along with that in Parliament House, Edinburgh.

Laing added the Y-traceried windows. The walls of the Hall have been altered, as has the chimney, and the fireplace dates from the nineteenth century. Mary, Queen of Scots held court in this Hall in 1564.

Darnick Tower

Darnick Tower, built about 1425, stands near the Tweed, at the foot of the Eildon Hills about a mile west of Melrose. The original tower rises to three storeys with a garret storey above the parapet. A square tower projecting from the south front rises a storey higher. It has a cap house on corbels. This contains a vaulted watch-room and, above the vault, a tiny dovecot. The building is of a purple-red local sandstone. The parapet rests on individual corbels, and cannon spouts drain the stone-flagged roof. There is a later addition to the east of two storeys and an attic floor.

A panel carrying the Heiton arms is inserted into the front of the stair tower just beneath the third-floor window. The lintel has the initials of Andrew Heiton and his wife Kate Fisher, together with the date 1569, when the rebuilding of the fifteenth-century structure was completed after destruction by Hertford in 1545.

The entrance is at the foot of the stair tower, wherein the turn-pike stairhead is vaulted. The watch-room is reached by a small newel stair in the wall. The basement, once also vaulted, has been altered when nineteenth-century modernisations were carried out; modernisations which probably included alterations to the parapet crenellation.

The Hall, on the first floor, has a large fireplace and a window in the south wall recessed for stone seats. Two bedrooms are on the second floor, while a garret room is reached from the parapet walk.

Sir Walter Scott is said to have coveted Darnick Tower so much that his friends dubbed him 'The Duke of Darnick'. The Heiton owners, however, refused to sell. Though still occupied, it is possible to visit Darnick Tower.

Dean Castle

Standing on the east bank of the Borland Water, a mile or so north of Kilmarnock, Dean Castle is doubly unusual; in having two separate towers built within curtain walling; and in its being an excellent example of romantically enthusiastic restoration which nevertheless pays due respect to medieval planning and detail.

The oldest surviving building is the tower of coursed rubble at the west side of the enceinte, built by the Boyd family in the fifteenth century. Robert Boyd strove hard to gain political control during the minority of James III, becoming his guardian. Boyd's son married the King's sister, Princess Mary, and became Earl of Arran. The father was himself elevated to Lord Boyd in 1459, at which time he probably began to build the Hall range, raising it upon a vaulted substructure on the south side of the enceinte. James, Lord Boyd, who died in 1654, added a tower fore-building and enlarged the windows of the original tower.

In 1609, Timothy Pont wrote of it as being: 'a staitly faire ancient building, arysing in tua grate heigh towers, and bult around courteways with fyne low buildings ... It belonged first to ye Locartts ... then to Lord Soulis, and now is the chaiffe dwelling almost for 300 yeirs of ye Lords Boyde.'

The original tower rises to three storeys, has a parapet flush with the walling, and above it a garret storey within the parapet walk. Entry is through an arched door in the east wall, which necessarily breaks the heavy basement course. The basement has two intercommunicating vaulted apartments. The main entrance would originally have been at first-floor level by means of a movable timber stair, but this is now built up. The thick wall contains a small guardroom beside this original entrance, with a trapdoor leading to a prison and a small stair descending to the laird's wine-cellar.

The Hall is a large and handsome room, with two stone benches running along the walls. There is a minstrels' gallery of sorts on the east wall reached by a passage from the turnpike stair in the south-east angle. The stair rises to the parapet, where it terminates in a seventeenth-century crow-stepped-gabled cap-house.

The second floor has another large room with a small chapel by the now built-up east window. Lord Boyd's extension has kitchen and cellarage in the basement, and a Hall on the first floor together with a small withdrawing-room and the usual bedroom accommodation above. There is a square projecting stair tower with a gabled cap-house at the south-east angle. The parapet is carried on individual corbels, and unlike those of the north tower, is not crenellated. The crow-stepped-gabled top storey provides access to the parapet walk.

James, Lord Boyd's three-storey house of the mid-seventeenth century joins this tower.

The Boyd family became almost as powerful as the Douglases, being created Earls of Kilmarnock. The last Earl was executed for his part in the Forty-Five, his end witnessed and described by Horace Walpole, and the lands were forfeited. In 1735, whilst this Earl was abroad, a serious fire, said to have been started by a careless maid, gutted the hall range. Later, what was left of the property was sold, changing hands several times until it became the property of the Superior of Kilmarnock, Lord Howard de Walden. In 1905 the eighth Lord Howard decided to restore the castle, a process which took thirty years. Among the architects involved were Henry Brown of Kilmarnock and later Dr James Richardson, inspector of Ancient Monuments for Scotland. The castle is now a museum, housing Lord Howard's important collections of armour and musical instruments.

Delgatty Castle

Delgatie, or Delgatty, stands on the side of a valley above a lochan, two miles east of Turiff. It was a seat of the Hays, the Earls of Errol, High Constables of Scotland. Its present owner is Captain John Hay of Hayfield. Although much altered by various additions, the original tower is a tall square keep five storeys high with a garret, a crenellated parapet and open rounds. It probably dates from 1570, the date over the Hall fireplace. In its planning and in its rib-vaulted lobby and first-floor Hall is plainly related to Craig, Gight and Towie Barclay even if not of the L-plan. To the west, an equally tall crow-step-gabled house was added in the seventeenth century, making it into a vast L-plan structure. Lower Gothic buildings to the east and west linked to the main block by in-and-out carriage arches were added in the mid-eighteenth century.

The original entrance on the west front has been covered over by the seventeenth-century house, and the entrance to the south, through a modern porch, gives access to a vestibule with a ribbed and groined vault. A passage leads to the turnpike stair, rising in the south-west angle of the keep. The original vaulted kitchen is in the basement, with the customary wide fireplace. The Hall above, also ribbed and groin-vaulted, has bosses decorated with the Hay arms. The fireplace lintel carries the date 1570 and the motto MY HOP IS IN YE LORD. There are numerous garderobes and mural staircases, and a fine tempera-painted ceiling on the second floor.

Mary, Queen of Scots spent three days at Delgatty after the Battle of Corrichie. A Hay of Delgatty was standard-bearer to Montrose.

Dirleton Castle

Dirleton Castle, in the village of the same name, was originally built in the thirteenth century by the De Vaux of De Valibus family, probably by John de Vaux, seneschal to Marie de Coucy, who married Alexander II in 1239. It stubbornly, if unsuccessfully resisted a siege by Bishop Anthony Beck, Edward I's fighting Bishop of Durham, in 1298, but was rebuilt during the following century. In 1650, it again came under attack, this time from the guns of Generals Monk and Lambert, who were seeking to oust its garrison of moss-troopers, three of whose leaders were subsequently hanged from its walls.

Dirleton Castle: a compact grouping conforming to a rocky contour.

The south-west towers, two of them circular, the third square, date from the thirteenth-century structure, being incorporated into the fourteenth century rebuilding. The old castle was grouped compactly round a triangular court, an example of what W. Douglas Simpson calls the 'cluster donjon' variety, the dog-leg later addition conforming to the contour of the rock. Its position was further strengthened by the deep moat, at least fifty feet wide, which surrounded it, and which, like the entrance gateway, is well preserved. The spanning of the moat involved a movable wooden bridge which rested on four piers; and there was the further defence of a drawbridge.

The south-west donjon rooms would originally be lit only by narrow loop-holes, though larger windows were added later to the upper floor. The rooms are polygonal, one on top of the other, the ground-floor room doubtless being for the soldiers, though vaulted like a dome, and having a harled fireplace decorated with dog-tooth mouldings of the thirteenth-century Early English style. The upper floor would be the solar or lord's room.

On the east side there is a range of building with a very thick outer wall, part of the basement of which has been hollowed out of solid rock. Loftily vaulted, the basement houses the bakery, with ovens and a well, and several large vaulted cellars. Above the bakery is the vaulted kitchen with roof ventilation, two large fireplaces and a service room leading to the Hall.

The Hall was seventy-two feet long by twenty-five wide. There would have been screens and a minstrels' gallery at the south end, the dais and the fireplace being at the north end. Food came up to a pantry behind the screens by means of a stair leading down to a hatch in the bakery vault.

The lord's rooms were at the north end, a stair linking the Hall and the cellars on one side and, on the other, a door leading down to the prison, beneath which is a dungeon reached only by a hatch. A window from which orders could be given overlooked the cellar, as at Linlithgow. Above, there would probably be additional bedrooms. It seems likely that there was also a wing along the north side of the court, which would no doubt contain further accommodation.

During the sixteenth century another Hall in the style of the Renaissance was built linking the old towers at the south-west corner with a stair leading to upper-floor bedrooms.

Set in a pleasant flower-garden, Dirleton is now an Ancient Monument.

Dornoch Castle

Dornoch Castle was once connected to a great cathedral, founded in the thirteenth century by Bishop Gilbert de Moravia. In 1570, the cathedral was burned by the Master of Caithness, ably assisted by Sutherland of Skelbo, Lord of Duffus, and Mackay of Strathnaver, over a quarrel about the wardship of the young Earl of Sutherland. What was left was further damaged by a furious gale in 1605. Thus the cathedral, across the road from the castle, is a comparatively modern reconstruction, except for the choir and the crossing.

At the same time the Bishop's Palace, as the castle was then called, was also sacked after a siege, its hostages for the surrender being then unscrupulously murdered. It remained ruinous until 1814, when it was partly restored to house the county courthouse and jail. Most of these institutions were pulled down to make way for the present early-Victorian county building. What survives is a five-storey keep with a circular stair tower added in the sixteenth century, its surface decorated with string courses, its roof conical. There is a moulded doorway at the base of the stair tower.

The lower building at right angles is probably also of sixteenth-century origin, but modernised. An enormous chimney-stack dominates the east end of the south front. A secondary stair tower projects from the north front and probably dates from the same time as the added buttress. The angle created by the surviving building probably once constituted the corner of a courtyard.

Doune Castle

One of the earliest and most impressive early Scottish castles to survive more or less intact, Doune Castle stands on an easily defensible raised site between the confluence of the River Teith and the Ardoch Burn, immediately below the little town of Doune. It was in all probability erected before 1400 for the second duke of Albany, the Regent Albany, Governor of Scotland from 1419 to 1424 during the minority of James I.

It consists of two massive towers linked by a lower range and built into the front of a free-standing forty-foot-high curtain wall to the rear, in which intended additional domestic buildings were never actually put up. There is a parapet walk on the wall, open rounds at the angles, and semi-circular bartisans on corbels midway.

The larger tower – that of the lord, which controlled the portcullis and acted as a gate-house – is a rectangular structure, its walls nearly nine feet thick, rising to a height of five main storeys

Doune Castle: with the Hall on the right.

and a garret, with a semicircular tower projecting in the north-east angle. There is a parapet flush with the main walls, and flanking a gabled roof to north and south. The wall walks of these are linked by open steps crossing the pitched roof at either end. The stairhead is topped by a high look-out platform reached by the eastern flight of steps, an arrangement as unusual as it is difficult to describe.

The north-west tower rises to four storeys and a garret, also with a flush parapet and a gabled roof.

The Regent was well provided for in the lord's tower. The splendid vaulted Hall is on the first floor, and at one end has a magnificent double fireplace and panelling, part of the Earl of Murray's restoration of 1883. The moulded segmental arches rise from substantial twin shafts with typically fourteenth-century moulded capitals and bosses. In front of the opposite wall there is a passage with a screen, restored in 1883, leading to the entrance, and with a gallery above it. Entrance to the Lord's Hall is by an outside forestair from the courtyard.

Next to the Lord's Hall is the retainer's hall, now linked by a door put in at the restoration but originally approached by a separate forestair from the courtyard. Here would be housed the mercenaries, under the Lord's control but without access to his private quarters.

The thick walls of Doune contain several stairs, one linking the Lord's Hall with the ample bedroom accommodation above. Doubtless for defensive reasons, many of the stairs cover short links. Garderobes were also built into the walls.

The kitchen in the west tower has an enormous arched fireplace, an oven area, slop drains and a remarkably modern-looking hatch-servery. Above these quarters, too, there was sleeping accommodation.

The entrance to the Lord's tower is by an arched gateway, giving access to a vaulted pend, with a vaulted porter's lodge on one side and a vaulted beehive prison cell in the other. There is an extensive range of vaulted basement cellars and store rooms, several with mural stairs leading to the floor above.

Work at Doune probably ceased when Albany was summoned to imprisonment and execution by James I in 1424, for an alleged family implication in the murder at Falkland of the King's brother, David, Duke of Rothesay.

Thereafter, the castle went to the Crown. James IV, however, settled it on his queen, Margaret Tudor, who in 1525 passed it to Henry Stewart, Lord Methven, a descendant of Albany. James V granted it to Henry Stewart's brother, Sir James. His son and namesake was created Lord Doune in 1581. It came, through marriage, to the Earls of Moray, with whom it has since remained, providing the title of the Earl's son and heir.

From time to time it was a residence of royalty, including Mary, Queen of Scots among its guests. During the 1745 rising it was garrisoned for the Jacobites by a nephew of Rob Roy, when a swivel mounted gun was added to its defences. For six days it imprisoned the Reverend John Home, the author of the tragedy of *Douglas*, the play that helped to break the anti-theatre grip of the Church of Scotland, and provoked an enthusiastic yell from the gallery on the opening night: 'Whaur's yer Wullie Shakespeare noo?' Home, however, made his escape with the aid of a rope of knotted blankets. Scott brings the eponymous hero of *Waverley* to Doune. It is now in State care.

Dowies House

Dowies House, otherwise known as Moure, stands in the valley of the Monreith Burn, two miles north-east of Monreith village. It is cross-shaped in plan, a square wing projecting to the south of the main block and a circular stair tower to the north. It has two storeys and an attic under a steep roof with plain gables. Though now stripped internally of interesting features, the turnpike stair remains, as does panelling in the window embrasures. Arrow-slits and shot-holes proclaim its defensive intentions.

Moure, as the house was then known, was a Maxwell possession, put up in the late seventeenth century near the site of an earlier castle. The descendants of Sir Edward Maxwell of Tinwald, second son of the first Lord Maxwell, occupied this castle until 1683, when they moved to the nearby ruined Myretoun Tower, which they bought from the McCullochs. Altered at the rooflines, Dowies House became a farmer's home. It has recently been admirably restored by Stewart Tod for the Landmark Trust.

Drochil Castle

Ruined Drochil, on the River Lyne, is one of the two most unusual Z-plan castles to be built in Scotland, the other being Noltland, in the Orcadian island of Westray. Drochil, 'designed for a palace more than a castle of defence', was built in the 1570s for his retirement by James, Earl of Morton. It carries his initials in raised lettering above the southern entry. As important a statesman as the Regent Morton (which he became in 1572) would certainly feel that his status demanded an imposing structure. In all probability he employed French craftsmen. Certainly, the 'tout une masse' plan is French, the massive, almost square, central block being of such proportions as to make the two projecting towers which form the Z seem much smaller than they really are.

The peculiarity of Drochil is that all four floors and the garret are divided down the middle by corridors running the full length of the building, from which access to individual rooms is gained; a major advance in domestic planning over the medieval system whereby one room led through to another. The ground floor has a barrel-vaulted ceiling of stone while the upper floors were timbered. The kitchen and the cellars were situated on the ground floor, the hall, the solar and the bedrooms on the upper floors.

The round towers, as at Claypotts, Dundee, have circular chambers and rooms in the basement. Above, however, both the interiors and the exteriors are square. The main wheel stair rises from one end of the ground-floor corridor. From the first floor upwards the wheeled stairs are carried by corbelled roundels overhanging the angles joining the towers and the main block. Some of the surfaces are enriched with decoration.

Morton, who was also responsible for the erection of the Portcullis Gate at Edinburgh Castle, which is similarly embellished with motifs, would undoubtedly have been in a position to command the best designer available. It has been surmised that the architect may have been William Schaw, Master of Works to James VI from 1553 until Schaw's death in 1602, and that his models might have been Chenonceaux and Martainville in France.

In any event, the Regent Morton did not live to enjoy his declining years at Drochil. In 1580, 13 years after the event, he was accused, tried and found guilty of taking part in the murder of Mary, Queen of Scot's second husband, Darnley. Morton apparently confessed to the fact that the Earl of Bothwell had apprised him of the Kirk o' Field plot, though Morton, Secretary Maitland and Bothwell are assumed to have conspired together at Whittinghame Castle. Morton was executed on 2 June 1581 at the Cross of Edinburgh by the Maiden, a Scottish variant of the guillotine. Drochil was never finished, and is now in sad disrepair, never having been taken on to the Ancient Monuments' estate.

Drum Castle

One of the oldest houses in Scotland continually occupied by the same family, Drum Castle stands above the Dee ten miles west of Aberdeen. The lands upon which it is sited had been a royal hunting preserve, but King Robert the Bruce awarded them to his armour-bearer and clerk-register, William de Irwin of Woodhouse, Dumfriesshire, for his part in the War of Independence. The charter is dated 1 February 1323, and was signed at Berwick-upon-Tweed.

When William Irwin – the family name was later changed to Irvine – took over his gift, he found a sturdy tower already built by Alexander III some forty or so years before. 'Bydand legend' asserts that one Robert Cementarius was associated both with the building of the old keep of Drum and with the construction of the Brig o' Balgonie.

The walls of Drum, twelve feet thick at the base but only nine feet higher up, allowing an increase in internal space, rise seventy feet above the ground. The angles are slightly rounded. The parapet, borne on individual corbels, has heightened open rounds. The roof may once have had a gabled attic storey, but now has a stone-flag roof slightly raised so that the water drains along the lower joins. Since this makes walking difficult, the inner face of the battlement is niched to facilitate movement.

The vaulted basement is reached from a mural stair on the first floor. The Hall, on the first floor, is barrel-vaulted. Surviving corbels show that there was an entresol floor which might have been the laird's bedroom, since its deeply set windows have stone seats and there is a garderobe. A turnpike stair winds upwards in the south-east angle. The original entrance would be by removable wooden stairs to the first floor. At a later date a stone forstair was substituted.

In 1619, the ninth laird, Alexander – all the lairds have been Alexanders, the only one not so christened changing his name to conform to the tradition – was prosperous enough to build on to the old tower a new L-shaped house of three storeys and a garret, with square towers on the outer angles and a circular conically capped stair tower at the south-west. Its more horizontal planning reflects the new custom of importing longer lengths of timber from the Baltic than were previously available in Scotland. Its internal arrangements, however, conformed to tradition, with the vaulted servants' quarters at ground-floor level, the high Great Hall on the first floor, reached by a straight stair opening into the screened serving area, and a small turnpike stair in the opposite corner connecting the Hall with the kitchen beneath. The upper-floor bedrooms were reached by several turnpike stairs.

In 1876, David Bryce reconstructed the barmkin courtyard with a new arched entrance to the north, retaining the original to the west. In 1878, his nephew, John, implemented his uncle's intentions for the main block. A new broad staircase and gallery were constructed along the northern side of the seventeenth-century house. The Hall in the old tower had its entresol removed and became the library. It was given a new heraldic plaster ceiling, and had its eastern window enlarged. The 1619 house was refitted

Drum Castle: ancient Bryce's entrance gatehouse.

with compartmented timber ceilings and Jacobean chimney-pieces in the fashion of the 1870s.

The lairds of Drum played an active part in Scottish affairs. Sir Alexander fell at the Battle of Harlaw in 1411, earning himself a mention in the ballad commemorating that event. The seventh laird was rewarded by James V for 'searching, taking and bringing to justice his rebels', but lost his son at the Battle of Pinkie in 1547.

The Irvines were Royalists in the troubled seventeenth century. Drum Castle was besieged and the family impoverished, though the son of the tenth laird, under sentence of death in Edinburgh, escaped his fate as a result of the Restoration. His successful involvement with a local girl 'beneath his station' made him the second member of the family to earn ballad immortality.

It is now owned by the National Trust for Scotland.

Drumcoltran Castle

Drumcoltran Castle, a mile north of Kirkgunzeon, is an L-shaped sixteenth-century structure the main block of which rises to three storeys and a garret. The parapet is carried on individual corbels. The stair tower, which has no parapet, rises a storey higher. There is a watch-room at the top of this, reached by a narrow turret stair built – not corbelled – into the re-entrant angle at the level of the parapet.

The doorway is in the re-entrant angle, and is defended by a gun-loop. A Latin inscription recommends the keeping of secrets, speaking little, being truthful, not drinking wine, remembering death, and cultivating piety; qualities not commonly practised over-prominently by the Maxwells, who owned Drumcoltran. It is now an Ancient Monument.

Druminnor Castle

Situated on the banks of the burn of Keron, in a sloping, steep valley two miles east of Rhynie, Druminnor is said to have been the original Castle Forbes, the oldest parts of which date from 1456, but the tower house of that date was completely demolished early last century. John Leyden said the ruins had consisted of 'a square tower united to a half-square and which contains the staircase'. A still older castle further up-river may have existed from *c*.1271, a grant of land to Duncan Forbes being made by Alexander III. The third Druminnor was built between 1440–70, and was originally a rectangular block attached to the second tower. Its doorway arch, made of five straight sections, is probably unique in Scotland, and the heavy corbelling which carries the circular stair tower squared out to provide the watch-room, above three Forbes crests, dates from 1577. There are wide-flanking gun-loops.

The castle is L-plan with a modern doorway in the middle of the north front. The walling is taken in at first-floor level, possibly where the fifteenth-century work ends. Much altered over the years, and having suffered many vicissitudes,[1] physical and historical, it was rescued by the late Honourable Margaret Forbes-

---

[1] Impossible to detail here, but traced by H.Gordon Slade in the *Proceedings of the Society of Antiquaria of Scotland, 1966/7*

Sempill, who carried out much painstaking restoration, initially with the advice of the late Ian G. Lindsay, removing the Archibald Simpson addition of 1841–43. All the basements are vaulted. There is on the first floor a particularly handsome Great Hall, in which reputedly fifteen Gordons were once murdered by a Forbes during a banquet in 1571, the two families having had a protracted feud. As if such an event were not enough for one family year, the Forbes also caused the battle of Tillyangus, the Master of Forbes repudiating his wife who happened to be the daughter of the Gordon Earl of Huntly. The Gordons won, Black Arthur, the brother of Lord Forbes, being killed in the action by William Gordon of Terpersie, and the victorious Gordons pursuing the fleeing Forbes right to the gates of Druminnor.

Drumelzier Castle

Drumelzier Castle stands by the Tweed, about three miles from Broughton. It dates from three periods. The oldest section, little of which remains, is that at the north-east side of the present complex and probably of mediaeval date. A rectangular south-west wing was added about the middle of the sixteenth century, extended by the addition of a small square tower at its southern angle.

The oldest section of the castle rises to two storeys, the south-west wing to three and an attic. The entire north angle of the building has been removed, probably providing a quarry for other buildings. The south tower remains, the best preserved and therefore the most interesting part of the castle, rising to three storeys and an attic.

The castle was abandoned when the nearby early-eighteenth-century house, now incorporated in farm buildings, was built. The old castle was already 'much out of repair' when Burn's friend Captain Grose drew it in 1790.

Drumelzier was a Tweedie stronghold. They held the lands from the fourteenth century until 1632, when Drumelzier passed to John, eighth Lord Hay of Yester, whose family retained it for a further two centuries.

Drumlanrig Castle

This splendid mansion scarcely qualifies for inclusion in a survey of castles all of which were built to be defended. It was built, however, towards the close of the seventeenth century, being begun around 1676, when fortalices were still thought to be necessary, and in a way forms a link between the 'real' castle and the country house 'pretend' castle which succeeded it. Indeed, with its sweeping *piano noble* staircase and its progression of rooms, such as was later to be copied in countless Victorian mansion-castles, it provides an example of architectural excellence of a particular kind scarcely rivalled anywhere else in Scotland, except perhaps in Robert Adams's Culzean Castle.

Drumlanrig consists of a great square built round the four sides of a courtyard. Towards the entrance front it has a vaulted arcade, which supports a terrace to which the great double stairs sweep round and up to the entrance on the first floor. Though the arcade is Renaissance in design, its roof has Gothic style groined and ribbed vaulting. The open vaulted door-porch is under a central tower. The door leads to a great entrance hall, now with a later handsome fireplace. There is an iron yett over the entrance doorway, and over the door at basement level.

Each angle of the court has projecting circular stair-turrets with doorways decorated with fluted pilasters and Renaissance entablatures. Where they rise above the courtyard, the dates of execution are cut on window lintels illustrating the progress of the building of the castle. Thus, the north-east tower, which is the oldest, carries the dates 1678, 1679 and, on the top storey, 1689.

The doorway to the dining-room has handsome Renaissance detail. The room itself has four windows facing south, two fireplaces and a richly ornamented ceiling. The drawing-room is immediately above the dining-room, its walls hung with tapestries. To the east of the dining-room is the main staircase.

The morning-room, at the south-east angle, has a plaster ceiling decorated with heart-shaped panels, doubtless an allusion to 'the good Sir James'.

In a survey of this nature there is no space to detail the many richnesses of detail, the great pictures and *objets d'art* all of which may be seen at Drumlanrig, now happily open to the public.

William, first Duke of Queensberry, commenced the building, incorporating some earlier seventeenth century work by William

Drumlanrig Castle: the garden front and terrace.

Wallace, with James Smith as architect and one Lukup as master-of-works. The Jacobean plan of inner and outer courts (as at Audley End, in England) was in English terms, already sixty years out of date. Such details as angle-turrets on corbelling, cable mouldings and mock gargoyles in the form of cannon spouts at the angles are similar to those more sparingly, but commonly used in the long native tradition of castle-building. It is often remarked that the north front of Drumlanrig bears some resemblance to William Bruce's design for the entrance front of Holyrood House, and it may well be that the real designer was Robert Mylne, Smith's father-in-law and the builder of Holyrood House.

In 1810, after the fourth Duke of Queensberry – 'Old Q', Wordsworth's 'Degenerate Douglas! O the unworthy lord', who cut down many of the estate's great trees – died, the estate devolved to the third Duke of Buccleuch, whose descendants still own it.

Drummond Castle

Drummond Castle stands on a rocky height three miles south of Crieff, overlooking Strathearn. Today, it consists of a tall fifteenth-century tower with a lower seventeenth-century extension and a late Victorian mansion, remodelled from the late-seventeenth- and eighteenth-century mansion which surrounded it. It is the work of the local architect G.T. Ewing, a more ambitious scheme by Sir Charles Barry, architect of the House of Commons, which would have turned it into a Scottish Penrhyn, not being carried out.

The tall keep was built soon after 1487, when Sir John Drummond of Stobhall bought the land. Five storeys high and with a garret, it has a rebuilt parapet with open rounds at the angles. There is a square tower on the east side, and a buttress tower at the north-west angle.

The Hall on the first floor, now used as an armoury museum, is the main feature in this much-restored building – badly damaged by Cromwell and, being garrisoned by Royalist troops in 1715, 'slighted' by the Jacobean Duchess of Perth in 1745.

The seventeenth-century extension, three storeys high and with dormer windows, takes the form of a gate-house block, its arched gateway pend still wearing its wrought-iron gates. The dormers carry the Drummond arms, the initials of the first Earl of Perth and the date 1630 and 1636. It was the work of John Mylne, who also provided the obelisk-type sundial of 1630, which is the centrepiece of the great garden to the south.

The builder was the twelfth descendant of a Hungarian Maurice, who came with Queen Margaret to the court of King Malcolm Ceanmore, and took his surname from the lands of Drymen (a corruption of Drummond) granted to him in west Stirlingshire. His descendant, Sir Malcolm Drummond, so distinguished himself at Bannockburn that he was rewarded by Bruce with the Perthshire lands.

The keep's builder, Sir John, had a daughter, Margaret, with whom James IV fell in love and wished to marry. The Scots nobles, who wanted him to marry the sister of the English King Henry VIII, had Margaret Drummond and her sister poisoned, to the king's lasting sorrow. He, like Mary, Queen of Scots after him, were frequent visitors to Drummond Castle. The fourth Earl, created Duke of Perth by James VII and II, followed his sovereign into exile. The estates were forfeited for Jacobite support in 1745, coming eventually through the female line to Lord Willoughby, and so to the present owner, Lady Jane Willoughby, daughter of the Earl of Ancaster. An attempt to claim them back on the grounds of male line descent by the Earl of Perth in 1868 was unsuccessful.

Dryhope Tower

Dryhope Tower – or what is left of it following the attempt of Scott of Goldielands to demolish it in 1592 on the orders of the King, the owner having been involved in a treasonable attempt against James VI at Falkland – stands stoutly, though roofless and ruinous, near the foot of St Mary's Loch. In all probability it was rebuilt about 1613, four storeys high. A panel, once by the entrance but now relocated, carries that date and the initials of Philip and Mary Scott, the parents of the song-celebrated 'Flower of Yarrow'.

The tower is entered at ground level through an arched doorway. The lowest storey provides a vaulted storehouse, the north corner of which was screened off to provide the approach to a round newel stair leading to the first-floor Hall. The fireplace, now in poor state, was in the north-west wall. The Hall was lit by three windows, two having stone seats. Above the hall was a mezzanine room with a wooden floor and a stone vault, the latter still intact and lit by a single window. No doubt the fireplace was above that in the Hall below, sharing its chimney.

Evidence suggests that the tower was once enclosed by a barmkin wall sheltering outbuildings.

Duart Castle

The earliest reference to Duart Castle, which stands on a peninsula jutting into the Sound of Mull, three miles or so south of Craignure, occurs in 1390, when the keep was probably built by Lachlan Lubanach Maclean, though the huge wall of enceinte is undoubtedly older, probably dating from the thirteenth century. Measuring eighty feet by sixty-five, it is six to ten feet thick, rises to a height of thirty-six feet and has a parapet and walk on the top, pierced at a later date by gun-loops. It fills out the surface of the rocky knoll on which the complex stands. The entrance to the courtyard is in the south front, originally protected by a drawbridge over the landward-side ditch.

When the original castle was cleared to make way for the Maclean tower house, heavily buttressed and unusually thick walls had to be used because of the nature of the site. The tower had a ground-floor cellar with a rock-cut well and three storeys, the first being the Hall. Entrance was by the north-east wall at first-floor level.

The present south-east range was added about the middle of the sixteenth century. It had four vaulted cellars and two storeys, including the first-floor Hall and a garret. The entrance gateway in the south-west wall was strengthened about the same time by the construction of a gate-house. The upper works of the keep were also remodelled and given angle rounds.

The postern doorway at the north corner of the castle having ceased to be used, what was probably a prison was erected at ground-floor level with a gun platform above.

Early in the seventeenth century the north-east courtyard range seems to have been dismantled. In 1633, this was rebuilt by Sir Lachlan Maclean, created a Nova Scotia baronet, to provide a three-storey structure with a kitchen on the ground floor and bedrooms above, the garret rooms having dormers.

In 1674, the castle was acquired by the Earls of Argyll. Though garrisoned, it was not used as a residence, and was abandoned after it had been garrisoned by Government troops during the '45. By the middle of the century the keep was roofless.

Over the next century and a half Duart became increasingly ruinous. It was reacquired in 1911 by Sir Fitzroy Maclean, the tenth baronet, who employed Sir John Burnet to restore the castle. Following a Royal Commission report and sketch-scheme by Thomas Ross and Frederick MacGibbon, the restoration was supremely well executed, but inevitably had to conceal some of the original features. Sir Fitzroy died in it at the age of 101. It has since remained the home of the clan chief.

Duchray Castle

Duchray Castle, on the right bank of the Duchray Water, stands three miles south-west of Aberfoyle. An oblong tower house with a round tower at the south-east angle and a round turret projecting on corbels at the top of the north-west angle, it dates from the end of the sixteenth century. The ground floor is vaulted. The windows have pointed arches, but these seem to date from late Georgian alterations. A battlemented wall containing the arched entrance is of the same age as the castle.

The lands of Duchray were bought by John Graham of Downie in 1569, who held them in life-rent, the eventual proprietor being his son, William Graham, who probably built the castle.

Duchray Castle was the rendezvous of the force which the Earl of Glencairn raised in 1653 to support Charles II in Scotland. They formed part of the troops who inflicted a defeat on a Cromwellian detachment at a pass near Aberfoyle a few days later. In recompense for these services, James VII instructed the Treasury of Scotland to pay Graham one hundred pounds sterling.

Dudhope Castle

Dudhope Castle, once the seat of the Scrymgeours, Constables of Dundee, stands in a city famous for the destruction of its stone-and-mortar heritage. The castle was planned as a courtyard fortalice, but so far as is known only two sides of the quadrangle were ever built, the south and the east. Round towers with conical caps finish each of the angles, but the north-western is as late as *c.*1700. Slezer shows an early-sixteenth-century tower house at its site. There is an entrance reminiscent of Fyvie, between two rather less imposing drum towers, surmounted by a pediment and a belfry.

Of the internal arrangements, only the vaulted cellars, reached by a vaulted passage running along the inner side of the main wing, survive unaltered. The largest room, at the west end, is the kitchen, which has a huge arched fireplace. Otherwise, the inside has been totally altered, since the building was adapted to act first as a woollen mill and then as a barracks. It has since suffered from neglect and vandalism, but is at last under repair.

The lands and title were conferred on the Scrymgeours in 1298. The present building, though dated 1600, may be older in parts, while the north-western section must date from the 1670s at the earliest. James VI visited Dudhope in 1617. Sir James, the eleventh Constable, was created Viscount Dudhope in 1641. The second Viscount died of his wounds fighting for Charles I at Marston Moor. The earldom went into abeyance for many years, but was restored to the late Henry J. Scrymgeour-Wedderburn in our own day. The building had long passed out of Scrymgeour hands, having belonged to Graham of Claverhouse, then the Duke of Douglas, and finally the Earls of Home before the estate was acquired as a public park.

Dunbar Castle

The red sandstone ruins of Dunbar Castle stand by the harbour on a promontory; they are too fragmentary to convey any real impression of its former strength and importance. It had a courtyard plan, its foundations probably dating from the twelfth century. A daughter of the Earl of Moray, 'Black Agnes', the Countess of Douglas, defended it for six weeks in 1539 against the English armies of the Earls of Salisbury and Arundel, using a giant catapult against the besiegers' stone-hurling mangonels, an event described with relish and at length in Blind Harry's epic poem *The Wallace*. The eleventh Earl of Dunbar was tried for alleged treason by James I, and had his estates forfeited to the Crown. James II bestowed them, including Dunbar Castle, on the third Duke of Albany, then an infant. Albany built the blockhouse on the landward hillock, but eventually yielded up the castle to the English.

After various violent vicissitudes, Dunbar Castle was burned by German mercenaries under the Earl of Shrewsbury in 1548. It must have been sufficiently repaired by March 1566, however, for two days after Rizzio's murder at Holyrood, Mary, Queen of Scots and Darnley arrived, 'hungry and clamorous for fresh eggs to breakfast', and from there she planned revenge for her favourite's death. In 1567, ten weeks after Darnley was blown up at Kirk o' Field, Mary spent a further ten days in the castle, this time with Bothwell, with whom she was to make a final hurried visit after her flight to Cakemuir disguised as a page, and her marriage to Bothwell. After the Battle of Carbury Hill, from which Bothwell returned alone to Dunbar, briefly, as a fugitive, the castle surrendered to the Regent, and in December 1567 was destroyed – more thoroughly, apparently, than in the traditional 'slihtings' of earlier times – by order of Parliament. The seaward end of the ruins was removed in the nineteenth century.

Dunbeath Castle

Dunbeath Castle, built in the first half of the seventeenth century perhaps on the remains of work two centuries older, stands on a cliff twelve miles north of Helmsdale, one of the few large fortalices of that date in Caithness to survive intact, albeit added to and altered internally. The original part is an oblong structure with two-storey conically capped angle-turrets at each of the frontal angles. Two semicircular turrets are corbelled out from first-floor level on either side of the main arched entrance, an enlargement of the original by John Bryce, who repaired and considerably remodelled it in later Victorian times. These are topped by square watch-rooms reached by tiny subsidiary corbelled-out stair turrets in the outer re-entrant angles between the large turrets and the main buildings. The southern turret is original and contains the stair. The northern or left-hand turret is a restoration by John Bryce, said to be correct, though the plan shows no obvious reason for a second turret at this point beyond a desire for symmetry.

There is a vaulted basement with four rooms, one of which has a mural stair to what would have been the original Hall.

In 1452, Sir George Crichton, Lord High Admiral of Scotland, heired Dunbeath and was created Earl of Caithness by James II. By 1507 it was an Innes possession, from which family in 1529 it passed to the son of the second Sinclair Earl of Caithness. It was bought by a wealthy merchant, John Sinclair of Geanies, in 1624. He is thought to have built the present castle. In 1652, the Royalists under General Hurry captured Dunbeath from Montrose, though after his defeat at Carbisdale the Royalist garrison capitulated a few days later having run out of water.

Dundas Castle

Dundas Castle, near Dalmeny, was begun by Dundas of Dundas in 1416. It is a massive five-storeyed rubble- built L-shaped tower, to which a further wing was added at the north-west angle, possibly about 1424. The doorway, in the re-entrant angle, had an iron yett. Though much altered internally for its nineteenth-century use as a distillery after it had been stripped of its seventeenth-century additions and superseded as the Dundas dwelling by William Burn's Gothic mansion of 1818, it is still in good condition. Within the garden is a spectacularly large sundial of 1623 set on a richly balustraded platform approached by steps.

Dundarave Castle

Dundarave Castle, by the roadside four miles north-west of Inveraray, is an L-plan tower house, with a square tower in the re-entrant angle and a round tower at the north-west angle. It rises to four storeys and an attic and was liberally provided with shot-holes. Angle turrets grace the corners of the wallhead.

The entrance is at the foot of the stair tower, guarded by a shot-hole and decorated with dog-toothed moulded ornamentation and the motto BEHALD THE END BE NOCHT VYSER NOR THE HIESTES, and I HOIP IN GOD, the family motto of the MacNaughton builders. There are also the initials I.M. and A.N. and the date 1596.

The vaulted ground floor contains the kitchen, with the usual wide arched fireplace, and two cellars with a vaulted passage between them. That next to the kitchen is the wine-cellar, with a straight mural stair leading to the Hall above.

The Hall had a garderobe in the south-east angle, and in the opposite angle a private turnpike stair leading to the bedroom accommodation above. There is a withdrawing-room next to the Hall. There are circular rooms in the round tower.

From the MacNaughtons, Dunderave passed to the Campbells

by an unusual method around 1700. The last MacNaughton pledged himself to marry the younger daughter of Sir James Campbell of Ardkinglas. For reasons difficult to appreciate, however, he found himself married to the wrong daughter. Thereafter, MacNaughton fled to Ireland with his true love, leaving Dundarave to the Campbells.

Dundarave provided the prototype for Neil Munro's novel *Doom Castle*. By the early nineteenth century it was abandoned and roofless. Sir Robert Lorimer, however, restored it , adding a low wing, so that it is today once again occupied.

Dunnottar Castle

Not even Britain's destructive planners of the late 1940s and 1950s would have had the temerity to knock down a church without permission and erect a private dwelling for themselves on the site. That, however, is what Sir William Keith, Great Marischal of Scotland, did to a church on a promontory jutting into the North Sea a mile south of Stonehaven, in order to establish Dunnottar Castle. The Bishop of St Andrews excommunicated him, but the damage was done. On payment of 'recompense' to the Church, and by agreeing to bear the cost of a new church elsewhere, the Great Marischal was reinstated on the instructions of Pope Benedict XIII.

The site is so obviously a defensive one that tales of Pictish battles long ago, however legendary, come as no surprise. The extensive works that now occupy the site date from various periods. Sir William exchanged Struthers, in Fife, for the lands of Dunnottar with Lord Lindsay of the Byres about 1382, but the oldest surviving portion of the castle is the early-fifteenth-century L-plan keep, four storeys high and once with a garret, at the south-west corner of the site. The walls have gun-loops. All angles have open rounds. This fortalice has a vaulted basement with the usual domestic cellars and a small prison under the stairs. There are two halls, that on the first floor being the Common Hall, with the original kitchen in the wing. Later, this room was connected with a private room, and the kitchen was moved to the longest of the vaulted store-rooms in the basement, which has a fireplace obviously inserted later. Possibly the buildings to the east may have been put up at this time to accommodate the stores thus displaced.

The Earl's own Hall, a well-lit room for the times, was on the

Dunnottar Castle: the early 15th century keep in the foreground.

second floor, with a withdrawing-room and other private rooms attached. In the sixteenth and early seventeenth centuries a large courtyard house of five ranges was built at the north-east corner of the site. The northern section contained the Hall and private apartment, the western a long gallery floor, entered by a stair tower at the south-west corner and, in the eastern on the opposite side of the quadrangle, more bedrooms, jutting out from the original staircase wing. From the external angle of this extended a salient range to the north-east containing a lobby and further bedrooms. At right angles to the end of the eastern extension, partially enclosing the fourth side of the quadrangle, was a large chapel. Further extensions included a stable block, barracks and a priest's house. Incorporated conveniences included a bowling-green and a forge for the casting of iron bullets. In its heyday, Dunnottar was thus both a dwelling of considerable comfort comparable with the great English palaces of Jacobean times, as well as a remarkably capacious stronghold.

The steep approach path to the gate-house, known as Benholm's Lodging, is defended by three levels of splayed gun-loops. The entrance is through a gateway defended by a portcullis, then up a flight of steps on which splayed gun-loops are trained. Without artillery it was unassailable.

Wallace captured Dunnottar. So did Edward III, but on that occasion it was quickly recaptured by the Regent Moray. Montrose besieged it, but by that date its entrance defences prohibited capture, so he burned the Earl Marischal's crops instead. The ninth Earl entertained Charles II in 1650. A year later, Dunnottar was chosen as the safest place in which to store the Scottish regalia while Cromwell stomped the land. His General Lambert besieged Dunnottar, but before the garrison was compelled to surrender for lack of food, the regalia were safely smuggled out by the wife of the parish minister and hidden in nearby Kineff Church. In 1685, one hundred and sixty-seven Covenanters of both sexes were packed into one of the vaults during the height of a hot summer. Nine died, twenty-five escaped – though two of them met their deaths falling off the cliff – and the others, when freed, were found to have been tortured.

The Earl Marischal threw in his lot with the Stewarts in 1715. A year later Argyll partly destroyed Dunnottar and it was finally rendered harmless in 1718. Between the wars the castle was carefully consolidated and partly reroofed under the supervision of Dr William Kelly (as at Birse with the advice of Dr W. Douglas Simpson) for Annie, Lady Cowdray. It is now an Ancient Monument, privately managed by the Rt Hon. Viscount Cowdray.

Dunrobin Castle

Dunrobin Castle, poised commandingly above the coastal plain a mile north-east of Golspie, the principal seat of the Sutherland family, goes back to the fifteenth century. The old part of the castle, at the north-east corner, is a seventeenth-century tower vaulted on each floor, an extension of the square keep now embedded in later work.

This 1401 tower, with its iron yett, is still preserved, but visible only from internal courtyards. The seventeenth-century L-shaped addition was built to the south and the west, thus forming a courtyard, and resulting in a mansion of the E-plan variety with three storeys and a garret and stair towers at the outer angles. A larger circular stair tower links this with the earlier keep. The initials of the 14th Earl of Sutherland and his wife are on window pediments, together with a bronze plaque recording its building after it had been 'defast in ye late Troubles', thus dating the addition to 1672–82.

A later addition was made before 1785, but the castle owes its present somewhat French-château-like appearance to the second Duke who, between 1845 and 1851, had Sir Charles Barry, the architect then rebuilding the Palace of Westminster, redesign the whole edifice in association with William Leslie of Aberdeen, turning it into the largest country house in Sutherland and, if any of the Sutherland structure believed to exist in the eleventh century is incorporated in the foundations of the early corner, also the oldest inhabited castle in the country.

Internally, the castle is arranged in suites named after members or relations of the family, but includes a suite designed by Sir Robert Lorimer after a fire.

The Sutherlands, descendants of the Freskins of Moravia, came to Scotland in the time of William the Lion. One of them was created Earl of Sutherland in 1235. They turned themselves into Celtic chieftains, their symbol, the Great Cat, producing the name Caithness. An heiress married the second Earl of Huntly, and so brought the Sutherland lands to the Gordons. This lady's grandson took part in Huntly's rebellion in 1562, but eventually returned from exile only to be poisoned along with his wife by his uncle's wife. Their son survived, but was kidnapped by the Earl of Caithness and forced to marry his kinswoman, Lady Sinclair, a woman of more than doubtful reputation and twice his age. On achieving his majority, he organised a divorce and married instead Lady Jean Gordon, whom the Earl of Bothwell had recently discarded in order to marry Mary, Queen of Scots.

The thirteenth Earl built the seventeenth-century extensions. The eighteenth Earl died young, leaving an infant daughter who eventually married the then most powerful landowner in these islands, the Marquis of Stafford. Their agent, James Loch, instituted the Clearances, burning crofters' cottages over their heads and deporting the former inhabitants overseas to make way for more profitable sheep, the ultimate blame, however, being placed by Highlanders on the Sutherlands.

The Countess became Mistress of the Robes to Queen Victoria, who visited Dunrobin on the Countess's death to lay the foundation stone of a memorial in the form of an Eleanor cross. Another visitor was Harriet Beecher Stowe, the author of *Uncle Tom's Cabin*, who, curiously, thought the slave trade obnoxious but the eviction of helpless Highlanders sound economic practice!

In 1984, Dunrobin was bought for conversion into an international holiday club establishment.

Dunskey Castle

Though 'quite ruinous' as long ago as 1684, Dunskey Castle still provides a dramatic skyscape, standing gauntly on a precipice at the head of Castle Bay, a little to the south-east of Portpatrick. It was built about 1510 by Adair of Kilhilt on the site of an older stronghold which had been plundered and burned in 1489 by Sir Alexander McCulloch of Myrtoun. Dunskey passed from the Adairs to the Blairs in 1648.

Dunstaffnage Castle

Dunstaffnage Castle stands on a rocky plateau on a promontory in the Firth of Lorne three miles north of Oban, at the mouth of Loch Etive. It incorporates building work of several periods, beginning in the thirteenth century with the construction by the MacDougal Lords of Lorne of a massive wall of enceinte, sixty feet high in places, conforming to the irregular contours of the rock, and crowned with a parapet walk. The walk was pierced with arrow slits and garderobe flues.

The curtain was interrupted at the north and west angles by round towers and by an entrance. Two-storey buildings were built against the north-west and east walls internally, in addition to the accommodation provided by the towers. The Hall was along the east side of the courtyard. The north tower was much the larger, in all likelihood containing four floors. The west tower also had four storeys.

In the late fifteenth or early sixteenth century the castle was

Dunstaffnage Castle: a corner of the curtain wall.

transferred to the Earls of Argyll, and held on their behalf by a succession of hereditary captains. They reconstructed the entrance, providing, in effect, a gate-house, the upper works of which were later altered towards the end of the sixteenth century. At about this time the domestic range was also much altered. Early in the seventeenth century the ground floor of the gate-house was subdivided, the entrance narrowed and lintels and slit embrasures in the curtain wall altered for defence against firearms. The upper storey of the west angle tower was probably also rebuilt at this time.

Small alterations continued to be made throughout the seventeenth and eighteenth centuries, but in 1725 there was a major addition in the form of a two-storey house by the north-east end, probably replacing the accommodation in the two towers, which were by then becoming ruinous. The 1725 house is now also ruinous. In 1810, the gate-house was accidently gutted by fire and Dunstaffnage ceased to be the principal residence of the Captains of Dunstaffnage, although tenants continued to live in the place until almost the end of the nineteenth century. In 1962, the Castle passed into the care of the State.

The gate-house tower, formerly reached by a drawbridge but now by a stone forestair, has a small guardroom to the right of the entrance passage. Above this is the modern-looking sixteenth-century house of two storeys and an attic, with a conically roofed stair turret to the east rising above the main wall. This was partly restored by the Duke of Argyll in 1903/4, and further restored in the 1930s by Angus, twentieth Captain of Dunstaffnage, after a legal wrangle resulting in the restoration of the hereditary nature of the office under the Argyll owners. Across the courtyard was the circular north-west tower, which was in effect a keep, square within and having three storeys. The other round tower could be entered only through the battlements.

Bruce besieged and took Dunstaffnage, an event commented upon in Barbour's eponymous poem. Always on the side of government, Dunstaffnage was garrisoned during the Civil War and the Commonwealth by government troops, as it was during both Jacobite risings.

Duntarvie Castle

Ruined early-seventeenth-century Duntarvie, a mile north of Winchburgh, was a house rather ahead of its time in matters of symmetry and domestic convenience, whoever built it being generous in his provision of public rooms and bedrooms. It is virtually two L-plan tower houses linked together by a straight central stair, resulting in a four-storey main block with a near symmetrical south front with a central entrance. At each end are set back square towers which once had balustraded platform roofs rising a storey higher than the rest of the building. Though intact when MacGibbon and Ross saw it, little of Duntarvie except the shell now remains. One of its owners, the Marchioness of Abercorn, was incarcerated in the Canongate prison of Edinburgh in 1628 for her religious beliefs.

Duntreath Castle

Duntreath Castle, in the Blane Valley a mile and a half north-west of Blanefield, near the Blane Water, was once a courtyard castle of considerable proportions; an intended quadrangle, in fact, which was never completed on the south side.

The Duntreath estate once formed part of the earldom of Lennox. At some time prior to 1364 it was granted to Murdoch, the son of Malcolm, Earl of Lennox, by his brother, Earl Donald. Murdoch's daughter, Isabella, succeeded to the estate, but in 1434, after the execution of Earl Duncan, James I made over Duntreath to his brother-in-law, William Edmonstone of Culloden, husband of Princess Mary Stewart, a daughter of Robert III. In 1452 the grant was confirmed by James II, the charter being made out to the son of the laird who had been the beneficiary of James I, his father holding only the life rent. It has remained with the Edmonstones ever since.

The first part of the castle they then built was the oblong tower which stood at the north-west corner of the courtyard. It is a massive structure, with three main storeys and a garret. Internally it is a 'double tower', each floor containing two rooms divided by a thick cross wall. The crenellated parapet rests on individual corbels, and there is a later crow-stepped-gabled roof. The original door, no longer used, was in the built-out porch that continued upwards as a buttress to end in a cap-house, part of which housed the turnpike stair.

The later additions of the seventeenth century have gone, including the gate-house, once one of the largest and most complete examples of its kind in Scotland, built by Sir James Edmonstone, sixth of Duntreath. So, too, has the tower in which the Dumb Laird, who died at the end of the seventeenth century, was confined. The Edmonstones then lived mainly on their property in Ireland. After 1740 the castle was allowed to fall into ruin, the chapel, according to one report, having 'undergone a crash' during this time.

Though the Edmonstones came back to Scotland in 1783, they lived in Colzium, near Kilsyth, until 1857, when Sir Archibald Edmonstone, thirteenth of Duntreath and third Baronet, restored the castle as the family seat, beginning with a new south-west range and eventually encompassing a vast scheme of reconstruction by Sydney Mitchell in the 1880s, including a new gate-house. In 1958 almost all but the original tower and the Victorian north-west range and gate-house was demolished. Two iron yetts of a Dutch pattern have been preserved, as have pediments incorporated from an older structure.

Duntroon Castle

Duntroon Castle stands on a promontory projecting into Loch Crinan, on the north side of the Crinan Canal, four miles or so south-west of Kilmartin. Like so many West Highland fortresses, it stands within a twelfth- or thirteenth-century wall of enceinte, rounded at the angles, pentagon shaped to the contours of the rock, and with a broad parapet walk on top. The original buildings were doubtless of the lean-to variety. The entrance is on the north-east side and furthest from the sea, an approach strengthened at a later date with a lower crenellated wall enclosing two sides of the enceinte.

In the southern angle of the courtyard an L-shaped house of the late sixteenth century has been erected on the site of a former building. The corners of this house are also rounded, though corbelled-out square just beneath the eaves. The doorway is in the re-entrant angle, now protected by a more modern porch. The barrel-vaulted basement houses the old kitchen and other cellars, now converted to the laird's bedroom, a modern kitchen and a bathroom respectively, the bedroom having a small stair to the Hall above.

The Campbells of Duntroon owned the castle, besieged by Colkitto and his Ulstermen in 1644 during the Montrose campaigns. When the Ayr Bank collapsed in 1792, the last Campbell laird of Duntroon had to sell his property to his neighbour Neill Malcolm of Poltalloch. Since the unroofing of Burn's Poltalloch House in 1959, the Malcolms of Poltalloch have restored Duntroon, modernising the interior, and made it their home.

Dunure Castle

The jagged stumps of mainly fourteenth-century Dunure Castle survive overlooking the fishing village of the same name. It once formed part of a strong fortalice and was an important early seat of the Kennedys. It was here, in 1570, in what became known as the Black Vault, that Alan Stewart, the Commendator of Crossraguel, was roasted by the Earl until he signed away his lands. Kennedy, described as 'and werry greidy manne' who 'cairitt nocht how he got land', was fined £2000 by the Privy Council, after it had been assured by Stewart that he would 'never be able or weill in my lifetime', and instructed to pay the Commendator a pension, though Kennedy kept the lands.

The castle originally consisted of two parts; a keep of irregular shape on top of a rock, in a wall of enceinte following the rocky contours, and a flanking range of buildings at lower level built at a much later date and once containing two kitchens, the lord's apartments and rooms for retainers. There was once a drawbridge at the entrance and, apparently, a chapel, both now gone. All that is left is now badly ruined.

Sir John Kennedy of Dunure was the second husband of Princess Mary, Robert III's daughter – she married four times. Sir John's brother, James, was a Bishop of St Andrews and founded St Salvator's College.

Dunvegan Castle

Dunvegan Castle, on the island of Skye, stands on Loch Dunvegan. It is much altered but still inhabited by the family of its first owners, the Macleods. Originally, it consisted of a wall of enceinte built round the edge of a rocky platform. There was a sea-gate to the north of the rock. Only a small section of that wall remains.

The oldest surviving building is the square keep in the north-east angle, dating probably from the fourteenth century. The ground floor consisted of vaulted cellars, and the first floor of the Hall, now the drawing-room. Above was the laird's apartment and other bedrooms. The flagpole tower, like the turrets, is a later decorative addition. To this was built by Alexander Crotach ('Crookback Alastair') the wing now known as the Fairy Tower in the sixteenth century. Not long afterwards a larger building was added. By the eighteenth century the keep was ruinous, and was rebuilt as a westward extension to the Fairy Tower. The Hall in the Fairy tower replaced that in the old keep.

In the 1840s, the castle was extended again and largely remodelled with a big gate-house porch in a somewhat dour plain

Dunvegan Castle: as remodelled in the 1840s, a view from the sea.

crenellated manner to designs by the younger Robert Brown. Thus this, perhaps the most famous castle in the Highlands, is architecturally a somewhat unhappy essay in the Picturesque, only the continuity of its tradition as the seat of the Macleods, its housing of the Fairy Flag – a crusading relic of the fourteenth century captured by the fourth chief – and the drinking horn given to the sixteenth laird linking it with the more distant past. Its visitors, however, have included James V, Johnson in the company of Boswell, and Sir Walter Scott.

Earlshall

Earlshall, half a mile or so east of Leuchars, is one of the best examples of Scottish Baronial castles to come down to us intact, though restored in 1892 by Sir Robert Lorimer.

The castle is built round a courtyard, the main house occupying two sides of it. There is a smaller detached tower which rises to

Earlshall Castle: one of Sir Robert Lorimer's remodellings.

three storeys, the lower two being vaulted, and a range of seventeenth-century outbuildings. The entrance to the courtyard is by a defensive archway which has a panel carrying the arms of Sir William Bruce, who began the building in 1546. Added to at various times in the sixteenth and seventeenth centuries – Bruce's great-grandson more or less completed the original in 1617 – it was uninhabited and near ruinous when Lorimer carried out his restoration for R.W.R. Mackenzie, a Perth bleacher, cousin to the Marshall Mackenzies in Aberdeen.

The main building is an elaboration of the L-plan layout; a principal block with three storeys and a garret, and a slightly higher wing with a round stair tower corbelled square at its top to provide a watch-room. On the other corner of the main block there is a large roundish tower with a small stair turret in the angle between it and the principal block. Dormer pediments over the windows of the main block carry the initials w.b. and d.a.c., as well as carved heraldic devices.

Entrance is by a door in the stair tower, above which are more armorial bearings. The rooms on the ground floor are vaulted. The Hall on the first floor has a nine-foot-wide fireplace, heraldically decorated, and the walls are handsomely panelled.

On the second floor there is a gallery containing a wooden ceiling dated 1620 and painted in *tempera* with real and fantastic heraldic devices; animals, including an ostrich and an armadillo, and improving proverbs, such as 'A NICE WYF AND A BACK DOORE OFT MAKETH A RICH MAN POORE', capable of several interpretations. During the Lorimer restoration the ceiling had to be taken down with great care and the missing parts replaced, the whole being most skilfully touched up.

Sir William Bruce, the original builder, lived to be nearly a hundred. He fought and survived Flodden, and eventually saw James VI crowned James I of England. Having outlived his son, his grandson, Alexander, made his additions to the building, though the effulgent decorative work was done for the great-grandson, another Sir William, who died in 1636. Sir William's son died at the Battle of Worcester fighting on the Royalist side; which perhaps explains why the next in line was one of the leading persecutors of the Covenanters. Known as 'Bloody Bruce', he and his men killed Richard Cameron at Airds Moss. Bruce then 'hagged off with a dirk' the Cameronian leader's head and hands, carrying them in a sack to Edinburgh, where he had them brought before the Council on a halbert. His action is commemorated in Sir Walter Scott's 'Wandering Willie's Tale', where the Laird of Earlshall sits 'with Cameron's blude on his hand' among the revellers at Redgauntlet Castle.

Sir Robert Lorimer not only restored the house of Earlshall, but relaid and replanted the formal garden, with its yew hedges, topiary and clever use of levels and spaces.

In 1926, R.W.R. Mackenzie sold Earlshall to Mr and Mrs Purves (née Rachel Nairn, of the Kirkcaldy linoleum-family). In 1983 now noisily close to R.A.F. Leuchars, it again came on the market, and in Major Baxter found a caring purchaser, though the tapestries, decorative paintings and Lorimer furniture were unhappily dispersed by the outgoing owners.

Earl's Palace, Kirkwall, Orkney: the entrance, circular turrets and one of the oriel windows.

Earl's Palace

The Earl's Palace, built next to the Bishop's Palace (now much more ruinous) and within a hundred yards or so of St Magnus Cathedral, in Kirkwall, Orkney, was the work of Earl Patrick Stewart, bastard son of James V. It is a splendid edifice, more or less complete up to the wallhead, showing much of the French influence encouraged in Scotland by Mary of Guise and her daughter, Mary, Queen of Scots, to whom Earl Patrick was an illegitimate half-brother.

This large fortified palace is U-shaped, the main block having a wing to the south and shorter one to the north. The western angles of both wings have circular turrets. The walls are constructed of Orkney flagstones with freestone dressings. A remarkable feature

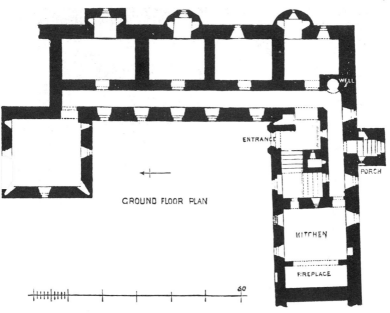

Earl's Palace: plans of the ground and first floors.

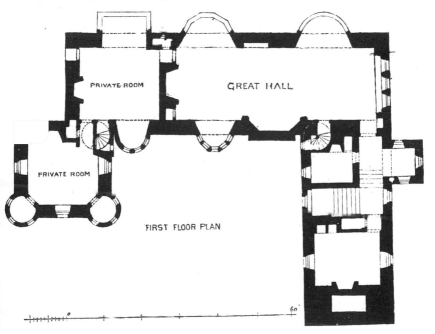

Earl's Palace: proposed reconstruction as a Sheriff Court, from the south-east, as drawn by Thomas Ross.

is the oriel windows at first-floor level to east and west, which have moulded mullions and transomes treated in an ornamental manner, though with a quatrefoil shot-hole under each window for defensive purposes. The ground floor is vaulted throughout. The upper floors, now gone, were of timber.

The entrance is in the south-east angle of the courtyard, flanked by elaborately moulded shafts with, above, several now weathered panels, one of them topped by the Royal Arms. There is a subsidiary entrance at the south side of the building. The main entrance opens into a vaulted lobby, with a handsome stone stair to the right ascending to the first floor, turret staircases once providing access to the upper floors. The gables are crow-stepped and steep, as may be seen from the drawings by David Bryce when there was a proposal, later dropped, to reroof the building for use as a Sheriff Court.

A long corridor to the left of the entrance leads to four cellars, and to a cellar in the base of the north wing. The south wing has a vault beneath its stair. The main room is the kitchen, with a large fireplace in the gable. Unusually, the polished stone well is in the southern corner of the corridor. There is also what appears to be a servants' room down some steps, off which is a service hatch. The magnificent Guest Hall, on the first floor, is reached by the broad main staircase. It has a huge fireplace with P.E.O., for Patrick Earl of Orkney, inscribed on the wall above it. The Hall is exceptionally well lit, with the oriel windows on both sides. To the north, the drawing-room also has oriel windows, and leads to another room, probably the Earl's bedroom, with a turret stair up to the family apartments. Above the entrance lobby, at the main stair landing, there is a handsomely arched little room sometimes called the chapel. More likely, it would have been a waiting-room, since when justice eventually caught up with Earl Patrick and he was condemned to be executed in Edinburgh, that event was postponed at the request of the clergy to allow him time to learn the Lord's Prayer. The accommodation for the other guests could only be reached by crossing the Hall, where their movements could easily be overseen.

Ecclesmagirdle House

This strangely named fortified house – also known at various times as Exmagriddle or Eglismagirdle, meaning 'the church of St Grill or Grillan' – stands on the south shore of a small lochan in Glenearn estate, in Lower Strathean. A T-plan house of two storeys and an attic, it was built in 1648 for Sir David Carmichael of Balmedie and Dame Anne, his wife, the initials s.D.C. and D.A.C. being carved on a panel above the arched gateway. The coat of arms which accompanied them has been stolen. The doorway is at the foot of the centre entrance tower, in one of the re-entrant angles of which is a corbelled stair turret leading to the attic floor. The dormer heads built into the retaining wall are nineteenth-century copies of originals.

The vaulted ground floor would once have housed the kitchen. The Hall is on the first floor, and there are bedrooms above. Some original interior work, including ribbed ceilings, survives.

The Abbey of Lindores held the lands in the twelfth century. Saint Grill was allegedly one of the twelve supporters of Columba who landed with him on Iona. Grill's small church was in what is now a grove of yew trees, having been superseded by a late Pre-Reformation rectangular chapel, now a roofless ruin. The graveyard contains the remains of two Covenanters, one, Thomas Small, according to his memorial, having 'died for Religion, Covenant, King and Countrie' on 1 September 1645.

The lands of Lindores Abbey went at the Reformation to Sir Patrick Leslie, son of the fifth Earl of Rothes, who married one of the daughters of the royal bastard Robert Stewart, Earl of Orkney. Becoming Commendator of Lindores, Leslie thus acquired Ecclesmagirdle, or 'Eglismagirdle', as he called it when selling the property to William Haliburton of Pitcur. In 1629, James VI confirmed a charter passing the lands from Haliburton to Carmichael of Balmedie, the builder of the present house. It now stands in the policies of Glenearn House, built about 1831, and is the property of James Drummond Hay.

Edinample Castle

A one-time MacGregor stronghold acquired by the Campbells while the MacGregors were a proscribed clan, Edinample Castle stands a few miles east of Blaquhidder, at the mouth of Glen Ample, overlooking a double waterfall on the Ample Water.

It is an interestingly designed Z-plan castle of late-sixteenth-century construction, though there may be a smaller older MacGregor tower enveloped in the eastern part. The towers are circular, the south-eastern corbelled to a single square corner at the top over the main entrance. It is not easy to see how it was originally roofed.

There are vaulted cellars on the ground floor, and one in the north-west tower. The stair to the first floor rises in the south-east tower, though from the Hall there are stairs within the wall down to one of the cellars, perhaps once the kitchen, and another to what may have been the wine-store. There is a bottle-dungeon in the south-east tower walling, accessible with difficulty through a small trapdoor from the guard-room above.

Edinample was heightened, it is not quite clear when, and substantially remodelled in the late eighteenth century with high-quality classical interior work, the roofs of the towers being altered to monopitch. A high four-storey addition was attached to the south-east tower early this century, but by the early 1970s the house was unoccupied and in bad repair. Restoration was begun but not completed: the classical interior work was removed, demolition of the wing begun and the roofs altered to a sixteenth-century form at the heightened level. Mr Nicholas Groves-Raines, who has recently acquired it, is now endeavouring to bring it to a better state.

Edinburgh Castle

The most frequently visited castle in Scotland, Edinburgh Castle stands on a cliff of basalt rock – an extinct volcano – towering above the city. There may have been fortifications on the rock from the earliest times. An earlier castle was occupied by Malcolm Canmore, lived in by Alexander I and declared a royal domain by David I. That castle, in all probability a timber structure, was destroyed by Bruce. The wall of enceinte that encloses the summit of the rock certainly retains some medieval work, but most of it belongs to the seventeenth and eighteenth century.

The narrow street at the top of the Royal Mile, beyond the Lawnmarket, broadens into the Esplanade, replacing a lower defensive space called the Spur, similar to that which once confronted those who approached Stirling Castle. By special decree of Charles I, this ground was temporarily declared Nova Scotia soil while the monarch's sixty-four new barons of Nova Scotia (frequently referred to in connection with other castles) took sasine of their colonial inheritance. The esplanade was levelled to provide a parade ground in the mid-eighteenth century, using waste from the site of what is now the City Chambers. To the right, a granite block commemorates Ensign Charles Ewart, the Scots Guard Sergeant who at Waterloo seized the French Eagle Standard. In front, over a drawbridge – incidentally, one of the last to be constructed in Scotland – and through the gate-house arch of 1887 is the Half Moon battery, built by Regent Morton in 1574 to allow artillery to defend the approaches from the town.

The arched portcullis gate, once said to be defended by two portcullises, is also probably Morton's work, but features Renaissance decoration. The upper section dates from 1886.

The level nature of the ground of the lower part of the castle is post-seventeenth century, before which time the terrain within the early curtain-wall was uneven, as can be seen from old prints. Further up, on the right, is the six-gun Argyll Battery, constructed in the 1730s on the orders of the famous General Wade, the builder of many military roads throughout Scotland. Defending a more

Edinburgh Castle: the familiar view from Princes Street, the castle dominating the city.

northerly approach is the Mills Mount Battery which, when constructed, looked over open country. Below is the low defence, probably built in the 1540s to give flanking protection to the Spur.

On the west side of the rock two levels of defence were constructed. The Western Defences as they now stand date from the 1730s. The terrace above dates from 1858. To the south, Butt's Battery was constructed by Theodore Drury, after a French fleet had sailed into the Forth in 1708 in support of the Jacobites. The Old Back Parade is overshadowed by the plain, even grim-looking, barrack block dating from the 1790s. A long flight of steps leads up to Drury's Battery, behind which is the Military Prison put up in 1842, but unused since 1923. Even more unpleasant are the vaults, originally constructed to provide a level surface for the Great Hall, and used for a variety of purposes down the years, but most notably as a prison for captured French, Dutch and American soldiers during the late eighteenth and early nineteenth centuries. One of these vaults now houses Mons Meg, probably cast at Mons in Belgium, and presented by the Duke of Burgundy to James II in 1459. It was taken to the tower of London to punish Edinburgh for the Porteous Riots, but eventually returned on the insistence of Sir Walter Scott.

Hawk Hill leads up through the strangely named Foog's Gate, guarding the royal heart of the castle, grouped round what is in effect an upper plateau of the rock. This quadrangle, formerly called the Palace Yard, is nowadays known as Crown Square. Of the four buildings which surround it, only two have medieval links. The Great Hall is perhaps the third Hall to be built on the site. It seems that there was a timber Hall in which the soldiers of the British King Mynyddog gathered around the year 600, and certainly a Hall re-roofed on the orders of Robert II in the fourteenth century. The present Hall was built on the orders of James IV; no longer for communal use, as in former times, but for ceremonial occasions. The rectangular Hall was lit by large windows on the south side and entered through a door near its west end, timber screens keeping out the draughts. At the east end, the king and the principal members of his court had their place on a raised dais. The most impressive feature of the Hall – which, fortunately, has survived – is the elaborate hammer-beam open-timber roof.

As early as 1650 the Hall was being used as a barracks, with subdivisions and inserted floors. Such a use continued well into the nineteenth century, until William Nelson, the Scottish publisher, paid for its restoration by Hippolyte Blanc between 1887 and 1891.

The personal accommodation for the monarch and his house-hold was located in the south-east corner of the rock. Here, David II began a tower house in 1368, augmented and extended through the reigns of many monarchs. David's tower, or the stump of it, is now embedded in the Half-Moon battery. Once again, it was probably James IV who was responsible for the present structure. It has been twice remodelled; once for Mary, Queen of Scots and Darnley, the date 1566 and the initials M.A.H. appearing over a door. Half a century later it was again reconstructed, and the king's lodging heightened, for the 'hame-coming' of James VI in 1617. Royal monograms, later erased on Cromwell's orders, were carved on the window pediments by the master mason William Wallace. The stone-work still bears the scars of Cromwell's siege of 1650.

The Palace is now used for several purposes. Part of it houses the

Scottish United Services Museum. A ground-floor room, leading off what used to be the Queen's bedchamber, is that in which Mary, Queen of Scots bore the future James VI and I. A vaulted room at first-floor level houses the Scottish Regalia of Crown, Sword and Sceptre. Hidden in Dunnottar Castle, and then in the parish church of Kineff to escape Cromwell's designs, they were later ceremonially walled up in the castle room after the Union of 1707. In 1818, however, again partly as a result of Sir Walter Scott's successful efforts in stimulating interest in the visual emblems of Scotland's past, they were put on display.

The most recent building in the square is the Scottish National War Memorial, which stands on the medieval site of the Church of St Mary. The envelope of the building was put up in 1755, but it was converted by Sir Robert Lorimer to its present function in 1924. It is now a colonnaded and vaulted cross hall with an apse opposite the entrance, in which there is a casket containing the names of the dead in two World Wars. The stained glass windows are by Douglas Strachan.

I have left to the last the oldest building, St Margaret's Chapel. It is probable that the fabric dates from the reign of David I, and is therefore of early-twelfth-century origin. Though once linked to other buildings and at various times used for secular purposes, it was restored in 1845. It is divided by a vaulted arch with the apse and altar at the east end.

Edzell Castle

Edzell Castle, seven miles north of Brechin, in the foothills of the Grampian mountains, was the ancient seat of the Lindsays, Earls of Crawford. The castle, of complicated structure, consists of an early-sixteenth-century keep, enlarged in the later decades of that century into a spacious courtyard mansion. In 1604 a larger garden or pleasaunce was created and surrounded by an ornamental wall to which a summerhouse and a bath-house were attached.

The L-plan tower, at the south-west angle of the main courtyard, replaced an older castle, and was once known as the Stirling Tower, after the family from whom the estate came to the Lindsays by the marriage of one of them in 1357 to Catherine Stirling of Glenesk. The keep rises to four storeys, with a garret inside the wallhead gable.

The parapet corbels, a double chequered arrangement of individual and continuous corbelling, are one of the earlier instances of this structural device being employed for purely decorative purposes. There are open angles at each corner. Small projecting half-rounds provide additional defence midway along each wall. The entrance, reached through an arched doorway from the courtyard, is in the re-entrant angle. It gives access to two vaulted cellars in the basement, the cellar to the east having a private mural stair to the Hall above. The Hall is a noble one, lighted by two windows, one having stone seats. The presence of two fireplaces, one larger than the other, suggests that the east end with the smaller fireplace may once have been screened off. There is an elegant little vaulted closet inserted in the north-west angle. The floors above have gone, but were reached by an unusually broad-stepped stair.

The late-sixteenth-century addition, erected by David, ninth Earl of Crawford, consisted of an L-shaped range three storeys high with gabled roofs but no parapets to the east and north of the keep. They are extremely ruinous, but once housed a series of spacious rooms above domestic offices. Those on the remaining sides have either been removed or were never completed.

The pleasaunce, a hundred and seventy-three feet by a hundred and forty-four, was added by the son of the ninth Earl, Sir David Lindsay, Lord Edzell, a Session judge. His initials, and that of his wife, Dame Isobel Forbes, are inscribed above a gateway along with the date 1604. The garden is enclosed on three sides by a remarkable wall, featuring a checked pattern of masonry which, like the three stars also to be seen, are part of the Lindsay crest. It is banded into compartments which feature individual niches with carved cubicles surmounted by pediments to accommodate busts or plants, and bas-reliefs representing the Celestial Deities, the Liberal Arts and the Cardinal Virtues, copied from designs which Lord Lindsay had acquired in Nuremberg.

The summer-house, a self-contained oblong two-storey building with its own stair tower, gun-loops and angle turret, has handsomely carved tympanums over the windows. The moulded doorway in the front of the stair tower has been superseded by a modern entrance. Of the two vaulted rooms in the basement, one is ribbed. The bath-house tower at the south angle has a stone sink for emptying water.

Mary, Queen of Scots held a Privy Council at Edzell in 1562 and stayed in the castle. Cromwell garrisoned it in 1651. When the

Edzell Castle: a keep enlarged to a courtyard mansion.

Lindsays had to sell it in 1715 because of huge debts, it was bought by the Earl of Panmure, who forfeited it after the 'Forty-Five Rising, but re-purchased it in 1764. It is now in the care of the State.

Eilean Donan Castle

The photogenic Eilean Donan Castle stands on a small island at the mouth of Loch Duich, opposite Skye. It was the chief stronghold of the MacKenzies of Kintail, and was latterly kept for them by their cadets, the MacRaes.

It began as a castle of enceinte in the thirteenth century on lands said to have been given by Alexander III to a son of the Irish Earl of Desmond for help in defending the king against the Norwegians at the Battle of Largs. In the fourteenth century a rectangular keep was built in the north-east angle.

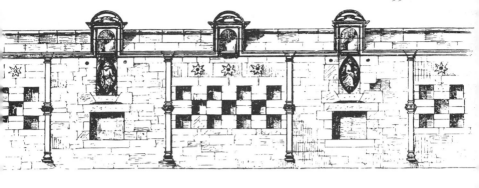

ELEVATION AND PLAN

OF A PORTION OF EAST SIDE OF GARDEN
WALL.

SCALE OF _____ FEET

Edzell Castle: MacGibbon and Ross's drawing of a section of the east
side of the garden wall.

In 1331 Randolph, Earl of Moray, executed fifteen men over a
territorial disagreement and 'decorated' the castle walls with their
heads. Eilean Donan was captured by the Earl of Huntly in 1504. In
1579 it was besieged by Donald Gorm, a claimant to the Lordship
of the Isles, but was saved when a stray arrow fired from the castle
killed the principal assailant. It was less fortunate, however, in
1719, when William MacKenzie, fifth Earl of Seaforth, had it
garrisoned with Spanish troops during the abortive Jacobite rising
of that year, and three English warships battered it into ruin.

It remained ruinous until Colonel MacRae-Gilstrap restored it
early this century to designs by George Mackie Watson as the seat
of the MacRaes and, later, also to shelter the Clan MacRae War
Memorial. The bridge dates from this time.

The keep, which rises to three storeys and a gabled garret, and
has open rounds and a projecting missile-device (though not above
the modern entrance) is a reconstruction.

Elcho Castle

Elcho Castle, on the south bank of the Tay four miles east of Perth, is one of the most interesting of later Scottish castles which, while still maintaining something of a defensive posture, managed to provide palace-like comforts.

In plan, this castle consists of a long oblong block with a square stair tower at the south-west corner and three other towers projecting on the north side. Two of these are round stair towers squared on corbels at the top into watch-rooms, the third containing small apartments. A large angle turret looms out of the south-east angle at roof level.

The square tower, with a crow-stepped gable on the southern side, dates from the fifteenth century, and has open rounds at the parapet angles. It was once thought that substantial reconstruction of the main block had been carried out in the latter half of the sixteenth century, but experts now believe it to be a homogenous structure of the late sixteenth century. There is certainly no trace of the castle that was supposed to have sheltered Sir William Wallace, so presumably an older castle once stood on the site. The entrance is in the re-entrant angle, and gives access to a generously proportioned turnpike stair with steps seven feet wide in the south-west tower. The ground floor houses a very large kitchen which has a fireplace itself almost the size of a small room, its flues a feature of the roofscape on the north front. A corridor on the ground floor links the kitchen with two stairs, from one of which there is another turnpike stair.

From the Hall on the first floor, which has relics of fine plaster work, three stairways lead up to bedroom accommodation, most of which has its own private lobbies and garderobes.

The Wemyss family held the lands of Elcho for more than five hundred years, James III having granted them in 1468 to John de Wemyss, heir to Sir John Wemyss of that Ilk. Sir John de Wemyss later became the first Earl of Wemyss when Charles I had his Scottish crowning. Surprisingly, the new Earl took the side of the Parliamentarians in the ensuing Civil War.

David, Lord Elcho, heir to the fifth Earl, was not only 'out' in the 'Forty-five, but survived Culloden to escape to France. The earldom thereupon passed to his younger brother, who had taken the surname of Charteris. By the 1780s, Elcho Castle was abandoned and fell into decay. Fortunately, it was reroofed in 1830, and, though it still belongs to the Earl of Wemyss and March, is in Guardianship, and still possesses the original wrought-iron grills protecting its windows.

Elphinstone Tower

Elphinstone Tower stands – or once stood – on a long ridge that runs south-westwards from Tranent, unfortunately over coal-bearing seams. It suffered as a result of subsidence, and indeed became so dangerous that part of it had to be demolished in our own day: a pity, because it was one of the most interesting of all the old tower houses. More has since crumbled away.

In plan, it was oblong, three main floors and at least two entresol floors being contained within walls nine feet thick. There was a sub-divided basement vault and above it three timbered floors. The Hall, twenty-nine feet by twenty, on the first floor, had a fine fireplace, with elevated flanking windows. There was richly decorated work on the lintel and cornice. At the other end of the Hall was a second large fireplace within an arched recess which, once screened, formed the kitchen. The second floor contained two main rooms, one of them the solar approached by a long gallery. Each had its fireplace and small chamber latrine. There was a wide parapet walk, stone-flagged.

The fascinating aspect of Elphinstone, however, was the manner in which stairways and small chambers were honeycombed into its thick walls, an outstanding example of clever utilisation of space. From the ground-level entrance in the north wall, the vaulted basement was approached. Two straight stairs rose from this lobby. To the right, one stair led to a little entresol room, complete with latrine, window and lamp recess. The left stair led to the Hall on the first floor, providing access from the screen end. The turnpike stair in the south-west angle, which led to the upper floors, rose, however, from the dais end, so that anyone wishing to gain access to the private apartments would have to cross the Hall, where his passage could be observed through a concealed port in the flue of the hall fireplace.

The Elphinstones held their lands from the thirteenth century, though the completion of the tower dated from the marriage of a female heiress to Sir Gilbert Johnstone in the fifteenth century. In 1545 the Protestant martyr George Wishart was brought from nearby Ormiston and at Elphinstone handed over to Cardinal Beaton, who took Wishart back to St Andrews for trial and execution by burning; an unpleasant fate, though not less so than that which soon afterwards overtook Beaton at the hands of the Protestants.

Elsieshields Tower

Like Amisfield, which was probably designed by the same master mason, Elsieshields Tower, which stands on raised ground two miles north of Lochmaben, is a fine example of a tall late-sixteenth- or early seventeenth-century tower designed to pile as much accommodation as possible on top of a relatively small base. The original L-plan fortalice rises to three storeys with an attic, has three large angle turrets and, on the fourth corner, a square two-storeyed tower rising above the main block. There is a slim stair tower, rising two storeys higher, corbelled out in the upper re-entrant angle thus created. The original doorway is in the re-entrant angle at the front of the stair tower.

A Johnstone stronghold, the usual arrangements would pertain, with the Hall on the first floor and the bedrooms above; although in this case the ground floor is, unusually, not vaulted. There is a nineteenth-century extension to the main block. Elsieshields is still occupied, for some years the home of the historian Sir Stephen Runciman.

Erchless Castle

Erchless Castle, ten miles west of Beauly, is a tall L-plan fortalice of four storeys with the stair tower rising a storey higher. Steep-roofed and with crow-stepped gables, it has a mural stair turret corbelled from first-floor level. There is also a turret at the south-west angle. The structure was doubled in size in 1895 and has been considerably modernised at various dates, an oriel window having been added to the west gable and a new entrance provided in the south face of the stair wing.

It has a vaulted basement, a Hall on the first floor and the usual accommodation above.

Originally owned by the de l'Aird family, the lands of Erchless passed through the marriage of an heiress to the Chisholms, who rented the present castle at the end of the sixteenth century. It was garrisoned by Government troops during the Jacobite rising of 1689. The laird of the day was 'out' in 1715, and his son was killed at Culloden in 1746. The family died out in the male line and the castle came to the last laird's sister, Mary Chisholm, a champion of the oppressed Highlanders during the dreadful days of the Clearances. Though no longer in the Chisholm family, Erchless is still occupied.

Ethie Castle

Ethie, five miles north of Arbroath, now a large and handsome mansion, has been so much altered since it came into being as a large square keep in the fifteenth century that it is difficult to be sure of the original plan. There does seem to have been a castle on the site at an even earlier date. The oldest portion now forms the south-west corner, though the balustraded tower above its stair dates from Sir Rowand Anderson's refurbishment in the 1890s and the roofline has been altered. An extension to the east, probably put up in the mid-sixteenth century, turned the original tower house into a large L-plan structure. Later sixteenth- and seventeenth-century extensions to north and north-east produced an irregular court of complex plan, which may have been two – the present division is much later – filling up the original barmkin. The round tower at the north-west angle, where filled-up gun-loops can be seen, may have been part of it.

The ground floor of the original tower house has two vaulted cellars; one, the original kitchen beneath the massive flue (though a new kitchen was provided in the first extension); another, the wine-cellar, with its private mural stair to the Hall above. There is a 'loupin-on stane', to assist mounting a horse, near the entrance to the outer courtyard.

Ethie was inhabited by Cardinal Beaton whilst he was Abbot of Arbroath *circa* 1530, and again when he was a Cardinal between 1538 and 1546, so must have been involved in his forceful attempts to hold down the boiling-up Reformation. In 1549 it passed to Sir Robert Carnegie, grandfather of Sir John Carnegie of Ethie, created Lord Lour in 1639 and Earl of Ethie in 1647. After the Restoration he exchanged this and other titles for those of Baron

Rosehill and Inglismaldie and Earl of Northesk. Though no longer with the family, Ethie Castle is still inhabited.

Evelick Castle

The substantial ruins of Evelick Castle stand amongst the foothills of the Sidlaws five miles or so from Perth. It was the seat of the Lindsays of Evelick, and probably dates from some time after 1560. An L-plan structure with its two wings joined at the corners, it rose to three storeys, and once, no doubt, also had an attic storey. A semicircular stair tower rises in the south-west re-entrant angle, and contains the entrance. The vaulted basement and the floors above have collapsed.

One of its early owners, Andrew Lindsay, was made a baronet in 1666. His second son, Thomas, was stabbed five times during a game with a step brother, James Douglas, who then held the dying youth's head under the water of a burn before finally knocking his brains out with a rock.

The last of the Evelick Lindsays was accidently drowned in 1799.

Fairburn Tower

On a ridge five miles north-west of Muir of Ord, Fairburn is a lofty tower four storeys tall with a garret and crow-stepped gables. It dates from the late sixteenth century – Coxton and Hallbar have been not dissimilar though less tall in proportion – but has a high square stair tower added in the seventeenth century. Fairburn has a watch-room at the top. There are circular angle turrets on the north-east and south-west angles and numerous gun-loops and shot-holes.

The original entrance to the keep was at first-floor level, by movable stair. The later entrance is in the south face of the stair tower.

The first-floor Hall has several mural chambers. A straight stair in the north-east angle led to the vaulted basement below, which had no entrance at ground floor level. Above the Hall, one room per floor, were bedrooms, each with a garderobe.

Fairburn was a Mackenzie castle, long since a ruinous landmark.

Falkland Palace

There are ancient references extant to a Macbeth, Thane of Falkland; but the Falkland that has come down to us today was owned by the MacDuff Earls of Fife, and so in 1371 came to Robert Stuart, Earl of Fife and Menteith, who, as Duke Robert of Albany, twice became Regent of Scotland during the minority and captivity of James I. He used Falkland as his residence for thirty-four years and probably bestowed on it the title of Palace. His son and successor, Duke Murdo, was under suspicion of murdering his nephew, David, Duke of Rothesay, at Falkland in 1424, and was executed by James I on his return to Scotland. Falkland was then annexed to the Crown.

It became a favourite residence for the first three Jameses, Jameses III and IV carrying out work on the courtyard palace. It may be that the front of the south range facing the street belongs to the latter half of the fifteenth century, built during the reign of James IV. James V was responsible for the Renaissance front facing the courtyard, and for the interior of the bulding. At one time there were ranges on the north and east sides, the west side being completed by a wall. The east range, rebuilt by James IV and added to by his son, has little now to show but the vaults, though above them once were the king's guard hall, the royal audience chamber and the privy dining-room. At the junction of the east and north ranges, there was once a stair leading up from the royal kitchen. The cross house of the east range, in the original room of which the dying James V heard of the birth of a daughter, the future Mary, Queen of Scots, and made his famous prophecy – 'It cam' wi' a lass, and it will gang wi' a lass' – now houses a reconstructed and refurbished king's bedchamber. In it is the 'golden Bed of Brahan', an early-seventeenth-century four-poster bought from abroad as a gift to the Earl of Sutherland from a wealthy clansman.

The east range had on its east side two sumptuously painted galleries, begun by James IV but completed by James V's French craftsmen, from which there was a view over the Howe of Fife and the surrounding forests; a view that must have been familiar to the poet William Dunbar. Only the south range and fragments of the east now survive. The west range, which contained James II's hall, was burned down in 1654 while occupied by Cromwell's troops.

The approach to the Palace is through a great twin-towered gatehouse, similar in defensive posture to those at Dirleton,

Falkland Palace: the gatehouse of the restored south range, contrasting with a typical vernacular East Coast house.

Caerlaverock and Tantallon, though without a portcullis. There are guard-rooms on both sides, however, and on the western side a dungeon underneath a trapdoor. The upper rooms were probably servants' quarters.

The basement of the two-storey building consists of the usual vaulted cellars. The first floor contains the large Hall. It has fine mullioned windows and an oak screen at the west end, above which is a minstrel's gallery. There is also an impressive seventeenth-century timber ceiling.

To celebrate his second marriage to Mary of Lorraine (or of Guise, as she is sometimes known) in 1538, James V caused Scottish masons to add Renaissance fronts to both the east and south ranges, the first of their kind in Scotland, though much of the detail was probably the work of a Frenchman, Nicholas de Roy, who had been recommended by the bride's father. The overall architectural charge was in the hands of Sir James Finnart, beheaded on a probably trumped-up charge of treason in 1560 before the embellishments were fully completed.

James VI used Falkland as a holiday retreat, giving it to his bride, Anne of Denmark, as a wedding present in 1589. Charles I stayed for a time when in Scotland to be crowned in 1633, as did Charles II under similar circumstances in 1650. He returned in 1651 and again the following year, when the decision was probably made to invade England behind Cromwell's back, as it were; an adventure which ended disastrously in the Battle of Worcester and foreign exile for the monarch.

The burning of the north range and years of neglect followed, despite a visit by George IV while in Edinburgh in 1822, until in 1887 the third Marquess of Bute bought Falkland and its hereditary custodianship and restored what was left of the Palace over the next thirteen years; a process carried on by his successors in the family until, in 1952, the National Trust for Scotland was appointed Deputy Keeper and effectively assumed responsibility.

Falkland, like Linlithgow Palace and parts of the castles of Stirling and Edinburgh, represents the Renaissance flowering which over a period of sixty years or so came between the two eras of fortified tower-house building.

Farnell Castle

Four miles south of Brechin, Farnell in part represents the original Bishop's Palace for the See of Brechin. In 1512 Bishop Meldrum called it 'Palatium Nostrum'.

In 1566 Bishop Campbell disposed of the lands of the bishopric, and Catherine, Countess of Crawford, turned it into a secular fortalice.

In the east section that was the Bishop's residence there are gables with large gabletted crow-steps, a projecting garderobe and sanitary flues on the north side, a double row of corbels on the east gable at the level of the floor and corbels clearly intended to support a one-time roofed timber gallery. There are small carved shields on the northern skewpots with the initials I.M. for Jesu Maria, and M, above which is a crown.

The circular stair, part of the post-Reformation addition on the south front, is corbelled to the square above the level of the eaves to provide a small watch-room. On the ground floor, near the new gable, there is a curious projection with a battlemented cornice which may have been meant to contain a closet.

There are two rooms on each floor, though the inside of the castle was much altered in late Georgian times and again in the recent restoration. The Earl of Southesk acquired Farnell by purchase.

Fawside (or Falside) Castle

Fawside Castle stands dramatically on a ridge two miles south of Tranent, overlooking Musselburgh and Tranent. Until recently it was an imposing ruin, which started off, probably in the early fifteenth century, as a plain rectangular tower four storeys high, with an entrance at ground level through the west wall. To the left of the door a straight stair in the thickness of the wall led to the first floor, and a spiral staircase in the north-east corner continued the ascent. Only the stair is capped. The main tower is vaulted and has a flat roof over the vault.

Named after the de Fauside or Falsydes, who owned or rented the land in the twelfth century, it appears to have been gained by the Crown through forfeiture. At any rate Robert the Bruce granted it to his nephew, Alexander de Seton, after the War of Independence. Nevertheless, the Fausides managed to remain the tenants of the tower for what we would nowadays describe as a peppercorn rent. They must have been a remarkable family, for Nigel Tranter[1] tells us, quoting from an unspecified contemporary English source, that the day before the Battle of Pinkie, fought near the tower in 1545, the inhabitants 'shot at the invaders with hand guns and hakbutts till the battle lost when they pluct in their peces lyke a dog his tails and then crouched themselves within, all muet; but by and by the hous was set on fyre and they, for their goodwill, brent and smootherid within.'

As a result of this experience, so disastrous to the gallant occupants, the structure had to be rebuilt, probably around 1547, when it was enlarged by a matching extension to the south.

[1] Nigel Tranter, *The Fortified House In Scotland*, Edinburgh 1962-65

Fawside Castle: a once roofless tower house well restored in our own day.

An L-shaped tower, larger but less massive, was then added, with a new entrance set, not in the re-entrant angle, but in the west face of the jamb, and opening into a scale-and-platt stair. Fawside well illustrates the ingenuity of its owners in extending their accommodation by lateral extension on a similar scale to the original building, thus creating an apparently unified and homogenous structure.

The newer section shows French-influenced corbelling, turrets and decorated mouldings. Within the last few years the whole building has been restored for reoccupation, though at the time of writing it is for sale.

Fenton Tower

Fenton has its place in history because its laird, Sir John Carmichael, when Scots Warden of the Marches, took objection to a remark by the English Warden about his patron, the Regent Morton, at one of their statutory meetings in 1575. The supporters of the English Warden thereupon replied with an assault known as the Raid of Redeswire, in which Sir John was killed, but the English were routed by the timely arrival of the Provost of Jedburgh with a small force, crying 'Jethart's here!,' a slogan which still provides the rallying cry for the annual Common Riding ceremony in the town.

The now ruined building cannot have been quite completed when its owner fell, for over the doorway in the wing the initials J.C. are accompanied by the date 1577. The tower stands on Kingston Hill, two miles south of North Berwick. It rises to three storeys and a garret.

Its interior has collapsed. A wide turnpike stair once led to the first floor. Access to the upper floors was by the usual narrower turret stair.

The main block has two vaulted rooms in the basement, the larger with a door affording direct entrance through the west gable. A small separate turnpike stair links the eastern room with the first floor. The semi-circular tower which carries this has a room on each of the floors above. In the western angle a garderobe, carried on corbelling, allowed what was deposited therein to fall straight to the ground; an arrangement crude even by sixteenth-century standards.

Fernie Castle

Fernie Castle, about three miles west of Cupar, was once part of the territory of the MacDuffs, Earls of Fife. In the fourteenth century the lands were divided into Easter and Wester Fernie and owned by branches of the Balfour family. By the fifteenth century, however, Wester Fernie, in which the Castle stands, was owned by the Fernie of that Ilk. Not for long, though. They failed to produce a male heir, and their daughter married a Lovell, who in 1586 sold the castle to Arnot of that Ilk.

Fertility and Fernie do not seem to have agreed with each other, for within the century the Arnot family also failed for want of an heir. Fernie then went to a distant relation, the third Lord Balfour, who gave the castle to his second son, Colonel John Balfour. The Colonel, however, was on the losing side in the Jacobite rising of 1715 and had his lands attainted, though in 1720 they were granted back to his elder brother, who had had the foresight to fight with the Hanoverians (a kind of insurance device practised by more than one Scottish family at the time).

Though the castle was incorporated in a later mansion and the whole harled, the original L-plan structure is clearly visible, the tower to the west having a main block rising to four storeys with a stair wing rising a floor higher and containing a watch-room. There is another circular tower to the north-west, squared at the top by corbelling, and containing yet another watch-room. The round tower with the conical roof is later work, as are many other features, including the enlarged windows.

In recent years the castle has become an hotel, and there is a modern addition.

Ferniehurst Castle

Ferniehurst Castle, on the right bank of the Jed Water, two and a half miles south-east of Jedburgh, dates from the late sixteenth century, and was the home of the Kerrs of the Lothian line, (the home of the Roxburgh Kerrs being Cessford), both offshoots of Anglo-Norman stock, who wrangled for centuries on the issue of family seniority.

The original Ferniehurst was built around 1476, probably by the father of Sir Andrew 'Dand' Ker, who was taken prisoner by the English under Lord Dacre in 1529. The son, Sir John, with French aid, recaptured the castle in 1549. Sir John's son, Sir Thomas, invaded England on 22 January, 1570 (the day after Queen Mary's half-brother, the Regent Moray, had been murdered at Linlithgow), hoping to start a rising that might lead to Mary's release from Fotheringay. All that happened was that in April the Earl of Sussex invaded Scotland, wrecking havoc and totally destroying Ferniehurst. James VI destroyed it yet again in 1593, on the grounds that the laird had succoured the Earl of Bothwell.

The oldest part of the rebuilt castle, an L-shaped tower of 1598, now forms the north-west angle cornered by a circular tower, producing a Z-plan effect. Later in the century a rusticated Renaissance arched gateway was built adjacent to the entrance jamb, as well as additional, but now roofless, outbuildings at right angles to the also roofless kitchen range.

The tower has four storeys and an attic, each angle being neatly finished with circular turrets. The original doorway is situated in the re-entrant angle. The main doorway now leads by a timber stair to the first floor, with higher ascent gained by means of a turret stair in the re-entrant angle.

There are six vaulted cellars in the basement of the wing and one in the tower. The room on the first floor of the tower was the original Hall, from an angle of which a straight stair leads to a cellar beneath, which may either have been a wine-cellar or an extremely unpleasant prison. In the seventeenth-century east wing there is a large room known as the Great Hall, with fireplaces at both north and east ends. At the east end of the room a smaller chamber gives access to the little room in the circular tower known as the Library, which is richly panelled and has shelves supported by finely carved brackets and a handsome carved wooden ceiling.

The upper floors house the usual bedroom accommodation. The fourth-floor rooms in the tower have gun-loops in the angle turrets.

A systematic restoration was planned in 1898, to which end the Hall was gutted, but the scheme fell through.

Sir Thomas's two sons were created respectively Earl of Somerset (after 1603) and Lord Jedburgh. The present Lothian line descends from Lord Jedburgh. Ferniehurst, though still in the Lothian family, has been a Youth Hostel since 1928, prior to becoming which further work was carried out.

At the moment of writing, the reroofing of the roofless lower wings is in hand.

Fiddes Castle

Four miles south-west of Stonehaven, Fiddes Castle is an L-plan tower house with the addition of a large circular stair tower at the south-west end of the block, corbelled out squarely to carry a crow-step-gabled watch-room. An even more unusual feature is the circular main entrance stair tower in the re-entrant angle, reaching round to encompass the main gable. This tower is partly a storey lower than the main building with an open platform opening off the crow-stepped higher part, which is an oversail from the main roof, containing the head of its turret access stair. In the drawing by MacGibbon and Ross, the platform had been roofed over but it has since been restored. Midway along the north front another stair tower projects, also corbelled out to carry a square watch-room. Two-storey angle-turrets, conically roofed, adorn the wing gable.

The castle has three storeys and an attic and is well equipped with shot-holes. The basement is vaulted, the kitchen, to the east, having a large fireplace. The neighbouring wine-cellar has the usual private stair to the Hall above. This has a private room off it in the wing, leading to another very small room with a finely decorated ceiling. Above, there are many bedrooms. The main stair rises to the first floor, the only ascent thereafter being by the round tower and the stair turret.

The Arbuthnots came from the Borders in the twelfth century when a Swindon married an Arbuthnot heiress and took her name. For two years, though for reasons unknown, they were 'alienated' from their lands, which were returned to the family by James III. The castle, now a farmhouse, has been carefully restored, and so saved from the decay foreseen as its fate by MacGibbon and Ross.

Fingask Castle

Four miles north of Errol, Fingask Castle dates from about 1594. There is an older portion, but it is incorporated in the wing of this L-plan building and the wing to the west, added in 1674. There were eighteenth-century additions behind the main block, and further extensions added in the nineteenth century. The reddish-brown coursed rubble building once had a square stair tower in the re-entrant angle, but this has disappeared in the many vicissitudes that have befallen the building. The present door, however, is probably in much the same position relative to the structure as the original.

The vaulted kitchen is in the basement of the wing. At the back of the arched fireplace is a gun-loop, one of many defensive devices in this building. There is a fine first-floor Hall with a smaller withdrawing-room in the wing, equipped with garderobe and mural closets. There is the usual bedroom accommodation above.

The earliest owners were a branch of the Bruces of Clackmannan, who sold Fingask to the Threiplands, a family from Peeblesshire. In 1674 Patrick Threipland, Provost of Perth, was knighted for his part in suppressing conventicles. He was made a Nova Scotia baronet in 1687, yet died a prisoner in Stirling Castle two years later. Sir David, his son and heir, was one of the first to join the Earl of Mar on the raising of the standard on behalf of the Old Chevalier in 1715. There, too, was his eldest son, also Patrick, who was captured while taking part in Mackintosh of Borlum's abortive raid on Edinburgh Castle. The Old Chevalier stayed at Fingask in February and again in March 1716. On the suppression of the Rising the estate was forfeited and dragoons occupied the castle. Lady Threipland bought it back from the York Building Company, to whom the government had sold it.

The Threiplands were 'out' again in 1745, and the eldest son, David, died in the Battle of Prestonpans. The youngest son, Stuart, survived the whole campaign and for a time shared his Prince's wanderings, escaping to France disguised as a bookseller's assistant. Once again there were dragoons in Fingask. In 1747 the laird returned to Edinburgh and set up in practice as a physician. The forfeited baronetcy was restored to his son Patrick in 1816.

Although the Threiplands died out in 1882, their place was taken by a Kerr cousin who assumed the name. In 1914 Fingask went to Sir John Stewart, who committed suicide. From 1925 until 1967 Fingask was in the hands of the Gilroys, who commissioned the Dundee architects John Donald Mills and Godfrey Shepherd to reduce it back to its original state, an aim in which they were not wholly successful. In 1967 Murray Threipland, grandson of the last family owner, bought back Fingask and carried out further restoration, some of which, however, some experts feel has 'no historical basis'. At least he restored, and indeed added to, the splendid nineteenth-century figure groups (including Prince Charles Edward and Flora MacDonald) by David and William Anderson, and perhaps by James Thom (who carved some of the figures for the Burns Monument at Alloway) in the formal garden, famous also for its elaborate display of topiary.

Fordell Castle

Fordell Castle stands about three miles west of Aberdour, on the edge of a ravine above the Keithing Burn. A sixteenth-century fortalice of coursed rubble, it comprises an oblong block running east and west, with two square towers carrying stairs at the north-west and south-east angles; almost, but not quite, a Z-plan castle. The tower to the south-east has a later gabled roof with crow-stepped gables, that to the north-west a flat roof and parapet. Angle turrets are corbelled out at appropriate ends of the towers.

The entrance is at the foot of the north stair tower, leading to a vaulted corridor along the north front, from which there is access to the three vaulted basements. The east room was once a kitchen, egress from it to the Hall being by a small stair in the wall's thickness.

The first floor, reached by the north-west stair, contains, as well as the Hall, a withdrawing-room. The turret stair provides access to the remaining floor. A vaulted and panelled room above the main stair-head is known as Queen Mary's room, the vault serving to support the flat roof of the tower above. Queen Mary visited Fordell on the occasion of the marriage of one of her Maids of Honour, Marion Scott, to George Henderson, laird of Fordell. Over the lintel of the door in the north tower are the initials of James Henderson of Fordell, along with the date 25 M C H. A.D. 1580. The Hendersons acquired the land in 1511. By the nineteenth century their descendants had built themselves a new mansion in the grounds, keeping the old castle wind- and water-tight as a folly. In our own day it was acquired and restored by the first Solicitor-General in Mrs Thatcher's first Conservative administration, Nicholas Fairbairn, Q.C. M.P.

Fordyce Castle

Fordyce Castle stands in the centre of the still almost unspoiled village of that name three miles south-west of Portsoy. The main part is an uncommonly well-detailed L-plan tower house, the oldest part dated 1592. It was built by Thomas Menzies of Durn, an Aberdeen merchant. The west wing of two storeys and an attic extending it to T-plan form, was added in 1700. Menzies' house, has three storeys, with a circular stair tower, corbelled out heavily

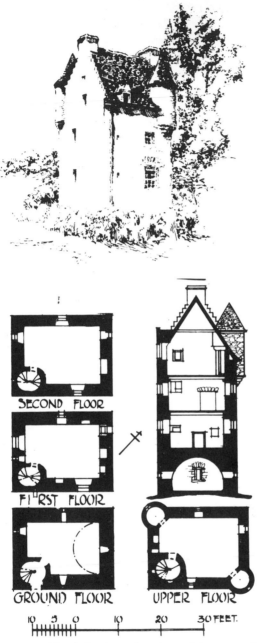

Fourmerkland Castle: a drawing of the tower house with a cross section and the floor plans.

in the re-entrant angle above the first floor and topped with an oversail from the south-wing roof. The corbelling, eleven members deep, is of several different designs. The top storey has conically capped angle turrets.

The entrance is in the re-entrant angle, at the foot of the stair wing. The basement is vaulted. The main-wing stair rises to the first floor, after which ascent is by the turret stair in the south wing. The usual arrangements would then originally have applied, although the house has since been much altered internally. The defensive arrangements provided shot-holes of four different types, giving a wide range of fire-angles. Long in a picturesquely but hazardously forgotten state, it has lately been repaired.

Fourmerkland Tower

Fourmerkland Tower, five miles west of Dumfries, was built in 1590 as a simple oblong of red rubble, rising to three storeys and an attic, each floor having only a single room. It is similar in design to nearby Isle Tower, familiar to Burns. Fourmerkland lands belonged to the Abbey of Holywood, but on the Reformation came to the Maxwells, whose arms are on a panel over the doorway. It has conically capped angle-turrets corbelled out on the north-west and north-east corners. The door, in the south front, carries as well as the date and the initials R.M. for the builder Robert Maxwell, and his wife, I.C. The turnpike stair is in the south-west angle, and rises the full height of the building. There is a vaulted basement kitchen. The well-lit Hall is on the first floor. The large window on the first floor is of a later date, as are the roof dormer and the upper courses of the turret masonry.

In 1720 the tower was bought by Robert Fergusson, who also acquired the similar nearby tower of Isle a little later.

Fourmerkland was occupied until about fifty years ago, and after several decades of abandoned neglect has, happily, now been re-roofed and made wind-and-water-tight by the late Sir John H. Keswick of Portrack.

Fowlis Castle

Six miles north-west of Dundee, Fowlis Easter – as it is called to differentiate it from Fowlis Wester, a village near Crieff, and Fowlis Castle, Ross-shire – is all that remains of a powerful courtyard fortalice, the seat of the Lords Gray. This early-seventeenth-century oblong structure with a later wing attached was known as the Lady's Tower. An unusual stepped chimney-stack, housing the kitchen flue, rises up the south front, and is a striking feature.

The castle is three storeys high with an attic and a stair tower topped by a modern conical cap. The stair tower rises a storey higher than the rest. A re-sited date slab carries the year 1640. The building, once a village tavern, fell into bad repair, but is again an inhabited house.

Fowlis Easter was given by David I in 1130 to William de Maule for his part in the Battle of Sauchie. It went to de Maule's son-in-law, William de Mortimer, but in 1377 passed to Sir Alexander Gray of Broxmouth by marriage. He became the first Lord Gray of Fowlis, whose other possessions included nearby Castle Huntly and Broughty Castle. In 1669 the ninth Lord Gray sold Fowlis Easter to the Murrays of Ochtertyre.

Much of the scheming to betray Mary, Queen of Scots, and persuade English Elizabeth to execute her cousin was probably carried on by the Master of Gray at Fowlis Castle.

Freswick House

A substantial late-seventeenth-century fortified laird's house, Freswick stands on an inlet in the Caithness coast about five miles south of Duncansby Head. It was built by the Mowatt family to replace Buchally Castle, now completely ruinous, a little to the south.

An L-plan castle of four storeys, Freswick has a short wing extending south from its northern end and a central stair tower with its own gable rising in the middle of the north elevation.

A low door in the wing leads to a vaulted ground floor, though there was once probably an entrance at the foot of the stair tower. The south-east elevation faces a courtyard, closed by a sea-wall and by an eighteenth-century office range. The windows of the house were replaced in the nineteenth century with lying-panes. Inside, the house was virtually gutted earlier this century, with the reported loss of much fine panelling.

The Mowatts sold Freswick to the Sinclairs in 1661. It then remained with Sinclair owners. It stood empty for many years, but was recently acquired by a restoring purchaser.

Fyvie Castle

Fyvie Castle, on a mound beside the River Ythan near the village of Fyvie, on the Aberdeen to Banff road, goes back to the thirteenth century, when it was a royal hunting-lodge, occupied by Edward I during his invasion of 1296. Among the early Scottish kings who stayed there were William the Lion, Alexander II and Robert the Bruce, who held court in it. It was held by the Crown until 1380, when Robert III gave it to his cousin, Sir James de Lindsay, from whom it passed to his brother-in-law, Sir Henry Preston, in 1397. The remains of the original castle are thought to be included in the Preston Tower, built at the east end of the southern façade about 1395, the castle and lands having been granted to Sir Henry Preston for valour at the Battle of Otterburn.

In 1433, Fyvie passed to the Meldrum family. Sir Alexander Meldrum built the Meldrum Tower, at the west end of the southern façade, and probably the whole range of the south front.

The castle was bought in 1596 by Sir Alexander Seton, Lord Fyvie and first Earl of Dunfermline, godson of Mary, Queen of Scots, and guardian to Charles I, who spent part of his childhood at Fyvie. Seton added the double Seton towers, as well as the pinnacles, parapets and corbelling of the elaborately ornamented upper works. These front the arched entrance, a magnificent façade. The south range was also rebuilt on the north side with a crenellated parapet removed in 1898.

Sir Alexander, Chancellor of the Realm, was created first Earl of Dunfermline in 1605. His castle forms two sides of a quadrangle, the ultimate plan remaining unfinished. The fourth and last Earl was outlawed in 1690, and his land forfeited. In 1726 the castle was sold to William, second Earl of Aberdeen, who neglected it. The Honourable General Gordon, second son of the second Earl of Aberdeen, who found it 'greatly dilapidated', demolished the north and east wings, built the further matching tower on the north side named after him, and laid out the policies and lake. His son, William

Fyvie Castle: a view of the magnificent entrance in the front elevation.

Gordon, added the small crenellated porch and entrance corridor in the 1830s.

In 1889, when Sir Maurice Duff Gordon got into financial difficulties, Lord Leith, great-grandfather of the last private owner, Sir Andrew Forbes-Leith, and a distant descendant of Sir Henry Preston, acquired the castle and the estate, and commissioned John Bryce in 1890 to add the fifth tower, the Leith Tower, adjoining the Gordon Tower, and to refit the interior. The small clock tower at the back of the south front was added by Marshall Mackenzie in 1899. In 1984, with a grant from the National Heritage Memorial Fund, the National Trust for Scotland became the owners of Fyvie on behalf of the nation.

Fyvie, a palace rather than a castle, is now a huge L-shaped building, the wings being one hundred and forty-seven and one hundred and thirty feet long respectively. The towers, despite their differing periods, are remarkably similar in style if not in detailing. Singularly impressive is the magnificent high-arched entrance between the double Seton Towers, facing south. As with the other major palaces, detailed description is impossible in a survey of this scope. Internally Fyvie abounds in Jacobean and genuine Scottish baronial detail. Its magnificent main stairway is amongst the finest in Scotland. It is constructed with a series of arches between the newel and the outer wall, each successive arch being at right angles to, and several steps higher than, the preceding one. The squares so formed are vaulted to form the rest of the steps. Near the top of the wall there is an inscription naming Lord and Lady Fyvie and the date 1603. The great staircase ends at an entresol over the second floor.

The basement of the house is vaulted, with both barrel and groined vaults. Many of the upper rooms are panelled and splendidly decorated with heraldic emblems in wood, plaster and stone. The castle abounds in fine plaster ceilings, including one in what is now the morning-room by Robert Whyte, done in 1683, and on the second floor, two with ovals.

The main drawing-room, which connects with an impressive gallery housing a nineteenth-century organ, has some outstanding English replica eighteenth-century furniture in the French style – 'better than the original', as one observer commented – together with some examples of the genuine article. The gallery walls are handsomely lined with tapestries. There is a fine collection of arms and armour, purchased, like most of the contents of value, by Lord Leith.

The many interesting paintings include the largest collection of portraits by Sir Henry Raeburn outside the National Galleries of Scotland, and the only known portrait of the kilted figure – the Honourable William Gordon of Fyvie – by Pompeo Batoni, painted in Rome in 1766.

Galdenoch Castle

Seven miles north-west of Stranraer, Galdenoch Castle is a ruined L-plan structure in a valley by a burn, surrounded by a farm steading. It is built with remarkably small stones.

The castle has had three main storeys with an attic above. The ground floor is vaulted. The door is in the re-entrant angle, opening to the main stair, the wing containing which rises a storey higher and would have been topped by a watch-room. The entrance was defended by a drawbar and socket. The Hall was on the first floor and a turnpike stair, only four feet in diameter, rose from a window near the south-east angle to give access to the upper floors. The crow-stepping of the gable, which MacGibbon and Ross noted as being peculiar to Galloway, is now less entire than when they saw it a century ago.

Galdenoch Castle was built between 1547 and 1570 by Gilbert Agnew, second son of Andrew of Lochnaw, who fell at the Battle of Pinkie. The family ruined itself supporting the Covenanters, for which they were heavily fined. An unsuccessful attempt to establish salt-pans on the Galloway coast incurred further insurmountable financial losses.

Gardyne Castle

Gardyne Castle stands above the Lunan Water, a mile south-east of Friockheim, a late-sixteenth-century tower originally a short oblong in plan, but with an extension virtually doubling the length of the building. What was a circular stair tower at the eastern angle, corbelled out to provide a square watch-room approached by a small stair in a corbelled-out turret in the southern re-entrant angle, is now a feature in the middle of the south-east façade. It is protected by several shot-holes. Two corbelled and crenellated angle-turrets of unique form, with conical stone-spired roofs, each with an elaborate finial, adorn the southern and western corners.

The basement is vaulted. The Hall has an unusual moulded square window.

On the west wall there is the date 1568 and the motto SPERAVI IN TE, DOMINE which in the time of MacGibbon and Ross had a still decipherable crest of the Gardyne family on a shield. These authorities date the addition as being of 1740, but there have been other additions since, mainly by H.O. Tarbolton early this century.

In any case the eponymous Gardyne owners were perpetually fighting with their neighbours at Guthrie Castle, a Gardyne stabbing his cousin to death in 1558, and William Guthrie of that Ilk slaying Patrick Gardyne of that Ilk in 1578, an event avenged a decade later, but this time leading to Gardyne's prosecution. Even that did not stop matters, and in the end James VI exerted his authority. The Gardynes disappeared, and their castle became Lyell property, which it remained until the present century.

Garleton Castle

Garleton, or Garmylton, two miles west of Athelstaneford (believed to be the birthplace of Sir David Lyndsay of the Mount, poet-diplomat and author of the famous morality play *Ane Satyre of the Thrie Estaties*, successfully revived on several occasions in our own day at the Edinburgh International Festival of Music and Drama, and elsewhere) once consisted of three separate buildings grouped round a courtyard. The main L-shaped block, now mostly gone, stood on the east front, with two detached 'wings' projecting westwards to north and south. The north-west wing, still clinging to three of its gun-loops, was once reduced to becoming farm cottages. The house to the south-west, however, is still entire.

Oblong, two storeys and a garret high, it has crow-stepped gables and a circular stair tower projecting to the south. Reduced in height, it now has an oversailing roof. An iron grille survives on a ground-level window, as do several gun-loops.

The basement has two vaulted rooms, once linked, the eastern having a hooded fireplace the corbels for the support of which remain. The other room, the kitchen, has had a wide-arched fireplace built in, to form a later partition. The door is of later date. The original stair has gone. There is a later external forestair. The upper floors have been much altered. Sections of the curtain-wall, and of a circular tower once attached to the main house, survive.

After its initial Lindsay (the i and the y were interchangeable until the eighteenth century) ownership, Garleton passed to the Towers of Inverleith, who sold it to the then Earl of Winton, who gave it to his fourth son, the founder of the Setons of Garleton. It became part of a farm steading, a sad fate for the birthplace of the founding father of Scots drama, though it has recently been repaired.

Gight or Formartine Castle

Gight, even in MacGibbon and Ross's day 'a shapeless ruin', would not qualify for notice here except for the fact that it eventually belonged to Catherine Gordon, the mother of Lord Byron, who spent some time in it as a boy. It was once a mighty tower with the rib vaults that distinguish Craig, which it closely resembled, Towie Barclay, Delgatie and Balbegno.

Gight occupied a commanding position on the summit of the 'Braes o'Gight' above the river Ythan, three miles from Fyvie.

The plan of the ground floor of this L-plan castle survives, with the door entered at the centre of one limb. A long passage ran right through the building to the turnpike stair. From a bend in the passage a shot-hole commanded the entrance, as at Craig Castle. Only the vaulting of the ground floor survives.

The estate in which this once strong castle was built came to William Gordon, third son of the Earl of Huntly, in 1479. The present castle must have been erected early in the sixteenth century. It was in notoriously bad condition when Byron knew it, and was not for long occupied again after the death of his mother.

Gilbertfield Castle

Gilbertfield Castle stands on the north side of Dechmont Hill, a mile south of Cambuslang. An L-shaped tower house dating from 1607, it rises to three storeys and an attic. There is no parapet, but two angle turrets defend the north-west and south-east corners. It is liberally supplied with shot-holes.

The doorway in the re-entrant angle opened on a lobby and a broad turnpike stair in a square wall. The vaulted basement in the main block housed a kitchen with a large fireplace, an oven and a window seat. From the western wine-cellar a stair rises to the Hall on the first floor, on which there was also a wing room in the wing beyond the stair. The two storeys above each contained three rooms.

Gilbertfield was owned in the seventeenth century by Allan Ramsay's friend Lieutenant William Hamilton, himself a minor poet. The castle is rapidly falling into irreversible ruin, particularly unfortunate since it was an uncommonly well-planned house for its date.

Girnigoe and Sinclair: two castles, once linked, their ruins grimly surviving on a North Sea cliff top.

Girnigoe Castle

Girnigoe is a long, narrow, double courtyard castle on a high peninsular promontory jutting into the Pentland Firth three miles north of Wick, its outer court on the landward side. The newer Castle Sinclair is now reduced to a jagged but tall stump. Rocks and sea-filled clefts must once have given this extraordinary double castle strong protection.

Girnigoe, the stronghold of the Sinclairs and a name once feared in the far north, is fronted by a huge tower house straddling the rock and pierced by an entrance passage, cranked for extra security, E-shaped in plan, one wing projecting further than the other. To the west, a drawbridge over the cut-away neck of the promontory separated it from the fortified forecourt subsequently developed as Castle Sinclair.

Girnigoe's main block rises to five storeys, like the south stair-wing. Together, these may have formed a late-fifteenth-century L-plan fortalice, to which the storey higher northern wing was added. The main-block basement, containing a vaulted dungeon, is a storey less deep than that of the wing. The door was in the front of the stair-wing, protected by gun-loops. The kitchen was in the basement of the north wing, with a private stairway leading to the Hall above, which occupies the first floor of the main block. It has a fine fireplace, and a very unusual corbelled-out oriel window surmounted with the Caithness arms. There was apparently once a *bretache* for calm-water defence against attack from the sea, the corbels for which are still visible. Similar corbels survive at a higher level on the south side, where the penetrating goe, geo or fjord (according to the particular local spelling used) fingers in. A private stair in the north-east angle once led to the rooms above.

The U-shaped court of Castle Sinclair was built in 1606 to provide extra accommodation. It too was of some strength with an outer ditch and a narrow pend protected by a portcullis. Traces of an oven in what would have been its kitchen survive.

The second son of William Sinclair, third Earl of Orkney, and later first Earl of Caithness, probably built Girnigoe. Cromwell garrisoned it. Attacked and badly damaged in 1679 by Sinclair of Keiss, the whole complex was abandoned to the elements in 1690.

Glamis Castle

Glamis Castle, by the village of that name, is famous as the fictional home of Shakespeare's Macbeth – a connection Sir Walter Scott vainly tried to establish when he visited the castle – and as the undoubted girlhood home of Queen Elizabeth, the Queen Mother.

At first glance it appears to be a structure of extreme complexity, but basically this is not so. It is simply a large L-plan tower house with a later circular stair tower in the re-entrant angle, the whole subsequently being much embellished, and extended into lower L-plan wings, producing an approximately symmetrical arrangement entered at the central angle.

The first identifiable building on the site was a three-storey tower house with a jamb on its south side, probably built by the man who became the first Lord Glamis in 1445. As it stands today, the castle is largely the result of augmentations begun by Patrick, Lord Glamis, in 1606, the year in which he was elevated to the Earldom of Kinghorn, and continued after his death in 1615 by his

Glamis Castle: the main entrance with, in the foreground, the statue of Charles I.

son and grandson. The result was one of the few houses, along with Fyvie and Huntly, which can compare in imaginative breadth and elaboration of detail with their Elizabethan and Jacobean English counterparts.

The two wings ending in round towers at the east and west of the lower extensions represent two sides of a courtyard, of which the other two sides were demolished by the third Earl, partly to reduce the house in size, but mainly to re-form the house as a formal symmetrical composition with a reorientated axial approach.

The first Earl Patrick was responsible for most of the shell of the castle, with the exception of the west wing. Over the central staircase tower is inscribed the year in which the work was begun, together with the Earl's name and that of his wife, Dame Anna Murray, a daughter of the first Earl of Tullibardine.

Earl Patrick planned for growth upwards, capped by an elaborate coping of bartisans, and for lateral expansion continuing the lines of the two blocks of the original tower, thus forming the angle of the V-shaped forecourt achieved by his grandson.

His son, Earl John, removed the walls of the barmkin to make space for the west wing and the round tower at the south-east corner. He was also responsible for the massively opulent plaster ceilings in the east wing and the Great Hall, executed in 1620/1, and 'signed' with a monograph of himself and his wife, Margaret Erskine, daughter of the first Earl Mar. On the death of her husband Lady Kinghorn remarried, resulting in a reduction in the patrimony that reached the four-year-old third Earl Patrick – later also created Earl of Strathmore – and a castle that had apparently again been reduced almost to the condition of a shell.

With great deliberation he in due course set about the continuation of his grandfather's plans, keeping a fascinating record of the progress of the work, a record now preserved in the Charter Room at Glamis. He married in 1660 Helen, daughter of the Earl of Middleton, at which time at Glamis, he tells us, there was 'nothing remaining but bare walls', some of them lacking even glazing, which was supplied in 1673 by a Dundee glazier, William Anderson. Among the Earl's additions was the small chapel to the rear of the house, first consecrated in 1688, and embellished with religious ceiling panels by Jacob de Wet (or Witt), brought over from Holland to do decorative work in Holyroodhouse. A Dutch woodcarver, Jan Van Santvoort, also a protégé of Sir William Bruce, was employed. The grounds were remodelled with the new formal approach already described and in 1683, to commemorate the completion of the work, the Earl had himself painted with his family in front of a distant prospect of the apparently completed castle at the far end of a paved avenue with three gates, a feature commented on by the poet Thomas Gray when he visited Glamis in 1765. The first of these gates, the work of Alexander Crow, survives intact, but was re-erected in its present position as the South Gate when the great avenue was swept away before 1772. The so-called Gladiator Gate was assembled from the third gate about 1770, and the second and least elaborate of the gates was used to mark off the present approachway.

Earl Patrick's fountain has disappeared from the once-formal gardens, but his larger than life-sized leaden statues of James VI and Charles I, have survived out of an original set of five, as has his elaborate polyhedron sundial.

The castle remained basically unchanged throughout the eighteenth century, and the Gothicising plan, devised by John Carr, following the marriage of the ninth Earl to the heiress Mary Bowes, fortunately remained unexecuted. In the last years of that century the west wing was gutted by fire, demolished and not reinstated until around 1800, reputedly by James Wyatt, the surviving wing being altered to match, with a flat roof and crenellated parapets substituted for the picturesque crow-stepped attic gables which had previously flanked the main tower. In 1891 the southern range of the office courts was remodelled to provide family quarters in proximity to the service areas, and nine years later the outer courtyard was similarly treated. The south and mid ranges were modernised in our own day for the present Earl and Countess by Professor James Dunbar-Nasmith.

Internally, the ground floor contains servants' rooms and stores. There is a series of unvaulted rooms, stripped of plaster and filled with arms, armour and furniture dating from 1900 on the first floor, as well as the huge dining-room of the 1840s and the billiard-room of 1903.

The best rooms are on the second floor. These include the barrel-vaulted drawing-room, with its 1621 plaster work; the Malcolm Room, named after Malcolm II, who traditionally (but improbably) died there, its frieze and ceiling also of 1621; and the remarkable chapel. There is also the Royal Suite, furnished in the 1920s when the Lady Elizabeth Bowes-Lyon married the Duke of York.

Above are the Canon's Room and the Muniment Room, fire damage early in the century leading to the stripping of the remaining upper rooms, which have not been reconstructed.

The lands of Glamis have been in the same family since 1372, when Sir John Lyon married the daughter of Robert II. Famous visitors have included Gray and Scott, the engraver Thomas Slezer (though in the 1719 edition of his *Theatrum Scotiae* the building claiming to be Glamis is, in fact, Dalkeith), the traveller and diarist Thomas Pennant and the Old Chevalier (James VIII), who stayed at Glamis in January 1716 before making his briefly triumphant entry into Dundee, and who later declared that during his Continental exile he had seen no finer edifice than Glamis; an opinion doubtless endorsed by its many visitors in our own day.

Glasclune Castle

The imposing ruins of Glasclune Castle stand three miles north-west of Blairgowrie. The castle was a Blair fortalice, Z-plan in design, but with an unusually narrow central block, only the foundations of which survive. Most of the circular north-east tower has collapsed since MacGibbon and Ross sketched the castle a century or so ago.

Glenbuchat Castle

Glenbuchat (or Glenbucket) Castle stands above the confluence of the Water of Buchat and the Don. A Z-plan tower house, now an Ancient Monument, it dates from 1590.

The main east/west block has large square towers at the north-east and south-west angles. In the two re-entrant angles facing north-west, large stair turrets rise from first-floor level. They are supported, unusually, on squinches. There are square-angled turrets with crow-stepped gables at the south-east corner of the main block and south-west corner of the north tower, and circular angle-turrets at the south-east angle of the south tower and the north-east corner of the north tower. There is a courtyard.

The door is in the re-entrant angle of the south-west tower, above which is the lintel inscription NOTHING ON ARTH REMANIS BOT FAIME. JOHN GORDONE – HELEN CARNEGIE 1590. The first part of the inscription – of dubious truth – is now illegible, but was recorded by Billings.

A guardroom lies at the foot of the tower. The ground floor is vaulted, containing the usual kitchen, with a wide fireplace and a wine-cellar linked by private stair to the Hall above. The first floor was later subdivided to provide dining- and withdrawing-rooms, as well as a bedroom for the laird in the north tower. Two stairs in the turrets lead upwards to the rest of the bedroom accommodation.

The Gordon family supported the Jacobite cause, Brigadier-General Gordon of Glenbuchat having been 'out' both in 1715 and 1745, though avoiding official retribution by escaping to France, where he lived to a great age. He commanded the Farquharsons and the Gordons for Prince Charles at Culloden. Though he kept his head, his lands, however, were forfeited, and were eventually bought by the Earl of Fife.

Glenbuchat Castle: a good example of a Z-plan tower house, now in State care.

Glenkindie House

Glenkindie House, on the left bank of the Don, is a Courtyard house open to the south, with low conically roofed towers on the south-west and south-east angles. The north side of the court may have been occupied by the house built in 1595 which was destroyed in 1644. The replacement of 1785 was in turn replaced in 1900 by the work of Sydney Mitchell. The surviving symmetrical wings probably date from the early eighteenth century, when the walls were erected round the gardens. The eastern wing has a fine columned stair. There is a sundial in the east section of the garden dated 'Leith Hall, 1722' which may well represent the date of the wings as now existing.

Greenan Castle

Greenan Castle is a familiar clifftop landmark on the coast two miles south of Ayr. The builder is believed to have been John Kennedy of Baltersan, his initials and the date 1603 being visible near the doorway. It is a simple rectangle in plan, once rising to four storeys without the parapet. It had three angle rounds with shot-holes, the fourth angle being taken up by the stair-head cap-house.

A vaulted basement entered by a doorway precariously facing the edge of the cliff, a first-floor Hall, well lit and with a large fireplace, and the usual accommodation above formed its internal arrangements. It is now weathering badly, and has suffered extensive collapse since MacGibbon and Ross drew it in the 1880s.

There seems to have been an earlier castle on the site, owned by the Davidsons, who sold the land to Kennedy. On 11 May 1602 Sir Thomas Kennedy of Culzean spent his last night at Greenan, before being murdered the next day by Mure of Auchendrane.

Greenknowe Tower

The tall, L-shaped ruined tower of Greenknowe stands on a grassy knoll just over half a mile from the little town of Gordon. It was built in 1581, and has a lintel carrying the initials of Seton of Touch and Edmondstone.

The main block rises to four storeys, the wing to five. Three of the angles have corbels supporting turrets with gun-loops. The door, which still carries its iron yett, is at the front of the wing, in the bend of the L.

The kitchen, with a large arched fireplace, is in the vaulted basement, through which a hatch in the vault passes to the hall above. The hall has a wide decorated fireplace. A broad turnpike stair leads to the first floor. A small stair running up the main angle tower provides access to the upper private apartments.

Greenknowe came to the Setons through marriage to an heiress of the Gordons of that Ilk, but in the seventeenth century passed to the Pringles of Stichel, one of whom was the Covenanter Walter Pringle, whose *Memoirs* were published in Edinburgh in 1723. Greenknowe is now in State care.

Guthrie Castle

Guthrie Castle began as a square tower two miles west of Friockheim. It was probably built by Sir David Guthrie, Lord Treasurer and Lord Justice General, in 1468, and is now the main element of a late-Georgian mansion completely reconstructed and enlarged as a rambling baronial pile of pleasing outline by David Bryce in 1848. Until very recently Guthrie was still the seat of Guthrie of Guthrie, despite the centuries of feuding described under the entry on Gardyne Castle, two miles away. While the Guthries also lost their lands as a result of the troubles that feuding caused, unlike the Gardynes, the Guthries recovered theirs.

Guthrie Castle's walls, eight feet thick, contained the staircase that leads from the original entrance in the centre of the south front to the first-floor Hall. The ground floor contains two cellars. The castle rises to three storeys and an attic within the parapet walk. The cap-house, dormers, crenellated parapet and open rounds drained by cannon spouts are all a successful Bryce replacement of the plain Georgian parapets which had been substituted for the originals. To what extent they are a correct restoration is not known. Briefly threatened by development in its grounds, mercifully, Guthrie has been resold as a private house.

Gylem Castle

Gylem Castle stands on the southern extremity of the island of Kerrera, four miles or so from Oban. It consists of a square tower with a stair tower wing making it the common L-plan pattern. With its courtyard, it occupies the entire surface of a rocky plateau jutting into the sea. The main tower is four storeys high, the wing a storey higher to accommodate a corbelled-out crowstep-gabled watch-room. Machicolated projections allow for the usual dropping of defensive missiles, though some appear to be chutes for garderobes.

A vaulted passage runs through the main block to the courtyard beyond on the south, and with a vaulted cellar on the west entered off the pend. Within the court the main door is in the stair jamb on the east face of the re-entrant angle and leads to the lobby at the foot of the stair wing. The main turnpike stair ascends to all floors except the watch-room, which is reached by a small turret stair corbelled out at third-floor level on the west front. The sculptured and moulded detail is of remarkable quality for such a remote situation.

The Hall, which also contains the kitchen, is on the first floor, and has a projecting garderobe in the north-west wall and a fireplace and cupboard recess in the south-west wall, as have the rooms on the floors above. There is a handsome oriel window at third-floor level on the defensive machicolation referred to above.

When Scott's friend John Leyden visited Gylem, he noticed a stone with the date 1582 (though he mistook the 2 for a 7). This, and two other carved stones, are preserved at Dunollie House, the present seat of the MacDougals. Gylem was attacked, taken and burned, by Covenanters under David Leslie, the Brooch of Lorne, a famous Celtic MacDougal heirloom, being stolen by Campbell of Inverawe, and not recovered until the nineteenth century. Gylem itself was never restored, though it has now been consolidated.

Haggs Castle

Now surrounded by an urban extension of Glasgow, though on the edge of the extensive parkland of Pollok estate, Haggs Castle, according to the arms and inscription, was 'biggit' by 'Sir John Maxwell of Pollock Knight and D. Margaret Conyngham his wife' in 1585. It was, and still is, remarkable for the richness of its cable and chequer mouldings at the first-floor string, wallhead, dormers and doorpipe. By the middle of the nineteenth century it was being described as 'a picturesque ruin', but soon afterwards was somewhat fancifully restored by the civil engineer Alexander George Thomson. A scheme by MacGibbon and Ross to restore it to a more correct state was unfortunately not executed. It is now Glasgow's Museum of Childhood.

An L-shaped fortalice of three storeys and an attic, it had a semi-circular stair turret projecting from first-floor level in the centre of the west wall, once with a corbelled-out square cap-house, now gone. The other stair turret in the centre of the south front was replaced by Thomson as a three-storey bay.

The ground floor has three vaulted rooms, one of which was the original kitchen, with a large fireplace. The fine first-floor Hall also has an impressive stone fireplace. In the west wall, a mural chamber led to a private stair down to the wine-cellar beneath.

The walls are filled with squared gun-loops and shot-holes.

Hailes Castle: once similar to Bothwell, but with a square donjon.

Hailes Castle

Hailes Castle stands on a promontory of the River Tyne at its confluence with a tributary near the village of East Linton. Built in the thirteenth century by the Northumberland family of Graydon – it resembles in some ways the fortified hall-house of Aydon Castle, on the English Tyneside – Hailes was once of substantial dimensions. It also had similarities with Bothwell, though the donjon, jutting out on the point of the promontory, is not round but square. The walls of enceinte are almost nine feet thick and have been strengthened by towers at strategic intervals.

The east courtyard range, which probably contained the Hall, was rebuilt in the sixteenth century. The north range along the river front dates largely from the fourteenth century. A vaulted and ribbed postern stair led down to the river, though the lower section from the half-way landing was probably movable and made of timber.

Hailes was a Hepburn possession for most of its existence, and the latest work dates from the time of the Earl of Bothwell, James Hepburn, Mary, Queen of Scots' third husband. Indeed, it was here that he first brought her after 'seizing' her at Fountainbridge on 24 April 1567.

It came to the Dalrymples of Hailes in the mid-eighteenth century, but was abandoned as a residence by Sir David Dalrymple, who acquired the fine mansion of Newhailes. In 1835, Hailes was being used as a granary. It is now in State care.

Hallbar Tower

A mile north of the confluence of the Fiddler's Burn and the Clyde, Hallbar stands on a commanding hilly site. Part of it is said to date from the eleventh century, although its ten-foot-thick walls in their present form appear to date from the sixteenth.

Square, and rising to four storeys with a garret above, it has a parapet only on the east and west wallheads, carried on individual corbels reconditioned in the nineteenth century. There is a square cap-house at the south-east angle. It has a stone roof, shaped like a pyramid. The main roof of the castle is stone-flagged. The garret is vaulted, to carry the weight.

The south-wall doorway leads to the basement, and to a mural stair which rises steeply round each side of the tower as it ascends.

The first-floor Hall has its fireplace and a garderobe with a drain. The second floor rests on heavy corbels. The third floor has gone.

Hallbar, a Douglas stronghold, was acquired in 1581 by Harie Stewart of Gogar, brother of James Stewart, Earl of Arran, on whose downfall Hallbar passed to Maitland of Thirlstane and then to Lockhart of Lee. Lived in in our own day, it is not beyond restoration.

Hallforrest

Hallforrest stands a mile and a half from Kintore. It is said to have been built as a hunting lodge for King Robert the Bruce and to have been granted by him to Sir Robert de Keith, Great Marischal of

Scotland, whose descendents became Earls of Kintore. Mary, Queen of Scots visited it in 1562.

One of the very few fourteenth century keeps to come down to us, it is a plain oblong structure, once having had two vaults divided by entresol floors, and a parapet. There was probably also a stone roof supported by an upper arch.

As at Threave, the entrance seems to have lead to the first entresol floor. There was possibly a cattle door in the basement, the gunloops of which are very small. The interior has long since been ruins.

Hallgreen Castle

Situated on the southern outskirts of Inverbervie, Hallgreen is a late-sixteenth-century L-plan castle, the main part of which survives, incorporated in an early to mid-Victorian mansion. The south front is original; the east has been rebuilt. Angle-turrets, dormers, gun-loops and a buttress at the south-east angle are also original. The castle, which has a vaulted basement, had the usual arrangements of the Hall on the first floor and bedrooms above.

Hallgreen Castle is supposed to have been built by the Dunnets in 1376, but it passed to the Rait family in the fifteenth century, and it was they who must have built what remains of the sixteenth-century castle. A stone carrying the date 1687 also survives. In recent years it has been deserted and in poor condition, but its restoration is now in hand.

Hallhead Castle

Five miles north-east of Tarland, Hallhead is a tiny T-plan house of 1688, the main block having two storeys and an attic. Its frontal eastern jamb houses the stair and rises a storey higher to provide a watch-room, reached by a small semi-circular turret stair corbelled semi-circularly out in the upper half of the re-entrant angle. The crow-stepped dormers are Victorian. An outbuilding on the site of the former courtyard, which was extant in Giles's view of 1838 but has since been rebuilt, carries the date 1703. The Gordons, later Wolrige-Gordons, became its owners in the middle of the nineteenth century. It is now part of the neighbouring farm.

Harthill Castle

Harthill Castle, a Z-plan structure with a square wing and a circular tower attached to diagonally opposite angles, stands by a burn a mile east of Oyne. It preserves the remains of an arched gate-house with a watch-room corbelled square on top. This is joined to part of an enclosing wall.

The tall main block rises to four storeys and a garret. The walls, of granite rubble, have several gun-loops. There are corbelled open rounds at the angles. The entrance, through an arched moulded doorway, still has its socket for a sliding bar. A guardroom adjoins the door, with shot-holes under the loops that light it. The ground floor, containing the kitchen and two cellars, is vaulted, the kitchen and the wine-cellar each having direct stairs to the Hall above, which occupies the whole of the first floor of the main block. The kitchen fireplace contains a shot-hole. There is a dome-vaulted cellar at the foot of the round tower.

The Hall has a large fireplace with ornamental jambs, stone seats and a saltbox. A door once opened to the former parapet on the barmkin. The two towers contain bedrooms, as did the upper floors reached by turnpike stairs in the thickness of the north-east and south-west angles of the main block.

Harthill is said to have been built by Patrick Leith in 1638. His great-grandson, also Patrick, was a leader in Montrose's army, but was captured and beheaded by Middltteon in 1647 when still only 25, leaving his brother, John, to inherit. John, according to Tranter, got himself into trouble by causing a fracas at public worship. 'By God's wounds', he is alleged to have roared out, 'I'll sit beside the Provost and in no other place!' At his trial for this disturbance John stated that the Provost was 'a doittit cock and ane ass', offering violence to the Clerk of the Court. Hardly a model prisoner, among other inconveniences he managed to set the jail on fire, and was only saved from execution by Montrose gaining victory.

The last laird deliberately set fire to Harthill, after which the estate passed to the Erskines of Pittodrie. Long roofless, Harthill has recently been well restored.

Hatton Castle

Hatton Castle, a mile or so above Newtyle, commanding the pass through the Sidlaw Hills, is a roofless Z-plan fortalice built in 1575 by the fourth Lord Oliphant. The main block has three stairs, and formerly also had a garret. Square towers without turrets project to north-east and south-west. Circular stair tower rises in the north re-entrant angles so formed. There is a moulded doorway in the inner re-entrant angle of the south-west tower and an empty panel space above. Indeed, an absence of ostentation about the window frames and upper works characterise this castle. The main block contains two vaulted cellars, the eastern one the kitchen, with a very wide fireplace arch.

A broad scale-and-platt stair occupies the south-west tower and leads to the now open-topped Hall. Off it, in the north-east tower, was the laird's bedroom. Access to the upper floors, now also gone, was by two stairs, one in the tower in the north-west re-entrant angle opening off the Hall. The other is now obliterated by the stabilisation of the west gable carried out by Lord Wharncliffe in the middle of the nineteenth century.

Robert the Bruce granted the lands to Isabella Douglas, the daughter of the 'Good Sir James'. She married Walter de Oliphant, Justiciar of Scotland. In 1627, Hatton passed to Halyburton of Pitcur, and then to the son of Mackenzie of Rosehaugh. The Earl of Crawford gained it for the Covenanters in 1645. It has for many decades shared a garden with a farmhouse of the 1840s, but in 1983 it was bought by Roderick Oliphant, whose purpose is to restore the fabric of the castle as a centre for the Clan Oliphant.

Hawthornden Castle

This castle, made famous because the poet William Drummond of Hawthornden was born in it and lived there most of his life, clings to a cliff that overhangs the gorge of the River Esk just over a mile from the village of Rosslyn.

To a ruined fifteenth-century tower there is attached an L-plan seventeenth-century house. The house is of harled rubble, three storeys high and with a garret. Three splayed gun-loops defend the doorway, in the east wall next to the tower; an arrangement augmented by a further gun-loop set in a window in the tower. The door, which carries an iron knocker inscribed with the initials of Sir William Drummond and Dame Barbara Scott (whose impaled arms are to be found on a panel above), leads through a pend to a courtyard, on the north side of which the main block of the seventeenth-century house stands. Internally, it has been modernised and its original height has been increased. A Latin inscription states that Drummond, the poet, restored the house in 1638.

In 1618, Ben Jonson was a guest at Hawthornden, having walked all the way from London. The tree under which the two poets are reputed to have met still survives. 'Welcome, welcome royal Ben', the retiring scholarly host is reputed to have said , by way of greeting to his more famous poetic colleague, who is supposed to have replied: 'Thank ye, thank ye Hawthornden.' Drummond, who kept a record of his conversation with Jonson, not surprisingly found the English poet somewhat tiresome by the end of a stay of several weeks. Unfortunately, what Jonson wrote during his Scottish tour was destroyed when the poet's London home caught fire.

Drummond, blighted in love by the death of his fiancée, Mary Cunninghame of Barns, in Fife, on the eve of their wedding, became a learned recluse. 'Content with my books and the use of my eyes.' he declared, 'I learnt even from boyhood to live beneath my fortune; and, dwelling by myself as much as I can, I neither sigh for nor seek aught that is outside me.' His melodious verses, and equally melodious prose work, *A Cypress Tree*, have sustained the literary fame of one whose devotion to the Stuart cause led to his despair at the execution of Charles I, and to his own melancholy death a few months after he was compelled to sign the Covenant.

Knox is alleged to have preached from a flat stone above the gorge. Dr. Johnson came to Hawthornden a hundred and fifty years after Ben Jonson's visit. An eighteenth-century Bishop of Edinburgh, Dr William Abernethy Drummond (1720–1809), has placed on a gable a tablet commemorating the valour of an ancestor, Sir Lawrence Abernethy of Hawthornden, who apparently captured Lord Douglas five times during one hectic day in 1338, yet was himself a prisoner by sunset; a state of affairs suggesting that his ability to organise security was less notable than his valour.

The caves and passages carved out of the rock beneath the castle are claimed to have been used by the Picts as a fort, and were also reputed to have been used by Bruce during the War of Independence.

Until very recently, Drummonds continued to occupy Hawthornden. It has recently been extensively repaired for its new owner, Mrs Heinz.

Hermitage Castle

Hermitage Castle, most perfect of the medieval castles on the Scottish Border, stands four miles north of Newcastleton, in wild and remote Liddesdale. It is still one of the most impressive, and oppressive-looking, medieval ruined castles to survive in Scotland. It is said to have begun its existence as a manor house of the Dacres between 1538 and 1365, possibly built on the site of a castle that existed in 1296. Oblong in plan, it consisted of a small central court enclosed by cross-wings on the east and west, and by screen walls on the north and south sides. The south screen contained the entrance and the north a turnpike stair rising only to the first floor. All that remains of this structure is the lower part of the walls facing the courtyard.

Some time before 1388 the castle was reconstructed, a large tower covering roughly the same area as the original building having a small square projection housing, at first-floor level, two sets of portcullises. The open court of the first castle was covered in, its surviving walls, suitably reduced, becoming internal partitions. A form of the fourteenth-century small square towers were added at three corners of the main tower.

About 1400 an oblong wing, which incorporated the west entrance on the third floor, was built out from the south-west corner. As it now stood, the castle had four main storeys.

Part of the grimness of the place is conveyed by the smallness of the windows, the wide, splayed sixteenth-century gun-loops, and, above all, by the great high frowning arch that couples the east and west towers together. The strongly fashioned coursed ashlar walls still rise to four storeys. There are crow-stepped gables over a small attic in the east elevation. There was once a timber gallery, or *bretache*, dating from the 1400 additions, projecting round the whole building at third-floor level, the socket-holes to support its joists being still visible. The wallhead and its parapet were restored in the nineteenth century, and some of the masonry, including much of the north wall, was rebuilt.

The entrance is now on the south front. The original entrance

Hermitage Castle: an aerial view, showing the outline and the
strength of this Border stronghold.

was that in the south-west tower, and at first-floor level, protected
by a portcullis. It leads into a central court, which formed part of
the original structure and has dooorways leading to large unvaulted cellars. The stair rises to the first floor, but as the interior
has been partly dismantled, leaving much of the building a powerful shell, it is not really certain how access was obtained to the upper
floors. There were two rooms in the main block at first-floor level,

Hermitage Castle: the entrance, from ground level.

Hermitage Castle: the courtyard and stair.

that to the west a Hall, that to the east probably a private apartment. The north-west tower and the south-east wing are reached by a stair from the west Hall, from which a stair leads down to the kitchen, with a fireplace, an oven and a drain for slops.

Once, there was a great room on the second floor, perhaps the main Hall, though it was later divided. The rooms in the towers at second-floor level all have attached garderobes. The third-floor rooms are smaller but better lit with regular windows.

The de Saulis family first converted the Dacre manor to a castle, Sir Nicholas de Saulis being Lord of Liddesdale in the reign of Alexander II and Alexander III. Reputedly, its construction led Henry III to assemble an army for the invasion of Scotland in 1243, on the grounds that the castle would be a constant menace to England.

By all reports de Saulis was a man of singularly ill repute. Legend gives us a choice as to the manner of his death; either in a cell of Dumbarton Castle, or, even more unpleasantly, boiled in lead at the stone circle of 'Nine Staine Rig', a mile or so away from the castle, though the authority for this second choice is merely a ballad by Scott's friend John Leyden, a minor poet born at nearby Denholm village.

Sir Nicholas's descendant, Sir John, was one of the Guardians of Scotland, but Sir William, his son, went over to the English and had his lands forfeited in 1320. Bruce then gave Hermitage to Sir John Graham, whose daughter and heiress conveyed it to her husband, Sir William Douglas, curiously named 'The Flower of Chivalry'. He seized Sir Alexander Ramsay of Dalhousie while that knight was at his devotions in the church of St Mary in Hawick, incarcerating his prisoner in the cell at the north-east tower of Hermitage, and leaving him to starve to death. The fact that a trickle of grain slipped from a granary above protracted the agony for seventeen days.

In 1492 Archibald Douglas, fifth Earl of Angus, exchanged Hermitage for Bothwell, on the Clyde, with Patrick Hepburn, first Earl of Bothwell. In October 1566 the fourth Earl of Bothwell, having been badly wounded in a skirmish with the Border reiver 'Little Jock' Elliot, was paid a surprise visit on his sick bed by Mary, Queen of Scots. She had been presiding over a Royal Court at Jedburgh, but on hearing of her lover's mishap, the Queen rode twenty furious miles to Hermitage, staying two hours with Bothwell 'to his great pleasure and content' before riding back again, an astonishing feat of horsemanship that cost her a ten-day fever.

In 1587 Mary's son, James VI, granted Hermitage to Bothwell's nephew, Francis Stewart, through whom it passed to its present owners, the Buccleuch family. It is now in care as an Ancient Monument.

Hill House

On a hillside in the southern outskirts of Dunfermline, this mid-seventeenth-century three-storey ashlar-fronted L-plan house has a five-storey re-entrant tower with lettered parapet, NI DEVS AEDIFICET DOMUM. The front windows have architraves enriched with a roll and hollow moulding pattern to be found in Fife from the close of the sixteenth century. Some of the pediments are defaced, but one has a seated figure playing a harp and another the upper part of a bearded man holding a book. Between the windows to which these pediments belong is a panel with the inscription in Hebrew, 'The Lord hath chosen them that fear him'. A third pediment on the south wall of the stair tower contains the initials W.M. Other inscriptions of a religious nature were above the original entrance doorway, but have been moved to an inner wall. Above the partition where it originally stood is a scrolled panel with the date 1623.

The house has been much altered internally. It now contains several fine fireplaces removed from seventeenth-century buildings in Culross.

William Monteith of Randieford acquired the lands of Hill in 1621, obtaining a charter for them the year after he built his house. Not surprisingly, in 1640 he seems to have been an elder in the parish.

Hills Castle

Hills Castle stands near the hamlet of Lochrutton, six miles south-west of Dumfries. The original structure is a rectangular tower of four storeys with a crenellated parapet and an attic, the parapet rounded at the angles, its walkway drained by particularly realistic-looking cannon-spouts. A two-storey addition was added in 1721.

The whole building is still enclosed in its original courtyard, with a gate-house which retains its iron yett.

The door in the north front leads to a vaulted basement, and to a turnpike stair in the north-east angle. The first-floor Hall has a garderobe and several aumries. There is a similar room on the second floor. The stairway is crowned by a conical cap-house within the parapet.

Sir John Maxwell, second son of Lord Maxwell, built the original tower in the middle of the sixteenth century. He married Agnes Herries, heiress to the third Lord Herries, and in his wife's right was duly made the fourth Lord Herries. Descendants included the heir to the Maxwell barony, the Nithsdale earldom, and the owners of Traquair, Peebleshire. Hills passed by marriage to the McCullochs of Ardwall, who still own it.

Hillslap Tower

Hillslap Tower, now referred to locally by its fictional name as the prototype of the legendary Glen Dearg in Scott's novel *The Monastery*, stands three miles north-east of Galashiels, at the head of the Allen Water. Over the lintel of the door in the re-entrant angle of this once roofless and floorless tower are the initials N.C. and E.C., together with the date 1585. It is an L-plan laird's house four storeys high with a fifth storey on its wing, and has a stair turret projecting at the re-entrant angle from first-floor level. The main stair leads to the first-floor Hall, large and well lit for so simple a tower; it once must have contained a wide fireplace.

Happily, in our own day the tower has been re-roofed for reoccupation.

Hoddam Castle

When last I saw Hoddam Castle, six miles south of Lockerbie, on the River Annan, the huge neo-Tudor mansion added by William Burn in 1827 and enlarged by Wardrop and Reid in 1878 had then recently been largely demolished, and the original mainly six-teenth-century tower left standing forlorn and derelict. Some repairs have been carried out since, but the site is now a caravan park. L-shaped, the main block rises to four storeys and a corbelled

Hillslap: once roofless, now restored, a Border tower house known to Scott.

parapet, with a garret above. In the seventeenth century the stair-wing was continued upwards for a further two storeys as a tower somewhat similar to that at Pinkie House, ending in a flat roof with a parapet clasped in a crenellated turret, an open round and two conically roofed angle turrets.

The entrance is in the re-entrant angle, in the south wall of the wing. The basement in the main block has two vaulted chambers. The wall that divides them continues upwards, providing two rooms on each floor.

The turnpike stair rises to the left of the entrance passage and ascends to the second floor. A turret stair in the re-entrant angle rises upwards from there.

The third floor of the higher wing has a room over the head of the main stair, which is vaulted. The thick walls have several mural chambers.

Hoddam was a stronghold of the Maxwells, held from the late fourteenth century by successive Lords Herries. The present structure, possibly incorporating part of its predecessor, is said to have resulted in the demolition of the chapel, causing such unease to the Lord Herries who ordered this action to be taken that he built a repentance tower to appease his conscience and the wrath of the Archbishop of Glasgow.

The sixth Lord Herries sold Hoddam in 1627 to Sir Richard Murray of Cockpool, who also owned Comlongan, and whose nephew, the second Earl of Annandale, conveyed Hoddam around 1653 to David, first Earl of Southesk. The fourth Earl of Southesk in 1690 sold Hoddam to John Sharp, whose line ended in four brothers one of whom was the writer Charles Kirkpatrick Sharpe, and another, General Matthew Sharpe, Liberal MP for the Dumfries burghs from 1832 to 1841. He brought in Burn to build the now demolished mansion.

Hollows Tower

Hollows Tower, sometimes mistaken for Gilnockie – the foundations of which are still just discernible a few miles away – was nevertheless also an Armstrong stronghold, the most famous member of the clan being the freebooter Johnnie Armstrong, celebrated in balladry. It stands on a beautiful site above the River Esk two miles north of Canonbie.

A sixteenth-century oblong tower with a vaulted basement, re-roofed in recent years by a member of the Armstrong family, it has four storeys beneath the parapet and a crow-stepped gabled garret. The parapet is carried on richly detailed corbelling in three tiers, capped by a cable moulding, and has angle rounds. A stone beacon for containing warning bale fires survives on the north gable.

The door in the west wall leads to the turnpike stair, which rises in the south-west angle. The Hall has a moulded fireplace, three windows and two window seats.

Horsburgh Castle

Standing on a prominent hillock three miles below Peebles, overlooking the Tweed and, distantly, Neidpath Castle, stands the small L-shaped sixteenth-century tower of Horsburgh. It is now a shell. The lands were owned by the Horsburghs of that Ilk – for

generations sheriff-deputies of the former county of Peeblesshire –
and remained in their hands until the beginning of the twentieth
century.

The Horsburghs also built Nether Horsburgh Castle, a mile
further down river, once a vaulted three-storey oblong keep
perhaps of the early seventeenth century, but now very ruinous.

House of Schivas

Schivas is a tall L-plan sixteenth century tower house in the Ythan
valley three miles east of Methlick. The wing is offset a little to the
west, apparently to give additional protection to the entrance in the
re-entrant angle. The house, once surrounded by an original
courtyard, now has a modern one. There are four groups of shot-
holes of various shapes round the doorway. A wide circular stair
tower projects from the north front of the main block and a stair
turret rises from first-floor level in the re-entrant angle.

The vaulted basement houses the kitchen, which is linked to two
cellars by a vaulted passage. There is a modern timber re-entrant
angle turret. The circular stair tower gives turnpike access to all
floors.

There is a panelled Hall with aumries and a garderobe, as well as a
chapel recess with the religious monogram I.H.S. and a cross.

The garden contains a seventeenth-century fountain, originally
from the town house of the Earls Marischal in Aberdeen.

The lands were owned in the fourteenth century by Schivas of
that Ilk. Heiresses took the property first to Lipps, then to
Maitlands. In 1467 the lands came to George, Lord Gordon, but by
1509 they were occupied by Thomas Gray of Scheves. The Grays
were undisputed lairds by the end of the sixteenth century, and
probably built the present castle. By 1721, Schivas was owned by
the Forbes family, who made many internal alterations. By the late
nineteenth century it had become a farmhouse. Burned out in 1900,
it was subsequently restored to designs by Sydney Mitchell for
Lord Aberdeen, and later greatly embellished to designs by the
antiquarian architect J. Fenton Wyness for Lord Catto.

Houston House

Houston, to the west of the village of Uphall, was originally a tall, unturreted L-shaped house of about 1601, built by Sir John Shairp, King's Advocate. Later in the century it was extended to the north and west, making it almost a square structure. The small stair tower projecting from the original east wing was added in the early eighteenth century, most of the interior being of that date, with good panelled rooms, although the entrance porch is of early nineteenth century date. There is a vaulted basement.

It is now an hotel, the old Hall being the dining-room. Internally it is, of course, much altered. A sympathetically designed extension, which complimented rather than copied the style of the original, was added in the 1960s, and has been enlarged again since.

Hunterston Castle

Hunterston Castle, two miles south-west of Fairlie, is now engulfed by two atomic power stations and a deep-water iron-ore terminal, mostly in the hands of the Hunterston Development Corporation. The Hunters, hereditary foresters of the offshore island of Little Cumbrae – the laird is known as The Hunter – held the peninsular estate from the twelfth century until recent times, and so are one of the oldest landowning families in Scotland.

The castle, once defended by a moat, is a small red sandstone rectangular tower rising to three storeys and a garret. There is a crenellated shoulder-high square-cornered parapet. One addition is dated 1679; a later addition resulted in the building forming three sides of a courtyard.

A square stair tower was added at the time of the first extension, projecting from the west wall, to serve both the older tower and the extension.

There is a vaulted basement with a large modern doorway on the outer wall. The main entrance was at first-floor level, giving access to the Hall, which has a fireplace and a garderobe and drain. Access above is by a turnpike stair in the south-east angle. Sir Aylmer Hunter-Weston, a general in the 1914/18 War and twenty-seventh of his line, was responsible for having Sir Robert Lorimer restore the tower as chauffeur's quarters and a garage, the latter in the ground floor! The tower was abandoned as a family seat in the late eighteenth century in favour of the nearby rather ugly Victorian-ised Georgian mansion. The Hunterston Brooch, found in the grounds in 1826, is now in the Museum of Antiquiaries in Edinburgh.

Huntingtower Castle

Three miles or so from Perth, near the south bank of the River Almond, is Huntingtower, formerly Ruthven Castle. It came into existence, probably early in the fifteenth century, as a gate tower, which was later modified to form a more conventional tower house. A plain L-shaped tower with an extra storey was added later in the century by the first Lord Ruthven, though it was not joined to the original other than by a wooden bridge linking the battlements. There may have been a defensive purpose in this arrangement. The space between the two towers was filled in towards the end of the sixteenth century.

The only vaulted section is the ground floor of the original tower. The stair in the L-shaped tower rises not in the wing but in a semi-curved turret at the north-west. Entrance to the first-floor Hall was by a movable wooden stair. The parapet and angle rounds are partly roofed in, providing a passage to the rooms and the garret.

In 1582 the fourth Lord Ruthven, who had been created Earl of Gowrie, made a sad miscalculation when, along with other Protestant nobles, he kidnapped the fifteen-year-old James VI, and imprisoned him in Ruthven Castle for nearly a year, misruling the country the while. The king, on a supposed hunting trip, managed to escape, thus ending the 'Raid of Ruthven'. In 1600, however, the Gowries were lured to a house in Perth, where, under the pretence of there being another plot, the Gowrie Conspiracy, James had both the young Earl of Gowrie and his brother, the Master of Ruthven, put to death. Their lands were forfeited and their name proscribed.

The castle, renamed Huntingtower, remained royal property until Charles I bestowed it on William Murray, who became the first Earl of Dysart. He fathered Bessie Dysart, the Duke of Lauderdale's second wife and reputedly Cromwell's mistress. The Earl sold the property to the second Earl of Tullibardine, through whom it passed to the Dukes of Atholl. It is now in the care of the State.

Huntingtower: an early example of 'infill' between two towers.

The castle contains some fine painted ceilings, mural paintings and plasterwork, as well as strikingly unusual decorative beams in the Hall. Until it was rescued from rot and ruin the interior had good seventeenth-century panelling, which was not reconstructed.

Huntly (or Strathbogie) Castle

What is left of the once even more substantial Huntly Castle stands above the junction of the Rivers Deveron and Bogie, just above Huntly town. Strathbogie, the first castle on the site, was a motte-and-bailey timber structure built by the Celtic Earls of Fife. Douglas, Earl of Moray, burned it to the ground in 1452. Evidence of the earthworks, however, survives.

The Celtic lords backed the losing side during the War of Independence. Consequently, the victorious Bruce conferred the lands of Strathbogie on Sir Adam Gordon of Huntly, Berwickshire, who transferred his hereditary title to his larger estate. The

Huntly Castle: the round tower and oriel windows.

first Earl of Huntly – the son of Lord Gordon, so created in 1436 – began the second castle in 1454, an oblong keep with a large circular tower at the south-west corner, rising above an extensive courtyard of secondary buildings. This first stone keep was partially destroyed in 1594, but the basement survived to support the main section above dating from 1553. The elaborate top storey dates from 1602.

The lower storeys are of rough coursed rubble while the upper works, with three handsome oriel windows on the main block – proudly linked together by inscribed friezes – and one on the large tower, line the French-influenced imaginative decorative stonework, are of dressed freestone. There is a splendid doorway, with a huge armorial panel above, at the foot of the north-east tower, which dates from 1602, and was put up for the fifth Earl and first Marquis of Huntly. The stair leads down to four vaulted basement cellars, the one in the larger round tower being a prison to hold the enemies of the 'Cock o' the North'. The ground floor above, housing the kitchen and two cellars, together with a bedroom and garderobe in the round tower, is also vaulted.

Of the two turnpike stairs that lead up from this bedroom, one rises to the first floor, the other to the roof.

The Hall, now subdivided and minus its fireplace, must once have been an impressive room. A fireplace dated 1606, however, survives in the room above to indicate what must have been the rich Renaissance character of the interior. The round tower rises a storey higher, and has a parapet on elaborate corbelling. The roof within the walk, reached through a pentagonal cap-house, has gone.

Huntly suffered despoliation at the hands of James VI's men, on one of his forays against too-powerful recalcitrant Catholic subjects. On that occasion the Marquis, still only an Earl, retreated to the Continent. His wife was the daughter of Esme Stewart, Seigneur d'Aubigny, a descendent of John Stewart of Darnley, who became constable of the Scots Guard to Charles VII and received from that French king the chateau of Aubigny-sur-Nère, near Bourges.

Huntly was rebuilt once more, but the constancy of the Marquis to the cause of Charles I led to the destruction of the Jacobean restoration; since when, Huntly has remained a reduced and roofless ruin, though the main tower appears to have been complete when Nattes drew it in the 1790s. Huntly is now an Ancient Monument.

Inchdrewer Castle

High on raised ground three miles south-west of Banff, the main tower of Inchdrewer Castle was one-third fallen, but was rescued from total collapse by Robin de la Lanne Mirrlees, who restored it externally in 1966. It was originally a sixteenth-century L-shaped tower with a door in the re-entrant angle, over which, on a squinch arch, was a thin stair turret. An extension to T-plan was made early in the seventeenth century to the main block, a round stair tower being added and the roofline altered. An irregular parallelogram of courtyard buildings extended south-eastwards, the main tower forming the east range. The courtyard remains in ruins.

The builders of the castle were Sir Walter Ogilvie of Dunlugas and his son, who bought the estate after the Reformation. One of their successors was created Lord Banff in 1692. In 1713, a later Lord Banff was murdered in the castle, probably by thieving servants, who set the building alight to destroy the evidence. It was later rebuilt. The last Lord Banff died in 1803. The Abercrombys of Birkenbog succeeded. By the end of the nineteenth century the remains of the castle were being used for farming purposes.

Inglismaldie Castle

Originally a late-sixteenth-century L-plan fortalice doubled in size by the insertion of a long seventeenth-century wing of the same height into its re-entrant angle, Inglismaldie stands near the North Esk six miles north of Brechin. Recast as a mid-Victorian mansion by the Aberdeen architect James Matthews, it has three storeys, an attic and a garret.

Both externally and internally it was much altered by Matthews. The turrets, on elaborate label corbelling, and the matching half-turret in the centre of what is now the front of the house, previously had oversailing roofs, probably a mid-Georgian alteration. These were restored by Matthews though to Victorian rather than seventeenth-century profiles. The label design is echoed in an unusual string-course at second-floor level. The kitchen premises, to the east of the present front, were once a chapel.

Internally, the basement is vaulted. The main stair ends on the first floor, which would have been the original Hall. Some fine original carved woodwork survives, although most is Matthews's work.

The Livingstones got Inglismaldie in 1588 by Royal Charter. In 1635 the lands passed to Sir John Carnegie, first Earl of Ethie, who later changed his name to Earl of Northesk and Baron Rosehill and Inglismaldie. In 1693, David Falconer bought the property. By his cousin's death he became fifteenth Lord Falconer of Halkerton. His sister married Joseph Home of Ninewells, and became the mother of the philosopher, David Hume. In 1778, the eighth Lord Falconer became the fifth Earl of Kintore. In 1925, Inglismaldie was bought by Major Adrian Keith-Falconer. Since 1960 it has been in the hands of the Ogilvie family.

Innerpeffray

Four miles south-east of Crieff, near Innerpeffray Library, above a bend in the River Earn, stands ruined Innerpeffray Castle. An L-plan tower of coursed rubble with a square stair tower in the re-entrant angle, it is still almost complete to the level of the wallhead. The gables are crow-stepped and although unturreted it has a memorable profile thanks to its huge gable and wallhead stacks. The entrance in the stair tower is protected by gun-loops. There is a porter's bench in the entrance lobby and a vaulted basement beneath. The kitchen in the wing has a large arched fireplace which incorporates an oven. There is a service stair from the laird's wine-cellar to the Hall above.

The turnpike main stair leads to all floors. The Hall, lit by windows on three sides, must have been an impressive room. Next to it is a withdrawing-room with garderobe and aumry, and there was once also a bedroom on this level in the wing. It was once Church property. The powerful local Drummond family provided the Commendator at the Reformation, the lands being settled on the baby son of the second Lord Drummond. In 1609, the son become Lord Madderty and built this his castle almost at once. The third Lord Madderty made a bequest to, and endowed, the famous Innerpeffray Library which, among other treasures, possesses Montrose's pocket Bible.

Innes House

Innes House was built originally between 1640 and 1653, when it was an L-plan fortalice with a tall square stair tower in the re-entrant angle. From the beginning, no expense seems to have been spared in its construction, as the laird's account book shows. The architect, William Aytoun, was responsible for the completion of Heriot's Hospital, Edinburgh. There are similarities, for instance, in the pediments of the windows and in other ornamental detail.

There are similarities, too, between Innes and Leslie Castle, both in the general plan and in the design of the chimneys; examples of Renaissance feeling making an early appearance in the north.

Internally, the original arrangement was also normal; the Hall and withdrawing-room on the first floor, a private stair down to the wine-cellar, and the bedrooms above. There have been so many later additions and alterations in later years, however, that the castle now wears the fashion of a younger age than its original con-struction justifies.

It was the seat of the Innes family from its building until the twenty-fifth chief (who became Duke of Roxburghe in 1805) sold it to the second Earl of Fife in 1767. The lands had been with the Innes family from 1160. James III visited an earlier castle in the grounds. One Innes chief was beheaded, one murdered, one put to the horn and another was a distinguished Covenanter. It was he, the twentieth chief, made a Baronet in 1625, who probably built the present house. He was amongst those who welcomed Charles II back to Scotland in 1650.

Inverkip Castle

Situated above the Clyde in the grounds of the house of Ardgowan, which replaced it as the family residence, Inverkip is a square tower of the late fifteenth century which once had three storeys and a garret, but is now roofless and floorless. It has a crenellated parapet on chequered double individual corbels, and open rounds on three corners, the cap-house no doubt occupying the fourth. The original main doorway was at first-floor level, reached by removable wooden stairs, though these were replaced at some stage by a later stone forestair. Enclosed in the platform of this is an entrance to the vaulted basement.

The illegitimate Sir John Stewart got the lands in 1390 from Robert III, his father. His descendants, the Shaw-Stewarts, still have the property. The tower was abandoned when the mansion by Hugh Cairness, an ex-assistant of Robert Adam, was built early in the nineteenth century. A previous castle on the site was garrisoned briefly by the English during the War of Independence.

Invermark Castle

This is a plain oblong tower at the east end of Loch Lee, mountainously situated near the head of Glen Esk and once guarding several hilly passes. In the sixteenth century the castle was of three storeys with a corbelled parapet and parapet walk. Another storey and a garret, together with a two-storey angle-tower, were added early in the seventeenth century. The walling has rounded corners. An interesting feature is the two massive chimney-stacks in which window openings give light to the garret storey.

The entrance is at first-floor level, reachable by movable timber stair or bridge. It has an iron yett. This entrance led to the Hall, attached to which is a small room. From the Hall, a private wheel stair – the only access – led to the vaulted basement below. The upper floors were also subdivided, perhaps when the addition was put on. They were reached by a now non-existent turnpike stair rising in a corner of the Hall.

Invermark was an outpost for the Lindsays of Crawford, to keep Highland marauders under control. The ninth Earl of Crawford died in it in 1558.

Invermay Tower

Invermay stands in the grounds of the tall Georgian house of the same name, three miles from Dunning, where the River May joins the Earn. An L-plan house of the late sixteenth century, its main block rises to three storeys and has a square stair tower at one end corbelled above second-floor level to house a small watch-room. This is reached by a diminutive turnpike stair carried in an equally diminutive semi-turret. There is a semi-circular tower on the opposite front dated 1633 and a later two-storey extension west of the main tower.

The house was owned by the Belshes of Invermay. Though no longer occupied, it is maintained in good condition.

A waterfall on the May is known as the 'Hubble-Bubble' because of the sound made by its gushing. The minor Scots poet David Mallet, or Malloch, wrote a song about it, 'The Birks of Invermay'.

Inverquharity Castle

Inverquharity Castle stands by the Carity Burn four miles east of Kirriemuir. It was originally an L-plan fortalice of the fifteenth century, but unfortunately the wing was pulled down in the late eighteenth century (or a little later) to provide materials for the nearby farmhouse of Inverquharity. Some fifteen years ago, when the castle was restored and reoccupied by Mr and Mrs A.C. Grant, the demolished wing was rebuilt with a pitched roof and dormer heads in seventeenth-century style to designs by W. Murray Jack. The main jamb that survived, however, remained intact, rising to four storeys with a parapet and stone-flagged parapet walk, drained by cannon-spouts, within which is an attic storey. This, alas, lost its original roof of scissors trusses just a year or two before the restoration. There are three open rounds on the angles.

The turnpike stair is in the re-entrant angle with the rebuilt wing. Next to it, the entrance has a pointed arch and above it, at parapet level, a device for dropping missiles. It also has an iron yett. These required a licence from the king, and exceptionally, this one, granted by James II, has survived. Dated 1444, it allows 'Al.Ogilvy of Invercarity' – the second baron – 'to fortalice his house and put an iron yett therein'.

Basement and first floor are vaulted. The lower vault has a timber entresol, entire when MacGibbon and Ross saw it, but lost earlier this century and replaced in the recent restoration. According to them the 'lower room was probably used for sheltering cattle in at night when any apprehension of a visit from lawless Highland neighbours was anticipated. The herds and servants usually found their accommodation in the loft in the vault', both levels being poorly lit by slits in deeply splayed arched recesses.

The vaulted Hall also showed a concern for security, access being by mural turnpike stair continued round a corner of the castle by a narrow dog-leg stair in the thickness of the wall before reaching the doorway. No one is sure of the purpose of the stone porch which projects into the Hall. Within it, there are a few steps leading only to a window. Above are the usual bedrooms.

Sir John Ogilvy acquired Inverquharity in 1420. A descendant, Alexander, was executed in Glasgow in 1626 after being captured at Philiphaugh fighting for Montrose. Another, Captain Ogilvy, fought for James VII right through to the Battle of the Boyne, and wrote the well-known song 'It was a' for our rightful King'. The family received a Nova Scotia baronetcy in 1626. The fifth baron sold the estate towards the end of the eighteenth century.

Isle of Whithorn Castle

This castle overlooks Isle of Whithorn's harbour, by the Drum-mullin Burn. It is a small L-shaped fortified dwelling of three storeys and a garret, and indeed one of the last to be put up in Scotland. It has a substantial rounded stair tower in the re-entrant angle, probably an eighteenth-century replacement. A modern porch covers the original entrance in the stair tower. The basement of the main block is barrel-vaulted. The first floor has two rooms, now with eighteenth-century decoration and an eighteenth-century fireplace. A single-storey nineteenth-century range at the rear carries a panel dated 1674, with the initials of Patrick Houston and Margaret Gordon, his wife. Two turrets crown the western angles, to cover any hostile approach from the sea.

During the 1820s, the building was occupied by Sir John Reid, Superintendent of Customs, at a time when smuggling was rife. Alterations were made by Sir John. The castle is in good condition and still occupied.

Isle Tower

Isle Tower, about five miles north-west of Dumfries, originally stood on an island of the River Nith. It adjoins Ellisland, once farmed by Burns. Isle was built in 1587 for John Fergusson and is an oblong structure of three storeys and an attic with a single room on each floor. His initials and those of his wife are inscribed over the doorway. It is now joined to a later house. The ground floor is vaulted. The turnpike stair is in the south-east angle, projecting inwards. The Hall has three windows, fireplace, garderobe and several mural cupboards. Arrangements above are similar. There are tiny rooms in the turrets; good examples, as at Spedlins, of what W. Mackay Mackenzie[1] believed to be a stage in the evolution of the open round to the roof turret furnished with windows.

Jerviswood House

Jerviswood stands in a good defensive position a mile north-east of Lanark, above the Mouse Water. Originally an L-shaped tower house, its two wings standing at right angles to each other, it has been extended eastwards.

It rises to three storeys and a garret beneath a steeply pitched roof. An older building has apparently been incorporated, in accordance with later seventeenth-century fashion. There are now no turrets or stair towers. The basement is not vaulted. The main rooms in the west wing were the kitchen, on the ground floor, with its fireplace and oven, and the dining-room on the floor above. The connecting staircase rises in straight half-flights to the second floor, and then continues round a newel. Although the interior was greatly altered when the building was used to provide accommodation for farm workers, several well detailed original fireplaces survive as well as an original shutter, found in a blocked-up window, and a panelled door opening from the first floor of the north wing on to the stair well. During the 1970s Jerviswood found a restoring purchaser.

The Baillies, descendants of the Baliol family, bought Jerviswood from ths Livingstones in 1636. The original tower would thus be Livingstone work, the additional extension probably that of George Bailllie, an Edinburgh merchant, who married Margaret Johnstone and had a large family, one of whom, Robert Baillie, the Covenanter, was hanged, drawn and quartered in 1684 for his faith, portions of his corpse being put on public view at Edinburgh, Jedburgh, Lanark, Ayr and Glasgow.

His son, also George, married Lady Grizel Home, daughter of the first Earl of Marchmont. She kept her father alive by secretly bringing him food through the crypt under Polwarth Church, where he was hiding from the government troops, until he managed to escape to the Netherlands. On the accession of William

[1] W. MacKay Mackenzie: *The Mediaeval Castle in Scotland*, Edinburgh, 1927

of Orange, Baillie returned to Jerviswood (though he lived latterly
at Mellerstain, near Haddington, to which Baillie's sixth descendant succeeded as the tenth Earl of Haddington in 1858), becoming
a Lord of the Admiralty and a Lord of the Treasury. Lady Grizel
wrote the beautiful song 'O werena my hert licht I wad die.'

Johnstone Castle

Johnstone Castle, now in the middle of a housing scheme in the
town of Johnstone, is an L-shaped fortalice of the fifteenth century
originally called Easter Cochrane and put up by the Cochranes,
later the Lords Dundonald. The Hunters of Johnstone bought it in
1733, renamed it, extended it and 'Gothicised' the original. By
1830, it had become a huge rambling Gothic mansion, but after the
Second World War it was reduced to the original tower proportions. What remains of the castle is now used as a local authority
store.

Kames Castle

Kames Castle, on the shores of Kames Bay, by Port Bannatyne, is a
tall sixteenth-century fortalice perhaps resting on fourteenth-
century foundations, considerably restored at roof level by David
Bryce. It has four storeys and an attic with a crenellated parapet on
individual corbels, the parapet walk drained by cannon-spouts.
The original entrance was by movable wooden stairs to the first
floor, the arched ground-floor present entrance being a later
addition, though by no means a modern one. Internally, the usual
arrangements pertained. The building has been much restored and
added to. Carlyle found it 'a kind of dilapidated baronial residence'
to which a farm was attached. It is now part of a holiday house for
the Scottish Council for the Care of Spastics.

The Bannatynes of Kames had their lands in the time of
Alexander III, and were apparently Chamberlains to the Stewart
kings when Bute was a royal demesne. One seventeenth-century
Bannatyne was a Scots MP. The last of the line died in 1780. His
nephew, who took his name, was the advocate who became Lord
Kames in 1799, and a founder member of the Bannatyne Club,
which produced printed volumes dealing with Scottish history and
literature.

Keiss Castle

As was the fashion in Caithness, where attack could come from either land or sea, Keiss Castle stands on a rocky promontory eight miles north-east of Wick, and on the opposite side of Sinclair Bay to Girnigoe. A Z-plan fortalice, Keiss had round towers at the north-west and south-east angles. The former is a stair tower, corbelled out square at the top to provide a gabled watch-room. There is a circular angle-turret with shot-holes in the south-west corner.

Keiss, though now badly ruinous, had four storeys and an attic, and so was exceptionally tall, though for the period it did not have very thick walls. The whole of the north-west corner fell into the sea more than a century ago.

Keiss, of early-sixteenth-century construction, was at one time owned by the Earls of Caithness, though its final owners were the Sinclairs of Dunbeath, who replaced it with nearby Keiss House.

Keith Hall

This large and impressive building, originally called Caskieben, stands on the southern outskirts of Kemnay village. Originally, it was a Z-plan fortalice with a square tower projecting to north-east and south-west, dating from the early seventeenth century. It was bought from its Johnston builders in 1662 by Sir John Keith, third son of the Earl Marischal and later first Lord Kintore. The tower survives, largely intact, at the back or north side of the house, but in front of it is the great symmetrical mansion with ogee-roofed towers erected between 1697 and 1699, of which Caskieben is now but a part. There have been many internal refittings, the first in 1730, and additions, one before 1811 involving the construction of stables and a semicircular well-stair in the former courtyard. In 1851 David Bryce made additions, as less successfully, did an anonymous architect around 1900. Keith Hall is now the subject of a major restoration scheme by Kit Martin. It will be used as multiple residences.

Kelburn Castle

The seat of the Boyle family, Earls of Glasgow, Kelburn Castle
stands two miles south of Largs. Although the Boyles have owned
the land since the thirteenth century, the existing house is basically
a tall sixteenth-century fortalice to which a large symmetrical
mansion was added in 1700 by David, the first Earl of Glasgow.
The 1692 contract between the Earl and the mason, Thomas
Caldwell, has survived. The distinction between the two buildings,
however, remains obviously clear, since the new house lies at an
angle to the old. The original tower was described by Timothy
Pont as being ' a goodly building, well planted, having very
beautiful orchards and gardens'.

The building is an oblong block with circular towers projecting
at the north-east and south-west angles, making it a Z-plan
structure. It rises to four storeys with rough-cast walls. The north-
east tower houses the main stair, and rises a storey higher than the
main building to accommodate a small conically capped watch-
room, which is reached by its own little turnpike stair corbelled out
in the west re-entrant angle.

The original doorway with its double-arched lintel, now a
window, was in the north wall, and carries the initials of John Boyle
and Marion Craufurd with the date 1581.

The vaulted ground floor would once have contained the
kitchen. A service stair by the west tower gives access to what
would have been the original Hall. The house has been several
times modernised internally and contains much fine early-eighteenth-century interior work.

David Boyle, created Lord Boyle of Kelburn in 1699 and Earl of
Glasgow in 1703, was one of the Commissioners for the promotion
of the Union of 1707.

Kellie Castle

Kellie Castle, three miles north of St Monans, has been described by
W. Douglas Simpson as one of 'the masterpieces of Scottish
Baronial'. As it has come down to us – happily, with its
seventeenth-century exterior virtually complete and unspoiled,
even its great square domed ceiling surviving nineteenth century
dereliction – it is now roughly T-plan in shape. There is a three-

Kellie Castle: Lorimer's Fife home, which he restored.

storey main block with three large square towers, two of which make up the cross-piece of the T. The third tower is placed at the bottom of the leg. There are also two smaller stair towers which project from the north front. The main towers are five storeys high, those in the north-west and south-west having sixteenth-century angle-turrets.

The oldest part of the house seems to be the north-west tower, perhaps incorporating a previous square tower with curtain-walling forming a courtyard. The height of the tower was increased in the late sixteenth century, when the curtain-wall provided a basis for additional new outbuilding work. 1583 is the date recorded on a wall of the east tower. The main block and the large south-west tower were added, and connected to the older parts of the building, in 1606.

The ground floor is entirely vaulted. An impressive square stair rises from the main doorway at the front of the south-west tower to the first floor, where the Hall, fifty feet long by twenty feet wide, is situated. Four different turnpike stairs give access above the Hall level.

An earlier castle belonged to the Sewards, but it was the Oliphants who began the present structure, owning its lands from 1360 until 1613, when the fifth Lord Oliphant squandered his inheritance and the property was sold to Sir Thomas Erskine, later Viscount Fenton, and later still the first Earl of Kellie, a favourite of James VI, though a man tarnished with unsavoury involvement, if not actual murder, in the Gowrie Conspiracy. The third Earl was responsible for the many fine ceilings in the castle.

With his death in 1829 the title merged with that of the Earl of Mar and Kellie and the castle was abandoned.

Fortunately, in 1878, before it had decayed too far, Professor James Lorimer, the father of the architect Sir Robert Lorimer, leased Kellie as an almost roofless ruin and proceeded to restore it. He described his acquisition in these terms: 'As it now appears it is a Jacobin residence of great elegance of form and possesses special interest from the fact that no external alterations appear to have been made on it later than 1606. The western portion is flanked by two towers with turrets supported by corbels or brackets and projecting boldly from the angles. The turrets are of considerable size, and are each lighted by two windows. The eastern portion is plainer and bears the date 1573.'

Young Robert Lorimer spent much of his boyhood at Kellie and was responsible for part of the layout of the garden, as well as for the design of an ogee-roofed gazebo. In 1958, on the death of the twelfth Earl, Hew Lorimer, the sculptor son of Sir Robert, bought the castle, and in 1970 made an arrangement with the National Trust for Scotland to maintain it, he himself remaining in residence as custodian.

The Victorian novelist Mrs Oliphant used Kellie as the setting for one of her most popular stories, *Katie Stewart*.

In June 1975 Queen Elizabeth, the Queen Mother, lunched at Kellie when visiting part of Scotland's contribution to European Architectural Heritage Year.

Kelly Castle

Kelly Castle, once known as Auchterlony, stands on the right bank of the River Elliot, two miles or so south-west of Arbroath.

Probably the Elliots had some kind of a castle here. In 1714, however, Alexander Irvine of Drum bought the estate, and the

Irvines turned whatever originally existed into the present T-plan five-storey tower, making up one side of a courtyard, which has survived remarkably complete. Lower buildings, one of them attached to a circular tower with gun-loops, made up the remaining sides. Access was gained through a pend which has since been enlarged, probably in 1864.

The castle has no parapet, but a steeply pitched crow-step-gabled roof. There is a conically roofed circular turret with shot-holes corbelled out over the courtyard corner and, at the opposite corner of the same face, a rectangular turret of three storeys, two of which rise above the level of the eaves and are reached by a small turnpike stair corbelled out in the re-entrant angle created by this turret against the main building. Behind, there rises an impressive chimney-stack and the stair tower added by Sir William Bruce's right-hand man, Alexander Edward in 1699. It contains a fine oval turnpike.

The doorway is in the re-entrant angle, approached from the south-east. The ground floor is vaulted, but the upper floors lost Alexander McGill's interior of 1701–5 in 1864, when the Dundee architect James Maclaren was called in by its Maule-Ramsay owner to rescue the building from a now derelict condition. His work has been modified since.

The barony of Kelly was owned by the Moubrays, from whom it passed to a Stewart supporter of Bruce. In 1402, it came to the Ochterlonys or Auchterlonys, who altered the name of the castle. Sir William Ochterlony eventually sold it to the Irvines, who got into debt as a result of the Civil War and sold it to the third Earl of Panmure, who gave it to his son, Henry Maule, Deputy Lord Lyon King of Arms. He took part in the 1715 Jacobite Rising, led by his brother-in-law, 'Bobbing John', Earl of Mar. Maule's elder brother, James, was wounded at Sheriffmuir. Both brothers were outlawed, but escaped to the Continent. The title was attained and the estates forfeited. Henry Maule's second son eventually bought back Kelly, having been given an Irish barony. The Panmure title merged with that of the Earl of Dalhousie.

Keltie Castle

Keltie Castle lies at the northern base of the Ochil Hills, not far from Dunning. It was built in 1686, a three-storey L-plan tower, reconstructed with a widened principal jamb in 1712. It has a corbelled rectangular turret, rather like a projecting window or cupboard, with a lean-to roof. The west windows on the first floor were enlarged in 1820. The interior was remodelled about 1920. The castle is said to have been built by John Drummond, whose uncle seems to have bought the lands in 1692 from the Bonars, the landowners since 1454. The castle passed by marriage to the Earl of Airlie in 1812. After the death of the eighth countess in 1833, it was sold to Lord Rollo, and has since had several owners.

Kemnay House

Kemnay House, on the southern outskirts of the village of the same name, was originally a tall L-plan tower dating from the middle of the seventeenth century. The lands belonged to the Douglases of Glenbervie in the sixteenth century, but passed to Sir Thomas Crombie, who built this tower house. He sold it to Thomas Burnett, of the Leys family, in 1688, who put on the south-west wing with a bell gable added to the jamb. The south-east wing probably dates from the late seventeenth or early eighteenth century. In a remodelling of 1808, the house was raised from two to three storeys and piend roofed, with an unusual junction at the jamb of the old house.

The granite water-tower and the porch on the west front date from 1833, and are thought to be the work of John Smith, who largely remodelled the interior in the classical style, though the first floor in the north-west wing retains original panelling, the painted panels, depicting architectural and landscape subjects, dating from about 1780.

The original doorway was in the re-entrant angle, but has been superseded by the main porch entrance. A stair turret on corbels rises above second-floor level in the re-entrant angle. The new windows are larger than the old. The gables are plain. The first Burnett was a stauch Hanoverian. Jacobite enemies had him seized and imprisoned in the Bastille while he was passing through Paris. The Duchess of Orleans ordered his release. A later Burnett of

Kenmay became a well-known pioneer agriculturist who is credited with having introduced the turnip into Aberdeenshire.

Kenmure Castle

Built on an isolated knoll at the head of Loch Ken less than a mile south of New Galloway, Kenmure Castle was reduced in the 1950s from an impressive mansion to a mere shell by contractors; something which would not now be allowed.

The present castle dates from the sixteenth and early seventeenth centuries, with later additions. The oldest part is the long main block of three storeys and an attic, a slightly later wing extending eastwards. A square stair tower rises at the north-east angle of the main block, the upper storey offset on corbelling. There is a later semi-hexagonal stair-tower in the re-entrant angle. Kenmure has much fine ornamental stonework. The doorway at the foot of the semi-hexagonal tower carries the Gordon arms and a viscount's coronet, together with the motto DREAD GOD. Apparently dreading enemies rather more immediately, the castle's walls are defended by circular shot-holes.

Kenmure was the seat of the West March Gordons of Lochinvar. John Balliol may have been born in Kenmure, and certainly used it as a headquarters, his mother being Devorgila, daughter of Alan, Lord of Galloway. She was responsible for founding both Sweetheart Abbey and Bailliol College, Oxford. A union of the West March Gordons with those of the north-east came when the sixth descendant of Sir Adam Gordon was created first Earl of Huntly, from whom descended the first Viscount Kenmure. The Kenmures were Stewart supporters. Kenmure Castle was burned after Sir John Gordon had hosted Mary, Queen of Scots, a fate it suffered again at the hands of Cromwell. The sixth Viscount was beheaded in the Tower of London for supporting the Jacobite rising of 1715, though not before Kneller had painted his portrait in prison. His grandson bought back the lands, and had the family honours restored, in 1824. In 1847, on the extinction of the peerage, the lands passed to an heiress. Mary, Queen of Scots visited Kenmure on her fatal flight to England, with the inflamatory consequences already mentioned. Burns also visited it, afterwards setting there his Jacobite song 'Kenmure's up and awa', Willie'.

Kilchurn Castle

This picturesque ruin occupies the end of a low-lying peninsula at the head of Loch Awe, two miles or so west of Dalmally, and was once surrounded by water, the level of Loch Awe having been lowered in 1817 by the clearance of the river bed at its outflow into the Pass of Brander. It was the seat of the Campbell lairds of Glenorchy, later the Earls and Marquesses of Breadalbane. It comprises a fifteenth-century keep built by Sir Colin Campbell, the Black Knight of Rhodes, augmented by adjoining ranges in the sixteenth century and again in 1693, when additions to the north and west were added, probably to house a garrison, but now more ruinous than the keep itself.

The oblong keep, a four-storey tower house with a garret, went up before 1475, the year of Sir Colin's death. It was set at one corner of a barmkin surrounded by a curtain fall with a postern in the south sector. Sections of this wall survive.

The keep probably had a main entrance at first-floor level reached by movable staircase, access above being by a mural stair in the south-west and north-west walls. The ground floor was entered by a door near the north angle. The two lower storeys each had one room with a garderobe, the upper floors, now fallen in, being subdivided. The upper works were remodelled in the latter half of the sixteenth century by Sir Colin Campbell, sixth of Glenorchy, who added angle rounds. A turnpike stair was inserted in the south-west side in 1691.

This laird also added the 'North Chalmeris' on the north-west side of the courtyard, but these have totally disappeared. There was apparently a Laich Hall and kitchen in the south corner of the courtyard, rebuilt in 1614 to a height of two storeys, and in 1616 further buildings, including the chapel, went up on the south-east side. The cylindrical angle-towers and the two ranges of barracks were added in the 1690s when John, first Earl of Breadalbane, did much remodelling to the castle. It was he who foreclosed on the Earl of Caithness for a vast debt, an action which led to that nobleman's premature death and the marriage of his widow to the debt collector.

Kilchurn was abandoned in 1740, when the family moved to the Castle of Balloch, later Taymouth Castle. Struck by lightning in 1769, shortly before the traveller Thomas Pennant saw it, Kilchurn was unfortunately deroofed a year later, after which it deteriorated

Kilchurn Castle: the corner keep and curtain wall, as seen across Loch Awe.

rapidly. It came into State care in 1953.

Kilchurn was originally in MacGregor territory, but once the Campbells had helped to bring about the downfall of that clan, it passed to Sir Duncan Campbell of Lochow, whose son was the builder of the keep. It was garrisoned in 1715 by government troops, though Lord Breadalbane was assisting both sides, and again in 1745 by government troops, to whom the owner afterwards unsuccessfully tried to sell it.

Kilcoy Castle

Kilcoy Castle, ruinous when MacGibbon and Ross saw it but restored in the 1890s by Colonel Burton MacKenzie to designs by Alexander Ross, stands at the northern neck of the Black Isle peninsula, three miles east of Muir of Ord. It is a fine example of a Z-plan fortalice, the main block lying east/west with circular towers of different dimensions at the north-west and south-east corners, the former being the larger, housing a cellar with shot-holes in the basement and a bedroom on the first floor, the latter being a stair tower squared out on corbels to carry a gabled two-storeyed superstructure above first-floor level. Circular angle-turrets are placed at the two opposite corners. The two south-facing re-entrant angles are both filled with conically shaped stair turrets above first-floor level. Two decorative dormer windows, mullioned and transomed, set in pinnacled buttresses, are replace-ment copies, and have most unusual details.

The present doorway is in the centre of the south front, though the original entrance was in the re-entrant angle with the south-east tower.

The vaulted basement has four cellars opening off a passage. That to the east is the kitchen with the usual appurtenances, the centre cellar being the wine-cellar, with its private stair to the Hall above. All the basement rooms have shot-holes.

The first floor contains the Hall, with a private room adjoining and the north-west tower bedroom with aumry and garderobe. The Hall mantlepiece has carvings of three MacKenzie shields with mermaids playing harps, a greyhound and a rabbit at the ends. There is also the date 1679. The turret stairs provide access to the rooms above.

The lands of Kilcoy were acquired in 1618 by Alexander Mackenzie, fourth son of the eleventh Baron Kintail. This Mackenzie built the castle. His family achieved a baronetcy which, however, became extinct in 1883.

Kildrummy Castle

Kildrummy, the 'noblest of northern castles', stands in undulating ground one and a half miles south west of the village of the same name, near the river Don, in a valley that has known habitation

Kildrummy Castle: a once powerful castle of enceinte.

since Stone Age times. Though now very ruinous, it was once one of the largest and most powerful castles in Scotland.

The original castle was built by Gilbert de Moravia, Bishop of Caithness and an ancestor of the Murrays, in the reign of Alexander II. We are in the peculiar position of having a verse-journalistic account of what happened when Edward I of England attacked it in 1306, setting it on fire. The luckless defender was Sir Nigel Bruce, the Scots King's younger brother. When John Barbour, Archdeacon of Aberdeen, wrote his chronicle poem *The Brus* in 1376, the traditions of the events of seventy years before must still have been common currency. Barbour details how the castle held out, until a traitor, 'Osbourn to name', set on fire the hall, which was full of corn. The fire soon spread over the whole castle, causing the defenders to take to the walls which, says Barbour, 'at that tym' had inner as well as outer battlements. So great was the heat of the conflagration that the attacking English could not get in; but without food, the Scots survivors eventually had no choice but to surrender.

All that, suggests W. Mackay Mackenzie, indicates that the Kildrummy described by Barbour was a wooden castle within the enciente, since had the castle possesed any of the towers which adorned it in its final form, any one of them would have provided a safer retreat than the walls.

The castle was restored before 1333, when it was again besieged by the Earl of Atholl, though this time it was successfully defended by Bruce's sister, Dame Christian. It was in Royal hands from 1361 to 1368, when Robert III allowed the Wolf of Badenoch, bastard son of Sir Alexander Stewart and self-styled Earl of Mar, to retain it. Its other owners included James III's luckless master-mason and favourite, Thomas Cochrane, and the Elphinstones through 1507 to 1626, when they were compelled to return it to the Erskine Earls of Mar.

The castle in its final form resembled Bothwell, like it, suggesting the Château le Coucy, built by Alexander II's father-in-law. This Kildrummy was vaulted on all floors and therefore fireproof. The high curtain walls enclosed the enceinte flanked by six round towers at the angles and the gateway. One of these, the largest, called the Snow Tower, at the north-west corner, was 53 feet in diameter and may have been the donjon. It had a well, now filled in, at its centre. Not much more than its foundations survive.

Most of the buildings within the enceinte have been almost completely destroyed. The English-style gatehouse to the enceinte has totally gone, except for the foundations. Opposite it was the two-storey Great Hall, the walls of which are the best preserved section of the castle. To the right, at an oversailing angle, there was a chapel on the first floor, its three tall lancet windows surviving on the only remaining wall, that to the east. The towers at either end of this wall survive in part.

There is evidence that some of the renewal work after 1306 was carried out by the English, possibly by Master James of St. George, who received from Edward I the vast sum of £100 – about £20,000 today – 'more than likely', according to W. Douglas Simpson in his guide book to the castle, for services rendered in building the now vanished gatehouse.

Kildrummy was badly damaged again in 1690, when it was set on fire by Viscount Dundee. It was still able to shelter the plotting that led to the Jacobite rising of 1715. In 1731 it passed to the Gordons of Wardhouse.

After the collapse of the Jacobite cause Kildrummy was

dismantled and used as a quarry, the gatehouse, as the nearest source, being removed first, stone by stone. This damage was stopped by the beginning of the 19th century, but the ruins were not systematically maintained until they were acquired by Colonel James Ogston in 1898. He built the mansion across the ravine in 1900. In 1951 the Colonel's niece, Mrs. Yates, gave over the castle to the care of the State.

Kilhenzie Castle

Standing by a tributary of the Girvan Water a mile south of Maybole, Kilhenzie Castle is a sixteenth-century tower house of two storeys and a garret, built of rubble, with an attic and conically capped corbelled-out angle-turrets at each corner. A seventeenth-century addition to the east made it into an L-plan structure, the wing, though lower than the tower, also rising to three storeys. In the re-entrant angle a circular stair tower carries a wide turnpike stair to the top. The house was a ruin until the nineteenth century, and some modernisations have occurred in the subsequent restoration as part of a larger baronial mansion.

Kilhenzie was owned by the Baird family, but by the mid-seventeenth century had passed into the hands of the ubiquitous Kennedys.

Killochan Castle

Killochan Castle, in the valley of the Girvan Water, about three miles north-east of Girvan, is a tall L-plan tower house excellently preserved. The main block rises to five storeys with a slightly higher wing at the east end and a square stair tower in the re-entrant angle. There is a conically capped circular tower at the south-east corner which has a parapet carried on continuous corbelling. There are two ashlar angle-turrets on the west gable, and one on the north. A machicolated projection high on the stair tower guards the entrance below. All the turrets have shot-holes. There is a deeply recessed small window splayed out on both sides to let extra light into the first-floor Hall without weakening the defensive posture. Over the door at the base of the stair tower is the information: THIS WORK WAS BEGUN THE 1 MARCHE 1586 BE IHONE

CATHCART OF CARLTON AND HELENE WALLACE HIS
SPOUSE. THE NAME OF THE LORD IS ANE STRONG
TOUR AND RYTHEOUS IN THEIR TROUBLIS RINNES
UNTO IT AND FINDETH REFUGE PROVERBS 18 VERS
10. A panel above encloses the arms of the two families.

From the entrance lobby there is a wide scale-and-platt stair, rare
for the period, rising in the north wing to the first floor. Above this
level, access is by a turnpike stair in the stair tower. The vaulted
basement contained the original kitchen and two cellars. The Hall
has a private room off it in the circular tower. This room, now the
dining-room, was once the scene of a number of conventicles in
Covenanting times. A turret stair tower rises from the first floor in
the re-entrant angle between the round tower and the east wall.
There is an eighteenth-century addition of two storeys to the north.

John Cathcart, who built the castle, was a Reformer, strongly
opposed to Mary, Queen of Scots. Cathcarts occupied Killochan,
though not continuously, until 1954.

Kilmartin Castle

A Z-plan tower house of the late sixteenth century near the
Oban/Lochgilphead road, by Kilmartin Parish Church, this
ruinous fortalice has a main block lying north/south, round towers
at the north-east and north-west angles, and a smaller stair tower in
the west front. Three storeys high, and entered by a door in the west
front, it had the usual vaulted basement, first-floor Hall and
withdrawing-room and bedroom accommodation above and in the
north-east tower, the other tower containing the main stair. The
previous house was the home of that Rector Carsewell who later
became Bishop of the Isles and moved to Carnasserie. It later
became a Campbell property.

Kilnmaichlie Castle

Kilnmaichlie Castle stands in the Avon glen four miles south of
Ballindalloch, part of the estate of which it became in the eighteenth
century. Kilnmaichlie is a T-plan house, extended from an L-plan
house in the early eighteenth century as an oblong main block of
three storeys with a square stair tower, once the arm of the L,

projecting from the centre. It is gabled, rising a storey higher to give access to the attic and provide a watch-room. There is an attractive string-course to relieve the plainness of the house. An angle-turret at the south-east corner of the castle has gone.

The original entrance at the foot of the tower has also gone, as has the stair inside. In the mid-eighteenth century windows were enlarged and new entrances provided. Internally, the house is entirely altered.

The estate of Kilnmaichlie came to Alexander Stewart, Earl of Buchan, from Robert II. The Earl gave it to his bastard son, Sir Andrew Stewart, with whose descendants the castle remained until sold to Ludovic, Laird of Grant, in the eighteenth century. In the 1780s and '90s, Mrs Pennell Grant, widow of Captain Alexander Grant of Ballindalloch and grandmother of Henry Mackenzie, the friend of Burns and Scott, lived in it. Mackenzie, the author of *The Man of Feeling*, has left a picture of the place so vivid that it is worth quoting:

> Her house was formed out of the remains of an old Gothic castle, of which one tower was still almost entire; it was tenanted by kindly daws and swallows. Beneath, in a modernized part of the building, resided the mistress of the mansion. The house was skirted with a few majestic elms and beeches, and the stumps of several others shewed that they had once been more numerous. To the west, a clump of firs covered a ragged rocky dell, where the rooks claimed a prescriptive seignory. Through this a dashing rivulet forced its way, which afterwards grew quiet in its progress; and gurgling gently through a piece of downy meadow-ground, crossed the bottom of the garden, where a little rustic paling inclosed a washing green, and a wicker seat, fronting the south, was placed for the accommodation of the old lady, whose lesser tour, when her fields did not require a visit, used to terminate in this spot. Here, too, were ranged the hives for her bees, whose hum, in a still, warm sunshine, soothed the good old lady's indolence, while their proverbial industry was sometimes quoted for the instruction of her washers. The brook ran brawling through some underwood on the outside of the garden, and soon after formed a little cascade, which fell into the river that winded through a valley in front of the house.
>
> Her husband's books were in a room at the top of a screw stair-case, which had scarce been opened since his death; but her

own library for Sabbath or rainy days was ranged in a little book-press in the parlour. It consisted, as far as I can remember, of several volumes of Sermons, a Concordance, Thomas a'Kempis, Antonius's Meditations, the Works of the Author of the Whole Duty of Man, and a translation of Boethius; the original editions of the Spectator and Guardian, Cowley's Poems, Dryden's Works, Baker's Chronicle, Burnet's History of his own Times, Lamb's Royal Cookery, Abercromby's Scots Warriors, and Nisbet's Heraldry.

I could draw the old lady at this moment! – dressed in grey, with a clean white hood nicely plaited (for she was somewhat finical about the neatness of her person), sitting in her straight-backed elbow chair, which stood in a large window scooped out of the thickness of the ancient wall. The middle panes of the window were of painted glass, the story of Joseph and his brethren. On the outside waved a honeysuckle tree, which often threw its shade across her book, or her work; but she would not allow it to be cut down. 'It has stood there many a day,' said she, 'and we old inhabitants should bear with one another.'"

Kilravock Castle

Kilravock Castle, like Brodie and Cawdor occupied continuously by the founding family – in this case the Rosses – stands on a steep bank above the river Nairn seven miles south-west of the town of Nairn. In 1460, the Baron of Kilravock was licensed by the Lord of the Isles to 'fund big (build) ande upmak a toure of fens with Barmkin ande bataling upon quhat place of strynth him best likes within the Barony of Kylrawok'. What got 'upmakit' was a massive tower, five storeys high with a gabled garret, walls seven feet thick, open rounds at three of the angles of the parapet and a squared cap-house at the top of the turnpike stair in the south-west corner.

Two additions were made in the seventeenth century. A square scale-and-platt stair tower with a gabled roof was tacked on to the south-west corner. A little later, the main block was erected at right angles, producing a kind of Z with the stair tower as the link. The main block has a steeply pitched roof with dormers, a stair in a squared turret at the extreme south-west angle and a semi-circular stair turret corbelled out of the centre of the south front at first-floor level. The original entrance door is now enclosed by the

Kilravock Castle: the varied profile of a much added-to castle.

linking square stair tower, and was defended by splayed gun-loops. Later and lower buildings abut the stair tower and the original keep.

The basement of the keep is vaulted, with three cellars and a vaulted passage to the north. There are mural chambers in the thickness of the walls. The basement of the south block is also vaulted, connected by a vaulted passage.

The upper rooms run the full length of the castle, and access to individual rooms is thus by means of the two stairs.

The Ross family probably descended from the Celtic Earls of Ross, although some say they sprang from the de Ross Norman family. In 1219 a Hugo de Ross, Lord of Geddes, near Nairn, was certainly a witness to Sir John Bisset of Lovat on the charter founding Beauly Priory. His son married Bisset's heiress granddaughter and so acquired the Kilravock estate.

Mary, Queen of Scots visited Kilravock in 1562. Hugh, the sixteenth laird, played a minuet on the violin for Charles Edward Stuart two days before Culloden, but presumably the prince had other matters on his mind. The Duke of Cumberland appeared after Culloden. While doubtless he did not encourage such musical entertainment, uncharacteristically, he spared both the castle and the laird. Robert Burns paid a visit in 1787 during his Highland tour.

An interesting correspondence between Burns's friend Henry MacKenzie, author of *The Man of Feeling*, and his cousin, the laird's daughter, Elizabeth Ross of Kilravock, survives, as does her *Journal* of the 1760s.

Kininvie House

The castle of Kininvie, to which extensions were made in the eighteenth century and to which later a new house was added in 1840 to designs by William Robertson, stands in lower Glen Fiddich, three miles north of Dufftown. Although it is said to have been built in 1480, in its present form the house dates from the late sixteenth century. The L-plan fortalice comprises four storeys and a garret. There is a circular stair tower in the re-entrant angle crowned by a corbelled-out square gabled watch-room a storey higher. The doorway, beside the stair tower, is in the re-entrant angle. There are arrow slits at basement level.

The basement is vaulted, and a turnpike stair rises to all floors. The internal arrangements would have followed the traditional pattern, but have been altered to link the old house with the newer house.

The estate belonged to the Leslies, Alexander Leslie having received a charter from the third Earl of Atholl, completing the castle in 1525. The eldest daughter of the fifth Leslie of Kininvie became the mother of Archbishop Sharp, murdered on Magus Moor, near St Andrews, in 1679.

Kinkell Castle

This small castle, a mile south-east of Conon Bridge, was built as a variant of the Z-plan pattern, with a large circular tower at the south-east angle of the main block and a thin stair tower corbelled above first-floor level at the north-west corner. Constructed in 1594, the main block was extended beyond the circular tower in the seventeenth century to produce the T-plan arrangement then common in the south of Scotland.

The entrance is in the front of the now near-central stair tower, in the re-entrant angle. The tower rises to four storeys to contain a conically capped watch-room, the main block having three storeys and a garret.

The basement has two vaulted rooms in the original block, one a kitchen with fireplace and drain, with a stair to the hall above. The basement of the extension is unvaulted.

The Hall fireplace has had its decorative work defaced during the castle's empty years, or even before, when it was a farmhouse. There is a corner garderobe and, in the north-west corner turret, a turnpike stair to the private quarters. Kinkell was owned by Mackenzie of Gairloch, whose family in 1763 received a baronetcy. Long derelict, it has now been carefully restored by the sculptor Gerald Ogilvie Laing.

Kinlochaline Castle

This ruined castle occupies a striking situation at the head of Loch Aline, that finger of the Sound of Mull that reaches into the sparsely populated lands of Morvern. Of oblong plan, with the western side shorter than the eastern, its thick walls rise to four storeys with a parapet and a walk forty feet high. It seems to have been built early in the fiftcenth century, though the entrance front was altered a century later. It is approached by a forestair, and the corbelled parapet walk with open rounds has a machicolated device above the entrance for the dropping of missiles. The forestair would once have been simply a movable timber one, leading, as does its successor, to the first floor. To the right there is a mural guardroom. The Hall has an arched fireplace to the north over which, surprisingly, there is a stone panel featuring a nude woman, thus disproving the claim that the first such feature to appear in Scotland was in the Renaissance statuary decorating the Palace at Stirling Castle. From two west windows, stairs lead to vaulted cellars lit only by slits. There has apparently been a half-floor at some stage. The turnpike stair rises in the south-east angle to the parapet. There has also been a complicated arrangement of mural stairs and passages. The parapet has small window embrasures in place of the usual crenellations. The garret floor has gone.

The castle was the seat of the Macinnes Clan, vassals to the Lords of the Isles and hereditary bowmen to the chiefs of MacKinnon, in Skye. Following an unsavoury family murder of the Laird and his sons by the said Mackinnons of Skye at nearby Ardtornish, the lands were given to Maclean of Duart in 1319, and it was therefore presumably the Macleans who built the present castle, badly damaged by Montrose's Ulster Lieutenant Colkitto in 1644, and later on by Cromwell, after whose attentions it was never repaired.

Kinnaird Castle

Ten miles west of Dundee, on the Sidlaw Hills overlooking the Carse of Gowrie, is Kinnaird Castle, an oblong tower rising to four storeys and with a gabled garret above the parapet. At the south-west angle is what appears to be a stair tower, at the front of which there is an entrance reached by a stone forestair. It is not, however, a stair tower at all, but a form of buttress with small apartments inside its walls at first-, second- and third-floor levels, the top providing a watch-platform. The parapet has machicolated projections, apparently to facilitate the dropping of things on unwelcome guests seeking admittance at the arched ground floor entrance below. There is an open round at the south-eastern angle, octagonal in shape.

The ground floor is partially vaulted, the central section once having had a timber ceiling on corbels. There is a subterranean dungeon cut out of the rock, and another in the thickness of the buttress base. A stair rises to the first floor in the thickness of the wall leading to the Hall, which has two stone window seats, a mural chamber and a garderobe with a drain. A turnpike stair in the wall of the south-west corner leads to the upper floors, each room also being equipped with mural chambers and garderobes.

To the east of the tower, though free-standing, is a seventeenth-century two-storeyed building containing the kitchen, with a hatch at the gable next to the tower. A dormer window on the second floor has the initials P.T. 11 M.O. and the date 1610. The estate was bought by Sir Patrick Threipland of Fingask in 1674, so the earlier date is something of a mystery.

The Kinnaird family built a castle here in the thirteenth century. It must have been replaced by the present one, which was visited by James VI in 1716. Roofless by the mid-nineteenth century, it was restored in the 1880s, and is still inhabited.

Kinnaird's Head Castle

As its name implies, Kinnaird's Head Castle, now a lighthouse, stands on the top of Kinnaird's Head, as the Aberdeenshire coastline bends into the Moray firth. An oblong tower, it was built about 1570 by Sir Alexander Fraser of Philorth. A four-storey tower with a corbelled parapet and round bartisans at the angles and square ones in the middle of the flanks, it has been much altered to fit it for the purpose it has served since 1787, when the lamp was superimposed on its roof. There are single-storey outbuildings by Robert Stevenson dating from 1830, and a puzzling adjacent three-storey tower called the Wine tower, further down the promontory. Reduced in height, it now has three vaulted stories but, very curiously, no internal stair. MacGibbon and Ross suggest that the father of Sir Alexander (also Sir Alexander) may have begun this with a view to having a residence near Faithlie, as the hamlet which he had created into a burgh of barony in 1564 was called, later becoming Fraserburgh. Finding it too inconvenient, he abandoned it incomplete. The upper room has three carved heraldic pendants with mottoes, the Fraser arms, those of James V and the inscription THE GLORY OF THE HONORABLE IS TO FEIR GOD. This room might have been intended as the Hall, with two further storeys above it, but the richness of the pendants is perplexing in relation to so primitive a structure.

Kinnairdy Castle

Kinnairdy Castle stands above a ravine two miles south of Aberchirder, L-shaped, though the stair tower is of a later date, and having five storeys and a garret.

The original entrance was at first-floor level reached from the courtyard wall parapet walk by a removable timber bridge. A straight stair ran down to the vaulted basement. The Hall contains an oak-panelled aumry, with carving amongst the finest in Scotland showing the heads of Sir Alexander Innes, thirteenth of that Ilk, and his wife Dame Christian Dunbar, together with the date 1493. Some of the heraldic decoration in the house was introduced in post-Second-War years by its owner at that time, Sir Thomas Innes of Learney, the then Lord Lyon.

Sir Alexander Innes was, it seems, well known for his love of fine

Kinnairdy Castle: a characteristic tower house and wing profile.

Flanders panelling, a taste which got him into debt and imprisonment on the initiative of one of his creditors, the Earl of Caithness, of Girnigoe Castle. Kinnairdy was sold in 1629 to Sir James Crichton of Frendraught, who became involved in a quarrel with Sir John Innes of Crombie and Gordon of Rotheimay, who burned the Tower of Ferndraught with three people inside it.

Kinnairdy came to the Reverend John Gregory in 1647. His brother, a well-known doctor and the constructor of the first barometer (actually made at Kinnairdy) succeeded. His third son, an Oxford professor, sold Kinnairdy to an Elgin merchant, Thomas Donaldson, who, in the eighteenth century, restored and reroofed the castle, altering the upper storeys.

Kinneil House (or Palace)

Kinneil House stands on the edge of a ravine on the western outskirts of Bo'ness, its policies now a public park. The lands were bestowed on the Hamiltons by King Robert the Bruce. The building dates from three periods: the 1542-44 tower, put up for James Hamilton, second Earl of Arran and Governor of Scotland from 1542-44, and the north-eastern wing or palace, originally a separate building, begun in 1553. Around 1600, two storeys were added to the northern wing of the palace. Further alterations were made about 1677 when the Duke of Hamilton had the interior of the tower and tower-head remodelled and added four-storey pavilions to each end, thus linking the two separate parts of the house. He also added the present tower windows. Within the last few years the roofs of the central block have been restored so that all is once again externally entire. A great formal forecourt, with two flanked blocks, now also restored, completes the late-seventeenth-century composition. The tower was entered from the forecourt at ground level. It had vaulted cellarage, the unaltered western wall still showing the gun-ports. Before interior demolition, the first floor contained the Hall.

The palace, three storeys high with an attic, is built of harled rubble. Its main block is, so to say, a double house divided down the middle on each floor. The stair, in the re-entrant angle, is now enclosed by later building.

The first floor has five rooms, the north-west room having two mural chambers one of which has a curious rectangular projection on corbels. Its matching room on the north-east carries a similar projection, almost a forerunner of the oriel window.

The house fell into disrepair and in 1936 was to be demolished. Mural tempera paintings were then discovered in the two north-west wing rooms. In what is now called the Parable Room there are six cartoons with life-size figures depicting episodes from the story of the Good Samaritan, while in the Arbour room Samson and Delilah, the sacrifice of Isaac, David and Bathsheba and the temptation of St Anthony are all depicted on roundels. The vaulted ceiling has a frieze decorated with animals and birds, and scrolls carry quotations.

Kinneil occupied an important place in history when its Hamilton owner became the Regent Arran. There is a record of his obtaining from the Lord High Treasurer 'drynk silver at the laying of the grund stanes at the palice of Kynnele' in 1553. It retained its importance when its laird was James VI's favourite 'Captain Jamie' Hamilton, who became Earl of Arran and Chancellor of Scotland.

The philosopher Professor Dugald Stewart, Burns's Edinburgh friend, lived in it for a time, as also in the eighteenth century did Dr

Kinneil House: a treasury of painted murals.

Roebuck, the founder of the once famous Carron Ironworks, which survived in operation until our own day. Roebuck once had as his guest the great James Watt, the perfecter of the steam engine, whose workshop survives at the rear of the house.

Since 1975, the property has been fully in State care.

Kirkconnel House

A Maxwell stronghold, Kirkconnel House stands near the estuary of the River Nith two miles north-east of New Abbey.

The original structure was an L-plan three-storey tower with an attic above the corbelled parapet and a square corbelled cap-house, reached by a small wheel stair in the wall to the south-west of the main stair.

The original entrance is in the re entrant angle, giving access to the foot of the turnpike stair, which is contained within the north-west jamb. There is a small mural guardroom to the right and a vaulted basement lit only by cross-slits.

The Hall, on the first floor, like most of the rest of the interior, has been Georgianised.

The builder, Aylmer de Maxwell, second son of Sir Herbert Maxwell of Caerlaverock, married Janet Kirkconnell. The property remains in the hands of the descendants.

Adherents to the Catholic faith, the Maxwells do not seem to have been well off. Thus, when changing needs and fashions demanded more accommodation, they built themselves a new addition without demolishing the old. A low two-storey range (only part of which is now visible) provided the east side of the present courtyard when it was added in the seventeenth century. This wing was much altered and added to in the eighteenth century.

The Georgianising of the main block was undertaken by James Maxwell after he returned from exile on the Continent following the 'Forty-five. He also added a substantial new three-storey house at the same time. About 1800 an even larger two-storey north wing of brick was added. This part contains a fine Georgian chapel.

The old fortalice, still well profiled, is situated at the south end of this complex.

Kirkhill Castle

Kirkhill Castle stands hard by the nineteenth-century mansion which succeeded it, near Colmonell, on the River Stinchar. An L-plan tower, it rises to three storeys and a garret and has circular turrets, closed originally, corbelled out at the angles of the main block. A lintel in the south face carries the initials of Thomas Kennedy and his wife Janet, together with the date 1589. All that remains of the interior is the vaulted basement. The stair is of the scale-and-platt type.

Kirkhill was built by the son of Gilbert Kennedy, who acquired the lands after the Reformation. A descendant was Sir Thomas Kennedy of Kirkhill, Edinburgh's Lord Provost in 1680. In 1843 it was bought by a hero of Waterloo, Colonel Barton of Ballaird, who built the new mansion and abandoned the old.

Kirkhope Tower

Kirkhope Tower stands on a hillside a mile or so south-west of Ettrickbridge and seven miles from Selkirk. An oblong sixteenth-century keep, probably built soon after 1535, it has been constructed out of hill stones and is four storeys high with a garret above the parapet, which does not, however, extend to the west side, where the chimney is placed. There are rectangular turrets at the north-west and south-east angles, the latter a cap-house for the turnpike stair. The door is in the south wall, leading to the basement. The Hall on the first floor must have been approached by a removable wooden stair. Sadly, the roof has fallen in, bringing down with it the floors of the bedrooms above.

Kirkhope was once the home of the eldest sons of the Scotts of Harden, and maintains its place in balladry ('The Dowie Dens o' Yarrow') even if its physical disintegration seems unlikely to be arrested.

Kisimull Castle

There is controversy as to the date of Kisimull Castle, hereditary home of the chief of the MacNeil of Barra, which stands on an islet in Castlebay, on the south coast of Barra. It lies within a wall of enceinte shaped to fit the contours of the islet, and circled by the sea at high tide. The forty-fifth MacNeil of Barra, who restored the castle from its ruined state in recent years and himself practised as an architect in America, considered the curtain wall to date from the eleventh century. W. Mackay Mackenzie[1], however, disagrees, thinking nothing earlier than 1427. There are, of course, similar examples of very old Celtic castles at Dunstaffnage, Tioram, Mingarry and elsewhere, to lend support to the earlier date.

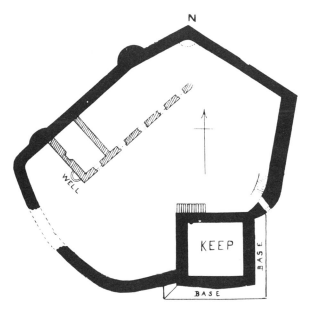

Kisimull Castle: the plan of a Celtic stronghold.

The first structures within the curtain-wall would be lean-to thatched buildings. St Ciran's Chapel was then built of stone against the north-west wall. To the north was added the semi-circular watch-tower, and is now the lesser tower of the castle. The curtain-wall was raised, and the Great Hall was added to the west. The heir's house at the western corner of the enceinte came next, and finally the Great Tower in the south-east angle, which became, and has remained, the main feature of the castle. Although it looks no older than the fourteenth century, the restoring MacNeil

[1] *op. cit.*

believed it to date from 1120. Square, five storeys high, it has a vaulted basement, a cellar with a trapdoor from a storehouse above. Above this was a room for the garrison, and on the third floor the chief's apartment, reached by a removable timber platform and an outside stair. There was also accommodation for the keeper of the castle, as well as both kitchen premises and, outside the curtain wall, accommodation apparently for the crew of Kisimull's galley.

The MacNeils claim descent from the famous Irish King Niall of the Nine Hostages in 397. The first of the family known to have settled in Scotland was Hugh Aonrachan, King of Airleach and Prince of Argyll, whose son is claimed to have begun the building of the castle in 1030.

Kisimull passed out of MacNeil hands in the nineteenth century, and lay ruinous for more than a hundred years before its present-day restoration.

Knock Castle

A small tower near the junction of the Muick Water and the Dee two miles from Ballater, Knock, built of rough coursed granite rubble, is an oblong fortalice with angled turrets on label corbelling at the two southern angles, and a gabled watch-room corbelled above the stair-head in the north-west angle. The door was to the north, within a courtyard. The turnpike stair rose to the north-west angle. The windows were well defended with shot-holes.

Even in the days of MacGibbon and Ross, Knock, a Gordon stronghold, was ruined internally. Once, however, it was important enough for the third Earl of Huntly, who fell at Flodden, to put one of his sons in command of it. In the Queen's ownership, it is now in State care.

Knockhall Castle

This L-shaped castle stands near the mouth of the River Ythan, four miles or so south-east of Ellon. Very unusually, the square stair tower projects from the flank at the junction of the main block and the wing. More or less complete to the wallhead, it has wide splayed gun-loops.

The doorway is in the re-entrant angle. On the lintel is the date

1565, although MacGibbon and Ross cite the 'raised fillet round the windows, the deviation from the traditional L-plan . . . and the character of the building generally' to suggest that Knockhall was reconstructed in the seventeenth century.

Also unusual is the placing of the kitchen in a vaulted basement at the front of the wing. This has a wide fireplace, a sink and a drain. In the basement of the main block there is another vaulted room with the same appurtenances but no fireplace, though with a hatch to the Hall above.

Knockhall waa built by a supporter of the Reformation, Henry, third Lord Sinclair of Newburgh. It was sold in 1633 to a son of Udny of that Ilk, but in 1639 captured by a band of Covenanters under the Earl of Erroll and the Earl Marischal. It was attacked a year later by a gang from Aberdeen, but not defended by Lady Udny, who was alone in the place at the time. It was accidently burned in 1734 and left a ruin with the upper floors gone. During the fire the Udny family, along with their important Charter Chest, were saved by Jamie Fleeman, 'The Laird of Udny's Fool', thought to have been the last family jester in Scotland.

Part of a courtyard wall, including a circular flanking tower, survives.

Lauriston Castle

Lauriston Castle now stands in the Edinburgh residential suburb of Davidson's Mains, gifted by its last owner, Mr and Mrs William R. Reid, to the people of Edinburgh. Though arranged as a house very much as the Reids left it, it is in fact now a museum, gracing an agreeable park by the Forth.

The original rectangular building had three storeys and an attic, with a circular stair tower to the north. A small square watch-chamber enters from the stair above the second floor. Two large pepper-pot turrets are placed at the southern angles, each containing a small room.

The ground floor retains its two original vaulted rooms. The first-floor Hall at its west end has a little hidden stair leading to a spy-hole; a convenience, no doubt, during the uncertainties of the Reformation years when Lauriston was new.

The castle was built by Sir Archibald Napier of Merchiston, father of John Napier, the inventor of logarithms. A pediment above the Renaissance-style window in the south front carries the initials of Sir Alexander, together with those of his second wife, Dame Elizabeth Moubray.

In 1656, the property was bought by Charles II's solicitor, Robert Dalgleish, who made some alterations to it. Though the original entrance, on the south front and at ground level, is now a window, it still carries the names of Robert Dalgleish and his wife Jean Douglas. In 1683 Lauriston was sold to an Edinburgh goldsmith, William Law. It became the home of John Law (1671–1729), the financier who founded the Banque Nationale de France and became Controller General of that country's entire financial system. He achieved a spectacular bankruptcy, dying in poverty in Venice, though somehow contriving to leave Lauriston to his descendants, with whom it remained until an Edinburgh banker, Tom Allan, acquired it in 1827, when substantial additions to it were made for him by William Burn. The porches were added in 1845 by W.H. Playfair for a later owner, Lord Rutherfurd. Burn's screen wall and octagon were raised a storey in 1872 to provide a library when the Crawfords of Cartsburn acquired it. An overlarge curator's house was built by E.J. Macrae once the city had acquired it.

Lauriston Castle

Lauriston Castle, near the coast, about seven miles north of Montrose, was a courtyard castle tower house of various dates fronted by a late-eighteenth-century mansion. Two sections of the castle survived, linked by a section of the barmkin which completed the courtyard. The more intact of the two was an L-shaped seventeenth-century structure, probably erected on the foundations of an earlier castle, incorporated into one end of the Georgian house. All became ruinous, the main mansion being partially demolished in the 1970s.

Lauriston belonged to the de Stivelyn or Stirling family, and then to the Straitons, who held it until 1605.

Law Castle

Standing on the 'law', or hill, above West Kilbride, this castle dates from the later part of the fifteenth century. Oblong, with four storeys beneath a parapet on a corbelled course and with four open rounds, the garret storey above has collapsed. The arched doorway on the south face at ground level is protected by two wide-splayed gun-loops.

The vaulted basement has two cellars. From that to the east a stair rises to the Hall above. The Hall on the first floor has a screened-off section with a wide fireplace which would have provided the kitchen. The second floor contains two rooms with garderobes and drains. There is a turnpike stair in the south-east angle, by the door.

The castle – also known as the Tower of Kilbride – is thought to have been built in 1468 for James II's daughter, Princess Mary, on her first marriage to the ambitious Thomas, Master of Boyd, afterwards Earl of Arran, who eventually had to flee the country. Proposals are under consideration for its restoration by Ian Begg.

Lennoxlove

Lennoxlove, near Haddington, was originally known as Lethington. It incorporates a fifteenth-century L-plan three-storey-and an-attic tower house built for the Giffords, which originally had a barmkin wall. The Maitlands bought the estate from the Giffords in the fourteenth century, and in 1626 enlarged the windows and provided an easier stairway. The original iron yett survives at the foot of the main stairway. At this time, too, the wallheads of the tower were raised and a two-storey cap-house added, blocking the parapet walk. The range, which projects to the east, contains a further two storeys. The date 1644 on the sundial on a corner of the south-east tower perhaps commemorates its building. The parapet is drained by gargoyle spouts, and has open rounds at all corners except that at which the cap-house provides a watch-room.

Further building work followed when the Duke of Lauderdale inherited Lennoxlove in 1645. Between 1673–4 a small northward extension now much altered was added to the seventeenth-century east wing by a Musselburgh mason, Patrick Wetherspoon. A Dutch joiner, Mathias Jansen, made the sash windows, amongst the earliest in Scotland. In 1676–7 a new domestic range was added to the north and west sides of the castle. Early in the nineteenth century, an upper storey was added to the seventeenth-century range, and the south-east tower was castellated by William Burn. There are two ground-floor entrances, the main entrance in the re-entrant angle rising to the first floor. It carries over the door a Latin inscription commemorating the improvements made by John Maitland in 1626. The door in the wall of the main block leads to a vaulted basement. In the wing, the vaulting is lower and was once topped by a floor with a hatch in it, providing a cell and a guardroom.

The first floor of the main block is vaulted, and possesses three orifices which, when filled in during 1912–14 restoration work by Sir Robert Lorimer, were found to contain soot. There must therefore once have been a central fireplace in the Hall floor, perhaps suggesting that the tower was originally of two storeys. The Oak room in the east range dates from Lorimer's period. The chimney-piece in the Tower Library came from Châtelhérault, the hunting lodge in the grounds of the former Hamilton Palace. The dining-room in the east range, with its columned screen, dates from the 1960s. An old kitchen is in the wing, on the same level as the Hall, where a stone wash-basin survives. A turnpike stair rises from the hall to the cap-house. The main turnpike stair rises to the third floor of the wing, level with the springing of the Hall vault. This room has a fine plaster ceiling. Over the fireplace are the arms of the first Earl Maitland and his wife, Isabel Seton, with the date 1618. There is additional domestic accommodation above.

Lethington was the home of the poet Sir Richard Maitland, in whose time it was burnt by the English; later the home of Mary, Queen of Scots's Secretary of State, William Maitland. Though the Duke of Lauderdale had his main Scottish seat at Thirlstane, he caused refurbishments to be undertaken to Lethington for the visit of the King's brother, James, Duke of Albany and York, and his wife, Mary of Modena, in 1679.

Lauderdale had no male heir, Lennoxlove was renamed by Charles II's mistress, Frances Stewart, who married the Duke of Richmond and Lennox and enabled her relative, Lord Blantyre, to acquire it by giving him the purchase money: hence presumably, the curious name 'Lennox love to Blantyre' of the old folk air adapted by Burns to match his last great love lyric, 'O wert thou in the cauld blast'.

Lord Blantyre's descendants, the Bairds, sold Lennoxlove in 1947 to the Duke of Hamilton, since when it has been that family's seat. Among the treasures it contains are the death mask of Mary, Queen of Scots; the casket purporting once to contain the forged letters which helped to bring about her end; and the patent creating the eleventh Duke Duc de Châtelhérault – a title conferred upon him by Napoleon III – as well as two cabinets once owned by Frances Stewart.

Leslie Castle

Standing on a haugh on the north bank of the Gadie, three miles south-west of Insch, Leslie Castle is one of the most interesting fortalices to be built in the north-east. Until recently ruinous, it is being generously restored by the architect David Leslie. Originally roofed in Foudland slates, it has now been re-roofed in green Westmoreland slates, thus making it unique in this respect in Aberdeenshire.

It is a stepped L-plan house of 1661, built by William Forbes, interesting in its internal planning, and with a generously proportioned stair tower in the re-entrant angle. It is also the latest known example of a fortified house of its type, albeit with details borrowed from the houses of the less defence-conscious south. It was once surrounded by a moat and wall, provided with a gate-house and drawbridge. Part of the gate-house was seen by MacGibbon and Ross, but has now gone.

There are three storeys and an attic, the stair tower reaching a storey higher. The entrance is in the re-entrant angle at the foot of the tower.

Even at this late date, it was thought necessary to defend the house with numerous shot-holes. A well-worn quoin carries the inscription FUNDED JUN 17 1661, and there are several uses of the Forbes arms.

The basement is vaulted, and contains the kitchen in the main block. This has a large fireplace, a trough for the water supply and a stone sink and drain. The east wing contains two vaulted cellars, the wine-cellar having the customary private stair to the Hall above.

There is a wide square main staircase. The Hall, in the main block, has a large fireplace bearing the arms and initials of the

Leslie Castle: an important L-plan house, before restoration.

founder. There is also a withdrawing-room and a private passage from both leading to the stair to the wine-cellar and to the garderobe. The withdrawing-room has, unusually, a vaulted strong-room with an inner safe in the north-east angle, as well as an outer door which would have been connected to the garden by means of a movable stair. The upper floors allow ample provision for bedrooms.

The upper external finishings show a departure from the old Scottish vernacular forms and a following of the English style, as at Heriot's Hospital, Edinburgh, and Winton House. The gables have flat overlapping skews instead of crow-steps, and the chimneys are groups of diagonally placed single flue-shafts, Tudor Jacobean fashion. The old form of angle-turrets at the main angles was, however, retained, albeit with fish-scale slates, as were the iron grilles over the windows.

The lands of Lesselyn were acquired in the twelfth century by Bertolf, a Fleming, whose descendants took the name of Leslie. At

Leslie Castle: restoration almost complete, one of several tower houses given new life in the late 20th century.

the beginning of the seventeenth century the last of his line married a daughter of Lord Lindores, another branch of the Leslie family. Outliving her husband, she then married John Forbes of Monymusk, who redeemed the debts on the Leslie estate. His son was the builder of the castle. William's son, John, sold Leslie to the Leiths of Leith Hall.

Lethendy Tower

Four miles south-west of Blairgowrie, flanking a Victorian Scottish Baronial mansion designed by Andrew Heiton, is the three-storeyed and garreted L-plan Lethendy Tower. The original door on the east front, now covered by a modern building, had a defensive splayed gun-loop, the Heron arms and the date 1678. Since it is unturreted it may perhaps be a late example of its type but is perhaps more likely to be a late-sixteenth- or early-seventeenth-century house modernised at that date. The interior has been completely altered. Viscount Graham of Claverhouse, Bonnie Dundee, was descended from a daughter of Heron of Lethendy.

Liberton House

Tradition has it that Provost William Little built Liberton House early in the seventeenth century, prior to abandoning Liberton Tower. Experts consider the date of the Little family's building to be 1675, the date of a dormerhead now on the wing. It has an L-plan main block of two storeys and an attic, and two slightly later single-storey and attic service wings, also L-plan, ranged round three sides of a court open to the north-east. A massive dovecot on the approach, an extensive walled garden and a small pantiled mill served by a dam, restored in 1936, still retain its seventeenth-century atmosphere.

The Hall has three tall windows on its south-east flank, though the details are mostly later restoration work. A turnpike stair leads to the first floor, the top level of the tower opening off the attic. Some of the upper rooms retain their original chimney-pieces.

Liberton Tower

A square tower, four storeys high, two of them vaulted, with a stone-flagged pitched roof, enclosing an integral parapet-walk, not supported on corbelling. Three straight stairs with windows where they turn the angle at the corners are encased in the thick walls, one leading to the vaulted basement from the first-floor Hall, the other two to the private rooms above. Entrance to the hall would have been by means of a removable wooden stair.

In 1587 an Edinburgh merchant, Provost William Little, bought the property from the Dalmahoy family, and early in the seventeenth century built himself a more comfortable 'modern' residence, which now stands across the road.

Lickleyhead Castle

Lickleyhead Castle stands by the banks of the Gadie at the foot of Ben Achie, a little south of the village of Auchleven. This handsome tower house, added to and modernised, preserves its distinctive modified L-plan exterior. The main block lies east/west and the wing juts out southwards so as to provide cover along two faces. The main block has strikingly corbelled two-storey turrets on the north front, the upper floors of which have oval windows. Such rounds are only found in houses of consequence, such as Castle Fraser, Craigievar and Glamis. In the west re-entrant, a long, narrow, semi-circular stair turret rises on heavy corbelling, and being corbelled out at the top, both provides access to a watch-room in the wing and echoes the main line of the crow-stepped gable of the wing. The castle rises to three storeys, an attic and a garret. It has crow-stepped gables and decorated pediments above the dormer windows. Though, in common with many Aberdeen area castles it has no gun-loops, it does have twelve shot-holes.

The entrance, in the main re-entrant angle to the south, gives access to a vaulted basement having kitchen and cellar lit by slit windows. The turnpike stair, reducing in width, rises to the first floor, after which the ascent is by the turret stair. The Hall is an excellent example of its kind, and the castle as a whole has been well restored.

The rebuilding of the hall fireplace produced evidence to suggest that Lickleyhead contained the nucleus of a tower older than that of the present castle, 1629 being the date engraved over the entrance. 1560 or thereabouts is Slade's suggestion for this nucleus. The estate was originally Leslie property, but in the thirteenth century George Leith sold[1] Lickleyhead to William Leith of Barn, twice Provost of Aberdeen, with whose descendants it remained until in 1625 Patrick Leith sold Lickleyhead to William Forbes of nearby Leslie. Forbes, perhaps employing John Bell of Aberdeen, is assumed to have restored what is today the main element of the present structure. In 1723, Lickleyhead was bought by Patrick Duff of Craigston. During the next forty years he and his son remodelled the interior of the tower and built a new wing at right angles to it. Further additions were made *c.*1825–30 by Henry Lumsden of Auchendoir, who bought Lickleyhead from the Ogilvie-Maitlands.

In 1645 the house was lived in by William Forbes, illegitimate son of John Forbes of Leslie. This William shot off his own hand while firing a gun, thought by some, including John Spalding the historian, to be a judgement on him for accepting 5,000 marks from the Covenanters for shooting Alexander Irvine, a supposed supporter of Montrose. After the Restoration, Forbes was tried and executed for the murder.

Linhouse House

Linhouse stands above the north bank of the Linhouse Water, three miles or so south of Midcalder. The original L-plan house, now the section to the west, was probably built by Francis Tennant, Provost of Edinburgh, in 1571, though we know from legal documents that there must have been an earlier house on the site. A second L-plan house, like its predecessor joined only by the corner of the wings, was added a century or so later, resulting in an E-plan structure.

The rubble building rises to three storeys, with the northern wing of the older section carrying an extra garret storey. The original door, in the re-entrant angle, though now a window, carries the date 1589 on the carved lintel, along with Edinburgh's motto, *Nisi Dominus Frustra*. This former door led to the vaulted basement in the north wing, and upwards to the spiral staircase crammed into a turret rising between the two wings. The contrast

[1] Leading H. Gordon Slade (*Proceedings of the Society of Antiquaries of Scotland, 1974, 75*) to suggest that either year might be that of the sale.

between this and the scale-and-platt later stair in the addition is noteworthy. There is an unvaulted kitchen in the basement of the main block. The first floor carried the Hall and a private bedroom. Above are further bedrooms, with an additional one in the north wing. The vaulted stair-head supports a parapeted look-out position reached by a stone turret on corbelling above the original entrance.

Linhouse came to the Royalist Muirheads early in the seventeenth century, and the initials of a member of the family, W.M., are to be found over the doorway of the look-out. The Muirheads sold the castle in 1767, and though it has since had several owners, it is still occupied.

Linlithgow

Linlithgow Palace qualifies for relatively brief mention in this survey in that, although not latterly a castle seriously equipped to defend itself, it once incorporated a wall of enceinte and is, in its final form, a product of the Court School; that interregnum between the building of the earlier and later tower houses to which Stirling and Falkland also bear witness.

The palace stands on a knoll projecting into the south end of the Loch of Linlithgow, and replaces older structures on the site; possibly a Roman station, and certainly a castle built by David I, occupied by England's Edward I in the winter of 1301–2 and demolished after 1313, when it was retaken by the Scots. It remained a ruin – total demolition of huge buildings was almost impossible in those days – until about 1350, when David II had it repaired. From then on it became a favourite residence of the Scottish kings.

It is designed round a courtyard. The oldest part of it is probably that within the walls of the south-west corner. The original entrance was from the east, defended with folding gates and a portcullis. There was also a drawbridge. The entrance leads under the Great Hall into the courtyard. To the left is the guardroom, with a dungeon beneath. There is a gun-loop in the attached garderobe to help defend the drawbridge.

To the right, a passage leads to a staircase descending to a lower floor, the ground at the north-east angle sloping away. There is a well-room in the north-east angle, with recesses in the wall to

Linlithgow Palace: an aerial view, showing the extensiveness of this royal dwelling by the shores of Linlithgow Loch. St Michael's Church is in the foreground.

contain the buckets, and a fireplace added later. The next room, barrel-vaulted and with a fireplace and oven, is probably the original kitchen. There is a large wine-cellar along the west side, with a shelf for the barrels, and a linked lower cellar. From there, a private stair leads to the dining-room above.

The main rooms are all on the first floor. The east side is given

Linlithgow Palace: the impressive entrance.

over to the Great Hall (or Parliament Hall, as it is sometimes called). It was a handsome timber-ceilinged room originally entered by the north end, but later by stairs in an angle-turret built, with other similar features and corridors, by James IV, when a taste for architectural symmetry was beginning to emerge.

At the north end of the Hall were the screens, a wall supporting the minstrels' gallery, and a turret stair going down to the original kitchen. When the north side was rebuilt by James IV, a large room north of the screens, however, was converted to a new kitchen.

At the south end of the Hall was the dais, a splendid Renaissance fireplace with a stone canopy supported on Gothic pillars with carved capitals and doors leading to two private rooms beyond. A narrow mural passage in the west wall provides a link to the staircase at the south end, and to the portcullis room. On the floor above, a similar passage has open apertures, turning it into a gallery from which the proceedings in the Hall below could be watched.

The south side of the courtyard has the chapel on the first floor, once richly decorated with canopied niches containing statues, mosaic work and fine glass; all, of course, now gone. On the west side of the courtyard were the King's private dining-room and drawing-room, the former with its stair to the wine-cellar already mentioned. There is another handsome fireplace in the drawing-room and stone window seats in both rooms. There is a further private drawing-room in the south-west angle. The room in the north-west angle was the royal bedroom.

In 1617 James VI came to Linlithgow and finding the north side of the quadrangle in a ruinous state, ordered it to be rebuilt. His mother, Mary, Queen of Scots had been born in a room in the north wing. The new building is dated 1619 and 1620. It is a 'double tenement', with central wall, the rooms thus lit from one side only. The basement contains six bedrooms, the first floor a banqueting hall with two large fireplaces, and adjacent further bedrooms with garderobes. The second floor contained the upper part of the Parliament Hall. The floor above that, now gone, provided further bedrooms or sitting-rooms.

The angle stair turrets continued a storey above the building, rising to the battlements, which run all round.

Space does not permit any detailing of the decorative work with which the palace was enriched in the various stages of its development. After the Union of the Crowns in 1603, the palace was left in charge of a keeper. Cromwell garrisoned it. Prince Charles captured it. Finally, the defeated Goverment General Hawley retreated there with his dragoons in 1746. The soldiers heaped up great fires to dry themselves. The caretaker, an old woman, remonstrated, though to no effect. 'General Hawley, ye're no the ainly one wha kens when to rin before fire,' she is said to have declared before leaving the palace. That night, it caught fire and its great and colourful interior was destroyed.

Various proposals have been made to reroof and restore it for use as County Courts, a Register House and other purposes. First safeguarded in the later nineteenth century by the Commissioners of Woods and Forests, it is now in care as an Ancient Monument.

Little Cumbrae Castle

Like Fairlie, Law and Skelmorlie, Little Cumbrae Castle, on the east side of the island of Little Cumbrae, was originally an oblong keep of the early fifteenth century and, with the others, intended to guard the entrance to the Clyde. It rises to three storeys and has a garret within the parapet walk, open rounds and numerous shot-holes. The parapet rests on continuous chequered corbelling.

The entrance is on the first floor, now reached by a stone forestair, but once by a removable wooden stair. At one time the only approach to the ground floor was down from the first, but a later entrance at ground-floor level was added.

There are two cellars on the ground floor. The high vaulted Hall and kitchen were both situated on the first floor, the kitchen fireplace being screened off from the Hall. They were latterly reached from the turnpike stair leading from the ground-floor door, and rising to the second floor, where the rooms above were reached by a mural corridor. Each bedroom has a garderobe, a fireplace and a window seat. The gabled garret has long since lost its roof.

Little Cumbrae Castle was in the keepership of the Hunters of Hunterston, on whose estate across the water two nuclear power stations and an iron-ore terminal are now located. In 1515, the Privy Council appointed Hew, Earl of Eglinton, as keeper following a dispute between the Crown and Hunter over the ownership of falcons. Robert Hunter, however, married the Earl's daughter, and so retrieved Little Cumbrae, keeping it until 1535, when Eglinton bought it back. It was this Earl who probably built the present structure. MacGibbon and Ross quote an entry from the burgh records of Glasgow for 1568 indicating the degree of comfort this castle could provide. 'Hew, Earl of Eglintoun, contracted with George Elphinstoun, glassin-wricht, burges of Glasgow, that the said George suld uphald and mantane the places of Ardrossan, Eglintoun, Polone, Glasgow and Cumbray in glassin worke ...' During the Cromwellian occupation of Scotland, Principal Baillie of Glasgow University found refuge 'in the Isle of Cumbrey with My Lady Montgomerey'. The sixth Earl confined Cromwell's friend Archibald Hamilton in the castle before dispatching him to Stirling to be hanged. Cromwell thereupon had Little Cumbrae sacked, since when it has been ruinous.

Littledean Castle

Unique among Scottish castles in that it is D-shaped, Littledean, two miles east of St Boswells and immediately below an old ford crossing the Tweed, includes work of two periods, both sixteenth century. The earlier section was an oblong block of four storeys and a two-storey attic, to the west of which a massive D-shaped tower was added, well provided with shot-holes, now, however, a shell. Only the west ends of the tower block survive.

The entrance to the tower – over which is a small guardroom – once had two doors, and opens into a narrow vaulted passage. On the north side, a door was broken through to give access to the vaulted storeroom in the older block. A circular stair led to the first-floor Hall, which has a large fireplace in the centre of the inner curve of the D, and a recess at either side, each with two shot-holes.

There appears to have been a barmkin attached to the tower.

Marcus Ker of Litil Dene had the lands in 1525, and perhaps built the main block. In 1550, he resigned the lands to his son and heir 'cum turre, fortalice' suggesting that the tower had been added by that date, perhaps in 1544.

On or around 1265, an earlier structure on the Littledean lands was the birthplace of the scholar Duns Scotus.

Lochhouse Tower

Lochhouse Tower stands on low-lying ground a mile south of Moffat. Rubble built, it once had three storeys and an attic, and has the basement course often found in the Dumfries area. The angles are rounded. The walls are taken in a little above second-floor level. The parapet once rested on individual corbels.

There is a vaulted basement, now partitioned. The original door is in the east front, that in the south wall being a modern addition to give access to the part of the vault now used as a store. The south section of gable remains. Lochhouse has been reroofed and completely altered internally, except for the turnpike stair in the north-east angle, which is no longer in use.

The Johnstones of Corehead, in Annandale, probably built the tower in the sixteenth century.

Lochindorb Castle: the surviving angle of an island castle of enceinte.

Lochindorb Castle

Lochindorb Castle stands on an island an acre in extent which it fully occupies, in the stretch of water of the same name, in Gaelic meaning 'lake of trouble', seven miles from Grantown-on-Spey. It is a quadrilateral enclosure forming a slightly irregular parallelogram, its walls seven feet thick and twenty feet high, with a round tower at each angle. Only one of the towers survives in reasonable condition, though all were still standing in 1793, when the first *Statistical Account of Scotland* was written. There were garderobes in the angles between the wall and two of the towers, no doubt for the use of the garrison. The castle is entered from the east, where there is a landing-place. The main arched entrance has traces of its portcullis grooves. An outer enclosing wall extended along the south and east sides.

Whatever buildings may have been within the walls extended along the south side of the courtyard and included a chapel. All is now too ruinous to be determinable as to function or date.

In the thirteenth century the castle was owned by the Comyns, Lords of Badenoch. Edward I penetrated as far north as this in 1303 and occupied Lochindorb for a month. It remained in English hands for some years, during which time it was probably extended. In Scottish hands again, it became a royal castle. It was held for Edward Baliol by the Regent Moray. In 1372, it was the stronghold of the Wolf of Badenoch, fierce son of Robert II. When Archibald Douglas became Earl of Moray, he strengthened it further. On the fall of the House of Douglas, James II ordered the Thane of Cawdor to destroy Lochindorb; which, in 1458, he did, transporting the 'iron yett' to Cawdor, where it still is.

Loch Leven Castle

Loch Leven Castle stands on an island at the west end of the loch, providing a viewpoint to Sir William Bruce's masterpiece, Kinross House, on the shore.

All that remains of Loch Leven Castle is a small early-fifteenth-century keep set into a barmkin with the north and east sides at right angles and the other two multi-angular. In the corner almost opposite is a small circular tower with gun-loops. There have been other buildings within the curtain wall, including a hall and kitchen range.

The oblong keep has five storeys, its walls of squared rubble being five feet thick. The walling has been intaken with a set-off above first-floor level, and corbelled again at the crenellated parapet – a kind of corset effect. The parapet, which has windows in it to light the top floor, has three open rounds, but in the south-east angle the stair rises. It may once have had a gabled roof.

The entrance to the courtyard is through an arched gateway near the main tower. The original entrance to the keep was by a movable staircase to the second floor above the basement, reached through a hooded arch on the east side. The Hall has a fireplace and stone window-seats.

From a screened area at the end a turnpike stair leads down to the vaulted kitchens on the first floor, and there is a trapdoor, presumably for the lowering of supplies. The kitchen has a fireplace, salt-box, sink and drained wall-closet. At basement level, and also vaulted, is another room with a trapdoor from the kitchen and now with its own modern ground-level door, which serves as the entrance to the tower.

Loch Leven Castle: a tower and barmkin known to Mary, Queen of Scots.

The room above the Hall has four windows, that to the east having been an oratory with altar-shelf and piscine, so may have been in the room in which the twenty-five year old Mary, Queen of Scots was imprisoned by the Protestant Lords on 17 June, 1567, from which she escaped on 2 May of the following year. This was not, however, her first visit. Two years before, while staying there voluntarily, she had had an interview with John Knox, presenting him with a watch as a gesture of goodwill.

The castle had been a royal residence as early as 1257, when Alexander III and his youthful queen were brought forcibly to it from Stirling. The English besieged it in 1301, until Sir John Comyn relieved it.

Not all its prisoners escaped. Archibald, Earl of Douglas, died in it in 1429, as did Patrick Graham, Archbishop of St Andrews, in 1477. The English Earl of Northumberland was confined there two years after Queen Mary's escape. He had offended Queen Elizabeth, and was eventually handed back to her for execution.

Lochnaw Castle

The story of Lochnaw Castle is a strange one. The castle is situated on a hillock by the shores of the White Loch. It replaces a medieval royal castle on an island in the loch, forcibly taken and blown up by Archibald Douglas, 'the Grim', in 1390. The Agnews of Lochnaw were appointed Constables of the Castle in 1360, and hereditary sheriffs of Wigtownshire in 1456, an office which survived until 1743.

The oldest part of the present castle is a small square tower of the sixteenth century, to which in the seventeenth century was added additional domestic accommodation to the west, making it L-plan, and to the north, making it U-plan. The north range, built in 1704, was demolished after the Agnews, by then an Australian family, bought back the original castle in 1957, the previous occupants also having demolished the neo-Tudor castle by Archibald Elliot, built on further to the west side in 1822.

The tower has four storeys and a garret, a vaulted ground floor, a turnpike stair in the north-west angle with a gabled cap-house and watch-room, a crow-stepped-gabled roof and a high machicolated parapet (curiously extended outwards to get it round the chimney-stack on the north gable) drained by cannon-spouts and open rounds at the other three angles.

Internally, the original moulded fireplaces, garderobes and aumries have survived, though only the beams of the painted ceilings on the Hall floor and the floor above are still there.

The earlier surviving addition is three storeys high with a projecting stair tower and the date 1663 on a dormer. The interior has been largely modernised.

Lochranza Castle

Standing on a small peninsula that juts into Loch Ranza, this is an L-plan castle, of complex and unusual plan, as it now stands probably of sixteenth-century construction. It is said originally to have been a hunting-lodge of the early Stewart kings. That there was an older castle on the site is attested to by both Fordun, who mentions it around 1400, and Dean Munro of the Isles, who in 1594 calls it 'an auld hoose callit the castil of the heid of Lochrenesay'. This 'auld hoose' must be incorporated in the new – more of it, according to Cruden, then is obvious to the eye.

The main block lies north and south, rises to three storeys and once had an attic. The south west jamb rises two storeys higher. The north, or kitchen end, of the main block is vaulted and was roofed transversely with a turret at the north-west angle. Its eastern third rose a storey higher as a north-east tower but has crumbled. Over the door in the west front, which is protected by an iron yett, is a corbelled and machicolated device at eaves level for dropping missiles on unwanted guests.

The basement to the south has a large unvaulted room, that to the north two vaulted rooms. A mural stair to the Hall on the first floor has been built in. In the Hall itself there is a raised dais. A partition divides off the kitchen at the north end, connected by a service hatch. There is a mural garderobe off the Hall, and what seems to have been another entrance, perhaps approached by a movable stair. The turnpike stair from the door gave access right up the castle, as did a mural turnpike stair to the bedrooms. Both towers had watch-rooms.

John de Monteith, Lord of Arran, conferred Lochranza Castle on Sir Duncan Campbell of Lochaw, ancestor of the Argylls, in 1433. James II granted it to the first Lord Montgomerie. James IV made him Earl of Eglinton. James VI used it as a base for his assault on the dangerous power of the Lords of the Isles. Cromwell garrisoned it. In 1705 it was bought by Anne, Duchess of Hamilton, but was deserted before the end of the eighteenth century.

Luffness

Luffness House, as it is now known, is a T-shaped building much altered since the original castle on the site was erected, probably by the Earls of Dunbar and March, in the thirteenth century. Standing at the head of Aberlady Bay – incidentally, formerly called Luffness Bay – it was once a large and powerful fortress surrounded by a moat, its purpose being to defend Haddington. The castle was presented to the Church in memory of the crusading eighth Earl, and a Carmelite monastery was established in the grounds. Among the relics surviving from this period is a recumbent effigy of the Crusader. Partly demolished by the English in the middle of the sixteenth century, it soon had a stair tower and turret added, as well as a new roofline. Mary, Queen of Scots is reputed to have visited Luffness, her third husband, the Earl of Bothwell, being head of the Hepburn clan. A panel on the corbelled south-east angle turret carries the date 1584 and the initials of Sir Patrick Hepburn and his wife, Isabel Haldane, who acquired Luffness at the Reformation. Further additions were made early in the seventeenth century.

In 1739, the Luffness estate was bought (for £8350) by the Earl of Hopetoun, who made many internal alterations to the tower, as did his nineteenth-century descendants. It is still in the possession of the Hope family, and lived in.

MacLellan's Castle

MacLellan's Castle stands in the centre of Kirkcudbright, by the River Dee. Once in a dire state, though still ruinous, it is now stabilised as an Ancient Monument.

It is a variation of an L-shaped fortalice, but a large one, with a main east/west block, a wing extending to the north, a rectangular tower projecting at the south-east angle, and two projecting towers in the re-entrant angle. Part of the main block rises to five storeys, but the rest of the structure is four storeys high. There are angle-turrets at the western corners of the main block, and at the two corners of the northern extension. The stonework is coursed rubble, with some decorative detail. There are several splayed gun-loops.

Entrance is through a door in the smaller of the two towers in the re-entrant angle. Above the door there are three large heraldic

MacLellan's Castle: an elaborate L-plan castle in the middle of a town.

panels in a moulded frame. The upper panel, now illegible, is
believed to have carried the royal arms. The other two carry the
arms of MacLellan and Maxwell, the initials G.M. and the date
1582.

A straight stair leads to the Great Hall, and a corridor provides
access to three vaulted basement cellars. A further passage at the
east end leads to the vaulted kitchen, which also has a direct door
into the courtyard, and to another room at the foot of the south-east
tower. The kitchen has a large wall-long fireplace, as well as a stone
sink with a drain.

The Great Hall is over forty-two feet long and almost half as
wide. The handsome fireplace has an eleven-foot lintel carved out
of a single stone. There is a peep-hole at the back of the fireplace
where, from a tiny room, a smoky watch could be kept on those in
the Hall. The Hall is lit by four windows, one of which has a

garderobe off it and another a private stair leading to the floor above.

A small turnpike stair in the west wall leads to three private rooms; one in the main block, one in the south-east tower and one in the wing, by the stair landing. A turnpike stair in a turret rises from the main stair.

The second floor has a well-lit withdrawing-room, possessing a window with stone seats, above the Hall.

Now roofless, the building had several crow-stepped gables, the angle-turrets were conically roofed, and, as might be supposed from the size of the kitchen and Great Hall fireplaces, the chimney-stacks are massive.

In 1569 Sir Thomas MacLellan of Bombie, Provost of Kirkcudbright, acquired the lands and buildings of the Franciscan Greyfriars Monastery, demolishing all but part of the chapel, now the Episcopalian Church, which contains an effulgent Jacobean memorial to its sponsor, put up in 1597 by his son. Sir Thomas married the daughter of the fourth Lord Herries, Dame Grizel Maxwell, whose initials adorn the doorway of the castle. Their son, Sir Robert, was a Gentleman of the Bedchamber both to James VI and Charles I, the latter creating MacLellan Lord Kirkcudbright in 1633. Lord John Kirkcudbright, the third to hold the title, lost most of his fortune supporting the Royalist cause, and the rest of it supporting Episcopalianism after the Restoration. Poverty forced the abandonment of his house, one of the finest examples of sixteenth-century fortified domestic architecture in Scotland. As Burns noted with astonishment, the Lord Kirkcudbright of his day kept a glove shop in Edinburgh.

Mains Castle

Mains Castle – it was called Fintry by its Graham owners until they transferred the name to Linlathen House some miles to the east – is a sixteenth-century courtyard castle on a steep bank above the Gelly burn, in Strathdichty, only three miles north from the heart of Dundee. Not surprisingly, in view of that city's until recently dismal record in looking after its heritage, the castle was long allowed to decay, but over the last decade the north and east ranges have been excellently rebuilt, where necessary, and reroofed as a Manpower Services scheme.

The castle is constructed round the north, east and south sides of the courtyard, the west having a high wall and a parapet continuous with the north-western arm of the south wing. The entrance gateway has a segmented arch, above which is a massive corbelled projecting bartisan for the dropping of missiles on enemies without. Before the time of MacGibbon and Ross the initials D.G. and D.M.O., for Sir David Graham and Dame Margaret Ogilvy, his wife, were apparently discernible on the keystone, along with the date 1562.

The main buildings, and the earliest within the courtyard, are those on the north side. The oldest part is what has been a small square house in the north-west corner, its east gable absorbed in the higher range which occupies the eastern two-thirds of the north side. The most impressive part of it is the high, square stair tower, which rises to six storeys and, above original corbelling, has a watch-room rebuilt in 1630 with four gables. The date is at the skews. The main building is remarkable for its big gabbleted crow-steps, similar to those at Farnell. The entrance was in the foot of the stair tower, and a turnpike stair, now fallen but to be rebuilt, led to the Hall and a private room on the first floor. The unvaulted ground floor of this range housed stables and stores, the kitchen with its oven being in the eastern range, which was rebuilt in late Stuart times and contained the dining-room and withdrawing-room. Over the door of the stair at the south end of this range was the inscription PATRIAE ET POSTERIS GRATIS ET AMICIS (Grateful for country, friends and posterity), but this part of the eastern arm was originally the north-east staircase wing of the south range, now so badly ruined that its form is hard to guess. The ground floor contained a bakehouse.

The Earls of Angus owned Mains in the fourteenth century, but in 1530 John Graham of Balargus, a cadet of the Grahams of Fintry, in Stirlingshire, acquired it. His son, Sir David, probably built the present castle and changed the name. He was a cousin of Claverhouse, and a nephew of the unpopular and eventually murdered Cardinal Beaton. Sir David himself was one of those who in 1596 sent blank signed letters to the King of Spain for that monarch to fill in his own terms for restoring Catholicism to Scotland, an affair known as the 'Spanish Blanks'. Its discovery cost Sir David his head.

Maxwelton House: Annie Laurie's one-time home, stripped of its Victorian accretions and restored.

Maxwelton House

Maxwelton House, until recently the home of the Laurie family, stands four miles east of Moniaive. The original house of the early seventeenth century forms three sides of a south-facing courtyard. A circular tower which contained a stair occupies the west re-entrant angle. The house was subjected to considerable Georgian and Victorian additions. When it was taken over by the late Hugh Stenhouse in the 1960s, however, all except the original exterior was demolished. The exterior has been carefully restored, the Georgian bow encased in a new gable and the interior splendidly modernised. Two panels preserved in the fabric are inscribed SIR. ROBERT. LAURIE. DOM. JEAN RIDDELL. Another, showing the impaled arms of the Lauries and the Griersons, carries the date 1641.

The literary interest of the house is that it was the home of Annie Laurie, the subject of an abidingly popular Scots song originally

written by her seventeenth-century lover, William Douglas of
Fingland, though polished and improved in the late nineteenth
century by Lady John Scott. In spite of the poet's well-known
protestations of ardour, one of which likened the lady's neck to that
of a swan, both parties married others.

Maybole Castle

This tower house of the Kennedys, one of the most turbulent
families in the south-west, was in fact a well-defended keep dating
from the late sixteenth and early seventeenth century, and probably
built by Gilbert Kennedy, fifth Earl of Cassillis and Lord High
Treasurer of Scotland. It is a tall L-shaped tower on the edge of the
town, four storeys high and with a garret. Large circular turrets are
corbelled from the north-east and south-east angles. The stair wing
projects to the south-west and there is a later, lower addition to the
north. The original entrance at the front of the stair tower has been
replaced by one in the east front of this addition.

There is a vaulted basement and, on the first floor, a well-lit Hall.
The upper floors have had their rooms subdivided. The room at the
top of the stair tower projects a little on corbelling, and has a fine
canted oriel. Since its interior is also panelled, presumably it was a
favourite of the owner of the castle. Oriel, skews and dormers are
uncommonly well detailed. It was a favourite source of inspiration
for Bryce, who reproduced it as the dominant element of several of
his larger houses, notably The Glen, Fotheringham and New Gala.

Some of the more famous outrages of the Earls of Cassillis are
noted under Cassillis House. At Maybole, however, the Lady Jean
Hamilton, daughter of the first Earl of Haddington and wife of the
po-faced sixth Earl of Cassillis, was imprisoned for life by her
husband after she had eloped with Sir John Fall, or Faa, of Dunbar,
the King of the Gypsies. Cassillis pursued the lovers and achieved
his end in true Kennedy fashion without regard to human cost, as
the anonymous ballad-writer records:

> They were fifteen well-made men,
>   Black but very bonnie;
> And they all lost their lives for ane,
>   The Earl of Cassillis Ladye.

In these days, anything was believable of a Kennedy.

Mearns Castle

A mile south of Newton Mearns, on the outskirts of Glasgow, stands Mearns Tower, a four-storey keep built under royal warrant by Herbert, Lord Maxwell, in 1449. An oblong fortalice, it survived to the wallhead prior to recent restoration. A section of the parapet corbelling is original. The entrance on the ground floor leads to a vaulted basement room. There is a straight mural stair leading to the first-floor Hall, which is also vaulted, once had a minstrels' gallery and still has stone window-seats. The original main entrance was through an arched doorway, now built up, reached by movable wooden stairs. The corbels to support a third floor survive, but the upper floors had gone by 1971, when the keep was converted to link two new Church of Scotland buildings serving the expanding Glasgow residential suburb of Newton Mearns.

The lands of Mearns came to the Maxwells through marriage with a Pollock heiress in 1300. One Lord Maxwell fell at Flodden. His son found himself in the Tower of London, having been taken prisoner at Solway Moss. James VI instructed the fifth Lord Maxwell to deliver up Mearns to the Crown. Mearns was sold in the mid-seventeenth century to Sir George Maxwell of Nether Pollock, from whose family it eventually passed to the Shaw-Stewarts.

Meggernie Castle

Attached to a larger hunting-lodge half way up Glen Lyon – reputedly the longest glen in Scotland – Meggernie Castle dates from the sixteenth century. The original tall square tower, possibly incorporating older fragments, rises to five storeys and has a steeply pitched roof with square pyramid-roofed turrets at each angle. There are shot-holes below the sills of many of the windows. The walls, five feet thick, are now harled and whitewashed. The door in the south front leads to a vaulted basement. First-floor Hall and bedroom accommodation above would have followed the usual pattern.

Meggernie was a Menzies stronghold, one of the most famous of its owners being Menzies of Caldares, better known as 'Old Caldares', the great tree expert. He was 'out' in the Jacobite rising of 1715, being taken prisoner at the Battle of Preston. Age prevented his participation in the rising of the Forty-Five, but he presented the Prince with a charger and sheltered several Jacobite fugitives on his estate at the same time as he was giving hospitality to the government soldiers sent to capture them! 'Old Caldares' left no heir, and the family of Stewart of Cardney, who adopted the name Stewart-Menzies, acquired the estate, which they retained until 1885. Meggernie is said to be haunted by the upper portion of the wife of a Menzies laird who sawed her in two in order to be able to dispose of her more easily, but apparently only managed to deal with the lower half; possibly because soon afterwards he himself was murdered.

Megginch Castle

Megginch, surrounded now by woodlands in the Carse of Gowrie, midway between Perth and Dundee, was originally a red sandstone rectangular tower of three storeys and an attic, with a semi-circular stair tower, corbelled square at attic level to provide a watch-room in the centre of the south front. There are conically roofed turrets at the north-west and north-east ends of the main block. The inscription PETRUS HAY AED FICIUM EXTRUXTI AN 1575 is recorded over one of the windows, though a late-fifteenth-century tower may be incorporated in the present building.

In the seventeenth century a south-west extension was added, turning the castle into an L-plan structure, and containing a scale-and-platt stair to first floor level. During the second decade of the eighteenth century an architect called Strachan carried out further work at Megginch. Later in the century a drawing-room wing with three storeys was added at right angles to the jamb, with a west bow in the castellated style. Unsubstantiated tradition alleges that this was the work of Robert Adam. The now-reconstituted ceiling was certainly good enough to be by him. This new wing was extended eastwards as a complete new front by the architect William Macdonald Mackenzie of Perth in 1817, with a Greek Doric porch, though this was removed in 1928 by J. Donald Mills, who built a crenellated substitute and made interior alterations. A restoration of 1966 brought the staircase back to its pre-Mills condition, but a fire in 1969 necessitated the replacement of much of the interior with reproduction copies and chimney-pieces imported from other houses.

Peter Hay, son of Hay of Leys, may have been the builder of the original castle, his namesake of 1575 turning it into what now survives as the oldest part. Sir George Hay of Megginch, the last of his line, sold the castle to John Drummond, Hereditary Seneschal of Strathearn. The third Drummond of Megginch was the first local member for Perthshire in the new and then highly unpopular United Kingdom parliament of 1707. He also exerted himself, more or less unsuccessfully, in attempting to hunt down the newly outlawed Rob Roy MacGregor. The Drummond family still lives in Megginch.

Melgund Castle

Melgund Castle, a mile east of Aberlemno, is a mid-sixteenth-century castle based upon an older plan, yet varied to provide higher than normal standards of convenience and comfort.

It was a stepped L-plan keep rising to four storeys with corbelling that supported open rounds. The stair wing was carried a storey higher to house a watch-room. The garret storey within the parapet has gone. The walls are well provided with gun-loops.

The entrance in the stair wing led to two vaulted cellars in the keep, and on the first floor to a private room off the small Hall with stone window seats, fireplace and recessed gun-loops. There is a garderobe with, off it, a recess which might either have been a prison or perhaps a safe. The upper floors once each had one room per storey.

The two-storey extension to the east also carried a parapet and walk. It housed the great Hall and withdrawing-rooms. The vaulted basement beneath accommodated the kitchen and four other cellars.

The Hall, with its large ornamented fireplace and high-position windows on the south side, must have been a handsome room. It is connected to the wine-cellar by the usual private stair. There has been building along the north face, but it is now totally ruinous. There is a secondary turnpike stair in the round tower at the north-east angle of the extension. There would be bedrooms above the Hall.

Tradition avers that Melgund was built for Cardinal Beaton, Archbishop of Scotland and Chancellor of Scotland. He was either married to, or had as his mistress, Marion Ogilvy, daughter of the first Lord Ogilvy of Airlie, and she bore him several children. After the Reformation, Melgund was in the hands of David Bethune of Balfour, a close relation of James Beaton, the last Catholic Archbishop of Glasgow and a nephew of the murdered Cardinal Beaton. Melgund passed in the late seventeenth century to the Marquis of Huntly, and then to the Lyons, the Maules and the Murrays, before coming through an heiress to the Earl of Minto and providing his son with the title of Viscount Melgund.

Merchiston Castle, Edinburgh

Originally an L-shaped tower dating perhaps from the fourteenth century, rising to four storeys with a corbelled parapet, rounds at each angle and a gabled attic storey, Merchiston has been much altered over the centuries. The ground floor has two unvaulted apartments, one a kitchen with a wide fireplace. A narrow stair runs down to a vaulted cellar, presumably a food-store or wine-cellar. In the south-west angle, a turnpike stair rises to the first floor and up to the parapet, where it is capped by a little roof turret. The first floor has three rooms, one with a plaster ceiling from the time of Charles II, similar to the decorative work introduced into Scotland by Dunsterfield and Halbert. The panelled Jacobean ceiling in another of the rooms was imported from a different house. A panelled closet is known as Queen Mary's room, she being reputed to have planted a pear tree in the gardens.

The walls, ten feet thick, had to endure many a siege, since Merchiston guarded one of the southern approaches to Edinburgh. In 1572, it was bombarded from Edinburgh Castle. Regent Morton's English commander, one Drury, shortly thereafter used it as a prison.

Though frequently under siege, particularly in 1572 during the struggle between Mary, Queen of Scots and the supporters of her infant son, its strongest associations are with the Napier family. Sir Archibald Napier refused to surrender Merchiston to the Regent Mar and it resisted 'smoking out'. He died in 1608. His son, John Napier, the inventor of logarithms, was born there in 1550. (Incidentally, he is reputed also to have devised an early version of the modern computer, known as 'Napier's bones', examples of which survive; a forerunner of the military tank; and an ingenious hydraulic screw, which advanced the development of water-pumping machinery for mines). The philosopher David Hume certainly claimed that Napier was 'the person to whom the title of a great man is more justly due than to any other this country has ever produced'. In 1593, Napier published *A Plaine Discoverie Of The Whole Revelation Of St John*, which apparently became a best-seller in those mysticism-obsessed times.

In 1614, his small but astonishing book *Mirifici Logarithmorum Canonis Descriptio* appeared. Napier's son rose to be Lord Justice Clerk and the first Lord Napier. The family also provided Edinburgh with no fewer than three Lord Provosts.

In 1833 the tower was let to Charles Chalmers, founder and first honorary member of Merchiston Castle School. Chalmers – brother of Dr Thomas Chalmers, who led the Disruption in the Church of Scotland – later conducted classes for boys intending to go to Edinburgh University. This private school was transferred to Merchiston, a castellated Gothic-style addition being added, which was described by Lord Cockburn in his *Memorials* as 'a recent and discordant front'. In 1914, house and grounds were sold by Colonel the Honourable J.S.Napier to Merchiston Castle School Ltd. In 1935, the old tower passed into the hands of the City. Used by the National Fire Service during the 1939–45 war, the tower was then threatened with demolition, but by 1958 restoration was under way for its conversion as part of the Napier Technical College, since 1974 the Napier College of Commerce and Technology, one of the largest advanced-education colleges in Scotland. During the restoration, an entrance drawbridge was discovered, and an original seventeenth-century plaster ceiling was uncovered and preserved.

Methven Castle

Methven Castle stands on a south-facing ridge five miles west of Perth. The present structure, which almost certainly incorporates earlier building, dates from the earlier part of the seventeenth century, and is one of the last fortified houses to be put up in Scotland.

The castle is square, with four ogee-capped stair towers at each corner, and much lower later additions to east and west. The coursed red rubble walls contain four storeys and a garret. The doorway in the north front was defended by a small parapet platform, the balustrade, however, being more decorative than practical.

Prior to 1323 the lands of Methven belonged to the Mowbrays, whose ancestor, Roger Mowbray, came to England with William the Conqueror. Unfortunately Sir Roger, the Mowbray in possession during the War of Independence, took the side of Baliol and the English interest, so in due course had his lands confiscated by the victorious Robert the Bruce. Bruce then bestowed them on his son-in law, Walter, the eighth hereditary High Steward of Scotland, whose own son became Robert II in 1371, his mother being Marjorie Bruce, Robert I's daughter. Robert II gave the lands of Methven to Walter Stewart, Earl of Atholl, who lost them by forfeiture in 1427. They remained with the Crown for a long time, the older castle being used as a dower house for the Dowager Queen. James IV settled Methven on Margaret Tudor who, when widowed as a result of Flodden, lived there. The lady then married Archibald, Earl of Angus, but divorced him in 1525, choosing as her third husband Henry Stewart, a descendant of Robert II's son. (Incidentally, it was through Margaret Tudor, Henry VII's eldest daughter, that her great-grandson, James VI, succeeded to queen Elizabeth's English throne in 1603.) For her third husband, the lady procured the title of Lord Methven in 1528. By him she had a daughter who died in infancy. She herself died in 1540, and was buried in Perth beside the body of James I. The widower, Lord Methven, then married Janet Stewart, a daughter of the Earl of Atholl, and had a son who became the second Lord Methven. He was killed by a cannonball from Edinburgh Castle in 1572, leaving a son, Henry, the third Lord Methven, who died without issue. Once again, the lands and property reverted to the Crown. James VI gave them to his favourite and distant cousin, Esmé Stewart, Seigneur D'Aubigny, who became Chancellor of Scotland and first Duke of Lennox, and whose son, the second Duke, built the present castle. In 1664 the Duke sold it to Patrick Smythe of Braco, whose grandson assumed the title of Lord Methven on being raised to the bench. After decades of uncertainty, Methven has now been restored by the architect Ken Murdoch.

Midhope

One of the saddest apparently unnecessarily doomed castles in Scotland, Midhope stands on the estate of the Marquess of Linlithgow. When first I saw it, it could still have been restored. Now it is a shell in danger of rapidly falling apart.

It consists of a five-storey-and-basement oblong tower house with a garret, topped by a steeply pitched sixteenth-century roof with corner turrets, subsequently extended twice eastwards by additions a storey lower to form a large rectangular house. The second of these additions was the work of Sir George Livingston, Earl of Linlithgow, in the 1660s. He completely remodelled the interior in a sumptuous Holyroodhouse manner, and inserted the fine Renaissance doorpiece with his initials and armoured cartouches. Substantial remains of superb woodwork and plasterwork are still extant amid the wreckage, but the building has become dangerous to enter. There is a vaulted basement in both tower and wing. It is approached through a courtyard with a fine arched gateway. On the outside of the courtyard a stone has the date 1582.

South of it is a fine walled garden with an arched alcove on the axis of the house.

Midhope, lived in until 1939 but abandoned after the Second World War, during which it was used (or rather abused) by the Fire Service and others, would have made a splendid contrast to the great and much visited mansion of Hopetoun House, across the park.

Midmar Castle

Midmar occupies a terraced site overlooking a big walled garden in a glen on the northern slope of the Hill of Fare, half-way between the valleys of the Dee and the Don. Originally a Z-plan castle of about 1565–75, possibly the work of George Bell, a member of the famous local family of master masons, though perhaps with seventeenth-century upper works, Midmar has a main block with diagonally opposite towers; that to the south-east being circular, that to the north-east square. Subsequently, it was extended around a courtyard open to the north. A seventeenth-century extension on its west side houses the vaulted kitchen and stables separated by the pend entry to the court. An L-shaped eighteenth-century extension

Midmar Castle: the circular tower of a castle carefully restored.

of the east side contains the dining-room, added about 1733. The stepped-up eighteenth-century terrace within the court leading to the entrance is also a later addition.

The main block rises to four storeys and a garret, the circular tower to six storeys. This has a flat roof with a crenellated parapet.

There are two stair turrets. One rises above first-floor level in the northern re-entrant angle, and has a conical roof. The other, in the opposite re-entrant angle, projects on label-formed corbelling from second-floor level, ending in an ogee-roofed cap-house giving access to the flat roof of the round tower. Round angle-turrets on corbelling and conically capped adorn the gables of the square tower to the west. Shallow square turrets with gabled roofs project on label mouldings on the north-east and south-west angles of the main block. The roof has a steep pitch.

The interior of the house preserves nearly all of its original features. The rooms open through one another, without corridors or passages. There are fine panelled rooms, some late seventeenth century, others of 1733, the former having plaster ceilings with simple geometrical ribbed patterns.

Midmar has had many owners. Brouns or Browns held the lands from the thirteenth century to 1422, when it was sold to Patrick Ogilvy. By 1468, however, it had been acquired by Alexander Gordon, first Earl of Huntly, who granted a charter in favour of his son-in-law, William, Lord Forbes. Early in 1484, Midmar was in the hands of Alexander Gordon. Ballogie was the castle's name when Alexander Forbes had Midmar towards the end of the seventeenth century. The next owners were the Grants, who called it Grantfield. About 1760, it was once again Midmar, having been bought by William Davidson, an Aberdeen provost. Margaret Davidson married an Elphinstone of Logie-Elphinstone, who sold it around 1795 to his brother-in-law, a banker, James Mansfield. One of his granddaughters sold it in 1842 to Colonel John Gordon of Cluny, with whose family it remained until 1977. Last occupied by them early this century, it presented a complete picture of how a seventeenth-century castle was lived in a century and a half ago, complete with antique stoves and lead-lined bath. Now it is in the hands of Rick Wharton who, with his wife, Jackie, has successfully completed the restoration, not only of the building itself but also of the walled garden, containing beeboles and other interesting early features.

Mingary Castle

This castle stands on a high rock close to the shore, guarding both the entrances to the Sound of Mull and Loch Sunart, a mile or so east of the Point of Ardnamurchan. It thus stands sentinel at the ancient division between the isles known as the Norderies and those which were the Suderies, including Man (hence the quaint surviving title of the Bishop of Sodor and Man).

Like other West Highland castles, it was erected inside a wall of enceinte shaped to the rock (in this case a rough hexagonal) and dates from the thirteenth century. On the top of this wall is a parapet, reached by stone forestairs from inside the courtyard. The main entrance was by sea, through a gate in the west side of the castle, up steps cut from the rock. There was also an entrance over a drawbridge across a wall ditch on the north-east approach. Three ranges of buildings stand inside the curtain wall, on the north, west

Mingary Castle: the later keep within the curtain wall.

and south-east sides. At a later date the north walling was heightened and built inwards to form an oblong keep. Renewed at a later date, it has been suggested that this building was used as a garrison rather than a residence. Several two-storey buildings, now very ruinous, were built against the west and south-east walls, the thickness being pared down to help accommodate them.

There is a slightly projecting semi-circular tower on the east face, with arrow slits and shot-holes. Alterations of various kinds were made in the sixteenth century, including the addition of two open rounds on the southern angles.

Mingary was probably built, or added to, by the MacIans of Ardnamurchan, descendants of that John of Islay who disposed of his legal wife to marry Princess Margaret, daughter of Robert II, and was involved in the Macdonald cause in 1588, when a Maclean of Duart captured the MacIan, then unsuccessfully laid siege to the castle with Spanish soldiers from an Armada galleon in Tobermory Bay. The Campbells, however, took Mingary from the MacIans, and received a charter for it from Lord Lorne in 1626. Taken by

Alasdair MacDonald in 1644 and recaptured by General Leslie two years later, the castle reverted to the Argyll Campbells in 1651, and their nominee, Alexander Campbell, sixth of Lochnell, probably built the keep around 1696.

The castle was garrisoned for the government in 1745. One James Riddell held the estate from 1770 to 1848, when it seems likely that the old castle was still habitable. It features in *The Lord of the Isles*, the last, and least successful, of Scott's long narrative poems which were a prelude to the Waverley Novels.

Minto (Fatlips) Tower

Minto Tower, crested on Minto Crags, four miles west of Jedburgh, is an oblong tower of three storeys with a garret above the parapet, which is rounded at each of its four angles. The parapet walk is drained by cannon-spouts.

The castle is entered by a door in the south wall with a vacant panel-space above it. The basement is vaulted, and still contains its entresol floor. The turnpike stair rises in the south-east angle, and has a cap-house with a conical roof.

The tower has been much restored, especially above the level of the parapet. It was reputedly the stronghold of a Border freebooter called Turnbull of Barnhill, who may have inspired the building's curious alternative name. After the days of the Turnbulls, this tower came briefly to the Stewarts, who in 1705 sold it to Sir Gilbert Elliot of Minto, a minor Scottish poet from whom are descended the Earls of Minto, who still own the tower.

Moncur Castle

Moncur Castle, in the Carse of Gowrie, within the Rossie Priory policies, is a small Z-plan structure of two storeys and an attic. At the south-west is a circular tower with a stair turret in the re-entrant angle, and a badly ruined square tower at the north-east. The ground floor has been vaulted. The castle was burned out in the eighteenth century.

Minto (Fatlips) Castle: a Border keep, heavily restored above the parapet.

Monkcastle

Monkcastle, a small ruinous T-plan structure, stands among woodland on a hillside midway between Kilwinning and Dalry. There is a main block of two storeys and an attic. From the centre of this a square stair tower projects, rising a storey higher. Although the walls remain intact the entire interior has gone.

Owned before the Reformation by the Abbey of Kilwinning, it fell into the hands of the second Earl of Arran, Duke of Châtelhérault, who gave it to his son Claud, the Commendator of Paisley. This is thought to account for the sculpted mitred head which survives on a panel above the doorway.

Monimail Castle

Monimail Castle, four miles west of Cupar, an example of the kind of edifice which superceded the castles, is all that survives of the former palace of the Archbishop of St Andrews. Like Myres, it shows evidence of Continental influence in the decorative roundels and the quality of the workmanship. Today, it stands in the grounds of Melville House, until 1939 the home of the Earls of Leven and Melville, and now a List D School.

A square tower of coursed rubble rising to four storeys, Monimail has a flat roof and a parapet without crenellations, though it has open rounds at the angles. There is a cap-house on the stair-head, possibly now reduced from its original size.

While there was an episcopal residence here, reputedly from about 1300, Bishop William Lamberton may have been responsible for the beginnings of the present tower, which Cardinal Beaton enlarged. The last Roman Catholic Archbishop of St Andrews, Archbishop Hamilton, was also a tenant. An Italian astrologer, using water from a nearby spring, known thereafter as Cardon's Well, administered a dose of his healing liquid to the Archbishop when that dignitary was suffering from what sounds like asthma. To his credit, Archbishop Hamilton tried hard to persuade Mary, Queen of Scots not to throw herself on the mercy of England's Elizabeth. Once he had failed, he himself was captured, wearing armour under clerical habit, when the Marian stronghold of Dumbarton Castle fell in April 1571. He was hanged five days later at Stirling Castle.

Monymusk Castle

Monymusk (now known as House of Monymusk) stands by the Don, near the village of the same name. Its nucleus is a five-storey L-plan house to which lower wings branching out to south and east were added early in the seventeenth century. The massive central tower was perhaps the guard-tower of Monymusk Priory, the last Prior being Robert Forbes. In 1587, William Forbes built the main house. In 1712, Monymusk was bought by Sir Francis Grant of Cullen. The house was remodelled in 1719 for his son, Sir Archibald Grant, to designs by Alexander Jaffray of Kingswells, his neighbour. The wings were heightened during this operation and an extra storey added to the tower. The original barmkin of the tower became a square court with paired gates between rusticated piers.

Early in the nineteenth century a Tuscan entrance porch was added. In 1838 William Burn drew up plans to 're-baronialise' the castle, but his plans were not carried out. In 1880 a two-storey wing was added to the south-east. The Tuscan porch was infilled and an oriel window was extended from the main bedroom and to some other rooms.

The present owner, Lady Grant, has been systematically restoring the house, resuscitating the library from what had become a lumber-room and removing the bow window from the smoking-room, amongst other improvements. Alexander Jaffray's seventeenth-century decorative internal work largely survives.

Monzie Castle

Monzie, a simple but finely detailed L-plan building, stands at the foot of Knock Hill, near Crieff. Two storeys and an attic in height and built of rubble, it is unturreted with crow-stepped gables and a moulded doorway in the wing dated 1634, with the arms of Campbell and Graham. The original turnpike stair has been removed.

The castle was gifted by Sir Duncan Campbell of Glenorchy to his fifth son, Archibald, and remained with his descendants until 1869, the house being the rear wing of a large bow-fronted Adam castellated mansion designed by Adam's ex-assistant John Paterson for General Sir Alexander Campbell *c.*1795. This was burned out in 1908, whereafter it was internally refitted in a sumptuous renaissance style by Sir Robert Lorimer. There has been some further restoration since. The Hall retains a fine fireplace with a swagged lintel.

Mounie Castle

Three miles east of Old Meldrum, Mounie Castle is a small seventeenth-century T-plan castle, its main block of two storeys and an attic, a circular stair tower projecting westwards, corbelled out at eaves level to contain a square-gabled watch-room once reached (but now closed) by a corbelled-out conically capped turret stair in the re-entrant angle above the original door. The basement has two vaulted rooms, one the kitchen with an arched fireplace and stone sink. The Hall has been subdivided and the interior modernised.

Mounie was, and again is, a Seton family possession.

Moy Castle

Moy Castle, formerly called Lochbuie Castle, stands at the north end of Loch Buie, on the south shore of Mull, and was the ancient seat of the Maclaines of Loch Buie.

Oblong, of rough course rubble and buttressed with a broadened base at the angles, it rose to three storeys with a flush parapet, each containing two deep crenels. There was a garret storey above, now ruined. Open rounds, which were roofed (as was the castle) when Dr Christison drew it for MacGibbon and Ross, adorn the north-east and south-east angles. There is a cap-house at the stairhead in the south-west angle and a gabled watch-room diagonally opposite. All within is now ruinous, though the usual arrangements no doubt pertained.

The castle probably dates from the fourteenth century, though the upper works are more characteristic of the seventeenth. Moy Castle was abandoned in 1752 when the nearby Georgian mansion was built. Its distinguished visitors included Boswell and Johnson, who arrived in 1773, but stayed in a small house nearby, now in the stable yard.

Muchalls Castle

Muchalls Castle, five miles north of Stonehaven and a mile inland from, but commanding a view of, the North Sea is a well-preserved early-seventeenth-century fortalice the basic dates of which are recorded on a panel over the courtyard gateway: 'This wark begun on the east and north be Ar.Burnet of Leys 1619, ended by Sir Thomas Burnet of Leys his sonne, 1627'. The Ar.Burnet is Sir Archibald, who brought the work at Crathes Castle to a conclusion.

Muchalls evolved from the L-plan castle type with a long wing extending at right angles from the west end of the main wing and a

Muchalls Castle: an L-plan castle, squared with a curtain wall.

short stair jamb jutting out from the east end. Curtain walling completes the square of the flagged courtyard.

There is a semi-circular secondary stair in the main re-entrant angle. Angle-turrets adorn the corners of the main gables, except at the eastern stair jamb. This carries the main stair to Hall level, and is then elaborately corbelled out to support a gabled watch-room. There are open rounds on the curtain walling, once crenellated but now plain, which was at one time properly served by a parapet walk. Two groups of shot-holes defend each side of the gateway.

The castle is entered by a door in the splay of the eastern stair jamb. There is a groined vaulted basement with several cellars, that at the north-east being the kitchen. At this level there have been some alterations. Access to the upper floors is by the stair in the re-entrant angle, which narrows after first-floor level.

The first floor contains the Great Hall, the withdrawing-room and the laird's study. The Hall is ornamented with ribbed plaster work and painted with heraldic designs of the Burnet and related families and the heads of Roman emperors, heroes of antiquity and scriptural characters. There is a splendid fireplace over which is a handsome coloured overmantel carrying the Royal Arms of Scotland and the date 1624. The other rooms are similarly decorated. The upper floors contain bedrooms, that at the west end of the main block housing a 'laird's lug', or listening, device leading to the Hall fireplace beneath.

Muchalls was Fraser property before it came to the Burnets in 1619.

Muckerach Castle

In the valley of the River Dalnain, a mile west of Dalnain Bridge, stands Muckerach Castle, a former seat of the Grants of Rothiemurchus. An L-plan tower house, its main block rose to three storeys and a garret. It had a circular wing containing the main stair corbelled out to the square to provide a two-storey superstructure and a small circular stair tower corbelled out on a squinch at second-floor level to serve it. There is a prominent splayed gun-loop just above the squinch. Once there was a large courtyard. Until the recent restoration, vaulted basement and Hall had survived, but the turnpike stair, reached from the door in the re-entrant angle of the main circular tower, had collapsed and the building was in a badly decayed state. Within the last few years it has been restored under the supervision of Ian Begg and reoccupied.

Muckerach was built and completed in 1598 by Patrick Grant, who married the Earl of Atholl's daughter, was knighted by James VI and died in 1626. It was abandoned when the Grants took over Rothiemurchus.

Mugdock Castle

Mugdock Castle, now much reduced from its former immense extent and great strength, is a ruin standing on a plateau on the south-west corner of the formerly more extensive Mugdock Loch, about two miles north of Milngavie. The loch in earlier times provided a defence on the west side, the rapid falling-away of the ground on the two remaining sides further adding to the castle's security.

There is evidence of extensive building on the site from the fourteenth to the beginning of the nineteenth centuries. The castle was of the courtyard type, and somewhat recalled St Andrews Castle, with which it was more or less contemporary.

Two towers on the west side of the courtyard and part of the gate-house, connected by a high curtain-wall, survive from the original fourteenth-century design. The castle was greatly enlarged in the fifteenth century by the addition of an outer court with another high curtain-wall, against which lean-to buildings were probably constructed. There is evidence that there was a chapel at the northern side of the enceinte.

Only the south-west tower is still entire. It rises to four storeys, each with a single room. It seems possible that the topmost was floored at parapet level to provide an attic, now gone.

The tower is of rubble, the walls above second-floor level being set out on a course of continuous corbelling on the south and west sides, and on individual corbels on the east. There is no communication between the basement and the floors above. The first floor is reached by a stone forestair, built partly against the curtain wall and partly against the east wall of the tower. There is an original fireplace, and, to the east, a door inserted at a later date to connect the tower with a modern house. The first floor has a ribbed and vaulted ceiling. A turnpike stair rises in the thickness of the south-east angle. The second floor is level with the high curtain-wall.

Of the north-west tower only the ground floor survives, with barrel-vaulted cellarage. A section of wall, which apparently once carried a parapet walk, also remains. The later building to the west, outside the courtyard, dates from 1655, though there were alterations in the eighteenth century and perhaps also later.

David de Graham acquired the ancient barony in the middle of the thirteenth century from Maldwin, Earl of Lennox. The builder of what remains of the present castle may have been Sir David de Graham, who died about 1396. From him the Montrose family descended. In 1458, the Grahams lands in the Lennox were erected into the barony of Mugdock, and Mugdock Castle became their principal seat; except, of course, for the short period during the forfeiture of the first Marquess of Montrose in 1645, when Mugdock passed briefly to the Marquess of Argyll, before being restored to its original owner. It was used until about the beginning of the eighteenth century, when it was replaced by Old Buchanan House.

In 1875, John Guthrie Smith had a large baronial mansion designed by James Sellars constructed beside and linked to the restored surviving tower. The preparatory work for this Victorian house destroyed much of the evidence of the extent of the fallen castle. Guthrie Smith's house also became a total ruin and is now demolished.

Muness Castle

Muness Castle, the most northerly in Britain, is a ruinous Z-plan fortalice built by Laurence Bruce of Cultmalindie in 1598, on the Island of Unst. Two storeys and an attic in height, it consists of an unusually long central block with round towers projecting at the north-west and south-east angles. The walls have been harled, a necessary protection against the northern climate, and are well supplied with shot-holes and gun-loops of various patterns.

Over the door in the south front is inscribed, with the date, Bruce's initials and his arms, as well as a quatrain: LIST YE TO KNOW YIS BULDING QUHA BEGAN: LAURENCE THE BRUCE HE WAS THAT WORTHY MAN: QUHA ERNESTLY HIS AIRIS AND OFFSPRING PRAYIS: TO HELP AND NOT TO HURT THIS VARK ALUAYIS.

The entrance lies at the east end of the south front, and leads to a vaulted passage which has the kitchen at the far end equipped with fireplace, stone sink and drain. The passage also leads to a room in the round tower. There are three other vaulted cellars . The eastern room has been the wine-cellar, having the customary stair to the Hall above.

The main stair to the first floor is of the square-plan scale-and-platt variety, intruding curiously between the Hall and a with-drawing-room, the castle being planned with no fewer than five rooms at first-floor level. A stair from the withdrawing-room gave access to the laird's family accommodation above, the floors of which have now gone. Access to the large room above the Hall on the second floor, and to the rest of the accommodation, was by scale-and-platt stair. Nothing remains of the former courtyard.

The reason for the construction of so strong and generously planned a castle in so remote an area is simple. Bruce's mother, a daughter of Lord Elphinstone, had an illegitimate child by James V, who became Robert Stewart, Abbot of Holyrood and Earl of Orkney. Though Bruce was implicated in a murder arising out of

Muness Castle: Z-plan castle on a northern island.

some affray in Perthshire, with the aid of his half-brother he was able to settle down well out of sight and mind. The castle was completed by Laurence's second son, Andrew Bruce.

Murroes Castle

Murroes Castle, standing in the hamlet of the same name, three miles north of Broughty Ferry, is a small late-sixteenth-century fortalice with a circular stair tower projecting westwards from the centre. The ground on which this tower stands is lower than that which carries the rest of the house, so the stair tower is supported by corbels on the inside. Until 1942, the roof of the tower was oversailed by that of the house. Towards the end of the last century, it had become a farm-worker's bothy. It has been completely restored in our own day, the stair tower now rising above the roof-line and being finished with a conical cap, probably a correct restoration. The addition at the south gable was built in the late 1960s.

The internal arrangements date from the Restoration, though the panelling in the drawing-room is said to have come from David Bryce's now demolished Fotheringham House (1859–61), the Fotheringhams of Fotheringham, Tealing, Powrie and Murroes being the owners of the estate of Murroes since the fourteenth century.

Murthly Castle

Murthly, or Murthy Castle, stands near the bank of the Tay four miles or so east-south-east of Dunkeld. It consists of an original free-standing tower of unknown age, though with alterations and the addition of angle turrets dating from the late sixteenth century. To this, extensions have been added at various times, occupying three sides of a square. The later additions include several pediments carrying seventeenth-century dates. No doubt to fill the open square of the courtyard, which it only does in part, a two-storey pedimented entrance hall with a Venetian doorway approached by an external staircase was added in the mid eighteenth century.

The original tower is claimed to have been a hunting-seat of the old Scottish Kings. Rubble built, it rises to a height of four storeys with an attic. Unusually, its conically capped angle-turrets are decorated with string courses.

Murthly came into the hands of the Stewarts of Grantully in 1605, and their arms appear on an heraldic panel near the roof level on the east front, together with the date 1617. They were descendants of Sir John Stewart of Bonkyl, a younger son of Alexander, the fourth High Steward of Scotland, as were James VI and the later Stewart kings as well as the houses of Lennox, D'Aubigny and Darnley. The baronetcy conferred on the Stewarts of Grantully in 1683 came to an end with the eighth baronet in 1890.

In 1829 the sixth baronet commissioned the architect Gillespie Graham to build a great new castle in the Elizabethan style a little to the south of the old castle, but in 1838 this laird died and Graham's building was never fully completed, some of its interior work subsequently being reused to refit part of the old castle. The new castle was demolished after the Second World War as, alas, was the Malakoff arch, a huge hilltop Arc de Triomphe in the grounds.

There survives a walled garden of 1699, laid out in the Dutch manner with terraces, ponds and clipped hedges.

Myres Castle

As the name suggests, Myres Castle stands in what was once marshland, just south of Auchtermuchty.

Originally a Z-shaped tower house joined at the angles, the round towers projecting from opposite angles, it was probably built on an existing structure dating from about 1490. Early in the seventeenth century the south-east circular tower was raised, the new upper section being square. A conical-roofed cap-house corbelled in the angle thus created contains the access to the upper storey and the small flat-roofed parapet. There are florentine inspired roundels amongst the decorative features. The seventeenth-century work is perhaps reminiscent of Earlshall, but on a smaller scale. Gun-loops of various patterns have survived modernisations.

When the poet-king James I was an English prisoner, he became so attached to an English page, Robert Coxwell, that he brought him back to Scotland with him. Coxwell received property in Auchtermuchty which included Myres Castle. In 1453, on Coxwell's death, Myres went to the widow, who took as her second husband John Scrymgeour, second son of the constable of Dundee and mace-bearer to the King. Myres stayed with the Scrymgeours until the early seventeenth century, when the father of another mace-bearer, Michael Paterson, feued it. Greatly enlarged in 1828, the house is still occupied.

Neidpath

Neidpath, L-shaped in plan though with rounded corners, which was once part ruinous, but was repaired in the nineteenth century though it is no longer habitable, stands near the road on a steep bank of the Tweed a mile west of Peebles. The tall rubble-built tower dates from the end of the fourteenth century, in part from the sixteenth, when the two upper floors were completely remodelled, the wallhead lowered, the associated barrel-vault removed and a new partially enclosed parapet walk provided. It is in fact a parallelogram with rectangular rooms in it. A more extensive scheme was carried out by the second Earl of Tweeddale (1653–86) when the ground floor was remodelled, a more spacious stair inserted in the south-east angle and an additional storey inserted

Neidpath Castle: a tower house by the Tweed, the right-hand jagged
edge marking the Cromwellian destruction.

beneath the vault of the Hall. It was once approached through a
door in the re-entrant angle, defensively an awkward arrangement
because of the nearness of the river. The fifth Earl moved the
doorway to the east wall, at forecourt level.

There are two rooms in the basement, one in the main block and
one in the wing. Both are vaulted. The turnpike stair is within the
thick south wall. The much altered first floor has had a wide
staircase added leading to the Hall on the second floor. There was
an adjacent room in the wing. The third floor is also vaulted. A
private turnpike stair in the north-west angle leads up from the
Hall.

There must have been a tower of some sort here when Sir Simon
Fraser, who defeated the English at Rosslyn Moor in 1302, owned

the land. His daughter and heir married Gilbert de Haya of Yester.
The Hays remained in possession until the end of the seventeenth
century, and the Fraser and Hay emblems – the strawberry plant
(*fraise*) of the Frasers and the goat's head of the Hays – are inscribed
on a stone in the courtyard. The builder of the existing tower was
probably Sir William Hay. James VI stayed at Neidpath in 1587.
The Hays were Royalists. In 1650, Neidpath was garrisoned by the
young Lord Yester, when it held out against Cromwell's army
longer than any other fortalice south of the Forth. Part of the upper
works and a substantial section of its southern face were battered in
this engagement, forcing the occupants to succumb. The jagged
edge and fallen stones of the damaged wing are still to be seen. It
was this which led to the fifth Earl's rebuilding of the main block,
his roofing in of the parapet in the north and south sides to form
galleries with square turrets and to provide an extra garret storey,
an arrangement unique in Scottish tower houses. He also planted a
noble avenue of yews along the approach to the castle.

In 1685 the first Duke of Queensberry bought the estate. He
made it over to his second son, the Earl of March, who used it as a
summer home. The third Earl of March died childless, and the
lands came to the fourth Duke of Queensberry; 'Old Q', the
'Degenerate Douglas' whom Wordsworth, at Neidpath on 18
September, 1803, vigorously castigated as the 'unworthy Lord'
who destroyed the trees. A successor, the seventh Earl of Wemyss
and March, later replanted them.

Sir Walter Scott's friend, the historian professor Adam Fergu-
son, was a tenant of the castle towards the close of the eighteenth
century, and Scott was a frequent visitor. Still in the hands of the
Earl of Wemyss, it is well cared for and open to the public.

Newark Castle

Four miles or so south of Ayr, Newark Castle is a sixteenth-century
harled rubble tower on a rocky outcrop. It rises to four storeys with
a garret storey above the parapet, which is carried on individual
corbels. There are open rounds on the two eastern angles, one of
which has a garderobe and drain. There is a square gabled cap-
house on the stair head of the north-west angle.

A seventeenth-century addition enlarged the original near-
square house to a rectangle which contains the present entrance,

and a tablet commemorating the marriage of James Crawfurd and Anne Kennedy in 1687. This section, similar in design to the original has, however, no parapet.

The stair, once reached through the west wall of the courtyard, but now, approached from the later entrance, is built into the thickness of the north-west angle of the original tower. There is a vaulted basement and a small mural guardroom off the lobby, a pattern repeated in the higher floors. The Hall is on the first floor. Extensive additions to the castle were made on the west and north sides about 1848, when the staircase leading into the courtyard at the north-east corner was removed.

The Kennedys of Bargany built this, their 'new wark', and by 1601 it was in the hands of the Craufurds of Camlarg. After Mure of Auchendrane murdered Sir Thomas Kennedy of Culzean – an event dealt with in Sir Walter Scott's play *The Auchendrane Tragedy* – it was to Newark that the murderer fled, and held out safely. Alexander Craufurd sold Newark to the Earls of Cassilis in 1763.

Newark Castle

Newark Castle, one of the most impressive fortified baronial residences, improbably survives surrounded by the paraphernalia of ship building and its related industries, on a spit of land projecting into the River Clyde in the town of Port Glasgow.

The castle began as a square keep, which went up in the fifteenth century. The gate-house block was in all probability added about the middle of the sixteenth century. This provided a west wing. The main block is dated 1597. The finished work thus occupied three sides of a square, the fourth side of which was completed with a curtain wall.

The keep rises to four storeys, the top storey being constructed out of the original parapet, which projected out a little on individual corbels, the cannon-spouts for draining the parapet walk still remaining. This storey is no longer roofed. The fenestration of the keep has been altered at some stage.

The entrance leads to a vaulted basement which once had an entresol, and to a turnpike stair in the north-east angle, serving all floors. There is one room per floor, each with its own garderobe.

The tall gate-house building has three storeys beneath a gabled roof. An arched gateway leads to a vaulted pend which opens into the courtyard. To the left, there is a guardroom with an arrow-slit for protection. To the right, there is a porter's seat. The turnpike stair rises to all floors from the guardroom. The room on the first floor has two windows with stone seats, a fireplace and a garderobe.

The Jacobean addition displays good Renaissance detail on doorways and dormer finials. All its angles have corner turrets and its walls are well provided with gun-loops. A large chimney on the east wall carries the bakehouse flue. On the south front, a conically capped semi-circular stair tower rises from first-floor level. The entrance, in the east re-entrant angle of the courtyard, has above it a panel dated 1597 with the monogram of Sir Patrick Maxwell, its builder, and the motto THE BLESSING'S OF GOD BE HEIRIN.

In the basement, three vaulted rooms open off a connecting corridor, that to the west the kitchen with a wide fireplace, sink and drain, the middle one a store and the third a wine-cellar directly linked to the Hall above. A service stair also gives access to the Hall, a handsome apartment illuminated by seven windows and heated by a richly decorated fireplace. A garderobe and a gun-loop are also provided. The main approach to the Hall, however, is by the main stair rising opposite the entrance to the building. The Hall floor also carries a service pantry and two other small rooms.

The second floor, made of pine, is a gallery which is divided into four rooms by means of movable partitions. All have fireplaces. The garret-storey floor has been taken out.

The lands of Newark were originally owned by the Danielstouns of that Ilk. One of Sir Robert Danielstoun's two heiresses married Sir Robert Maxwell of Calderwood in 1402. The Maxwells were therefore the builders of the entire castle as it now stands.

James IV was a frequent visitor. Records for the year 1497 detail four shillings and eight pence for 'ane bote to fetch wine fra the schip twys, quhenshe lay at the New Werk'; and another, dated the following year, for six shillings to carry 'the Kingis gere . . . to the New Werk' from 'Dumbertone', on which rock, almost opposite, there then stood a now largely-vanished royal castle.

Sir Patrick Maxwell sold the lands around the castle to the magistrates of Glasgow in 1668, the name of the hamlet, Newark, being changed to Port Glasgow and the new port being used to transfer goods to and from large ships to smaller craft that could travel the shallows up-river; a procedure essential until the construction of a deep channel late in the eighteenth century. The castle ceased to be lived in early in the eighteenth century, no doubt because of the growing industrial activity around it. By then in the possession of the Shaw-Stewarts, it was in danger of being destroyed by vandals until taken into State care.

Newark Castle

On the top of the steep right bank of the Yarrow Water, about four miles up from Selkirk, in the grounds of the Buccleuch seat of Bowhill, stands the roofless Newark Castle. It replaced an 'auld wark,' vanished without trace, and was built some time before 1423 by Archibald, Earl of Douglas. It was a royal hunting-seat in Ettrick forest, and the Royal Arms are to be found on the west gable.

The oblong tower was once five storeys high, with rubble walls ten feet thick. The parapet, only sections of which remain, is supported on somewhat rudely fashioned corbelling. Two-storey cap-houses crown the north-west and south-east corner angles. They may be a sixteenth-century addition, being similar to those of that period found at Oakwood and Kirkhope.

The door, now at ground level in the north wall, leads to a vaulted basement which once had a timber entresol floor. A straight stair, changing into a turnpike one, rises in the north-west angle. The Great Hall was on the first floor, having a section at the end screened off to provide the kitchen. The main entrance, by means of a removable wooden stair, was once at this level. There are three mural chambers in the north wall of the Hall, the largest probably being the original guardroom. The upper floors, now collapsed, were reached by a second turnpike stair in the south-east angle. The tower was defended by a barmkin wall, substantial sections of which survive. There was also a gate-house.

Lord Grey took the castle from the English in 1548. Almost a century later, after the Battle of Philliphaugh in which an army of six hundred Royalists under Montrose was defeated by six thousand Covenanters under Leslie, about a hundred wounded prisoners were shot in the courtyard of Newark, the ministers of the Kirk apparently unable, or unwilling, to persuade its Generals to show Christian tolerance to captives of a different religion.

Sir Walter Scott made his Last Minstrel recite his song to the

Newark Castle: a one-time royal hunting seat, where Scott made his Last Minstrel recite.

sorrowing Duchess in Newark. Wordsworth twice visited the castle; in 1814 with his sister and in 1831 with Sir Walter Scott. The ruin has now been secured against further decay.

Newmilns Tower

Newmilns Castle stands behind the Loudon Arms, in the burgh of Newmilns. A small sixteenth-century oblong rubble tower, it rises to three storeys and an attic above the parapet. The roof has been lowered at some time. Though in various states of incompleteness, the open rounds on triple corbelling remain. The castle has string courses at each floor level. There is a vaulted basement and one room on each floor.

A possession of the Loudon family, it was once used as a prison for Covenanters. A band of their fellows, among them John Low, attacked the castle and rescued the prisoners, but Low fell in the affray and his gravestone is in the wall surrounding the castle.

Niddry Castle

Niddry castle, a strong, once handsome and still impressive L-shaped tower house, at one time surrounded by a barmkin, stands on a small outcrop about half a mile south-east of Winchburgh. It is thought to have been built around 1500 by the third Lord Seton, who was killed at Flodden thirteen years later. Of rubble with dressed quoins, it had four storeys and a parapet, now gone, on corbelling, part of which survives. During the seventeenth century, elaborate additional accommodation was added to the top of the tower within the parapet to an even more extraordinary design than that which was placed on top of Preston Tower, but most of the Niddry addition has crumbled away.

The doorway is at ground level, in the re-entrant angle, opening into a guardroom-lobby with its own garderobe. The basement in the main block has one large vaulted chamber, though corbels at the level of the springing of the arch suggest that once there was an entresol timber floor. There is a similarly equipped dungeon in the wing.

Access to all floors was by means of a turnpike stair in the thick walling of the re-entrant angle. The first-floor Hall has an exceptionally large fireplace and a small adjoining kitchen. The upper rooms are mostly equipped with mural closets.

Niddry Seton, as the castle was once known, was the place to which Lord Seton brought Mary, Queen of Scots on the night in 1506 when he assisted in her escape from the Douglas stronghold of Loch Leven Castle. From there she sent a message to her cousin, Queen Elizabeth, before riding to Hamilton, defeat at the Battle of Langside, flight to England, Fotheringay and the executioner's block.

Niddry passed to the Hopes of Hopetoun. At the time of writing it is the subject of a possible restoration via the National Trust for Scotland by a private purchaser, several potential buyers having expressed interest. The eventual removal of a disused pit bing, between which and the Glasgow-Edinburgh railway line Niddry has been trapped for more than a century, would do much to improve its survival chances.

Nisbet House

This well-preserved fortified mansion built in the seventeenth century stands in well-wooded policies two miles or so south of Duns. It has many unusual features. The main block, running east and west, has round towers projecting at the two southern ends, and two square stair towers rising on the opposite north side. In the two re-entrant angles between the stair towers and the main block, facing north-east, above second-floor level there are small stair turrets corbelled out, and there is an angle-turret with gun-loops projecting from the north-east corner of the main block.

The castle rises to four storeys, and, unusually for the period, has a decorative cornice supporting the roof. The crow-stepped stair towers are corbelled out beneath their top storeys to provide small rooms reached by the stair turret.

For its late period, the house is notable not only for the number of gun-loops, but for the curious fact that they are down-tilted, suggesting that they were certainly not put there for decorative reasons.

The entrance is in the north front between the stair towers, is surrounded by moulding and carries above it the Kerr arms and their motto, 'Forward'.

Inside, the ground floor has a vaulted kitchen at the east end and several vaulted cellars. The first-floor Hall has a private room to the east and small linked rooms in the circular towers, each of which has turnpike stairs, that in the north-west tower being the principal stair while that in the north-east tower the private stair from the Hall.

The house has survived with comparatively little disfiguring alteration, although during the eighteenth century a large square tower with Gibbsian details was built on to the west end. It contains superb Rococo plasterwork.

The previous Nisbet Castle was removed when the present structure was put up, probably about 1630 by Sir Alexander Nisbet of that Ilk, though it is said to have been paid for out of the fortune of his heiress wife, Katherine Swindon of that Ilk. Ill-luck struck the family, however, during the Civil War; one of the sons was killed in action, two were executed and she and her husband had to flee their lands. The Kerrs then acquired the property.

Noltland

Noltland – with Drochil, Peeblesshire, one of the two largest Z-plan castles in Scotland – was built during the last quarter of the sixteenth century, though it has been claimed that it incorporates sections of the structure erected earlier for the princely prelate Bishop de Tulloch. It was besieged by Sir William Sinclair of Warsetter, and later seized by Sir Gilbert Balfour of Mountquhannie, brother-in-law of Adam, Bishop of Orkney. This was the time when, following the Reformation, Church lands and riches were being 'redistributed', providing previously impecunious lairds with funds for building. Sir Gilbert Balfour is probably responsible for the present imposing structure.

Noltland's main block had, or was intended to have, four storeys and an attic, which provided a bedroom reached by means of a walkway along the parapet wall. This block is flanked by two square towers. Sir Gilbert, whose family was implicated in much of the dirty business that characterised the reign of Mary, Queen of Scots, and who had to flee to Sweden, where he was eventually put to death, must have felt permanently insecure, for Noltland's seven-foot-thick walls have so many tiers of yawning gun-loops that some writers have compared them to the hull of a timber man-o'-war. Over seventy of these gun-loops can still be counted on the surviving structure.

The northern tower, which contains a bedroom, and what remains of the link section of the main block (which may never have been finished), rise to the full height, though now roofless. The rest of the main structure has lost its upper storeys. The northern tower and connecting wall are finished with a projecting parapet. It is, of course, possible that Sir Gilbert had to flee before he was able to raise the main part of the castle to the intended four storeys. Corbelling of an unusual design linked diagonally to the main block supports the upper storeys of the northern tower, projecting space for the stair above first-floor level.

In the seventeenth century a southern extension was added, across the courtyard. It consisted of an L-shaped block together with corbelling to carry a circular angle-turret. Additional eighteenth-century work extended these ranges to the east and the west.

Entrance to the courtyard was through an arched gateway. The moulded castle doorway itself was placed in the re-entrant angle of the south-west tower, and was flanked by shot-holes. A porter's chamber was cunningly fitted in beneath the turn of the unusually wide main wheel stair, which rises gently round a thick newel, itself pierced by a gun-loop and crowned by a capital. A vaulted passage to the right of the entrance led diagonally to the kitchen quarters, which were located in the west end of the block. The handsome stone-roofed Hall, sixty-two feet long and twenty-four feet wide, above the kitchen, has a moulded fireplace and stone seats in one of its windows. A pantry recess with two aumries and a gun-loop are situated in the north-west angle, near the kitchen flue. To the east, there is a withdrawing-room, also with stone seats and garderobes. Beside the top of the main stair there are the beginnings of a secondary stair which does not appear ever to have been finished.

Noltland was considered as a possible place of refuge for Mary, Queen of Scots after her escape from Loch Leven Castle, and preparations were made to receive her. In 1592 it was besieged by Earl Patrick Stewart. It made its final little historical gesture when it gave refuge to the last surviving officers of the Marquis of Montrose's army. Soon after, it was allowed to fall into ruin. For many more years, however, until well into the twentieth century, it was illuminated to celebrate births in the Balfour family.

Nunraw

Nunraw, half a mile east of Garvald, was originally a fifteenth-century peel tower built, allegedly, by Cistercian nuns, who must have been somewhat alarmed to be charged by James II with the responsibility of fortifying the nunnery and having 'guns aye loaded to shoot at our aulden enemies of England'. Whether the ladies ever did this is perhaps questionable. At the Reformation, the tower fell into the hands of the Hepburns, the family of the Earl of Bothwell.

The north tower, all that remains of the old structure, has walls six feet thick rising to four storeys, and with an attic beyond the parapet carried on corbelling, drained by cannon-spouts. There are open rounds in all but the south-west angle, where the tower is joined to the nineteenth-century mansion. The basement and first floor of the tower are vaulted, the original Hall floor having a garderobe. Nineteenth-century renovation uncovered the fine painted refectory ceiling, dated 1461, and bearing the arms of several Continental royal families. Part of the ceiling is now in the National Museum of Antiquities, Edinburgh.

In 1946, the Cistercians returned to take back Nunraw and construct the first monastery to be founded in Scotland since the Reformation, alongside their new Abbey of Sancta Maria.

Oakwood Tower

Oakwood stands on the edge of the steep right bank of the Ettrick Water, four and a half miles from Selkirk. It is an oblong tower without parapet or parapet walk, rubble-built, and rising to three storeys with an attic. There are rectangular turrets on the north-east and south-east angles supported on elaborate corbelling, and with gabled roofs. The steeply pitched roof itself has crow-stepped gables. The arched and moulded doorway still has its iron-studded door and iron tirling-pin, on the west wall at ground level. It opens on a lobby which leads to a vaulted basement, and to a wide turnpike stair with a remarkably thick newel, in the south-east angle.

The Hall is on the first floor and has an elaborate fireplace, three aumbries, a garderobe and two windows, an additional two having been built in. The small room on the same level has a fireplace and two wall cupboards. The second floor is similar to the first, though with a higher ceiling.

Oakwood was built by Robert Scott in 1602, on the site of the birthplace of the thirteenth-century wizard Sir Michael Scott of Balwearie.

Ochiltree Castle, or Place

Ochiltree Castle, about four miles south-east of Linlithgow, is an L-shaped rubble house of three storeys and an attic, its wing to the north, its stair within the re-entrant angle. It has angle turrets at the north-west and south-east corners. The original doorway, recently reopened, is in an unusual vestibule, outshot and clasping the front of the stair tower, but the present entrance is in the west wall, surrounded by a later porch ornamented with reused dormer heads containing the arms of Sir Archibald Stirling of Keir and his wife, Dame Grisel Ross, and the date 1610, from which the dormer windows probably also date. In the early eighteenth century the north jamb was doubled in length, the addition being a storey lower.

Its Ayrshire name doubtless derives from the sixteenth century, when it may have been the property of 'Captain Jamie' Stewart of Ochiltree in Ayrshire, who became Earl of Arran and Chancellor of Scotland. Ochiltree Castle became a farmhouse and was on the verge of dereliction when it was partially restored and reoccupied.

Old House of Gask

Four and a half miles north-east of Auchterarder stands the Old House of Gask, an extensive courtyard house abandoned in favour of Richard Crichton's early-nineteenth-century mansion nearby. The Oliphants of Gask got their lands from Robert the Bruce in the fourteenth century and became Lords of Gasknes and Aberdalgie. A Laurence Oliphant was created Lord Oliphant in 1458. But the fifth lord, said to be 'ane base and unworthy man', sold most of his lands except Gask, which was eventually bought in 1625 by his cousin, the first of the Jacobite Lairds of Gask and the builder of this house.

The west wing, of three storeys, contained the 'Jacobite Hall', and was reconstructed from the ruins in 1932. There is an arched northern gateway with a bellcote above, dated 1632. The ruined south wing is of two storeys with sculpted dormer heads dated 1641. There is a circular angle tower at the north-east. There are two seventeenth-century sundials in the garden.

On 11 September, 1745, Prince Charles Edward Stewart breakfasted at the 'Auld Hoose' – a lock of his hair was given to his host and became a family heirloom – and the following February Gask was duly ransacked by the Hanoverians. Caroline Oliphant, later Lady Nairne, was born in the old house in August 1766, celebrating it in 'The Auld Hoose, which, along with 'The Land o' the Leal', 'The Laird o' Cockpen', 'Caller Herrin' and 'Will ye no come back again?' has kept her Scotland's most celebrated song-writer after Burns.

Old Knock Castle

Old Knock Castle stands in the grounds of Knock Castle, J.T. Rochead's mansion built for the Greenock industrialist Robert Steele shortly after 1850, and for which the early-sixteenth-century tower house was abandoned. It overhangs a ravine on the Clyde Coast, about three miles north of Largs.

Originally it was a Z-plan tower, but only half the ruins survive. The main block of four storeys and a garret once had circular towers at its north-east and south-west angles. The northern tower and most of the main block have crumbled to a ruined shell. The southern tower, housing a turnpike stair, survives, having been restored, as does the section of the main block containing the entrance. There is still a dovecote still above the crow-step-gabled garret. There is generous provision of shot-holes and a splayed gun-loop above the door to the stair-tower. Almost all that is left of the curtain wall preserves a moulded doorway with an heraldic panel bearing the initials i.f. and i.b. and the date 1604.

John Fraser, son of Hugh Fraser of Lovat, came into the lands of Knock by marrying the heiress in 1380. The Frasers of Knock supported Montrose and suffered so severely that after Philiphaugh they had to sell out to the nearby Montgomeries of Skelmorlie, the first of many subsequent owners.

Old Leckie House

Six miles west of Stirling, in the Carse of Stirling, Old Leckie dates from the late sixteenth century. It is a T-plan tower house, the main block having three storeys and a wing which projects from the centre of the south front. A stair turret is corbelled out from first-floor level in the eastern re-entrant angle. A second stair in the western re-entrant angle rises to second-floor level. Formerly the wing contained a large stair to first-floor level. Beneath it is the original entrance sheltered by an arch, but still with its iron yett. A lower east wing was added in the mid-eighteenth century when the interior was refitted, though the fine columned Hall fireplace remains. The house, superseded as the laird's residence when New Leckie (now Watson House) was built in 1830, and is still occupied, having recently been restored.

There was a Mordaco de Leckie in a previous house on the site in

1406. It then came to the Crown, being given by James II in 1451 to Adam Cosure, a burgess of Stirling who had loaned the king money. The debt repaid, James III took successful steps to dispossess Cosure, and the lands went to the aptly named William, Lord Moneypenny who, however, sold them, months later to Andrew, Lord Avondale.

A century later a descendant of the original owner, John Leckie of Leckie, bought back the lands and built the present castle. Baillie David Moir of Stirling bought the castle from the Leckies in 1659, and his descendants retained it until the beginning of the present century.

Prince Charles Edward Stuart called at the house on 13 September, 1745.

Orchardton Tower

Four miles south of Dalbeattie, Orchardton is the only free-standing circular tower house in Scotland. Four storeys high, it has a parapet and a walk, and there is a gabled cap-house within the parapet. Substantial remains of barmkin building survive.

The original entrance to the south at first-floor level would be by movable wooden stairs from the courtyard. The ground floor is entered through an arched doorway facing west. The first floor is now reached by an external forestair through an aperture that was once a window.

The Hall on the first floor, like the rooms above, is circular. The upper floors have unfortunately fallen in.

The tower was built by John Cairns in 1456, but later bought by a member of the Maxwell family. The Jacobite grandson of Sir Robert Maxwell was captured at Culloden and taken to Carlisle. While languishing in prison, he was interrupted in the process of destroying his personal papers. These, however, proved his salvation, for his commission turned out to be signed by the King of France. He was thus a genuine prisoner of war, and not a rebel. Sent back to France, he later returned to Scotland to claim Orchardton. Scott made use of this story in his novel *Guy Mannering*.

Orchardton Round Tower: the only freestanding round tower in Scotland.

Peffermill House

An early-seventeenth-century house, L-shaped in plan, of three storeys with a garret built of harled rubble for Edward Edgar, possibly on the remains of an existing fortalice, Peffermill stands on land he had bought from the Prestons of Craigmillar. Edgar's master mason is thought to have been William Aytoun, the three sundials on its wall closely resembling those by Aytoun at Heriot's Hospital, Edinburgh. The house was owned by Osborns and Alexanders before being turned into a farmhouse in the early nineteenth century and much altered. In 1911/12 it was repaired and converted into three flats. Since then it again reached near dereliction, from which it was rescued by the architect Nick Groves-Raines, who uses it as both house and office.

It is said to have provided the prototype for the Laird of Dumbiedykes in Scott's *Heart of Midlothian*. It was the scene of one unusual occurrence. When the body of Margaret Dickson, hanged in Edinburgh for murder, was being carried to Musselburgh for burial, her relatives stopped at Peffermill House to refresh themselves. Meanwhile, a passer-by, overcome by curiosity, began to inspect the load on the cart, and discovered the corpse in the process of coming to life. When the mourners returned, it is said that she was quite herself again. For the rest of her days she was known as Half-Hangit Maggie o' Musselburgh.

Penkill Castle

Penkill Castle stands about three miles east of Girvan, a sixteenth-century square tower rising to three storeys and a garret with a seventeenth-century addition, making it into an L-plan fortalice. There was a circular stair tower in the re-entrant angle, but this is now replaced by a heavier Victorian tower. There are conically capped angle-turrets corbelled out at both the north-west and the south-east corners, each containing shot-holes. The 1628 wing also has three storeys and an attic, though it does not match the height of the original tower.

Above the vaulted basement, lit with arrow-slits, is the first-floor Hall. It has a large fireplace and a former garderobe, now serving as a link with a later wing. There are stone window seats in the second-floor apartment.

The tower was probably built by Adam Boyd, grandson of Robert, Lord Kilmarnock, early in the sixteenth century. The first addition was built by Thomas Boyd, Adam's great-great-grandson, who married a Muir of Rowallan. After the death of another Adam Boyd in 1750, the succession moved to a junior line of the family.

By 1857, Penkill was in poor repair. It was extensively and rather unsympathetically restored by Spencer Boyd, the designer being William Bell Scott, the pre-Raphaelite artist and poet, with the Glasgow civil engineer A.G. Thomson as executant. On Spencer Boyd's death his sister, Alice Boyd, succeeded, and invited Dante Gabriel Rossetti, then suffering from eye trouble, to stay during the summers of 1868 and 1869. William Bell Scott, who painted the staircase, became terminally ill at Penkill and died there in 1883. The castle thus has strong associations with the pre-Raphaelite brotherhood and until recent years was also rich in contents. Some of these were unfortunately dispersed in the 1960s and 70s, but the present owner, the American Elton Eckstrand, has reacquired as much as possible.

Pinkie House

The lodge gates of Pinkie House are visible from the High Street of Musselburgh. Though now it is one of the most impressive seventeenth-century houses to be found in Scotland, it began its existence as an L-plan tower, possibly based on an older fortalice. The tower is now the northern end of the main block, and was once the country seat of the Abbots of Dunfermline. It thus passed to Alexander Seton, first Earl of Dunfermline, Chancellor to James VI. In 1613 Seton proceeded to extend the building to the south and west, adding, amongst other external features, massive chimney-stacks along the east front, two little square-plan angle-towers on the north gable, and singularly opulent-looking three-storeyed oriel windows on the south gable. There is also a lower extension to the west of the palace – which is what the building became – put up later in the seventeenth century.

The main block has three storeys beneath a pitched roof. The ground floor is vaulted. A turnpike stair in the original tower gives access to the first and second floors, access above being by a turret stair corbelled on the north-west re-entrant angle and topped by a cap-house which leads to the flat roof of the tower. As at Fyvie, where Chancellor Seton was also active, a courtyard was planned by the Earl – perhaps with Hatfield, the English home of the Cecils in mind – but was never finished, though happily the English-inspired Jacobean fountain, destined to be its centre-piece, was built. The Tudor additions, put up in 1825, are by William Burn.

The outstanding apartment is the ninety-six-foot-long gallery, with its Italian-style tempera painted ceiling of cherubs and naked females. When Loretto School took over the building and it was proposed to use this room as a dormitory for boys, the then Headmaster thought it likely to exercise a disturbing influence on them and proposed to have it covered over or removed. Fortunately, better counsels prevailed. There is also a fine plaster ceiling in the Seton room, where the building Earl died in 1622

The 'King's Room', elaborately decorated with pendants and other fine plasterwork devices, is so named because Charles I is thought to have slept there. It is also said to have provided sleeping accommodation for Prince Charles Edward on the victorious night following his defeat of Sir John Cope at Prestonpans.

Pinwherry Castle

Standing on raised ground in the village of Stinchar, near the junction of the River Stinchar with the Muick Water, five miles or so from Colmonell, Pinwherry Castle, a much-ruined sixteenth-century stronghold, was an L-plan fortalice belonging to the Kennedy family.

The door is in the ground floor of the wing, beneath a square stair tower, corbelled from first-floor level in the re-entrant angle. There is a second turnpike stair within the south-west corner. The gables were crow-stepped, with circular angle turrets at the southern angles. The interior has collapsed.

John Kennedy built Pinwherry about 1596. The last of his line died in 1644. After a short period in the possession of the Earls of Carrick, it was bought by the Pollock family, but was abandoned before the close of the eighteenth century.

Pitcaple Castle

Pitcaple stands on the right bank of the river Ury five miles north-west of Inverurie. A Z-plan castle dating mainly from the early seventeenth century, it does, however, incorporate older work. By 1830 it had become semi-ruinous and was restored and extended by William Burn, his new wing extending southwards from the south-west angle.

The main block, lying north/south, rises to three storeys and an attic with higher circular towers at south-west and north-east. There is a turret at the south-east corner. A diminutive stair turret projects high up in the re-entrant angle between the main south gable and the south-west round tower. The north-east tower is for some reason known as the Thane's Tower. Gun-loops were discovered in its walls during reharling in our own time.

The original entrance is at the foot of the south-west tower. The main block's basement is vaulted, as are all four storeys of the Thane's Tower. The Hall as always is on the first floor. Among the bedroom accommodation above is the room in which Charles II spent a night in June 1650, having ended his Dutch exile by landing at Garmouth.

James II gave Pitcaple by charter to David Leslie in 1457, in all probability the date of the original castle on the site. The Leslies were a wild lot. George, the fourth laird, killed George Leith of Freefield, resulting not only in lasting enmity between the two families but leading to the laird's exile and death as an officer in a foreign army.

James IV and Mary, Queen of Scots both visited Pitcaple, the latter allegedly breakfasting in the castle while on her way north to destroy the power of the Gordons.

Another feud, involving James Leslie, the laird's second son, in 1630 led to the burning of the house of Frendraught, with considerable loss of life. James's father – he who had entertained his monarch just over a year before – died for him at the Battle of Worcester. Following his betrayal by MacLeod of Assynt, Montrose was lodged in another room in Pitcaple on his way to his execution in Edinburgh.

The Leslies remained lairds until 1757, when Jane, half-sister of the last Sir James, married Professor James Lumsden of the University of Aberdeen. Their daughters sold it to another branch of the Lumsden family.

Further additions, including the red granite Corinthian columns of the entrance hall and main stair, and the service court, were provided by Duncan MacMillan in 1870.

Pitcullo Castle

Pitcullo Castle, a late-sixteenth-century L-shaped tower house two miles or so west of Leuchars, began as a rectangular block extended, rather awkwardly, in the seventeenth century by the addition of an enveloping south-west tower. There is an half-oval stair tower at the rear of the building.

The main block is three storeys high with a basement at one end. The square south-west tower has an unusually small corner lantern turret with a conical roof set on corbelling just beneath the foot of the crow-step gable.

The main stair in the wing reaches to first-floor level. In the re-entrant angle, a turret on corbelling gives access to the floors above, this turret being squared at the top to form a cap-house or watch-platform. A stair tower on the north front was once also squared at the summit.

The main entrance is at the foot of the stair wing, guarded by a splayed gun-loop – indeed, the defensive features appear to have been remarkably varied when the castle was still in its ruined state. The vaulted basement had two rooms, that to the west being the kitchen with a gable fireplace and oven. The Hall was one of two first-floor rooms, and had a mural closet.

Pitcullo was originally the property of the Sibbalds, but came to the Balfours in the sixteenth century. In the late 1960s, it was bought by a restoring purchaser, Roy Spence. Because of the loss of much of its upper works, and the dangerous condition of the seventeenth-century wing, which was leaning away from the remainder, it had to be demolished. The building was perhaps reroofed rather than restored, the present dining-room, for example, being fashioned out of the vaulted basement, the stepped levels of which are a very unusual feature. While the renovation was hardly handled with quite the imaginative lavishness Sir Robert Lorimer bestowed upon similar tasks, the result, though it did not please all the purists, seemed commendable, since what would otherwise have remained a decayed ruin now has a new and useful life. In any case, further work has since been carried out on the castle by Ian Begg and Dorothy Bell for a new owner.

Pitfichie Castle

Sixteenth-century Pitfichie Castle, on the right bank of the Don, a mile north of Monymusk, is a rectangular block of four storeys with a large round tower projecting at its south-west angle. There is a semi-circular stair turret in the east re-entrant angle corbelled square to form a gabled cap-house. Its two massive chimney-stacks are a notable feature. The arched entrance is at the foot of the round tower. The hall is on the first floor with sleeping accommodation above. A large section of the castle fell in 1936, but had fortunately been well recorded. Pitfichie has since been sensitively restored, with assistance from the Historic Buildings Council for Scotland.

Pitfichie was owned by the Urrie, or Hurry family, from which came General Hurry, who featured in the Civil War. In 1650, an unpleasant Urrie got himself outlawed for raiding the homes of the tenants of Forbes of Forneidlie, stealing their cattle. In 1657, Pitfichie came into the hands of Forbes of Monymusk. John Forbes of Pitfichie raised taxes for the Jacobite army in 1715.

Pitfichie Castle: the seemingly doomed ruin . . .

Pitfichie Castle: . . . but sensitively restored from old records.

Pitkerro Castle

Pitkerro, three miles north of Broughty Ferry, is a long, narrow mansion dating from the later sixteenth century. Near the centre of the east front it has a round stair tower corbelled into a square gabled watch-room, as at Claypotts. This is approached by a tiny stair tower in the re-entrant angle above the later crowstep-gabled porch. There is a conically capped angle-turret corbelled out on the opposite corner.

The first floor contained the Hall and private room, but they are both of such length that they have been partitioned from the start. The usual stair led up from the wine-cellar to the private apartment.

Pitkerro was probably built by John Durham, second son of Alexander Durham of Grange of Monifeith. It remained in the hands of the Durhams until the beginning of the eighteenth century. In the early nineteenth century it was remodelled, the roof being cut down to a lower pitch. By 1902 it had come into the ownership of Colonel Douglas Dick, who engaged Sir Robert Lorimer to make it one arm of a large L-plan mansion with a fine garden. Lorimer gave it back its high-roofed crow-stepped profile, restored the dormers and reroofed the turrets with his characteristic bell-shaped roofs, but partly overlaid the east elevation with new buildings. Its future was in some doubt after the Second World War but it is now flatted.

Pitreavie Castle

Standing two miles south of Dunfermline, Pitreavie Castle was built by Henry Wardlaw, later Sir Henry, about 1638. The architect may have been his father, also Henry. A sundial on a terrace on the south side of the house bore the date 1644. After the Battle of Inverkeithing in 1651 – the last to be fought on Fife soil – when Cromwell defeated the Scots, it is said that some Highlanders, who had taken heavy casualties, begged for shelter within the castle. Wardlaw's family, however, killed them by throwing stones from the roof of Pitreavie. Legend attributes to this act of inhumanity the family's loss of their property, since it passed to the Blackwoods soon after.

Sir Henry's grandson, the third Baronet of Pitreavie, married Elizabeth Halkett, whose pseudo-archaic ballad of 'Hardyknute' played some part in arousing interest in genuine balladry in the early stages of the eighteenth-century literary revival. The estate passed from the Wardlaws to the Blackwood family, but by the mid-nineteenth century the house was deserted, though maintained.

Pitreavie, still basically externally an early-seventeenth-century double-plan mansion, is now in the hands of the Royal Navy and the Royal Air Force. A Dutch-style chimney-gable is a feature of the view of the house from the south-west. The entrance hall at the foot of the staircase has mouldings on the edge of the newel, which is finished at top and bottom in an unusual way. Much of the fine plasterwork and panelling has been retained, though extensive alterations were made as long ago as the late nineteenth century. The initials s.h.w. for Sir Henry Wardlaw, surrounded by knotted wreaths, survive on a decorative architrave over the Renaissance doorway in the re-entrant west wing.

Pitsligo Castle

Pitsligo Castle, a few miles west of Fraserburgh and half a mile east of Rosehearty, is a ruined but once powerful courtyard castle which developed from an oblong fifteenth-century keep on the south side. An arched entrance gateway in the high west enclosing wall of the outer court has a panel inscribed with the impaled arms of the Forbes and Erskines, the initials of Alexander, Lord Pitsligo, and the date 1656. Over the gateway to the inner court are the initials of Alexander, second Lord, and Mary Erskine his wife, and the date 1663, the year of his succession to the title. There is a tall flanking drum-tower at the north-east angle of the courtyard. The main tower had two main vaulted storeys with entresols, but virtually all above the upper vault has now gone. The stair tower and attached extension at the north-east corner is slightly less ruinous.

In 1723, Patrick Cook, in his *New History of Aberdeen*, wrote: '... The old tower of Pitsligo was built about three hundred years ago, eighty foot long, and thirty-six foot broad, the walls six foot thick. It was divided into three stories, of which two are yet standing. The whole house consisted of three rooms – the lowermost was the kitchen, and is twelve foot high; the second was the eating-room, and twenty-five foot high; the third, which was taken down about twenty years ago, was the sleeping apartment for the whole family and had in it twenty-four beds.'

There are panels dated 1577 with the initials of James VI (who was six in that year) over the courtyard doorway, and on the east wall of the tower a quartering of the arms of Scotland, England, Ireland and France and the date 1603.

The first Lord Pitsligo, Alexander Forbes, was so created in 1633. His great-grandson forfeited the title for his part in the Forty-Five.

Pitteadie Castle

Pitteadie Castle, originally a simple tower with very thick walls entered at first-floor level and dating from the fifteenth or early sixteenth centuries, survives as a ruin on a hill two miles north-west of Kinghorn. In the sixteenth century three substantial alterations were made, leaving the castle with three angle-turrets and a stair tower at the remaining corner, and also providing a handsome Renaissance gateway, dated 1686, which survives and carries the family crest and initials of William Calderwood, an Edinburgh apothecary who bought Pitteadie in 1671.

The basement is vaulted, as was the stone first floor, but the remaining floors have collapsed.

In 1564 the property belonged to William Kirkcaldy of Grange, but was owned around 1620 by James Boswell of Balmuto, who probably made the alterations. It has long been abandoned, although restoration has been considered in recent years.

Pittfirrane Castle

Pittfirrane Castle, two miles west of Dunfermline, home of the Halketts, began as a free-standing tower. In 1583 a member of the family removed the parapet walk, raised the walling and added a square stair tower and angle-turrets. His great-grandson, Sir Charles Halkett, put on an L-shaped wing to the east in the late seventeenth century; since when further additions and alterations have been made to a castle that now serves as a golf club house.

Several Halketts were provosts of Dunfermline. Through the female line the property passed to the Wedderburns, who then took the Halkett name. Sir Peter Halkett, an officer on the Hanoverian side, was taken prisoner by the Jacobite army at Prestonpans and released on parole. Ordered to break his parole by the Duke of Cumberland, he resigned his commission rather than so tarnish his honour, though he later fought with distinction in the American war as a colonel.

Pittulie Castle

Pittulie Castle, half a mile from Pitsligo and about four miles from Fraserburgh, consists of an oblong block with a square tower at the north-east corner. It appears to date from the end of the sixteenth century and probably replaces a previous castle on the site. It has remarkably low angle-turrets on the south-east and south-west gables and unique squared angle windows on corbelling – now unfortunately less intact than they were a century or so ago, as a comparison with the drawings by MacGibbon and Ross will show.

The main block had two storeys and an attic, the main stair in the square tower rising to the first floor, a turreted stair on the north front from the level of the large Hall rising higher. The upper floors of the tower were reached by another turreted stair corbelled out from the second floor. The original entrance is by the north front of the tower.

In spite of various dates on the building – 1658, 1677 and 1727 – the house was probably built for the marriage of Alexander Fraser and Margaret Abernethy of Saltoun in 1596. As a result of this marriage, the Frasers inherited the Saltoun peerage. The castle passed to the Cumine family, who enlarged it but abandoned it around 1850.

Place of Mochrum

In the centre of moorland, surrounded by a cluster of lochs, about five miles south of Kirkcowan stands Mochrum Castle, formerly Drumwalt; two towers, the western of early-fifteenth-century origin and the other a century or so younger, standing separately in a courtyard.

The older tower is oblong, of four storeys, its north and south sides having parapets on individual corbels with open rounds at the angles and cannon-spouts to drain the walkways. The crowstep gables contain a reconstructed garret, remodelled during a sensitive restoration by the Marquis of Bute, begun in 1873, with the local architect Richard Park working closely under the Marquis's supervision. A hall linking the two towers was added in 1877/8, and in 1902 the distinguished arts-and-crafts architect Robert Weir Schultz took over, refitting the building with superb woodwork, some of it made in the Marquis's Cardiff workshops, some by Ernest Gimson and Ernest and Sydney Barnsley.

The door to the east leads to the lower basement, above which is an entresol floor under the vaulting. The lower floor was the kitchen. The turnpike stair in the south-east angle leads to modernised rooms as it winds up to the cap-house, which gives entry to the parapet walk.

The east tower is also oblong, crowstep-gabled but with a square gabled stair tower projecting to the north. An underground passage links the stair tower with the modern north wing.

Mochrum was given to Thomas Dunbar, second son of the Earl of March, in 1368. A member of the family was Gavin Dunbar, James V's Archbishop of Glasgow and Chancellor of Scotland. The family received a Nova Scotia baronetcy in 1694, but then, or soon after, the Place of Mochrum passed to the Earls of Dumfries, later Marquises of Bute.

On an islet in Castle Loch there are the foundations of the still older Myrtoun Castle, a stronghold of the McCullochs.

Plean Castle

Plean Castle, a mile east of Plean village, is probably of fifteenth-century origin. The original walls rise three storeys to the parapet corbelling, above which would have been a garret within the gables. There would have been open rounds at three angles except the north-east, where the cap-house stood at the head of the stair in this angle.

Neither the present entrance in the south front nor the inscription above it is original. A straight stair leads to the Hall on the first floor, which has a window with stone seats, two garderobes and a fireplace. A turnpike stair rises to the now subdivided second floor.

The ground floor is unvaulted, though the remains of the sixteenth-century courtyard buildings show that once it was vaulted.

Badly restored a generation ago, when an ugly windowed storey was inserted in the parapet, Plean is again derelict.

The lands of Plean, or Plane, came to the probable builder of the tower, Lord Somerville, through marriage in 1449. In the late sixteenth century they passed to the Nicolsons of Carnock.

Plunton Castle

Plunton Castle stands on a farm three miles south-east of Gatehouse of Fleet. It is an L-plan tower house of the late sixteenth century, three storeys high beneath the wallhead and with an attic. A turnpike stair rose up the small wing projecting at the south-west corner, but has now gone. From the entrance in the re-entrant angle, at the foot of the stair tower, there was access to two vaulted basement cellars, the more northerly also having direct access from the courtyard to the west, presumably a store of some kind, though defensively a weak arrangement. The Hall is, as usual, on the first floor. The two bedroom floors above each had four rooms with fireplaces.

Plunton was the seat of the McGhies in the early sixteenth century, but passed to a family called Lennox, after whom the farm on which the ruined castle stands is now named. Sir Walter Scott used Plunton-Lennox castle, as it was later known, as the scene for his unsuccessful melodrama *The Doom of Devorgoil*.

Portincross Castle

Portincross Castle stands on a jutting rock in the Firth of Clyde two miles west of West Kilbride. It is of unusual plan, a red sandstone oblong block, with a tall wing appended to its east end, rising to three storeys with a garret in the tower block and an extra storey in the wing. The parapets, on individual corbels, are without rounds.

There are two entrances at right angles to each other in the re-entrant angle, that to the tower being arched, that to the wing leading to the first floor. There is a kitchen in the vaulted basement with a straight stair to the first floor and, in the linking wall of the two sections, a turnpike stair beyond. The Hall in the main block is vaulted, with an *entresol* floor at the base of the vaulting. There is an additional kitchen at first-floor level. The higher part of the building is now ruinous, having stood exposed to the elements since a gale stripped its roof in 1739.

The Ross family backed the wrong side in the Comyn/Bruce struggle, and the victorious King gave Portincross to a loyal follower, Sir Robert Boyd of Kilmarnock, with whose family the castle remained until 1785, when the line ceased. Several of the Stewart kings visited Portincross, signing and dating charters there.

Preston Tower

Preston Tower, which stands in a market garden near the road from Edinburgh to North Berwick, and not far from the site of the Battle of Prestonpans, was originally a Home fortalice, probably of fifteenth-century origin. It passed by marriage into the family of Hamilton, who thereafter were known as the Hamiltons of Preston.

Originally a strong L-shaped tower, its present somewhat strange, extended telescope-like appearance is the work of Sir John Hamilton who, around 1626, to increase his domestic accommodation simply built what amounted to a two-storey house with dormer windows within the parapet walk on top of the tower, a somewhat similar solution to that carried out at Niddry, West Lothian.

Preston's red sandstone walls, seven feet thick, originally contained three main storeys. The parapet is of dressed ashlar, supported on individual corbels, some of which are gargoyles. There are open rounds at each angle of the parapet.

The vaulted basement is entered by a door on the east wall, secured by an outer door and inner iron yett. It contains what must once have been a fearsome cellar prison, with ventilation but no light and accessible by a hatch from an entresol floor, also no doubt a prison cell, though a little less horrific. It, too, could be reached only by a hatch from above.

The entrance to the vaulted hall on the first floor is by the once circular-headed but now square-headed main door, which was secured by a drawbar, and could only be reached by removable wooden stairs. Corbels over the door suggest that there was once a projecting wooden hoarding round this part of the tower. The Hall has a large fireplace and a walled chamber. A trapdoor in the floor allowed the owner to inspect his victims in the upper cellar beneath. A passage from the hall leads to what was possibly the lord's private room, also on the first floor. The newelled turnpike stair to the higher floor winds up within the thickness of the south-west angle wall. There is a small vaulted apartment with fireplace and garderobe in the wing, no doubt the guardroom for whoever had the task of watching the unfortunate prisoners below. The third floor contains two unvaulted rooms. Another turnpike stair at the re-entrant angle led to the seventeenth-century addition, now wholly ruinous. The semi-circular pediments above its dormers carry the initials of Sir John and Dame Katherine Hamilton.

The tower was burned in 1544 during Hertford's invasion; again by Cromwell in 1650, to punish the laird of Preston Tower for having dared to raise a troop of horse to fight against the Protector at Dunbar; and finally, after being repaired, accidentally in 1663. It was then abandoned.

The Professor of Logic at Edinburgh University, Sir William Hamilton (1791–1856), claimed back the title (forfeited in 1684 because of a Hamilton refusal to take the oath to William of Orange) and also acquired the ruined tower, subsequently repaired and consolidated again by Miss Stirling Hamilton after it was scheduled as an Ancient Monument in 1936.

Provan Hall

Provan Hall, six miles east of Glasgow, stands on lands which were owned by the Prebendary of Barlanark, canonry of Glasgow Cathedral. One of its canons was the self-appointed James IV, an office he undertook as part of his penance for what he regarded as his share of blame for the death of his father after the Battle of Sauchieburn. By the sixteenth century, however, it was in the hands of the Baillie family, who erected the earliest part of the hall.

Provan Hall is thus a late-sixteenth-century defended house forming one side of a courtyard on the south side of which is a small but well-finished early-eighteenth-century house. High curtain-walls frame off the remaining sides. There is a moulded arched gateway with, above it, a lookout platform reached by a flight of steps within the courtyard.

The old house is oblong, with a conically roofed stair tower projecting from the north-east corner and containing shot-holes. The rubble walls rise to two storeys, though there is a garret within the steeply pitched roof. An outside forestair now replaces the original in the stair tower.

There are three vaulted rooms in the basement, the largest of which was the kitchen, and this has a wide arched fireplace, an oven and a drain. The vaulting of the other two rooms runs at right angles to that in the kitchen.

The first floor has two rooms, each with a hooded fireplace. The eastern room has a closet in the tower. The western room also has a closet with a window in the south-east angle. This floor was originally reached by an external stair, the only other link being a hatch to one of the basement rooms.

The house came to the Hamiltons through the marriage of a Baillie daughter to Sir Robert Hamilton. A date on the screen wall running along the east side of the court to the south, 1671, also bears the initials of Sir Partick Hamilton. The City of Glasgow bought it in 1667. After various vicissitudes, it was bought by a group of people in 1935 when again up for sale and given to the National Trust for Scotland.

Ravenscraig Castle

Ravenscraig Castle, built in the middle of the fifteenth century high on a promontory running out into the Firth of Forth, has the double distinction of being one of the first castles in Scotland built to withstand and return artillery fire, and the first to be overlooked, as it now is, by high-rise flats, on the outskirts of the town of Kirkcaldy.

It has two horseshoe-shaped towers, ashlar built, their walls fourteen feet thick, the windowless rounded section facing in a landward direction. On the seaward side, where the thick window embrasures have stone seats, there was a courtyard built out into the Firth of Forth on a spur of rock. The towers were linked by a building two storeys high, though with its landward fall extended upwards by an immensely thick parapet, pierced by gun-loops, thus providing an artillery platform.

The taller western tower was entered from a forestair at first-floor level to the south. A turnpike stair rises in the north-east angle. Because of the thickness of the walls, the single rooms on each floor are necessarily relatively small, though they are well provided with mural cupboards and garderobes. That on the first floor would presumably be the hall, though had the building been completed it seems possible that a more imposing hall was intended to run along the first floor of the linking building. There is a massive flue to the chimney in the existing Hall, its point of egress a feature of the roofline.

The lower eastern tower has a vaulted basement, in the floor of which a well has been constructed. There is a straight stair in the thickness of the west wall. This tower has two storeys with an attic floor and a parapet dating from the seventeenth century. Those interested in the detailed analysis of the fortifications of Ravenscraig, and of its intended part in the defence of the Forth, will find much to absorb them in Stewart Cruden's *The Scottish Castle*.

James II, whose interest in guns resulted in his own death from the explosion of one, started to build Ravenscraig before 1460 for Mary of Guelders, who died there in 1463, having spent the three years of her widowhood in it. It was thereafter involuntarily bestowed upon William St Clair, Earl of Orkney, by James III, in exchange for Kirkwall Castle, which the King wanted for himself on taking Margaret of Denmark as his bride. Ravenscraig remained in the possession of the Lord Sinclair, a senior scion of the family holding the Caithness Earldom. It is now in the care of the State.

Redcastle, or Edradour

David, brother of William the Lion, is credited with having built in the twelfth century the nucleus of the much-altered, but now, sadly, fast-decaying castle on the northern shore of the Beauly Firth, four miles east of Muir of Ord. What now nobly crumbles is roughly an L-plan fortalice of the sixteenth century with a taller tower in the re-entrant angle, altered in the seventeenth century. The gable of the wing is angled to the site. Later additions, however, particularly by William Burn in 1840, make precise dating difficult.

Sir John Bisset had it in 1230, and then the Douglases, one owner being the eighth Earl, stabbed to death at a 'Black Dinner' in Stirling Castle by James II. After the fall of the house of Douglas, the Black Isle was mostly taken over by the Crown. Mary, Queen of Scots visited the castle in 1562. It became Mackenzie property in the seventeenth century, and during the twentieth it came to the Baillies of Dochfour, who eventually abandoned it.

Redhouse Castle

The ruins of Redhouse Castle, two miles south of the village of Aberlady, are extensive. First came the tall four-storey late-sixteenth-century oblong tower at the north side of a rectangular courtyard: the remainder of the north and east sides are occupied by domestic ranges with vaulted cellars. At the south-east angle of the courtyard there is a double dovecot with a single pitch roof, also over a vaulted cellar.

Later, the house was extended on its north side by a tower and a Renaissance doorway was added. This moulded doorway carries the initials of Master John Laing and Rebecca Dennistoun, his wife. John Laing was Keeper of the Signet.

Though Redhouse must once have contained many interesting features, most of the interior has collapsed and rapid deterioration has wrought its toll. A Douglas property before the Laings acquired it, through Laing's son-in-law the house eventually came to the Hamilton family, and remained with them until the last of the line was executed for his part in the 1745 Rising, when his property was forfeited and allowed to fall to ruin. It is presently owned by Lord Wemyss.

Repentance Tower

A unique fortified watch-tower, Repentance Tower stands on the summit of Trailtow Hill six miles north-west of Annan. A square structure of coursed rubble, it rises to three storeys. There is a parapet walk – the parapet was rebuilt in the eighteenth century – drained by cannon-spouts, and a hipped roof with a storm beacon to contain a warning fire in the centre, a device lit whenever there were marauding Englishmen in the vicinity. The windows are minimal in size and there are several gun-loops and shot-holes.

The original door would be on the first floor, accessible by removable wooden stairs. The present access to the first floor is by a stone forestair. REPENTANCE is inscribed over the lintel. There is a vaulted basement reached from the first floor, a wooden stair between first and second floors, and a small watchroom with a fireplace under the stone roof.

The builder of this mid-sixteenth-century castle was John Maxwell, Lord Herries, whose seat was nearby Hoddam Castle.

Having pulled down a chapel to build Hoddam, he had to appease either (or both) his conscience and the Archbishop of Glasgow by providing a communal facility. It withstood English siege in 1570 though, as Herries told the King nine years later, it 'mon be mendit of the litill defacing the Englische army maid of it' on that occasion.

Rossend Castle

Rossend Castle, which stands on a rocky eminence above the harbour at Burntisland, commanding a splendid view over the Firth of Forth, began as a small square sixteenth-century tower, later heightened; later still, having added to it a taller eastward wing.

The original tower was three storeys high, with a parapet. The parapet walling was raised during the work of extension, when crenellations were constructed. The lower storeys were incorporated with those in the newer eastern section. It had two vaulted rooms, one being the original kitchen.

The entrance to Rossend was through the stair wing in the north front. The Durie arms and the date 1544 survive on an armorial slab over the porch. The Hall, on the first floor, was the northernmost of two rooms at this level. The other, Queen Mary's room, was panelled in pine, probably in the seventeenth century when other rooms were being similarly treated.

The main stair rises to the second floor, after which access is by turnpike stair in the walling. For most of its existence the castle was known as the fortalice of Burntisland.

There are various theories as to Rossend's age. Durie of Durie is said to have erected it in 1382. Certainly, the lower levels suggest at least as old an origin.

The Abbot of Dunfermline owned the lands, but in 1543 the then Abbot, George Durie, granted them to his legitimised son, Peter, who may have built the first tower. Mary, Queen of Scots gave the property to Sir Robert Murdocairnie. It was in 1563, while she was staying in the castle during his ownership, that the love-sick French poet Chastelard made his second, and fatal, attempt at secreting himself in the Queen's bedroom. This grand-nephew of Bayard had come over in the nineteen-year-old widow's train from France, to where he soon returned. Anxious to get back to Scotland, however, Chastelard was warmly received by Mary, who apparently flirted with him, if John Knox is to be believed, allowing the young man to lean on her shoulder during a dance, 'The Purpose'. A first attempt at hiding in her bedroom at Holyrood was discovered and pardoned and he was banished from the Court. His second attempt, a few days later, at Rossend, led, not to his instant execution at the hands of Moray, as Mary apparently ordered, but to his trial and death by beheading at the Mercat Cross at St Andrews. It is said that he went to his end declaiming his friend Ronsard's 'Epistle to Death':

> Such cruel martyrdom is love
>   No lover may contented live;
> But death true happiness may give
>   Since love no more his heart may move.

Sir Robert Melville had his lands forfeited during the reign of the Regent Morton, and for a short time the Duries returned. But Sir Robert persuaded James VI to give him back Rossend in 1587.

Garrisoned against Cromwell, Rossend was nevertheless taken by him in 1666. It was later acquired by Sir James Caskie, who was created Lord Burntisland when he married a lady with a title in her own right, the Countess of Wemyss. The Jacobite supporters of the Earl of Mar held it briefly in 1715. In the eighteenth century it was bought by a Skye man, Murdoch Campbell, who gave it its present name of Rossend.

At the beginning of the twentieth century, much altered and extended, it was the home of a Kirkcaldy merchant, James Shepherd. It ended its domestic life as a boarding house until 1952, when it came into the hands of Burntisland Town Council. It then became a *cause-célèbre* in defence of the new concept of conservation when the former Burntisland Town Council appeared determined to demolish it against all reason, political prejudice apart. In the autumn of 1971 a public inquiry found in favour of its survival. After further intervention by the Secretary of State, it was sensitively restored by Ian Begg of Robert Hurd and Partners, a leading conservation expert, as offices for his practice, and opened as such on St Andrews Day 1977. The Great Hall of the castle, which contains two striking fireplaces, is to be restored to 'regain the appearance it deserves'.

Rossend Castle: the ruin a Local Council was determined to destroy . . .

. . . but, following much controversy and Public Inquiry, restored by Ian Begg as his architectural firm's offices.

Rossend Castle: one of the painted ceilings.

Rosslyn Castle

Rosslyn, a fortalice of the powerful St Clair family, Earls of Orkney, stands precipitously above a loop of the North Esk, the river winding round three sides of the castle. The castle now consists of a sixteenth-century house altered in Carolingian times, flanked by a ruined square donjon keep to the south-east and other ruined foundations of walls commemorating the former extensiveness of a stronghold whose owners once led a princely life-style.

The first keep was probably built for Sir William St Clair (one of the knightly crusading company that carried Bruce's heart to Palestine) who died fighting the Moors in 1330. A great tower to the south-west was added by the second Earl. A domestic fire destroyed much of the castle in 1452. Hertford burnt it again during his invasion of 1544, and the Cromwellian General Monk similarly contributed his share of damage a century later. It was once again attached and damaged by a mob in 1688.

What survives all this is the imposing oblong eastern block, rising to five storeys, almost every window having its own gun-loop. The richly carved entrance, with a doorway dated 1622, is through the courtyard on the north side, giving access to the building at third-floor level. A corbelled stair turret is built into the south-west angle. There is an especially richly carved large window between the door and the turret, the window supporting the St Clair arms and the initials w.s.

Each of the lower floors has four unvaulted rooms, and there is a fifth in the tower. By the most northerly rooms, a wide squared stair rises from the basement to the top floor. The north room on each floor is larger than the others, that on the ground floor being the kitchen, with gable fireplace and adjacent draining facilities. The Hall, in the entrance-floor tower, is, of course, ruined, though it still has its large fireplace carrying the date 1597. The inhabited portion of the house has impressive panelling and decorated ceilings. A collateral branch of the original family still owns it.

Rosyth Castle

Rosyth Castle once stood on a small sea-rock just under two miles north-west of North Queensferry, connected to the mainland by a causeway. It is now situated in the middle of the Royal Naval Dockyard. It is a substantial L-plan ruined tower with a thickly projecting stair tower, but was once at the corner of a rectangular walled courtyard surrounded by later domestic buildings, some traces of which survive. The courtyard was entered by a gateway and pend in the north wall, protected by gun-loops. Above the entrance is a weather-beaten panel bearing the date 1561 and traces of the initials M.R. (Maria Regina).

The ashlar tower rises through three storeys to a parapet, which does not rest on corbelling and, indeed, overhangs the wall. The floor above is roofless.

Entered by an arched doorway in the re-entrant, at right angles to the tower itself, the lobby leads to a vaulted basement that once had a timber entresol floor, a recess for a guardroom and the stair to the first floor, which carried the Hall. This room had a lofty barrel-vaulted ceiling apparently with an entresol carried on corbels at the spring of the vault. The small windows have once had stone seats. There is a larger seventeenth-century window, at the time of the construction of which the fireplace was enlarged. The entresol floor had its own garderobe. The floor above was not vaulted.

The Stewarts of Rosyth claim descent from Walter, High Steward of Scotland, and from 1428, when the lands of Rosyth were given to Sir David Stewart by James I, they remained with the family for two hundred and seventy years.

Robert Stewart was a supporter of Mary, Queen of Scots, hence the initials on the court gateway. George, his son, died without issue, and his widow married twice, in both cases choosing ruffianly husbands; first, Archibald Wauchope, the younger of Niddry Marischal, who helped the Earl of Bothwell and the Master of Grey attempt the abduction of James VI in 1591; and second, Andrew Wood, whose piratical ventures against local seamen eventually led to his being outlawed. Possession of the castle was then gained by Henry, the last Stewart laird's brother, whose son married the daughter of Napier of Merchiston, the inventor of logarithms. His initials, j.s., and those of his wife, m.n., and the date 1639, indicate the date of the larger window in the Hall; but he was a Royalist, so Rosyth was attacked by Cromwell, and, much damaged, surrendered.

When Queen Victoria crossed the Forth on 6 September, 1842, she gave royal endorsement through her diary to what has remained a popular legendary belief: 'At eleven we reached the South Queensferry where we got out of our carriage and embarked in a little steamer ... On the opposite side you see a square tower, close to the water, called Rosyth, where Oliver Cromwell's mother was said to have been born ...'

Rothesay Castle

Rothesay Castle, on the Isle of Bute, is one of the most remarkable in Scotland. It consists of a great circular wall of enceinte strengthened by four round towers, the whole surrounded by a moat. The upper part of the wall would have had a bretasche, or defensive wooded boarding, traces of the puttlog holes for which still remain. Running out of the north entrance is a gate-house keep of later date. The early work is of finely coursed ashlar, the later of rubble work, an L-shaped tower of four storeys and an attic in height through which the entrance of the castle now runs.

It has generally been supposed that the towers were added after the Norse siege of 1230, led by Uspak, so graphically described in *Haakon Haakonson's Saga*. Failing to storm the castle, the Norsemen hacked their way through the walls, a part of the eastern wall showing signs of just such a disturbing and rebuilding. W. Mackay Mackenzie[1] disputes the possibility of such an action being feasible at that date, but Stewart Cruden advances substantial proof that it could,[2] at the same time disagreeing with W. Douglas Simpson[3] that the towers, each with a batter at the base, were not a slightly later addition to the curtain-wall added to provide extra strengthening. Only the north-west tower survives in good condition. Much of Cruden's argument relates to the evidence of the original crenellations sealed in when the curtain-wall was heightened when the forework was built, probably in James IV's time.

It is possible that the original castle, with a surviving chapel dedicated to St Michael and other buildings inside the wall of enceinte, now only identifiable in outline, was built by Alan, the High Steward, in 1204. A stair from the chapel rises to the ramparts. The castle was certainly in Norse hands for some period after Uspak's taking of it until the Norse grasp on Scotland was broken by Alexander III at the Battle of Largs in 1263. The castle was a favourite residence of both Robert II and Robert III. The forward keep was probably built by the master masons John and Huchone Cooper for James IV and James V, both of whom frequently visited the castle. It withstood the siege by the rebel Master of Ruthven, which in 1527 destroyed most of the Royal burgh of Rothesay.

The Earl of Lennox captured it on behalf of the English in 1544, and it was in turn garrisoned for Charles I and then for Cromwell, whose forces supposedly dismantled it when they left in 1659. What remained was burned by Argyll's men during his rebellion of 1685.

In 1498, the noble family of Bute had been appointed hereditary keepers. Their descendants moved to a nearby mansion after Argyll's attack. In 1816–17, the second Marquess cleared the castle of rubbish and repaired it.

The ground floor is almost wholly a vaulted passage, storage accommodation then being within the curtain-wall. To the east

[1] *op. cit.*
[2] *op. cit.*
[3] *op. cit.*

Rothesay Castle: the gatehouse tower of a castle which once held John Knox a prisoner.

side, a small guardroom adjoins the entrance, which would no doubt have been defended by a drawbridge, and still has a portcullis groove. The square tower forming the leg of the L, still with its crow-stepped gable and chimney head, contains chutes to the moat from latrines in the upper floor.

The upper floor of the keep was approached by a straight mural stair. The Great Hall, forty-nine feet long by almost twenty-five feet wide, still has its large fireplace to the west. There were windows on three sides. The south end was partitioned off to form a withdrawing-room. Its floors are now inaccessible. Traces of ribbed vaulting suggest that the royal apartments included an oratory. There were bedrooms on the upper floors.

Rothesay Castle was again repaired by the Bute family in 1872–9, and is now in State care.

Rowallan Castle

Rowallan Castle, three miles north of Kilmarnock, housed what was once one of Scotland's most important families, Robert II's first wife being Elizabeth Mure, daughter of Sir Adam Mure of Rowallan. She bore her husband a child, the future Robert III, before the marriage was sanctified. The castle, once made stronger by being surrounded by marshland now drained, is grouped around a mound which probably supported an earlier fortalice. The present castle is of the courtyard pattern, the three sides of its square facing the mound in the middle, the fourth side being closed with a curtain-wall. It dates from three periods. There is a wing to the south constructed early in the sixteenth century. The twin-turreted gatehouse with its conically capped roofs dates from 1562. Its towers are divided into four sections by string courses. They have undergone alterations, which may have been the work of Sir William Mure, the poet and Covenanter. The royal arms are to be found at the top end of the forestair, above the entrance. There is a seventeenth-century wing to the north, now ruinous.

The entrance block has three storeys and an attic, though the roof has been replaced at some stage. A passage links the entrance to the courtyard, between two guardhouses. A doorway on the south side of the courtyard leads to the main rooms. Both wings have a vaulted ground floor, the room in the west wing having been the kitchen with the dining-room and a small withdrawing-room above it on the first floor. The turnpike stair in the square tower provides access to the private rooms above. In the main block, the second floor is given over to a single room with a private apartment off it, a turnpike stair leading to the sleeping accommodation above.

Rowallan descended through the main Mure line until the death in 1700 of the sixteenth laird, a supporter of William of Orange. James VI knighted the twelfth laird. The fourteenth laird shared the Reverend Zachary Boyd's enthusiasm for improving Glasgow University. The sixteenth laird's daughter married the first Earl of Glasgow. Their daughter married Sir James Campbell of Lawers, thus taking Rowallan into that family. Acquired by the Corbetts early in the present century, restoration was considered, but a new house by Lorimer was built instead. Rowallan is now an Ancient Monument.

Rusko Castle

Three miles from Gatehouse of Fleet, Rusko Castle stands on a woody hillside above the valley. Basically it is an oblong early-sixteenth-century castle to which a long and lower seventeenth-century wing, now ruinous, was added. Within eight-foot-thick walls it rises to three main storeys with a garret above the parapet, which is carried on chequer corbelling. There is a gabled cap-house at the south-east angle.

Entry is in the east wall, beneath a weather-beaten heraldic shield with arms said to have been those of the Gordons and the Carsons. The doorway is unusual, semi-elliptically arched with joggled voussoirs. The northern half of the lobby was used as a guardroom. To the left, a turnpike stair rises in the south-east angle.

The basement is vaulted and has carried an entresol floor. The ground floor, now divided into two rooms, has a recess which may have carried a stair to the first-floor Hall above, a large room lit by four windows, three with stone seats and possessing a handsomely moulded fireplace. Rusko, once known as Glenskyreburn, was owned by the Cairns, but passed to the Gordons of Lochinvar early in the sixteenth century. The castle was inhabited until between the World Wars, became roofless but has recently been skilfully restored by W. Murray Jack.

Saddell Castle

Saddell Castle stands near the ruins of the Cistercian Saddell Abbey, four miles south of Carradale. As it now survives, it comprises an oblong keep of four storeys and a garret built in the early sixteenth century, and an extensive range of eighteenth-century outbuildings, the erection of which resulted in the dismantling of the original barmkin, the south side of which was incorporated into the south range.

There is an interesting parapet resting on individual stone

corbels beneath which there is a second course of corbels added purely for decorative effect. There are open rounds at the angles and an additional semicircular round above the door in the west front, reached through a moulded courtyard doorway surmounted by an image of the Galley of Lorne and the date 1508, obviously recast. In MacGibbon and Ross's day, the courtyard crenellations simply came down to a lower level over the doorway. Saddell, however, has been near ruinous more than once – was, indeed, probably roofless in the seventeenth century – and several times restored, extensively in the nineteenth century.

Immediately inside the castle, a hatch led to a prison pit. The basement below ground level, reached by a flight of stairs, has two cellars. The lobby gives access to the main turnpike stair in the middle of the west side, which rises to all floors. An entresol rested on the spring of the vault. The first floor was divided by a timber screen providing the Hall to the north with a rather narrow kitchen, having a deep fireplace, an oven and aumries within its broad moulded arch. The second floor, originally with two rooms, was subdivided later. The third had three rooms, one with garderobe and window seat.

Saddell stands on what were Church lands. Reginald, son of Somerled of the Isles, built the Abbey, which welcomed the still unvictorious Bruce in 1300. James IV made the lands into a free barony, and gave them to Bishop David Hamilton in 1507, together with a licence to build a castle. It was completed before 1512. In 1559, the Earl of Sussex landed in Kintyre from Ireland and burned Saddell, 'a fayre pile and strong', he called it. No doubt this would have led to the rebuilding of the upper works. The castle came to the Argylls after the forfeiture of the MacDonalds and in 1680 the first Marquis leased it to William Ralston of that Ilk, who had to reroof it. Towards the end of the century Saddell went to the Campbells, one of whom, in 1770, used stones from the Abbey to build outhouse buildings. Soon after, Saddell House, nearby, was built, and the castle was used to house servants. It was restored in the nineteenth century by Colonel Macleod Campbell and reroofed again just before the Second World War. Its final restoration in recent years has been by the Landmark Trust, and it is now on their list of holiday letting accommodation.

St Andrews Castle

The ruins of this once enormously powerful castle stand on a rocky headland washed on two sides by the North Sea, in the middle of the sea front of the town of St Andrews. It was a castle of enceinte enclosing a pentagonal courtyard with a tower at each corner and buildings all round.

The best-preserved section is the south front. This consists of a keep-like tower with a battered base and chequered corbelling under the parapet, cannon-spouts for its draining, and the base of what have been landward-facing angle-turrets. The original entrance, the built-up jambs of which remain, was evidently through the lowest storey of this tower over a moat. The later entrance, over a drawbridge, in the south front, adjoins the tower. There is a Renaissance-style gateway, probably put up in the mid-sixteenth century for Archbishop Hamilton, with vaulted guard-rooms to either side. Flanking this showy entrance façade at the other end was a circular donjon-like south-western tower, but this has all but vanished.

Little is left of the Great Hall, which lay along the east side. The kitchen tower is at the north-east corner, though little other than the remains of the vaulted cellars have survived the actions of wind and sea. The stairs to the upper floor were at this corner. The sea-tower, at the north-west, contained a vaulted room at the level of the courtyard and another on a lower level, from which was the entrance to the still-surviving bottle dungeon, cut out of the rock, its narrow neck making escape virtually impossible. Possibly its most distinguished prisoner was the poet Gavin Douglas, Bishop of Dunkeld, who did, however, manage to get out alive.

The first castle was built by Bishop Rodger in 1200, forty years after the founding of the great cathedral. This castle was fought over during the Wars of Independence and 'completely demolished' in 1336, after a siege of three weeks, when the English garrison was routed by Sir Andrew Murray. It lay ruined for more than half a century.

The second castle was probably begun early in the fifteenth century, and added to until its final destruction. Archbishop James Beaton (1523–39) lived in it in regal splendour, surpassed, however, by the style with which his nephew and successor, Cardinal Beaton (1539–46), surrounded himself. He was assassinated for opposing the will of Henry VIII, and the castle was subjected

The battered remains of St Andrews Castle.

to a destructive bombardment by French troops. Archbishop John Hamilton (1546–71) rebuilt the castle, but after the Reformation it passed to the Crown. Following a brief spell as an Episcopalian institution, it was simply deserted. In 1654, the Town Council ordered some of its stones to be used in repairing the harbour walls. The castle's jagged remnants are now in care as an Ancient Monument.

Sanquhar Castle

The little that is left of Sanquhar Castle stands by a bank of the River Nith, overlooking the village of Sanquhar. It was an extensive courtyard castle, probably dating from the early fifteenth century and first owned by the Rosses. In Bruce's time a Ross heiress, the last of her line, married the Lord of Creighton, with whose descendants it remained until 1630, when it was bought by Sir William Douglas of Drumlanrig. Sir William, later the first Duke of Queensberry, preferred his old castle to his fine new mansion of Drumlanrig, in which he is said to have slept only one night. The second duke, however, had more modern tastes and abandoned Sanquhar Castle. Incredible as it now seems, local people simply pulled the building apart to use its stones elsewhere, a process only halted in the middle of the nineteenth century. The third Marquis of Bute began rebuilding it in 1896, but work was abandoned on his death in 1900, before much had been done.

Sauchie Tower

Sauchie stands on a rise near the village of New Sauchie, two miles north-east of Alloa. A fifteenth-century square keep of ashlar, it has four main floors and an entresol, the tower topped by a parapet on individual corbels with open rounds at all four angles.

It is entered at ground-floor level on the west front through an arched doorway. To the left of the lobby there is a turnpike stair in the north-west angle, topped above the parapet with a hexagonal cap-house having a conical roof. To the right of the lobby there is a guardroom fashioned out of the thickness of the wall.

The ground floor has a vaulted ceiling, with corbels indicating the level of the former entresol floor at the spring of the vault. The basement beneath was probably a store, though there is a small prison built into the thickness of the west wall, and a former garderobe which appears to have been used at one time as a bakehouse.

The Hall is on the first floor, and has a wide fireplace and stone seats in three windows. There is a wall closet with a stone basin in the north wall. The second and third floors have fallen in.

Sauchie was the seat of the Schaws, Masters of the King's Wine-Cellar, who acquired the keep from the Annands. The tower has recently found a restoring purchaser.

Scalloway Castle

Scalloway Castle, on the west side of the Shetland mainland five miles west of Lerwick, now overlooks works connected with the retrieving of oil from the bed of the North Sea. It is an L-shaped castle, built in 1600 by Mary, Queen of Scots' nephew, the tyrannical Earl Patrick Stewart, who also built the Earl's Palace in Kirkwall. It was paid for by the simple means of extracting free materials and labour from his tenants on pain of forfeiture of their own lands and properties. The castle rises to four storeys. A stair turret projects at the north-west angle, and there is a smaller one in the north-west re-entrant angle. Angle-turrets grace the remaining corners. The entrance is in the main re-entrant angle and leads to a wide vaulted scale-and-platt staircase. A porter's room lies to the left and there is another vault beneath the stair, probably a temporary prison. To the right, a passage leads to the kitchen, which has a wide fireplace and a stone seat at one end and also a well; and to a vaulted store.

The Hall takes up the whole of the first floor of the main block, and has two fireplaces. Opposite the larger fireplace is a recess for a dresser or sideboard. Two turreted newel staircases, approached from opposite angles, lead to the second floor, which had two bedrooms in the main block and a third in the wing, each with a fireplace and a garderobe. The third floor had three, each similarly equipped.

Cromwell garrisoned the castle during the Commonwealth when he also built a barracks at Lerwick, only the walls of which remain – but after the Restoration, Scalloway Castle was abandoned and fell into ruin.

Scotstarvit Tower

Bulky-looking Scotstarvit Tower stands on raised ground three miles south of Cupar, a well-preserved L-plan structure carrying the date 1627. Narrow and defensive, this led some to believe it older, quoting a charter of 1529 which refers to a tower on the Hill of Tarvit. Possibly it was simply old-fashioned when its scholar-owner caused it to be erected, or perhaps remodelled from an earlier structure.

The ashlar tower rises to five storeys and a parapet carried on individual corbels. There are angle shot-holes and a parapet walk, which does not have rounds. Above the parapet, the garret storey is gabled and roofed with flagstones. The small wing carries the turnpike stair, and is topped with a conically roofed cap-house, by means of which the parapet walk is reached. There is a thick chimney-stack at the west gable.

The tower is entered through an arched door by the re-entrant angle, and from the lobby there is access to a vaulted basement as well as to the stair tower. There was originally an entresol floor at the spring of the vault, providing a room equipped with stone window-seats.

The Hall is on the floor above, with a fireplace (reduced in size at some later date), stone seats and a garderobe with a sink. A mural chamber leading off the stair provided a guardroom.

The second floor has also only one room, a vaulted apartment. The third floor has corbels to carry the garret storey, which once contained an heraldic fireplace removed to the later mansion of Hill of Tarvit (now in the care of the National Trust for Scotland). Its lintel has the date 1627, together with the motto SPE EXPECTO, suggesting that this might have been the study of the tower's owner, the famous Scots scholar, Sir John Scot of Scotstarvit. Apart from encouraging Timothy Pont, the minister of Dunnet, to carry out a survey of the country – the maps for which were beautifully printed by John Blaeu of Amsterdam in 1654 – Sir John Scot of Scotstarvit, Director of the Chancery in Charles I's day, produced one of the most famous unread books in the history of Scottish literature, *The Staggering State of Scots Statesmen*, the burden of which was that nearly every statesman from 1550 to 1650 had achieved his offices and acquired his estates through fraud and treachery – according to Carlyle, 'not a satire at all but a Homily on Life's Nothingness enforced by examples' – an accusation which could well have had much truth in it! Sir John also founded the Humanity Chair at the University of St Andrews.

Skelbo Castle

Skelbo, stronghold of the Lords of Duffus, stands on a rocky eminence in Loch Fleet, four miles north of Dornoch. The oldest part of the castle is supposed to date from the fourteenth century, though what remains seems to belong to the seventeenth. It is an oblong fortalice with vaulted cellars in the basement, one large room above and a garret. There is an arched entrance near the north end, still with its draw-bar slot.

The Sutherlands, Lords of Duffus, had a turbulent history; which is to say that their past encompasses one laird murdered by the Gunns in 1530; the sacking of the town of Dornoch in 1567 and 1570; and an unsuccessful attempt to steal the corn of the Earl of

Sutherland in 1616. The son of the laird who organised this particular theft against his kinsman was made a peer by Charles I and probably built 'modern' Skelbo.

Skelmorlie Castle

Skelmorlie Castle stands on the edge of a tree-covered cliff about five miles north of Largs. It is a red rubble oblong tower, now harled, rising to three storeys and an attic. There are ashlar conically capped turrets on the north-east and south-west angles, the upper level of the supporting corbelling adjacent to the eaves. On the east gable there is an imposing chimney-stack, carrying the kitchen flue. A stepped chimney by the centre of the northern wallhead is also a striking feature.

The original doorway was in the centre of the southern face, the present entrance in the north front being Victorian. The gables are crow-stepped. There is no parapet, though it doubtless had one originally.

The basement has two vaulted rooms, one of which is the vestibule for the Victorian entrance. The first-floor Hall had its kitchen to the east, screened off. The original turnpike stair rose within the south wall. A secondary turnpike stair rises from the Hall level to the second floor, which has two large rooms and a small one in the south-east angle, encapsulating a garderobe.

The castle was built in 1502, probably by a son of the second Lord Montgomerie of Eglinton, though its upperworks must have been remodelled about a century later. Robert Montgomerie of Skelmorlie was knighted by James VI and made a Nova Scotia baronet by Charles I. When Sir Robert's wife, a daughter of Sir William Douglas of Drumlanrig, died, he built for her an ornate mausoleum in the grounds of Largs Old Church. It still survives and is known as the Skelmorlie Aisle. It is sculpted out of Italian marble with much intricate detail. The ceiling of this vault is embellished with symbols ranging from the signs of the Zodiac to aspects of Skelmorlie Castle.

Robert Montgomerie's great-great-grandson died without issue, and the property was sold to Hugh Montgomerie of Busby, Lord Provost of Glasgow. He, too, died without a son. His daughter married Alexander Montgomerie of Coilsfield and their son heired the property as twelfth Earl of Eglinton in 1796.

In recent years it has been the home of the Wilson family. There was a disastrous fire in 1959, which did a great deal of internal damage, but revealed a number of concealed earlier structural details. The castle has, however, been restored.

A large Victorian addition was built on by an earlier tenant, the Glasgow merchant James Graham, in 1852, but this has now been demolished.

Skipness Castle

Skipness Castle stands strategically on a raised beach at the north-eastern tip of Kintyre, where Kilbrannan Sound, Loch Fyne and the Sound of Bute meet. It comprises a considerable quadrangle surrounded by a wall of enceinte, erected in the latter half of the thirteenth century. Earlier in the century a hall-house and a chapel had been built, and these were partially incorporated when the high curtain-wall was put up, the former on the north and the latter on the south, the chapel, however, being secularised, since a new church was erected near the castle. Other buildings in the court included three towers, the remains of two of which are to be found in the north-east and south-west angles, and another, a latrine tower, near the centre of the west front. The main entrance was from the sea, through the former chapel, to which was added a shallow gate-tower with portcullis and machicolation off-centre in the south wall, though there was also a postern gate in the east wall. The northern arched entrance through the hall-house is a later addition.

The main element in the castle as it now stands is a sixteenth-century tower house of four storeys remodelled and heightened from the late-thirteenth-century tower with gabled cap-house, open rounds at three angles and a garret within the parapet walk. The very small wing houses garderobes on each floor with a wide chute to dispose of the refuse. The basement, in which the walls of the earlier castle are incorporated, is vaulted, though the vaulting is a later addition. It is approached by an arched door which does not connect with the Hall above. This was reached by a stone forestair through the entrance in the south-east corner. The Hall now has no fireplace, but a chimney flue by the northern window suggests that there might have been one. A mural stair in the south-east corner rises to the second floor, where a window has been blocked and turned into a fireplace. The third floor, entered by an arched doorway, has similar heating arrangements and window-seats. The garret has lost its flooring.

The castle was believed to have been first put up by a member of the MacSween family around 1247, though there is good architectural evidence to suggest the more likely date as *c.*1290–1310. Evidently Skipness was given by the Crown to the second Earl of Argyll. It withstood a Colkitto raid, and, despite an order for its destruction, survived the Argyll rising of 1685. It ceased to be lived in at the end of the seventeenth century, and was converted to farm steading use by the removal of the early courtyard buildings. In 1898 the farm buildings were totally removed by R.C. Graham of Skipness, and what remained of the castle was preserved. It is now in State care.

Smailholm Tower

About six miles west of Kelso, 'seen and seeing all around' in Dr John Brown's words, Smailholm Tower stands on Sandy Knowe Crags above the farm of Sandyknowe, where Sir Walter Scott came when a boy to visit the farmer, his paternal grandfather Robert Scott. Smailholm was one of the most celebrated of all the Border castles. It was described by a nineteenth-century topographical writer as 'a conspicuous landmark to direct vessels to Berwick'. It directed the boy Scott's imagination to the force of history, it being recorded that once the 'lonely infant was found in a thunder storm, lying on the soft grass at the foot of the old grey Strength, clapping his hands at each flash and shouting 'Bonny! Bonny!' Scott featured much-fought-over Smailholm in one of his early poems, 'The Eve of St John', and again, more extensively, in 'Marmion', where he dubbed it 'that mountain tower/ Which charmed my fancy's wakening hour'. He paid it a farewell visit the year before his death, taking with him the painter J.M.W. Turner, who made a dramatic sketch of it for the author's *Poetical Works*.

The plain, oblong rubble-built tower of the Pringle family of Galashiels probably dates originally from the early sixteenth century, though it may have been partially rebuilt in the seventeenth century by the Scotts of Harden, who possessed it by 1645. It rises to four storeys, the basement and the upper storeys being vaulted. It has a parapet on the longer north and south walls, partial

Smailholm Tower: a Border keep that helped to awaken the sense of history in the boy Walter Scott.

on the north side and blocked by a curious dormer window on the south.

The tower is entered at ground level through an arched doorway in the south wall. The lobby leads to the usual high basement chamber which has corbels, indicating that there was once a timber entresol floor. The turnpike stair is encased in the thickness of the south-east angle. The hall on the first floor, entered from a small angled lobby, has a fireplace, a drain garderobe, two recessed window-seats, and a cupboard in the south wall. A hatch in the centre of the Hall floor must once have given access to the entresol bassment room. The second, unvaulted floor, a bedroom, is similar to the first, though without the hatch. The top floor was reconstructed early in the seventeenth century, or a little before. This perhaps accounts for the fact that parapet walks, reached from doors in the north-east and north-west corners, are confined to the side walls and do not overhang. The present north parapet wall has a watchman's seat and a recess for his lantern. Bartisan becons on

Border towers on the Scottish side date from 1587 when, following English example, an Act of Council of 1587 directed the lieges to 'keep watch nyght and day, and burn baillis (bales) according to the accoustomat ordour observit as sic tymes upoun the borderis'. This once rather strong tower was surrounded by a barmkin curtain-wall and small courtyard, traces of which remain, and within which there once stood a domestic chapel and other buildings, one of which was the kitchen. Since 1951, Smailholm has been in State care.

Sorbie Castle

A mile east of Sorbie village stand the ruins of once-powerful Sorbie Castle, an L-shaped fortalice allegedly built early in the sixteenth century on the site of Pictish fortifications. It is a tall building, with three storeys and an attic contained in its main block, and with its possibly seventeenth-century stair tower rising a storey higher to allow for a cap-house. The entrance, in the re-entrant angle, had a door defended by three drawbars, the sockets for which may still be seen.

The basement has four vaulted rooms, that to the north of the main block the kitchen. Beneath the main scâle-and-platt stair to the first floor is another vaulted floor which was probably a prison.

The once-handsome Hall had a large fireplace, the flue for which rises adjacent to the stair tower. A turnpike stair on triple corbelling in the re-entrant angle provided access to the bedrooms above.

The lands of Sorbie – a word in its original form meaning 'the house among swamps' – seemed to have belonged to Candida Casa, the Abbey of Whithorn, but the Ahannays or Hannays were in possession by 1529, and perhaps earlier.

Feuding with the Murrays and paying for their involvement in the Civil War forced them to sell Sorbie in the 1670s to the Earl of Galloway, to whom they were connected by marriage. After the death of the last Sorbie Stewart in 1748, the castle simply fell into ruin. It is now in the restoring hands of the Clan Hannay Society.

Incidentally, Patrick Hannay, who served the 'Winter King' during the Thirty Years War, was a minor poet whose *Poems* were published in Edinburgh in 1622.

Sorn Castle

Sorn Castle clings to a cliff on the north bank of the River Ayr two miles or so east of Catrine. Though the present mansion is rectangular, only the southern part is old, and of that only the western end was part of the original fortalice. This south-west corner dated from 1409, a tower of three storeys and an attic. Later, an addition to the north-east provided kitchen and cellarage at ground level, a Great Hall above and additional bedroom accommodation on top of that. The roof of the old portion and of this addition, running at right angles to the original, were both probably constructed (or reconstructed, in the case of the original) in the late sixteenth century, when a crenellated parapet with open rounds on ornamental chequered corbelling was added.

In 1864 David Bryce doubled the size of the castle by adding a large wing to the north-west side, on the whole respecting the exterior style of the original tower. In 1909 a Glasgow architect, H.E. Clifford, added the terrace overlooking the river, which is crossed to the west by a suspension bridge of 1837. The interior of the old portion has, of course, been greatly altered.

The lands of Sorn passed from Keith of Galston by the marriage of his heiress, Janet, in 1406 to the Hamiltons of Cadzow, ancestors of the Dukes of Hamilton. The marriage of another heiress brought them to the Setons of Winton. James VI is said to have set out from Glasgow on horseback to attend a winter wedding at Sorn, but his mount sank so deeply in moorland bog that he was forced to leave it stuck there. Sorn Castle was garrisoned by government troops during Charles II's troubles with the Covenanters. The second Earl of Winton sold the property to the Earl of Loudon about 1680. One of its most celebrated inhabitants was the Countess of Loudon, who, widowed in the eighteenth century, lived on until a few weeks before her centenary, setting to the end an example in estate management well ahead of her time.

Southsyde Castle

Southsyde, an L-plan fortalice three miles south of Dalkeith, dates from the first half of the seventeenth century. Before the Reformation, it belonged to Newbattle Abbey. The present structure may have been built by Patrick Ellis around 1640, his initials, with those of his wife, being inserted above a first-floor window in the west gable. Originally it was of four storeys with long corbelled angle-turrets extending through the upper three floors. By about 1840, though occupied by a farm tenant, it was partly ruinous. The rebuilding that followed involved lowering it by a storey and, in effect, turning it into a nineteenth-century castle-country house in the interpretative manner so widely desired by newly wealthy Victorian patrons.

Spedlins Tower

Spedlins Tower stands above the south bank of the River Annan four miles north of Lochmaben. The two vaulted lower storeys date from the fifteenth century, the roofless upper works from the seventeenth. Entry is now at ground-floor level through the north front, though the main entrance would once have been by a movable wooden stair to the first floor. Angle-turrets on triple corbelling adorn all four corners, and the surviving crow-stepped gables show the roof to have been a double one reflecting the double-pile plan superimposed on the hall vault, a very exceptional feature for that date.

The ground floor is vaulted, but has been subdivided at some later date. An angle stair rises within the east wall to the first-floor Hall. The stair is protected by a shot-hole from a window embrasure.

The vaulted Hall has a finely decorated Renaissance fireplace, five windows, two of which have stone seats, and a garderobe. In the south-east angle a turnpike stair leads to a trapdoor beneath which is a mural prison of a sort that would ensure that an occupant's confinement would be likely to be terminal.

The second floor has a corridor which leads to four rooms with fireplaces and garderobes. The third floor houses attic rooms, perhaps servants' quarters, reached by a turnpike stair at the north end of the corridor below. There were probably also more rooms in a garret floor above.

Spedlins stands in the grounds of Jardinehall, a nineteenth-century house on the completion of which the commodious old tower house was abandoned. It was thus a Jardine seat. A panel linking the arms of Jardine and Johnstones is dated 1605.

It has recently been restored by Stephen Yorke.

Spynie Palace

Spynie Castle, or Palace, two miles north of Elgin Cathedral, at the south end of Spynie Loch, was the residence of the Bishops of Moray, and must once have reflected their wealth and power.

The oldest part of the castle is the hall-house along the south side. The gate-house, defended by a portcullis, has a single stair leading to the battlements. Much of the design of the mouldings seems French or English rather than Scottish. As the castle was put up while the cathedral was being rebuilt after its destruction by the Wolf of Badenoch, it is probable that the masons employed on the cathedral may also have been deployed on the castle. The gate-house carries the arms of Bishop Innes, who was consecrated in 1406. One of his successors, Bishop David Stewart, who died in 1575, excommunicated the Earl of Huntly. That nobleman thereupon threatened to 'pull him out of his pigeon-holes'. To this the bishop replied that he would build a house out of which the Earl and his whole clan should not be able to pull him. The result was the keep, six storeys high and with walls more than ten feet thick, except where they face the courtyard. Although the parapet has gone, there are traces of the open rounds that once adorned the gables, and of a cap-house in the north-east angle.

There were extensions from the courtyard and from outside at basement level, connecting with the Hall above – a fine room with a large fireplace and window-seats – only by a small mural staircase. The main entrance, however, was on the first floor, over a removable drawbridge, close to the wall of enceinte. A turnpike stair in the thickness of the wall nearby leads to the upper floors, and to an entresol in the north wall housing a guardroom. There is also a tower in the south-east corner of the enceinte, possibly also the work of Bishop Stewart.

James VI gave Spynie, a temporal barony after the Reformation, to Alexander Lindsay, son of the Earl of Crawford, along with the title of Lord Spynie. The same monarch, however, later asked for it back, so that it could be used by the Protestant Bishops. During the religious troubles of the seventeenth century, Bishop Guthrie was in 1640 forced to surrender it to General Munro. Innes of Innes and Grant of Ballindalloch then held it for the Covenanters. It was to become an Episcopal seat again at the Restoration, though the last Bishop to occupy the building died there in 1686, after which it was allowed to fall into ruin.

Stair House

Standing on the banks of the River Ayr three miles south of Tarbolton, Stair is an L-plan tower house three storeys high, with a square tower projecting at the south-east angle and a circular tower in the north-west. It dates from the late sixteenth or early seventeenth century. An extension of two storeys to the south with a round tower dates from the late seventeenth century, from which period there also dates the three-storey extension to the east, with another circular stair tower. The round tower at the north-west angle, divided into four sections by string courses, is provided with several shot-holes. The entrance currently used is in the later re-entrant angle and is not the original. Though it fell into disrepair in the middle of the nineteenth century, Stair House is now restored and lived in.

By the marriage of a Kennedy heiress to Sir William Dalrymple in the mid-fifteenth century Stair became the Dalrymple family seat, from which the first Earl took his title. The fourth Earl was a Reformer, in 1567 supporting the party around the infant James VI against his mother. James, the eighth laird, was created Viscount Stair in 1689 and became President of the Court of Session as well as the author of a standard textbook on Scots law. His son, created Earl of Stair in 1703, bears responsibility for the pointless Massacre of Glencoe, which has remained a stain on his reputation. The second Earl rose to be a Field-Marshal, but resigned after George II had shown marked preference for his Hanoverian over his British troops at the Battle of Dettingen. Stair passed out of the family at the end of the eighteenth century. During the period when it was occupied by General Stewart, Burns paid several visits. The eighth Earl repurchased the property.

Stanely Castle

Stanely Castle, an L-shaped early-fifteenth-century fortalice, stands, a roofless and floorless ruin, surrounded since 1837 by Paisley Waterworks. It had four storeys beneath the parapet and probably a garret. The door, in the re-entrant angle, was protected by a projection at parapet level for dropping missiles on unwelcome arrivals.

The lands of Stanely, or Stanelie, belonged in the fourteenth century to the Dennistouns (or Danielstouns) of that Ilk, but the present castle dates from its Maxwell ownership, brought about by the marriage of one of two Danielstoun heiresses. The Maxwells also owned, among others, the castles of Newark, Haggs, Pollock, Dargarvel and Calderwood. Stanely went by purchase to Dame Jean Hamilton, Lady Ross of Hawkhead, in 1629. Her daughter, Elizabeth Ross, carried it to the third Earl of Glasgow by marriage in the middle of the eighteenth century. It was abandoned by the early 1800s.

Stapleton Tower

Three miles north-west of Annan, Stapleton Tower is an oblong sixteenth-century tower house to which, until the 1950s, a Victorian mansion was attached. Demolition of the house has left the shell of the castle, four storeys in height with a parapet which has nineteenth-century crenellations and possibly similarly re-moulded corbelling. There are open rounds at all four corners, but the roof, and whatever else was above the parapet, have gone. There is a vaulted basement. The interior has been stripped. Stapleton was an Irvine stronghold.

Stirling Castle

Stirling Castle, both in its situation and its role in Scottish history, has similarities to Edinburgh Castle. Both stand on basaltic rock faces carved out by the scouring glaciers of the Ice Age; both have long sloping 'tails' down to level ground, which provided a structure for the construction of medieval towns; and both were royal seats, 'the effective capital of the kingdom', as Richard Fawcett has remarked, being 'wherever the King happened to be in residence'.[1]

The poet Alexander Smith wrote: 'Stirling, like a huge brooch, clasps Highlands and Lowlands together'.[2] Before the physical process of unification could be repeated in the relationship between Highlander and Lowlander, Stirling was thus a key defensive site.

The earliest recorded castle at Stirling was that lived in by

[1] *Stirling Castle; Official Guide;* HMSO 1983
[2] *A Summer in Skye:* 1856

Stirling Castle: the 'brooch' that clasps Lowlands and Highlands together, long a military headquarters but now under extensive restoration.

Malcolm Canmore. Alexander I died in Stirling Castle, as did William the Lion, after a period when it was in English hands to secure his release from captivity. These castles were probably timber constructions. Stone, as an ingredient in castle construction here, is not referred to before 1287.

During the fourteenth century, Edward I took Stirling Castle, Wallace regained it, the English took it back again, and, following Bannockburn in 1314, fought to wrest it once more from the English. Bruce had it 'slighted' so that it could not again be used against the Scots. Only in 1347, after repair and a further spell in English hands following Bruce's death, did the castle finally come back to the Scots.

Nothing of the castle as it was when it was the centre of these stirring events survives, except possibly some of the stones of the North Gate, referred to as being in existence in 1381. Stirling was, however, the favourite royal residence of the Stewart kings. James II lured the eighth Earl of Douglas to it in 1452, murdered him and had his body tossed out of a window. James IV built the Forework across the approach to the castle in 1500–08, and laid out the courtyard now called the Upper Square, being responsible for the completion of the Great Hall in 1503, and forming the square with buildings that were to be altered or replaced by his successors. James V built the splendid Palace on the south side of the square between 1539 and 42 under the supervision of Sir James Hamilton of Finnart. The detailed accounts are missing; it was probably designed by Thomas French with James Nicholson as master of work. Robert Robertson the carver, was responsible for the ornamental woodwork, although John Drummond, master wright to the king, may also have been involved. Mary, Queen of Scots was crowned on the old chapel in 1533 and James VI was baptised there in 1566. Mary of Lorraine, whilst Regent, is said to have been responsible for the defences in front of the Forework known as the Spur, apparently similar to the Italian-designed Spur at Edinburgh, though, like it, built over or incorporated in later developments. Prince Henry, the son of James VI, in whom all Scotland's hopes were placed – he died aged twenty-three – was born in the castle in 1594. For his christening the king rebuilt the Chapel, but other schemes for glorifying the place were abandoned when, as James VI and I, he moved down to London to inherit the English throne in 1603.

After the Union of the Crowns, Stirling Castle declined in importance. James VI returned to it in 1617, and Charles II was there in 1650. It was nevertheless in a poor state early in the eighteenth century, although various plans for its restitution were drawn up, though not executed. After the Forty-five, the castle was subdivided for use as a barracks, Robert Billings replacing the fire-damaged northern end of the King's Old Building in 1855. The famous roundels which graced the ceiling of the Palace were taken down after one fell in the eighteenth century, killing a soldier. Only the action of the Governor of Stirling Prison saved them from destruction. Eventually, the castle became the depot for the Argyll and Sutherland Highlanders, although its importance was increasingly acknowledged following the intervention of Edward VII in

Stirling Castle: the Chapel Royal, with mural traces of its former grandeur.

1906. In 1964 the military finally left, and the long process of restoring Stirling Castle to something of its former glory began.

The outer defences, built between 1708 and 1714, largely the work of the engineer Drury, incorporated the east wall of the Regent Mary's Spur. The Esplanade, flattened to become a parade ground, provided a dangerous frontal approach for any enemy.

Sadly, there have been many alterations in James IV's forework, which old prints show to have been like something from a fifteenth-century French manuscript, with its rectangular towers at the corners and four semicircular towers with conical roofed caphouses flanking the gate-house. The Prince's tower, at the west end, survives; the Elphinstone Tower at the east end was largely demolished and the inner pair cut down and given commonplace crenellated parapets.

Inside, the lower square has the front of the Palace to the left, the south gable of the Great Hall straight ahead, and eighteenth-century or later military buildings to the right. A road leads between the Palace and the Great Hall to the Upper Square. The Chapel, rebuilt by James VI, stands partly on the site of its predecessor. The mural paintings by Valentine Jenkin, done in 1628 and subsequently overlaid, have been partially restored.

The King's Old Building, on the west side of the square, contains fragments of an early-sixteenth-century royal apartment, suggesting that once there were two well-lit rooms over a vaulted basement reached by a turnpike stair. That building now reflects its long use for military purposes. The room in which James II dispatched his most serious trouble-maker was damaged in the nineteenth-century fire, in the section restored by Billings. It is now part of the Regimental Museum and Headquarters of the Argyll and Sutherland Highlanders.

The Palace, also built on the site of an earlier construction, represents the first serious use of French masons in Scotland, the Renaissance detail of the sculptured figures mixing oddly with the late-Gothic cusped arches. The statues include the Devil (no doubt the work of a Scottish craftsman), the more important planetary gods and, of course, the commissioning monarch, James V himself. The entrance was through a porch in the north-west corner, and led to the King's Outer and Inner Halls and bedchamber, off which there was a study. The Queen's similar apartments were reached by a gallery, the bedrooms being adjacent. The roundels, finally returned except for three in the National Museum in Edinburgh in

1970, are on the walls of the Queen's apartments, awaiting reconstruction of the ceiling. The Great Hall is linked to the Palace by a nineteenth-century bridge. James III may have begun it, though it was completed during the reign of James IV. Five huge fireplaces heated this rectagular apartment. There was a magnificent hammer-beam ceiling, unfortunately now gone, and windows placed high in the wall to provide plenty of light while still allowing tapestries to be hung beneath, thus providing the reflective warmth of their decoration. Its restoration from a crude late-eighteenth-century barrack conversion has now reached roughly halfway, though it will still be many years before it again looks as it did in the time of the Stewarts. Other features of great interest are the kitchens restored in 1921; the central courtyard of the Palace, where James V kept the royal lion; the wall walk; 'the Lady's Hole'; and the nearby 'King's Knot', an ornamental garden which once adjoined a pleasure canal and still survives.

Stobhall Castle

Stobhall, known earlier as Stobshaw, stands on a ridge above the Tay about nine miles north of Perth. It is unlike most Scottish castles in that it does not possess a tower, but consists of four unconnected buildings at different angles and levels, the ensemble given unity by the courtyard wall, itself of an irregular shape, and largely retaining.

The entrance to the castle is through a pend beside a long two-storey block with dormer windows and crow-stepped gables. This was used as the dower house for Drummond Castle, and contained a large kitchen and a living-room, with bedroom accommodation above. The straight central stair has some original plasterwork, and there is still some good panelled interior work upstairs. It is thought to have been built, early in the seventeenth century, by John Drummond, the second Earl of Perth, whose arms, together with those of his wife, Lady Jane Kerr, a daughter of the Earl of Roxburghe, are carved above the entrance.

The L-shaped late-sixteenth-century building in the centre of the courtyard has a chapel and a turreted priest's house, the Drummond family remaining staunch Catholics after the Reformation and in the seventeenth century getting permission to hold services in Stobhall, when Catholic worship was otherwise generally banned. The priest's house rises to three storeys and has an attic and a two-storeyed conically capped tower projecting from the south-west angle. The chapel, with stone altar and aumry for the sacred communion vessels, has a fine tempera-painted ceiling depicting equestrian figures representing the kings of all the earth. David, second Lord Drummond, was responsible for this building, his arms, initials and the date 1578 being inscribed on the outside. The plate-traceried Gothic windows are mid-Victorian. Priests apart, the house once accommodated that strange *ménage à trois* John Ruskin, his wife Effie Gray, and her future husband John Everett Millais.

Next to the chapel is the laundry building, two storeys high and also having a brewery and bakery. To the east there is a later domestic range which housed the kitchen and stores, demolished after the Second World War but since re-erected as a library.

In all probability there was an earlier castle on the site, perhaps a tower, for Robert the Bruce granted the site to the Drummonds after Bannockburn, since the idea of scattering three-pointed spikes in the path of the English cavalry – Calthrops they were called, used again in the twentieth century by peacefully picketing miners against the horses of the mounted police – is credited to Sir Malcolm Drummond. Annabella Drummond, his great-grand-daughter, became queen to Robert III.

Stobhall was the main Drummond seat until 1487, when Sir John, the twelfth holder of the title, was made Lord Drummond and started work on Drummond Castle, by Crieff. Stobhall then served first as a dower house, and then as the residence of the estate factor. Because the estate was forfeited for Drummond Jacobite activities, Stobhall's owner the Willoughbys and later the Earls of Ancaster, although by a curious and happy quirk of fortune it is actually once again owned by the present head of the Drummond family, the Earl of Perth.

Stranraer Castle

Stranraer Castle (or Kennedy's Castle, as it was once called) stands at the centre of the town; once famous for its curving streets and eighteenth-century houses, but now somewhat straightened out by an undistinguished post-Second-World-War development, the only merit of which has been to better the view the old building, once hemmed in by nineteenth-century commercial development. A sixteenth-century L-plan fortalice of three storeys beneath a corbelled parapet, with an added seventeenth-century storey above, the building has been much altered and reconstructed internally, especially during the period when it was used as a prison. There are two ground-floor vaulted rooms, reached through the original door, and a large first-floor Hall.

The Castle is thought to have been built by Adair of Kinhilt in 1511, though it came into the ownership, first of the Kennedies of Chappel and then of the Stair family. Graham of Claverhouse, 'Bonnie Dundee', lived in it whilst engaged in suppressing Covenanters as one of his duties as Sheriff of Galloway.

Strathendry Castle

The old part of Strathendry Castle, a mile and a half west of Leslie, is a late-sixteenth-century tower built for the Forrester family, to whom the barony came by marriage in 1496 on the failure of the original Strathendry line. Three storeys high and with an attic, the tower is built of rubble. There are two entrances. That on the south front, though perhaps not original, has an heraldic panel over it with the arms of Thomas Forrester and Isabel Laremont, his wife, together with their initials. The entrance to the north, at the foot of the projecting stair tower, carries the initials S.E.D., probably those of Sir E. Douglas, who in 1675 had married the Forrester heiress on the failure of the line. The date is 1699.

The original basement was a single vaulted chamber, but has since been divided. There are two rooms on each of the second and third floors. The top storey, partly within the roof space, has been turned into a single room. The windows have been altered. There are crow-stepped gables and, on the east side, a parapet walk with two angle-turrets. The roof is modern.

There is a circular well in the courtyard and, nearby, a seventeenth-century dovecote.

William Burn built adjacent Strathendry House in 1824. The old castle was renovated in 1910, having been sold to the Tullis family five years earlier. It changed hands most recently in 1962. According to Dougald Stewart's biography of Adam Smith, it was from the northern doorway of this castle that the future author of *The Wealth of Nations* was kidnapped by gypsies when a boy.

Tantallon Castle

At about the same time that the Douglas family was building a new style tower-house castle for themselves at Threave, over in the west, William, the first Earl, on the East Lothian coast eight miles south of Haddington and facing the Bass Rock, was putting up Tantallon, the last medieval castle of enceinte to be built in Scotland, complete with keep-gatehouse and curtain-wall; a form of defensive structure which the use of artillery at Crécy in 1346 had shown to be ineffective.

Tantallon consists of a fifty-foot-high crenellated curtain of dressed ashlar twelve feet thick, blocking off the neck of a sea promontory from cliff to cliff, in front of which is a deep ditch cut out of the rock. Two towers stand at the ends of the curtain; one circular, one D-shaped. A massive rectangular keep-gatehouse looms out of the centre section of the curtain. It stands eighty feet high and has four storeys of living accommodation above the portcullis chamber. 'Red in colour', writes Cruden[1], 'the fabric seems to hang upon an expanse of green, and behind it the vast expanse of a massive sky sets off the composition.' With Hermitage and Bothwell, though perhaps in a more startlingly striking setting, it is one of the most impressive castles in Scotland. Its strength, indeed, begat a proverb of the impossible – 'Ding doun Tantallon – mak a brig to the Bass' (as easily knock down Tantallon as build a bridge to the Bass Rock) – and inspired Scott's description in *Marmion*:

> And sudden, close before them showered
>   His towers, Tantallon vast;
> Broad, massive, high, and stretching far,
> And held impregnable in war,
> On a projecting rock they rose,
> And round three sides the ocean flows.
> The fourth did battled walls enclose
>   And double mound and fosse;
> By narrow drawbridge, outwards strong,
> Through studded gates, an entrance long,
>   To the main court they cross.
> It was a wide and stately square;

[1] *op. cit.*

Tantallon Castle: all that survives of a castle once thought to be as impregnable as the Bass Rock, offshore.

> Around were lodgings fit and fair,
>   And towers of various form
> Which on the coast projected far,
> And broke its lines quadrangular;
> Here was square keep, there turrets high,
> Or pinnacle that sought the sky,
> Whence oft the warder could descry
>   The gathering ocean-storm.

It was described, more briefly, by Hugh Miller as being: 'Three sides of wall-like rock, and one side of rock-like wall.'

The gate-house tower was the defensive centre, the floor over the entrance passage being a fighting deck from which the drawbridge and portcullis were worked, the inner gates folding shut against the court. Above was the lord's Hall, and in the two storeys higher, his private rooms. There was additional, if perhaps rather cramped, sleeping accommodation in the rooms hollowed out of the frontal and tall oversailing turrets (referred to by Scott) of the tower, the small windows, however, each having their own stone seat.

On each side of the courtyard, east and west, were domestic buildings, but only the west range survives. It has a 'laich hall' on the ground floor and a 'lang hall' above; the lower for the paid soldiers or retainers (unusually well provided for with an entrance through a central door and a central fireplace), the upper approached through a smaller hall at the screen end, up a broad stair and through an elaborate doorway.

In 1479, twenty-four years after the Douglas forfeiture, James III gave Tantallon to Archibald 'Bell-the-Cat' Douglas, the fifth Earl of Angus. The sixth Earl married James IV's widow, lost favour with the young James V, and for his own protection shut himself up in Tantallon. The king went in person to capture it in 1528, but in spite of a siege that made use of 'thrawn-mou'd Meg and her Marrow' – two cannons brought over from Dunbar Castle – he only obtained it by doing a deal with the governor, Simon Panango, after Angus had fled to England. James then strengthened the defences with freestone, the better to resist cannon-ball. The castle was further strengthened in 1543, after it had been restored to Angus. Indeed, he died in it in 1556. In 1639, when it was held by the Marquis of Douglas on behalf of the king and prelacy, the Covenanters took it and 'dang doun Tantallon'; or much of it, though enough was apparently left for a garrison to hold out unsuccessfully against the king and his General Monk in 1659.

Early in the eighteenth century what survived this onslaught was sold by the Duke of Douglas to Sir Hew Dalrymple, President of the Court of Session, who carried out further demolition, though one might have expected him to have known better.

Said by the historian Major to be the birthplace of the poet Bishop Gavin Douglas of Dunkeld, the first translator into Scots (or, for that matter, English) of Virgil's *Aeneid*, Tantallon was visited by Queen Victoria in 1870. It is now in care as an Ancient Monument.

Terpersie Castle

Terpersie, a mile or so north-west of the village of Tullynestle, was built for William Gordon, a cadet of the house of Gordon, in 1561. It is a comparatively diminutive structure, but the earliest Z-plan castle in Scotland (after Huntly, *c.*1543, which, strictly speaking, was not originally so conceived), and, indeed, the earliest surviving dated Scottish castle. Terpersie's thin walls and the absence of vaulting in the basement of the main block suggest that comfort as well as defensibility was much in the owner's mind. The master mason was Thomas Leiper.

The main block, lying north to south, has two roofless but once conically capped, distinctly medieval-looking round towers projecting at opposite angles. The bases of these towers house polygonal chambers with shot-holes commanding the faces of the main building. The coarse rubble walls rise to three storeys and a garret, and are also well equipped with shot-holes. A seventeenth-century addition to the castle has long since totally collapsed.

The entrance to Terpersie is at the southern end of the east front, and links directly to the main basement apartment, which was probably originally a kitchen, and is lit by five slit windows. A straight stair inside the walling of the south gable leads to the first floor, at which level it seems that there may once also have been another entrance. Above, a corbelled turret stair in the angle between the south-west tower and the south gable reaches to the upper floors. The Hall on the first floor has two impressive windows. On this level, as well as above, there were private apartments and bedrooms.

Gordon accompanied his chief to the Battle of Corriche, the only victory Mary, Queen of Scots ever secured. Among the other battles on both sides in which he was involved was Tillyangus, ten years later, when he killed Black Arthur Forbes, the brother of Lord Forbes, and thus helped to win the day. After the Battle of Auldearn in 1645, General Baillie's Covenanting army burned Terpersie, though it was subsequently restored.

The Jacobite laird of Terpersie, generally supposed to be the last person to be executed for playing a part in the rising of 1745, had his property forfeited. The lands of Terpersie were absorbed into the Knockespock estate, and Terpersie was used as a farmhouse until the end of the nineteenth century, when it was abandoned. It has now been restored by Captain Lachlan Rhodes.

Terpersie Castle: one of the earliest, and smallest, of the Z-plan castles.

Terpersie Castle: the restoration almost complete.

Thirlstane

Thirlstane Castle, by the River Leader, situated on the ourskirts of the village of Lauder, possesses one of the most imposing frontages of any castle in Scotland, its symmetrically towered plan and, on the south side, its parapets entirely on arches, 'springing from tower to tower', being unique in Scotland. The original castle stood two miles to the east, and was probably abandoned in the seventeenth century. A solid tower called Lauder Fort, reputed to be constructed by Edward I during his invasion of Scotland, may possibly be incorporated in the leg of the T-shaped structure which has come down to us, though this is doubted by MacGibbon and Ross.

The oldest identifiable part of the castle was built by John, First Lord Maitland. It was, however, the first, and last, Duke of Lauderdale – he who assisted Charles II in his attempt to foist Episcopalianism upon Scotland, and who became virtually the 'uncrowned king' of the country – who in 1670 caused the old fortalice to be extensively remodelled, employing the great architect, Sir William Bruce, a family connection of the Duke's second wife. Bruce, who also rebuilt the Palace of Holyroodhouse – David Walker, indeed, has called Thirlstane 'a stretched version of James V's tower at Holyrood' – supervised the building operations at the Duke's other Scottish seats, Lennoxlove and Brunstane, and was involved with work carried out at the principal English Lauderdale seat, Ham House.

The third sixteenth-century extension involved the remodelling of the southern end of the house, rebuilding the kitchen wing to its earlier height, but carrying the remainder to four storeys and adding rounds to the south-west and south-east angles, as well as to the north-west angle of the mid-sixteenth-century stair tower, raised to give access to the floors above. A window lintel on the west front, dated 1599, commemorates this work with the initials of Sir William Stewart, fifth of Traquair.

John, the aforementioned first Earl, who became Lord High Treasurer of Scotland in 1636, raised the older northern portion of the house to roughly the level of the later southern portion.

The pre-Bruce sixteenth-century structure was oblong, with a circular tower at each angle, three storeys high and built of local red rubble. There were four stair turrets rising on corbelling in the four entrant angles. To the north, the two round towers are corbelled

Thirlstane Castle: perhaps Scotland's finest example of the grand symmetrical design: Sir William Bruce augmented by Bryce.

out from second-floor level, those to the south having been altered to merge with later additions. Above second-floor level, on the south side, there is, as already mentioned, a seventeenth-century parapet walk partly supported by substantial corbels and partly by arches leading from the semi-circular towers. Bruce's additions provide a splendid flourish to the entrance, dominated now by the ogee-capped tower added by David Bryce in 1840, when the ninth Earl of Lauderdale commissioned the rebuilding of the flanking blocks and the restoration of the main house.[1] At the same time the outer square towers and the dormer windows were also added. To a surprising degree, Bryce respected much of what Bruce had done before.

The threatened collapse of the ogee tower in post-Second-War years led to an extensive restoration scheme funded in part by the

[1] David Walker comments that the authorship of the 1840 additions is difficult, since preliminary pencil drawings in Burn's hand survive with the RIBA, much as built. Burn and Bryce did not go into partnership until 1841.

Historic Buildings Council for Scotland, prior to the formation of the Thirlstane Trust in 1984, in whose keeping this sumptuous castle now rests for the benefit of future generations, and on which the present laird serves.

Inevitably, the interior has been much altered during the centuries, though not the main arrangement of the rooms. Each floor has four rooms. There is a good seventeenth-century plaster ceiling on the second floor. The towers contain small chambers. The main Baroque plaster ceilings, featuring bunches of grapes, were probably executed by George Dunsterfield and John Halbert, Charles II's favourite 'gentlemen modellers', as such craftsmen were called in these days. They, together with the joiners who worked for Bruce, were imported by the Duke from England, where they had been employed at his English seat, Ham.

The private apartments above the public rooms were easily reached by a number of turnpike stairs.

Thornton Castle

This small castle lies three miles west of Laurencekirk, in the Howe of the Mearns. An L-shaped fortalice, it rises to three storeys and has a crenellated parapet on chequered corbels with open rounds at all angles and projections to allow the parapet walk to pass round the chimney-stack. There is a rebuilt garret storey within the parapet.

The probable date of the building is 1531. The Thorntons had the land first, but in 1309 a Thornton heiress brought it to Sir James Strachan. In 1683 a Strachan heiress carried the property to Robert Forbes of Newton. The last Strachan laird, incidentally, was the parish minister at Keith, Banffshire. The Fullertons had it next, then the Crombies, who altered the castle a great deal. In 1893, Sir Thomas Thornton bought back the property.

Threave Castle

Threave Castle stands on an island in the River Dee, about a mile west of Castle Douglas. It is a massive oblong keep of five storeys, with at one time also a garret, and with flanking drum towers at each angle (only one of which survives), linked by a curtain-walled

344 · *Threave Castle*

Threave Castle: the massive keep with the surviving drum tower.

courtyard and by a ditch and rampart beyond. There is an
impressive gateway in the curtain-wall on the east side.

The castle, which dates from the fourteenth century, rises to a
height of seventy feet and has walls eight feet thick. It is well lit for
the period. On the north, south and east sides sockets to support a
bretache, or timber gallery, survive.

The entrance was at *entresol* level by movable wooden bridge
from the gate-house in the curtain-wall; a room, used as a kitchen,
which was the upper section of the high vaulted basement, having a
fireplace and a stone sink in the window embrasure. The dimly lit
room beneath contains a well, another sink and drain, and, in the
north-west corner, a deep dungeon covered by a trapdoor.

A wheel stair rises to the Great Hall, forty-six feet by twenty-
five, with a fireplace and a garderobe placed in an angle. Once there
was a second entrance to this room, by wooden bridge from the
upper floor of the gate-house and the parapet wall.

The second floor is similar in dimensions to the first, but has a withdrawing-room for men-at-arms with ten windows and an elaborate fireplace. At this level, through passages in the walls, the bretache would have been fitted up.

Threave was built by the illegitimate son of Sir James Douglas ('The Good'), entrusted by Bruce with the task of taking the king's heart to Jerusalem in expiation for his murder of the Red Comyn. Sir James was killed in Spain fighting the Moors, and Bruce's heart was brought back to Dunfermline Abbey. The illegitimate son, Archibald ('The Grim'), was third Earl of Douglas and Lord of Galloway from 1369. His son married James I's sister. It was from Threave that the teenage sixth Earl and his brother rode to Edinburgh Castle in 1440 for the Black Dinner, at which they were murdered by Crichton and Livingstone, determined to put an end to the power of the Douglases once and for all. The castle was heired by their sister, who married her cousin, the eighth Earl. He was assassinated by James VI at Stirling.

Threave was much used as a base for raids into England. It was the scene of the beheading of the MacLellan Tutor of Bombie against the express orders of James II, as a result of which the castle was besieged, not by Mons Meg as has sometimes been claimed, but by another bombard. Thereafter, Threave became a royal fortress. It was besieged again by the Earl of Arran in 1545, and once more by the Covenanters in 1640, when the Earl of Nithsdale was forced to surrender it, as he had also to surrender his own castle at Caerlaverock. The Covenanters then 'slighted' it, though not so thoroughly as to prevent it being still used as a prison for French troops during the Napoleonic wars. It is now an Ancient Monument.

Tillycairn Castle

Tillycairn is an L-plan castle standing on high ground almost two miles south-east of Cluny, and now adjacent to a farm steading. In its present form it may have been strengthened in 1542 by Matthew Lumsden after he had his farm stock raided by Strachan of Lynturk, a thug who had been involved in the murderous quarrel between the Forbeses and the Gordons. Though relatively small, it has very thick walls, the lower courses being constructed of large boulders. It has rounded corners, angle-turrets on all the gables save one, a parapet walk (now gone) on the west side of the wing and a semicircular stair tower rising up the re-entrant angle, beside which is the entrance.

There are three vaulted rooms in the basement, one the kitchen with a wide arched fireplace. The Hall occupies the whole of the first floor of the main block. It has a fine fireplace, rather curiously a store sink and drain, and a 'laird's lug' above the fireplace to enable the owner to listen in on his visitors' (or relatives') conversation. The bedroom accommodation was, as usual, above.

The last of the Lumsden line died in 1672, when Tillycairn went to Thomas Burnett of Sauchen, but had Forbes connections thereafter until early in the eighteenth century it was acquired by the Gordons of Cluny. Ruined, it remained with the Cluny estates till 1973 when it was bought and restored by Iain Begg for David Lumsden, descended from a branch of the family of the original owner.

Within the last few years it has been reroofed under the supervision of Ian Begg and reoccupied.

Tillyfour, Place of

Standing on the east bank of the Don five miles north-west of Monymusk, the Place of Tillyfour is a small fortalice, a variation of the L-plan structure with the joining of the wings producing two re-entrant angles. In the eastern re-entrant angle there is a squat stair turret corbelled out on a squinch, a comparatively rare device in the north-east. The courtyard to the south has an arched gateway.

The door is in the west re-entrant angle, still with its drawbar and socket. A guardroom remains, along with some slit windows.

The original building probably had two storeys and a garret. The roof level was altered in the first half of the seventeenth century. By the mid-nineteenth century the castle was derelict. In 1884 it was sympathetically restored by Hew Montgomerie Wardrop and his pupil, Robert Lorimer, the new work being copied from the style and manner of the old. Once, there was a hunting-lodge for the Earl of Mar on the site. The present house, however, was probably built by John Leslie of Waterhouse in 1508. His grandson was falconer to James IV. His great-great-grandson was created a Nova Scotia baronet in 1628. The lands passed from the Leslies when Sir John died in 1640 and his widow married a Gordon within six months of her previous husband's death.

Tilquhilly Castle

Two miles south-west of Banchory, Tilquhilly Castle, built in 1576, is a Z-plan fortalice of three storeys and an attic. It has a central keep and two square towers. There is a slightly curved stair tower in one re-entrant angle, and a narrow semicircular stair-turret corbelled out in an unusual three-tier manner from first-floor level in the other. There are no turrets, but at third-floor level the rounded-off corners are corbelled out to the square near the eaves.

The ground floor is vaulted and contains the kitchen and the wine-cellar with its private stair to the Hall. All are well provided with shot-holes.

The Hall is on the first floor of the main block, and there is a private room in the east tower. The south-west tower has a separate room. The upper bedroom floors have been much altered.

Tilquhilly belonged to the Abbey of Arbroath, and then to the Ogstoun family, from whom it passed by marriage to David Douglas, son of Lord Dalkeith. His grandson is said to have erected the present castle in 1576. Sir Robert Douglas was a Royalist and the castle was garrisoned by Covenanters. In 1665, a Douglas heiress took the castle through marriage to George Crichton of Cluny.

Tilquhilly has been unoccupied for many years, although there have been schemes for its restoration as a residence. Restoration is now about to be put in hand.

Tinnis Castle

Tinnis Castle, a remarkable ruin, stands on a steep rocky knoll overlooking Drumelzier Haugh and Merlin's Grave, about eight miles from Peebles. It was built among the ruins of an Iron Age fort.

It was a courtyard castle with a wall of enceinte and two round towers at the north and south angles. Virtually nothing survives of the curtain-walls that protected the south-west and north-east sides of the courtyard, but sections of the north-west curtain still stand to a height of about three feet three inches. The north tower is better preserved than the south. The main residential buildings probably stood on the south-east side of the enceinte.

Legend claims that the castle was the residence of the poet Ossian's Dunthalamo, whom the Fingalian hero slew at its gates. Scholarship suggests that it was built in the fifteenth or early sixteenth century by a Tweedie of Drumelzier. An anonymous account of Tweeddale, written late in the seventeenth century, claims that: 'The House was blown up with powder by the Lord Fleming whose father Drumelzar had slain in a bloody feud that continued betwixt the families.' The murder victim was John, second Lord Fleming, killed by Tweedie of Drumelzier in 1524. Some confusion has arisen because, as it happens, in 1592 'the houss of Tynnies', in Yarrow, was also blown up, though by William Stewart of Traquair and on royal instructions. It has now totally disappeared. The distance away at which large mortar-bound fragments of the surviving Tinnis lie from the castle, as if violently thrown, suggest that it could very well have been blown up, as the anonymous writer stated, though it had no connection with those misdeeds of Bothwell which led to the destruction of the other Tynnies, along with Harden and Dryhope.

Tolquhon Castle

Tolquhon Castle stands two miles south of Tarves, an impressive though ruined fortalice of the Forbes family.

The original structure was a small but strong rectangular tower dating from the early fifteenth century, and built by the Prestons of Craigmillar, in Lothian. To this was added during the latter part of the sixteenth century a large quadrangular mansion (unusual in Aberdeenshire, where the big tower house was the norm) the tower then becoming the north-east angle of the courtyard.

To the south there is the main block of three storeys with a circular stair tower, corbelled out to a square top and projecting into the central courtyard. At the north-west, it projects L-plan fashion, into a square crowstep-gabled tower containing the main stair. Lower wings run to the east and west, and a balancing circular tower thrusts out from the north-west angle, diagonally balancing the old tower at the south-east.

Preston Tower, once a parapeted keep, is now largely collapsed, but the rest of the castle still survives complete to the wallhead. When James Giles drew it in 1838, all the sixteenth-century buildings were still roofed, but by 1887 McGibbon and Ross were lamenting the falling in of the roof and rapid deterioration of the structure.

There is a remarkable gate-house with two drum towers, armorial bearings and French Renaissance-style sculpture. The Castle itself is unusual in combining a wide variety of gun-loops and shot-holes, yet having courtyard windows large for the period, and evidence in general of a high level of domestic planning in its layout.

Entrance is through an arched doorway in the south-west square tower, approached from the courtyard. It gives access to a vaulted passage in the main block, off which are three vaulted cellars and the kitchen. This has a large fireplace, a stone sink and a hatch. Private stairs link both kitchen and wine-cellar to the Hall and to the laird's private room above. The bakehouse, with two ovens, was in the south-east tower. Beneath this level there was a prison.

A curved stair in the south-west tower had what may have served as a guardroom at the foot of it, as it provided the main approach to the Hall, a once handsome apartment with a moulded fireplace and a floor made up of hexagonal flagstones. The laird's room, leading off it, has a small oratory. Next to this is a secret chamber reached only by a trapdoor; a convenient hiding-place in troublous times. The turnpike stair in the central round tower provided access to the bedrooms above.

The lower ranges are more ruinous, but contained a long gallery with cellars beneath and, in the north-west circular tower, a vaulted bedroom and an unvaulted one above.

To the west of the gatehouse the outer wall carries the inscription 'Al this worke excep the Auld Tour was begun by William Forbes 15 April 1584 and endit be him on October 1589'.

Beyond, the castle is approached by a huge walled outer court of irregular pentagonal form. Its arched outer gate was protected by triple gun-loops.

The estate passed to the Forbes family by the marriage of Sir John, brother of the first Lord Forbes, in 1420. James VI was a guest in the castle and, indeed, lived in it during his excursion to crush the rebellion of the Catholic earls under Huntly. One Forbes fell at Pinkie; another saved the life of Charles II at Worcester and was knighted. In 1716, the castle was bought by Lt-Col. Francis

Farquhar, from whom it passed to the second Earl of Aberdeen. It was deserted as a residence by the end of the eighteenth century and was briefly a farmhouse. It is now an Ancient Monument.

Torthorwald Castle

Torthorwald Castle, on high ground overlooking Lochar Moss, about four miles east of Dumfries, though now very badly ruined, is a stark reminder of the feudal power of the Middle Ages. It has been an oblong keep with a tall pointed vault basement and an entresol floor resting on a circular vault. Virtually all the north gable and most of the west wall have gone. The entrance to the lower vault was apparently in the north wall, bricked up at some later stage. There is no way now of knowing how the upper floors were reached, but a straight flight of steps in the south gable led from the upper vault to the Hall above. A spiral stair in the north-east corner led only to the Hall. The castle is still surrounded by the remains of earthworks, probably raised for an earlier stronghold on the site.

The castle may have been built either by Sir William Carlyle early in the fourteenth century, or by Thomas Carlyle, who was killed at the Battle of Nevill's Cross in 1346. Froude tells us that the great Thomas Carlyle boasted of the fact that the blood of the Lords Carlyle of Torthorwald ran in his veins.

The Kirkpatricks had the castle after the Carlyles. In 1590, a bastard son of the Regent Morton was created Lord Torthorwald by James VI.

Torwood Castle

Torwood Castle, an L-plan structure built about 1566, which has had a now mostly vanished courtyard to the north, once containing seventeenth-century outbuildings, stands on high ground two miles north of Larbert. The long main block has three storeys, with a stair wing projecting northwards at the west end, rising two storeys higher. It would once have housed a gabled watch-room.

There is a square tower in the re-entrant angle which apparently rose a storey lower than the wing. A small corbelled-out circular turret housed the stair to the watch-room. The walls are well

supplied with shot-holes and gun-loops.
The moulded doorway in the re-entrant angle is guarded by gun-loops. The door leads to a lobby, from which the main turnpike stair rises. There is a guardroom in the gable to the right. A vaulted passage from the lobby leads along the north side of the main block to reach three cellars and the kitchen, all vaulted. The kitchen, at the far end, has an arched fireplace, an inlet for water and a serving hatch. The western room is the wine-cellar, with the usual private stair to the Hall above.

There is a curious vestibule half way up the main stair containing a basin and drain. The Hall has a decorated fireplace in the south wall and a withdrawing-room at the east end. The upper floor is now ruinous.

The Forresters of Garden, keepers of the nearby former royal forest of Tor Wood, were the lairds from the fifteenth century. The castle passed in the seventeenth century to the Forresters of Corstorphine, who probably built the courtyard extension.

Torwoodlee Tower

Torwoodlee Tower, two miles above Galashiels, was built in 1601 by George Pringle to replace an earlier structure, and stands in the grounds of Torwoodlee House, which in 1783 replaced the second tower.

Torwoodlee Tower was once a courtyard-plan structure two storeys and an attic high. The vaulted cellars on the north range are now fragmentary. Little more than a picturesque shell, the tower's former internal arrangements must largely be matter for conjecture. The circular entrance tower, corbelled out square at wall-head level, covers a two-storey watch-room.

Towie Barclay, Aberdeenshire.

Towie Barclay stands in the Ythan Valley, four miles south of Turriff. It appears to have replaced an earlier structure found by one Sir Alexander Barclay of Tolley, whose death in 1136 is commemorated in an inscription built into the castle, although the same stone adds a moral homily and the date 1593. It is, however, more probably of early sixteenth century date, like the

Towie Barclay: before restoration, a tower house wanting its top storey.

Towie Barclay: sensitively restored, including the garden approach.

other tower houses in the area with high quality rib-vaults. Cruden remarks that 'nowhere else in Scotland is the Gothic spirit to be found more strongly'. One of the descendants of the Barclay family became the famous Russian Field Marshal Prince Barclay de Toille, immortalised in Tolstoy's *War and Peace*.

Although it encorporates earlier work Towie Barclay is now an unusually proportioned L-plan fortalice. The main block lies north/south, the wing, projecting eastwards, carrying the date 1604 and the initials I.G. and E.B. above its doorway, one of two in the re-entrant angle.

There is a vaulted basement with four vaulted rooms entered from a ribbed and groined lobby. Such a lobby is also to be found at Gight and at Craig. There is a private stair in the south-west angle from the wine-cellar to the Hall.

The main staircase to the first floor begins straight, but wheels round inside the corner of the tower. The Hall is more ornately magnificent than is usual in the other castles of this group, having a groined and ribbed vault in two compartments, only that at Balbegno being comparable. There is a small but elaborate vaulted gallery in the south wall, probably an oratory since it contains the religious monogram I.H.S. and the carved heart and pierced hands and feet of Christ. The corbels from which the sides spring also have shields carrying emblems of the four Evangelists. The gallery is reached by a mural stair.

The wide fireplace has stone seats and an umbry, and there are stone seats in the window embrasures from the eastern of which there opens a small vaulted room.

In 1792, Towie Barclay had its two upper storeys, parapet and rounds removed, but the latter have been replaced. Towie Barclay has been well restored in our own day by its present owners, Marc and Karen Ellington, receiving both a Saltire Award and a European Heritage Award. The walled garden in front of the house has been restored by Karen Ellington.

Traquair

Traquair, the oldest inhabited house in Scotland and one of the loveliest, probably began as an oblong keep towards the end of the twelfth century. Alexander I had a hunting-lodge there for use when he was hunting in the Ettrick Forest. William the Lion signed

Traquair House: the approach, through the inner gates, to Scotland's oldest continuously inhabited house.

the charter which gave Glasgow its burgh status at Traquair. When Alexander and William knew the old tower, the Tweed flowed by its walls; but when James Stewart, the first Earl of Traquair, began turning his tower into a great formal palace, he diverted the Tweed into a new bed, about a quarter of a mile away.

The original tower, once freestanding and dating from 1492, is now incorporated into the north end of the main block. About the middle of the sixteenth century a south wing was added, with a rectangular stair tower projecting westwards. During the second half of the century, the building was again extended, the west wall aligned to that of the stair tower. Lower wings of late-seventeenth-century origin, the work of James Smith, built for the second Earl, reach westwards from both ends of the main house, providing a *claire-voie* and terrace with twin garden houses. Fortunately, his sketch of 1695 to extend and make symmetrical the main front was never carried out.

The main section of the house – big, tall and compact like a northern castle, and quite different from the slimmer Ferniehurst – rises to four storeys in height, and there is a garret. The later extensions are served by a circular stair tower at the south-west corner. There is a priest's room on the top floor of the tower, complete with secret stair. The library is impressive, as is the drawing-room, with its oak beams decorated with ballad quotations. There has been little alteration to the interior layout of Traquair since James Smith's work in the seventeenth century, a scheme prepared for the fifth Earl to Georgianise the structure happily also being abandoned.

Mary, Queen of Scots stayed there with Darnley in 1566, not long before his explosive end at Edinburgh's Kirk o' Field. She left behind a quilt allegedly embroidered by herself and her four Marys. After his defeat at Philiphaugh, Montrose was refused admission by the first Earl, who had been Charles I's Treasurer, but whose adherence to the Catholic faith and the Stuart cause resulted in his dying a beggar in the Edinburgh streets. The knocker on the door, said to have been sounded by Montrose, is, however, of later date, though it undoubtedly felt the hand of Sir Walter Scott, who believed the Montrose story to be true. Prince Charles Edward also came to Traquair, entering through the famous bear gates, which clasp the family arms. They are known now as the 'steekit yetts' (shut gates). Legend offers two explanations. One is that the seventh Earl closed and locked them after returning from the funeral of his young wife, swearing that they would not again be opened until another Countess of Traquair arrived to enter. His son, the eighth and last Earl, died childless, and the line itself died out with his sister, who expired in her hundredth year in 1875, after which the line passed collaterally to the Maxwell-Stuarts, who still own Traquair.

The more appealing version, approved by Scott, is that the gates were locked behind Prince Charles after his departure in 1745, the Earl swearing they would not be unlocked again until a Stuart sat once more upon the throne in London.

Tullibole Castle

Tullibole Castle stands a mile east of Crook of Devon. It now looks like a seventeenth-century house, but was probably originally a free-standing tower; perhaps the western end of the main block.

The eastern end is dated 1608. An Edinburgh Advocate, John Halliday, bought Tullibole in 1598, and he and his son, eventually Sir John, seem to have provided some of the defensive features. The castle has three storeys and a garret to the east, with an additional storey to the west. The stair-wing has two ashlar angle-turrets. High over the doorway, level with the eaves, is a little bartisan. There is a stair turret in the re-entrant angle prominently corbelled at first-floor level beside the entrance, defended by small shot-holes, above which are the initials of Master John Halliday and Helen Oliphant, his wife. The liberal provision of stairs marks an advance in domestic convenience over many castles of the period. The precision of dating, 2 APRIL 1608, is unusual, if not the sentiments of the motto, THE LORD IS ONLIE MY DEFENCE and PEACE BE WITHIN THY WALLES AND PROSPERITIE WITHIN THY HOUS. Over the years the interior has been much altered. Marriage of a Halliday heiress, Katherine, conveyed the house to the Moncrieff family in 1705. Their descendants succeeded to the Nova Scotia baronetcy of 1626, and the eleventh baronet, a Lord Justice Clerk, was created Baron Moncrieff of Tullibole in 1873. Three of the family became judges, one of whom presided over the famous trial of Madeleine Smith, the papers of which are now at Tullibole. Six others achieved prominent positions in the Church.

Udny Castle

Udny Castle stands four miles south of Tarves. For long deserted, it was made the dominant element of a large Victorian baronial mansion designed in 1874-5 by Maitland Wardrop, but this was in turn abandoned and eventually demolished in the mid-1960s, leaving the rectangular tower externally in much the condition it began. When that was has been a matter of conjecture. Some have said that the lower half with the rounded angles like Drum belongs to the fifteenth century, to which the addition was put on in the sixteenth and angle-turrets in the seventeenth. Since MacGibbon and Ross's analysis of the features of its plan in 1887, it has usually been dated in its entirety from the late sixteenth or early seventeenth century. Since Ronald of Uldney was given a charter to the lands by David II, there would almost certainly have been an earlier castle on the site. Udny, a hundred feet high, has five storeys and an attic flanked by corbelled parapets on the long side only. It

Udny Castle: a tower house freed from its encumbering Victorian mansion.

has an arched entrance in the east which penetrates walls eight feet thick, leading to a vaulted kitchen and wine-cellar. A newel stair rises to the first-floor Hall, which has window-seats, mural chambers and, off it down a mural passage, a small bedroom. The fine ribbed Jacobean ceiling applied to the sixteenth-century vault is Wardrop's work of the 1880s. A turnpike stair leads to the upper floor. Over the doorway is inserted the caution: LET NO ONE BEAR BEFORE THIS THRESHOLD HENCE, WORDS UTTERED HERE IN FRIENDLY CONFIDENCE, a couplet which hardly has a pre-seventeenth-century ring.

One laird of Udny raised men to fight for Mary, Queen of Scots against the English, while a successor fought for the King against the Covenanters. 'The Laird of Udny's Fool' was a renowned jester, Jamie Fleming, kept by the twelfth laird, and probably the last professional family jester in Scotland. An eighteenth century Udny was a pioneering agriculturalist.

Udny has now been splendidly restored by a direct descendant of the original owner.

Wedderlie

About a mile north of the hamlet of Westruther is Wedderlie, a mansion built in 1680 incorporating an L-shaped tower, probably also built in the later sixteenth century. Three storeys high, the top floor of the tower is built out upon a range of large corbels. There are three big wallhead stacks. The tall roof is of an unusual design for its date. The ground floor of the north wing is vaulted, and the hall in the first floor has two windows with stone seats in the embrasures.

It seems likely that a still older structure was incorporated in the sixteenth-century fortalice. Wedderlie, though owned in the thirteenth century by Sir Robert de Polwarth, was granted to one of King Robert the Bruce's followers, Sir Richard Edgar, in 1327 and remained in the Edgar family for four hundred years. In 1733 it was acquired by Lord Blantyre. Though in a ruinous state in the latter part of the nineteenth century, it has since been restored and is occupied.

Wester Kames Castle

This small late-sixteenth-century four-storey castle in the grounds of Kames Castle was an oblong keep with a projecting stair tower to the north-east rising a storey higher. There is a turret stair in the south-west re-entrant angle leading to the squared-out watch-room on top of the round tower; a conically roofed angle-turret on the south-east corner and, alongside this, a projecting device on the east front for dropping missiles on those at the ground-floor entrance below.

There is a vaulted basement. The main turnpike stair leads to the first floor, higher ascent being by the turret stair.

The MacKinlays had the lands of Wester Kames in Bruce's time, but the Crown repossessed them and gave them to the royal butler, or dispenser, a MacDonald who adopted the name Spens. In 1670 the castle came through the marriage of an heiress to the Grahams. In 1863 it was bought by the Marquess of Bute. By the early nineteenth century it was a ruin, in part only twelve feet high, but in 1897–1900 it was well restored, by the 'Arts and Crafts' architect Robert Weir Schultz for the third Marquess of Bute.

Westhall Castle

Westhall stands about half a mile north of Oyne, and is a modified L-shaped fortalice now attached to a nineteenth-century mansion. Three storeys and a garret high, it was extended to the north and east in the seventeenth century. The gabled extension included a large circular tower attached to the south-east angle of the original L-plan block. A large circular stair tower projects on a squinch, or corbelled arch, in the re-entrant angle. The corbelling is of the label variety, common in the north-east.

There is a high crenellated parapet with an open round. The basement is vaulted. The Hall is on the first floor, with the usual bedroom accommodation above.

Westhall belonged to the Diocese of Aberdeen from the thirteenth century. It came to Walter Gordon at the Reformation, but in 1681 was bought by James Horne, the Vicar of Elgin, later dispossessed because he refused to subscribe to the Test Act. He married a daughter of the Laird of Pitcaple. Horne's advocate son, a Jacobite, managed to have the lands erected into a Horne barony.

The property is with his successors through several female branches.

West Shield

West Shield stands among moorland three miles north-west of Carnwath. L-shaped and large for its time, it began as an oblong tower early in the sixteenth century. A lower wing was added in the seventeenth, projecting southwards. Perhaps a little later, an extension of the main block to the west was added on and a square stair tower with a lean-to roof inserted into the re-entrant angle of the L.

The main block rises to four storeys and a garret. There are steep crow-stepped gables, and no parapet. The ground floor of the original block has three vaulted rooms. There is an unvaulted room in the extension to the west. The turnpike stair reaches the third floor, after which higher access is by wooden stair.

The Hall was on the first floor of the original block, but the additions provided plentiful extra accommodation.

West Shield was built and owned by the Denholms before it passed to the Lockharts of Lee. Though still roofed, its upper floors now appear to be dangerous, and its remote position unfortunately makes its rehabilitation unlikely.

Whittingham Castle

Whittingham Castle, two miles from East Linton and about six miles from Haddington, stands by the mouth of Whittingham Water near the Greek-style house built when the estate was acquired by James Balfour of Balbirnie, with whose kinsfolk it still remains.

It is a squat fifteenth-century L-shaped tower with the wing constructed against the short side of the oblong, thereby leading W. Mackay Mackenzie[1] to deduce that the reason for the adaptation of the L-shape was in this case domestic convenience rather than defence, since the short flank could afford very little protection. It contains only the turnpike stair.

[1] W. Mackay Mackenzie, *The Mediaeval Castle in Scotland*

Entry is by the door carrying above it the Douglas arms, in the east wall of the stair wing. The ground floor is vaulted. The first-floor Hall, now a museum of old prints and documents, is panelled and has a fine painted ceiling. There is fine plaster work above. The parapet rests on individual corbels. Though the corners are curved, there are no defensive rounds. Some of the chimneys and windows have been modernised.

The lands of Whittingham were acquired by the Douglase's in the fourteenth century. James Douglas, Earl of Morton, eventually the Regent Morton, was the owner during the reign of Mary, Queen of Scots. Tradition has it that the plotting of Darnley's murder took place at Whittingham, which happened conveniently to be approximately mid-way between Bothwell's castle of Hailes and Secretary Maitland's Lethington. Colourfully, the final decision is supposed to have been taken under an enormous yew tree, more than seven hundred years old, which has achieved so great a girth and weight that some of its own branches have rooted, forming leafy caverns.

Balfour's most famous descendant was Arthur James Balfour, Prime Minister of Britain and the first Earl of Balfour, who lies buried in the nearby family burial ground.

Williamston House

One mile east of Madderty, Williamston House is a T-plan structure with a circular tower projecting from the north front of the main block, though not quite centred. This is corbelled out to form a square watch-room above, reached by a tiny stair in a small conically capped turret in the re-entrant angle.

The house, two storeys and an attic high, has a single-storey drawing-room wing added about 1800. It is now a farmhouse with a modern interior.

Williamston was bought by Sir Laurence Oliphant of Gask from Sir William Blair of Kinfauns in 1650 – at which time the house may well have been newly built – for his eldest son, Patrick, aged twenty-two, whom his father sought, through the Court of Session, to compel to marry a forty-nine-year-old sister of the Marquis of Douglas. Patrick, however, took matters into his own hands by secretly marrying Margaret Murray, the daughter of the minister of Trinity Gask; for which defiance he was disinherited except for Williamston House, his younger brother, Laurence, heiring Gask.

Appendix I

A glossary of architectural and Scots terms

Arcade A series of arches supported by piers or columns. A blind Arcade is such a structure built against a wall.

Arch A self-supporting structure capable of carrying a super-imposed load over an opening. The most common arches are:

a) Semicircular or Round

b) Segmental

c) Elliptical

d) Lancet or Pointed

e) Ogee

f) Flat

g) Cusped

Architrave A moulding surrounding, or framing, a doorway or window opening.

Ashlar Large blocks of masonry wrought to even faces and square edges.

Astragal Glazing bar, often wooden, between window-panes.

Attic A small top storey, usually behind a sloping roof.

Aumbry or aumry Originally Almry, 'a place for alms'. A recess or cupboard to hold sacred vessels for the Mass, but later also used for domestic vessels.

Bailey A term applied to the external wall surrounding a medieval castle or keep, and later to one of the internal courts of the castle-(hence 'Old Bailey', the London Criminal Court, after its position between the Lud Gate and the New Gate, when the street was part of the former medieval bailey).

Barbican Outwork defending a castle's entrance.

Barmkin (Scots) Enclosing wall.

Bartisan (Literally 'battlement') Corbelled turret, round or square, at the top angle of a castle.

Base Moulded part of a column.

Basement The lowest storey of a building, often wholly or partly below ground level.

Bastion One of a series of projections from the main curtain-wall of a fortress placed at intervals to enable the garrison to enfilade besiegers. Usually pentagonal or semicircular, but may be triangular.

Batter A slight inward inclination or tilt of a wall from its base upwards, either to add strength or to make tunnelling by attacking forces more difficult.

Battlement A form of parapet indented or crenellated for soldiers to shoot between the merlons, or solid sections. In medieval times the crenel was usually half the width of the merlon. After the invention of gunpowder, battlements continued in use as a decorative feature.

Bay A section or compartment of a building in medieval architecture. The unit of design between each pair of roof-trusses or transverse vaulting-ribs and their supporting buttresses.

Bay window A window projecting from the face of a building at ground level, either rectangular or polygonal. The name derives from the fact that a large bay window was frequently placed in the bay of the Great Hall, where the dais or high table stood. A bay window may be of one or more storeys. Where it rests above ground level, on corbels, it is called an oriel.

Belfry In medieval times a movable wooden tower used in defence, but now a bell turret.

Boss A knob or projection usually placed to cover the intersection of ribs in a vault.

Bow-window See Bay window; but bow-windows are curved in plan.

Bracket A support projecting from a wall or column. A corbel.

Bretasche (Scots) A defensive wooden gallery on a wall (English: Brattice).

Broch (Scots) A circular tower-like structure, open in the middle, the double wall of drystone masonry being linked by slabs to form internal galleries at varying levels. Found in north and west Scotland, most probably dating from the earliest Christian times.

Burgh A town with trading privileges. Royal burghs had a monopoly of imports and exports till the sixteenth century. Burghs of Barony were founded by barons to whom local trade dues were paid.

Buttress A vertical member projecting from a wall to stabilise it, or to resist the lateral thrust of an arch, roof or vault. A flying buttress transmits the thrust to a heavy abutment by an arch or half-arch.

Cable-moulding A Norman moulding imitating the strands of a rope.

Canopy A hood over an altar, niche or statue.

Cap-house (Scots) A small watch-room at the top of a turnpike stair, often opening into the parapet walk and sometimes rising from within the parapet.

Chevron A Norman zig-zag decorative motif based on an inverted V.

Close (Scots) A courtyard or passage giving access to a number of buildings.

Commendator The holder of revenues of an abbey *in commendum* (Latin for 'in custody') while no regular abbot is appointed. In the Middle Ages, the commendators were usually bishops, but after the reformation they were laymen.

Conservation A late-twentieth-century usage implying the prolonging of the life of a building, with or without physical renewal, and in some cases finding a new use for it.

Coomb Ceiling (Scots) A campsile or sloping ceiling, as in an attic.

Coping A protective capping of brick or stone on the top of a wall.

Corbel A projection, usually of stone, built into a wall and projecting from its face to provide a seating for a beam or roof-truss.

Corbie or Crow-step (Scots) A gable, or peaked wall, at the end of a double-pitch roof, the ascending surface of which resembles a flight of steps.

Crypt Underground room.

Cupola A small domed turret covering a roof or an internal stair.

Curtain-wall The connecting wall between the towers of a castle.

Donjon The keep or central fortress in a castle (Latin, *dominus*, Lord; hence, the dwelling of a lord.)

Doocot (Scots) A dovecot.

Dormer window A window standing up vertically from the slope of a roof and lighting a room inside. Hence, Dormer head is a gable or pediment above such a window.

Dressings Features such as quoins or string-courses made from smoothly-worked stone.

Drystane (Scots) Drystone construction without mortar.

Eaves The overhanging edge of a roof.

Embattled Provided with battlements.

Embrasure A small splayed opening in the wall or battlement of a fortified building.

Enceinte (French, girdle, enclosure) In military architecture the line of the wall encircling a fortress.

Entresol A mezzanine storey within or above the ground storey.

Feu (Scots) Land granted by the feudal superior to the vassal or feuar on condition that he pays an annual feu-duty. Many domestic feudal rights of this sort are now being disposed of by redemption in Scotland.

Fore (Scots) Structure protecting an entrance, as in forestair, forework.

Fosse A ditch.

Freestone Stone that can be cut in all directions, usually sandstone or limestone.

Fresco A painting executed on wet plaster.

Frieze A horizontal band of ornament.

Gable A vertical wall or other vertical surface, frequently triangular, at the end of a pitched roof, in Scotland often with a chimney at the apex.

Gallery A balcony or passage, often with seats, usually overlooking a great hall, church or garden.

Garderobe A medieval privy, usually built into the wall of a castle.

Gargoyle A waterspout projecting from the parapet of a wall, carved into human or animal shape.

Gazebo A round summer-house overlooking a garden.

Groin The line of intersection of two vaults.

Hammer-beam An elaborate type of roof-truss used in Gothic and Tudor buildings. To avoid tie-beams across an imposing hall, short timber cantilevers (or hammer-beams) are used.

Harling (Scots) Wet dash, or roughcasting, hurled or dashed onto a rubble wall to give additional protection against the weather.

Ilk, of that (Scots) Of that same place.

Jamb (Scots) A wing or extension adjoining one side of a rectangular plan, making it into an L- or T-plan.

Keep The principal tower of a castle. Also called a donjon.

Label Ornamental boss at the end of a hoodmould.

Laich, Laigh (Scots) Low.

Laird A Scots landowner.

Lancet window A slender pointed arch window.

Lintel A horizontal beam of stone bridging an opening.

Machicolation A series of openings in a stone parapet through which missiles or boiling liquid could be dropped on to the heads of assailants beneath.

Merlon One of the solid tooth-like projections of a battlement.

Mezzanine A low storey between two high ones.

Motte A steep mound, the main feature of eleventh- and twelfth-century castles.

Motte-and-bailey A defence system, Roman in origin, consisting of an earthen motte (mound) carrying a wooden tower with a bailey (open court) with an enclosure ditch and pallisade.

Moulding Ornament of continuous sections.

Mullion The vertical member between the lights (compartments) of a window opening.

Newel The centre post in a circular turnpike or winding stairway.

Niche A vertical recess in a wall, often to take a statue.

Ogee A double curve, bending one way then the other.

Oratory A small private domestic chapel.

Oversail A series of stone or brick courses projecting over the main face of a building.

Palimpsest The re-use of a surface, especially for carving or other ornament.

Pantile a roof-tile of curved S-shape section.

Pediment a formalised gable (derived from use in temples) over doors and windows.

Peel, Pele (literally, palisade) A stone tower near the Scottish-English border.

Pend (Scots) An open-ended passage through a building, on ground level.

Pendant A suspended feature of a vault or ceiling, usually ending in a boss.

Pepperpot turret A bartisan with a conical or pyramidal roof.

Piano nobile (Italian, noble floor) the principal floor, usually with a ground floor beneath and a lesser floor above.

Piscina A basin with a drain for washing the Communion or Mass vessels, usually set in, or against, a wall.

Pit prison A sunken prison approached from a floor-hatch above.

Pleasaunce (Scots) A walled garden.

Pointing Exposed mortar joints of masonry or brickwork.

Porch A curved projection protecting an entrance.

Portcullis A gate, usually sharp-pointed along the bottom, sliding up and down vertical grooves cut in the stone sides of a castle gateway.

Puthole Holes in a wall constructed to receive the short timbers, or puttocks, on which boards rested during the construction of a building, and not filled in after its completion.

Putto A small naked sculpted boy, often with wings.

Quadrangle The inner courtyard in a large building.

Quoins Dressed stones at the angles of a building.

Rake Slope or pitch.

Rampart A stone or earthen wall surrounding a castle.

Rib-vault Ribs used in medieval vaulting, usually to support the surface of a vault ('as the ribs of an umbrella support the thin fabric when stretched' – *Martin S. Briggs*).

Rococo The final playfully ornamental phase of the Baroque style.

Roll-and-hollow moulding Simple round edging formed at outside vertical corner of hewn stone at the side of door or window.

Roll moulding Moulding of near-circular or semi-circular pattern.

Round (Scots) A roofless bartisan.

Rubble Masonry the stones of which are wholly or partially left rough.

Rustication The indented ornamental treatment of stone surfaces to give an impression of strength.

Scale and platt A stair employing intermediate landings.

Scarp The cutting away of ground to form a steep slope.

Screen An erection to divide an adjoining kitchen from the Hall in a castle.

Section A view of a building or architectural detail displayed by 'cutting' across it.

Sill The horizontal projection at the bottom of a window.

Skew (Scots) sloping or sloped stones finishing a gable higher than the roof.

Solar (Literally, sun-room) Upper living-room of the lord in a medieval dwelling.

Splay Chamfer.

Spring Level at which a vault or an arch rises.

Squinch a small arch built obliquely across each internal angle of a square tower or other structure to carry a dome or octagonal splice. The device is of ancient eastern origin.

Steading (Scots) A group of farm buildings.

Stoup A vessel for the holy water.

String-course Intermediate course, or moulding, projecting from the surface of a wall.

Stucco (Literally, plaster) The smooth external rendering of a wall.

Tracery A pattern of arches and geometrical figures supporting the glass in the upper part of a window, or applied ornamentally to wall surfaces or vaults.

Tumulus (Literally, mound) A barrow.

Turret A small tower usually attached to a building.

Vault An arched ceiling of stone. Tunnel- or barrel-vaulting, the simplest kind, is, in effect, a continuous arch. Pointed tunnel-vaults are found occasionally in Scottish buildings with or without decorative surface ribs. Groin (or cross) vaults have four curving triangular surfaces created by the intersection of two tunnel-vaults at right-angles. Rib-vaults are separately defined.

Appendix II

Castles grouped by region

Dowies House
Drumcoltran Castle
Drumlanrig Castle
Dunskey Castle
Elsieshields Tower
Fourmerkland Tower
Galdenoch Castle
Hills Castle
Hoddam Castle
Hollows Tower
Isle of Whithorn Castle
Isle Tower
Kenmure Castle
Kirkconnel House
Lochnaw Castle
Maclellan's Castle
Maxwelton House
Old Knock Castle
Orchardton Tower
Place of Mochrum
Plunton Castle
Repentance Tower
Rusko Castle
Sanquhar Castle
Sorbie Castle
Spedlins Castle
Stapleton Tower
Stranraer Castle
Threave Castle
Torthorwald Castle

FIFE REGION
Aberdour Castle
Airdrie House
Balcomie Castle
Balgonie Castle
Balmuto House
Collairnie Castle
Couston Castle
Earlshall
Falkland Palace
Fernie Castle

Fordell Castle
Hill House
Kellie Castle
Monimail Castle
Myres Castle
Pitcullo Castle
Pitreavie Castle
Pitteadie Castle
Pittfirrane Castle
Ravenscraig Castle
Rossend Castle
Rosyth Castle
St Andrews Castle
Scotstarvit Tower
Strathendry Castle

GRAMPIAN REGION
Abergeldie Castle
Aboyne Castle
Achanachie Castle
Allardyce Castle
Arnage Castle
Balbegno Castle
Balbithan House
Balfluig Castle
Ballindalloch Castle
Balquhain Castle
Balvenie Castle
Barra Castle
Beldorney Castle
Benholm Tower
Birse Castle
Blairfindy Castle
Blervie Castle
Braemar Castle
Cairnbulg Castle
Carnousie House
Castle Fraser
Corgarff Castle
Corse Castle
Coxton Castle
Craig Castle

Craigievar Castle
Craigston Castle
Crathes Castle
Crombie Castle
Cullen Castle
Delgatty Castle
Dornoch Castle
Drum Castle
Druminnor Castle
Dunnottar Castle
Fiddes Castle
Fordyce Castle
Fyvie Castle
Gight (or Formartine) Castle
Glenbuchat Castle
Hallforrest Castle
Hallgreen Castle
Hallhead Castle
Harthill Castle
House of Schivas
Huntly (or Strathbogie) Castle
Inchdrewer Castle
Inglismaldie Castle
Innes House
Keith Hall
Kemnay House
Kildrummy Castle
Kilnmaichlie Castle
Kininvie House
Kinnaird's Head Castle
Kinnairdy Castle
Knock Castle
Knockhall Castle
Lauriston Castle
Leslie Castle
Lickleyhead Castle
Midmar Castle
Monymusk Castle (now known
as House of Monymusk)
Mounie Castle
Muchalls Castle
Pitcaple Castle

Pitfichie Castle
Pitsligo Castle
Pittulie Castle
Spynie Palace
Terpersie Castle
Thornton Castle
Tillycairn Castle
Tillyfour, Place of
Tilquhilly Castle
Tolquhon Castle
Towie Barclay
Tullibole Castle
Udny Castle
Westhall Castle

HIGHLAND REGION
Ackergill Castle
Ballone Castle
Balnagown Castle
Brims Castle
Brodie Castle
Burgie Castle
Cadboll Castle
Castle Grant
Castle Leod
Castle of Mey
Castle Stewart
Castle Sween
Castle Tioram
Cawdor Castle
Dalcross Castle
Darnaway Castle
Dunbeath Castle
Dunrobin Castle
Dunvegan Castle
Eilean Donan Castle
Erchless Castle
Fairburn Tower
Freswick House
Girnigoe Castle
Keiss Castle
Kilcoy Castle

Kilravock Castle
Kinkell Castle
Lochindorb Castle
Mingary Castle
Muckerach Castle
Redcastle (or Edradour)
Skelbo Castle

LOTHIAN REGION
Barnes Castle
Borthwick
Bridge Castle
Brunstane Castle
Brunstane House
(near Portobello)
Cakemuir Castle
Carberry Tower
Colinton Castle
Craigcrook Castle
Craigentinny Castle
Craigmillar Castle
Craiglockhart Castle
Cramond Tower
Crichton Castle
Dalhousie Castle
Dirleton Castle
Dunbar Castle
Dundas Castle
Duntarvie Castle
Edinburgh Castle
Elphinstone Tower
Fawside (or Falside) Castle
Fenton Tower
Garleton Castle
Hailes Castle
Hawthornden Castle
Houston House
Kinneil House (or Palace)
Lauriston Castle
Lennoxlove
Liberton House
Liberton Tower

Linhouse House
Linlithgow Palace
Luffness
Merchiston Castle
Midhope
Niddry Castle
Nunraw
Ochiltree Castle (or Palace)
Peffermill House
Pinkie House
Preston Tower
Provan Hall
Redhouse Castle
Roseburn Castle
Rosslyn Castle
Southsyde Castle
Tantallon Castle
Whittingham Castle

STRATHCLYDE REGION
Abbot Hunter's Tower
Aiket Castle
Ardchonnel
Ascog House
Auchans Castle
Baltersan Castle
Balcardine Castle
Barncluith
Barr Castle
Barr Castle
Blair Castle
Bothwell Castle
Breachecha Castle
Brodick Castle
Busby Peel
Carnasserie Castle
Carnell or Cairnhill Castle
Carrick Castle
Cassillis House
Castle Levan
Castlemilk
Castle Stalker

Cessnock Castle
Craignethan Castle
Crawfurdland Castle
Crookston Castle
Crosbie Tower
Dalquharran Castle
Dalyell House
Dargarvel Castle
Dean Castle
Duart Castle
Dundarave Castle
Dunderave Castle
Dunstaffnage Castle
Duntroon Castle
Dunure Castle
Gilbertfield Castle
Greenan Castle
Gylem Castle
Haggs Castle
Hallbar Tower
Hunterston Castle
Inverkip Castle
Jerviswood House
Johnstone Castle
Kames Castle
Kelburn Castle
Kilchurn Castle
Kilhienzie Castle
Killochan Castle
Kilmartin Castle
Kinlochaline Castle
Kirkhill Castle
Knock Castle
Law Castle
Little Cumbrae Castle
Lochranza Castle
Loch Sween Castle
Maybole Castle
Mearns Castle
Monkcastle
Moy Castle

Mugdock Castle
Newark Castle
Newark Castle
Newmilns Tower
Penkill Castle
Pinwherry Castle
Portincross Castle
Rothesay Castle
Rowallan Castle
Saddell Castle
Scalloway Castle
Skelmorlie Castle
Skipness Castle
Sorn Castle
Stair House
Stanely Castle
Wester Kames Castle
West Shield

TAYSIDE REGION
Aberuchill Castle
Affleck Castle
Airlie Castle
Aldie Castle
Ardblair Castle
Ashintully Castle
Auchterhouse
Balmanno Castle
Balvaird Castle
Blair Castle
Braikie Castle
Broughty Castle
Burleigh Castle
Careston Castle
Castle Huntly
Castle Menzies
Claypotts Castle
Colliston Castle
Comrie Castle
Cortachy Castle
Craig Castle

Drummond Castle
Dudhope Castle
Ecclesmagirdle House
Edzell Castle
Elcho Castle
Ethie Castle
Evelick Castle
Farnell Castle
Fingask Castle
Fowlis Castle
Gardyne Castle
Glamis Castle
Glasclune Castle
Guthrie Castle
Hatton Castle
Huntingtower Castle
Innerpeffray
Invermark Castle
Invermay Tower
Inverquharity Castle
Kelly Castle
Keltie Castle
Kinnaird Castle
Lethendy Tower
Loch Leven Castle
Mains Castle
Meggernie Castle
Megginch Castle
Melgund Castle
Methven Castle
Moncur Castle
Monzie Castle
Murroes Castle
Murthly Castle
Old House of Gask
Pitkerro Castle
Stobhall Castle
Williamston House

ORKNEY
Earl's Palace
Noltland

SHETLAND
Muness Castle
Scalloway Castle

WESTERN ISLES — BARRA
Kisimull Castle